MURROW'S COLD WAR

MURROW'S COLD WAR

Public Diplomacy *for the* Kennedy Administration

GREGORY M. TOMLIN

Potomac Books

AN IMPRINT OF THE UNIVERSITY OF NEBRASKA PRESS

Unless otherwise noted, all photos are from the National
Archives Collection, Box 19, E1069, RG 306.

Library of Congress Cataloging-in-Publication Data
Names: Tomlin, Gregory M., 1979– author.
Title: Murrow's Cold War: public diplomacy for the
Kennedy administration / Gregory M. Tomlin.
Description: Lincoln: Potomac Books, an imprint of the
University of Nebraska Press, 2016. | Includes
bibliographical references and index.
Identifiers: LCCN 2015036856
ISBN 9781612347714 (cloth: alk. paper)
ISBN 9781612348285 (epub)
ISBN 9781612348292 (mobi)
ISBN 9781612348308 (pdf)
Subjects: LCSH: Murrow, Edward R. | United States
Information Agency—Officials and employees—Biography.
United States—Foreign relations—1961–1963.
Classification: LCC E744.5 .T66 2016 | DDC 327.73009/046—dc23
LC record available at http://lccn.loc.gov/2015036856

Set in Sabon Next LT Pro by Rachel Gould.

For Elizabeth

CONTENTS

List of Illustrations | ix
Acknowledgments | xi
Introduction: Public Diplomacy for a New Frontier | xv
List of Abbreviations | xxxv

1. Good Night, CBS | 1
2. 1776 Pennsylvania Avenue | 27
3. From Fiasco to Progress in Latin America | 56
4. This . . . Is Berlin | 83
5. Mr. Murrow Goes to Hollywood | 112
6. The USIA and the Cuban Missile Crisis | 142
7. Advocates for a Test Ban | 170
8. Birmingham, the Story Heard 'Round the World | 190
9. Counterinsurgency Propaganda in Southeast Asia | 219
10. Good Luck, Ed | 245

Notes | 267
Bibliography | 327
Index | 341

ILLUSTRATIONS

Following page 82

1. USIA director Edward R. Murrow and President John F. Kennedy
2. Murrow with his son, wife, and President Kennedy
3. USIA deputy director Donald M. Wilson
4. Murrow at his USIA office
5. Murrow with Eleanor Roosevelt on *Prospects of Mankind*
6. Murrow addresses listeners on a Voice of America broadcast
7. Murrow administers oath of office to George Stevens Jr.
8. Murrow with CBS News president Richard Salant and producer Burton Benjamin
9. Murrow with Voice of America director Henry Loomis
10. Murrow with Thomas C. Sorensen
11. President Lyndon B. Johnson presents Medal of Freedom to Murrow
12. Visitors in Tokyo view memorial tribute to Murrow

ACKNOWLEDGMENTS

A tremendous group of mentors, colleagues, and friends has encouraged me through this endeavor, and I am proud to thank many of them at the forefront of this completed work. Dr. James Hershberg, my dissertation adviser, taught my first foreign policy course in graduate school at the George Washington University in 2008. For the next five years he prodded me to locate the most recently declassified sources, present research at conferences, and refine the arguments made in these chapters. The other members of my dissertation committee provided unfailing encouragement during the process. Dr. Eric Arnesen's detailed feedback greatly improved my writing, and his passion for social and labor history inspired me to explore intriguing angles into American history that I would not have pursued on my own. Dr. Steven Livingston, from the School of Media and Public Affairs at George Washington, provided the refreshing eye of a political scientist (and fellow artilleryman), and he urged me to make this study relevant to people beyond the community of diplomatic historians. Dr. Chris Tudda, from the Office of the Historian at the Department of State, wrote the book on public diplomacy during the Eisenhower administration, *The Truth Is Our Weapon*, thus providing me with a valuable example on how to approach this topic during the Kennedy years.

Throughout my three-year enrollment in the doctoral program at George Washington, I had the incredible fortune to be associated with another superb history department, in my fulltime job as assistant professor at the U.S. Military Academy at West Point. The freshmen in the American history survey courses and the upperclassmen in the Cold War America elective offered questions and perceptions that helped me to hone many of my own interpretations about U.S. foreign policy. Lieutenants Grant Kirkpatrick and Patrick Moesta joined me in a yearlong exploration of American public diplomacy through their senior colloquium and thesis. Their demonstrated maturity and scholarship, as well as their impressive performance on a conference panel with graduate students at Columbia University, leave no doubt in my mind that the U.S. Army has been enriched by commissioning them into the officer corps.

Were it not for Dr. Robert and Christine McDonald's warm reception in July 2005, I may never have even considered graduate work in history. The McDonalds welcomed me into their home and introduced me to the West Point history department upon my return from a year in Iraq. Spending time with the McDonald family will certainly remain one of the highlights of the Tomlin family's time in New York. The department's leadership, Brigadier General (Retired) Lance Betros and Colonels Matthew Moten and Ty Seidule, stalwartly supported this endeavor and trusted me with a variety of other opportunities unique to working at West Point, to include leading the Cold War staff ride (study abroad program) to four European countries for three consecutive summers. Colonel Gail Yoshitani has been the best boss that an academic or army officer could ask for. Beyond her help in improving my teaching, she read every draft chapter of this book and provided meaningful feedback about how to strengthen its quality.

Articulating my thoughts onto paper greatly benefited from several conferences that permitted me to introduce themes or topics from this work. Dr. Andrew Preston of Cambridge University and Dr. Anders Stephanson of Columbia University provided helpful comments on two of the chapters. Dr. Victoria Phillips of Columbia introduced herself, after I gave a presentation on U.S. Information Agency World Fair pavilions at the Society for Historians of American Foreign Relations, and she has since become a marvelous friend. Her dissertation on Martha Graham, as a U.S. cultural ambassador, helped me to expand my understanding of what comprises public diplomacy. Most impressively, she took the initiative to organize a conference on cultural diplomacy in April 2012 that brought West Point cadets and faculty together with graduate students and faculty from Columbia's Blinken European Institute and Department of History. Victoria has done much to improve civil-military relations!

Transforming my dissertation into a manuscript worthy of submission to a publisher benefited greatly from reviews provided by two public diplomacy experts who read every page of the original work. Dr. Nicholas Cull, the foremost public diplomacy scholar, whose *The Cold War and the United States Information Agency* serves as foundational reading on this topic, recommended several new angles to consider in analyzing Murrow's agency. Alan Heil Jr., author of *Voice of America: A History*, provided the keen eye of someone who lived this history and knew many of the players from his thirty-six-year career at the Voice. I remain indebted to both for their generosity in time and red ink.

Locating primary sources for this work led me to archives in five states and overseas. A fellowship from the General of the Army Omar N. Bradley Foundation and a generous research grant from George Washington's Department of History helped to offset the costs of the travel. Several archivists helped me to maximize my limited time in their reading rooms, especially Patricia Albright at Mount Holyoke College, Barbara Cline at the Johnson Library, and Dr. Stephen Twigge at the British National Archives. Dr. Susanne Belovari of Tufts University, who has worked with legitimate Murrow biographers, shared her own insights into Murrow's background and introduced me to Charles Casey Murrow, Ed's son. Casey generously gave of his time during a memorable interview in Vermont, where he shared his personal memories and showed me several of the Murrow family's treasured keepsakes from their three years in Washington DC.

A fine group of professionals from the University of Nebraska Press ensured that this work became available through Potomac Books. Acquisitions editor Alicia Christensen received my proposal enthusiastically, and Marguerite Boyles and Joeth Zucco helped me to navigate the technical components of publishing. Dr. Karen H. Brown's meticulous copyediting and cheerful correspondence made the final stages a true pleasure.

As with my first book, my family proved exceptionally supportive and interested in the writing process. When not asking, "How's the latest chapter coming?" they tolerated my absences from activities and gatherings. My brother Michael hosted me the night that I arrived in Virginia, after two and a half years in South Korea, to begin graduate school in July 2008 and again on the night before my dissertation defense in March 2013. So you could say that this venture began and ended on the army cot in his Arlington apartment. My parents, Professor Harry and Donna Tomlin, remained enthusiastic about the project, but they also knew when to caution me to find balance between scholarship and family.

Saving the most extraordinary for last, I cannot thank my wife, Elizabeth, enough for her patience, support, and love. She shuttled our children, Patrick and Hannah, to activities or to the park, just to give me a few quiet hours at the house on weekends. Elizabeth read every draft chapter, providing a refreshing nonhistorian's critique of the material, in addition to the sharp eye of an attorney (one of the perks of marrying a former legal writing fellow!). She also gave birth to our son, George, on December 6, 2012, and yet still continued to hold down the household as I wrote the final four chapters and began the revision process. As I have told Elizabeth since our days at the College of William and Mary, she is a superstar.

INTRODUCTION

Public Diplomacy for a New Frontier

> It has always seemed to me the real art in this business is not so
> much moving information or guidance or policy five or 10,000
> miles. That is an electronic problem. The real art is to move it
> the last three feet in face to face conversation.
>
> —EDWARD R. MURROW, August 4, 1963

Despite not being a lawyer himself, the representative of the John F.
Kennedy presidential administration who addressed the Federal Bar
Association on September 26, 1963, captured the undivided attention of its members. He could mesmerize almost any audience with
his deep voice and melodious delivery, just as he had in describing
the Blitz from London during the Second World War and the bullying tactics of Senator Joseph McCarthy (R-WI) in 1954. Formerly
the most recognizable journalist in America, Edward R. Murrow
did not appear before them as a CBS reporter but, rather, as head of
the United States Information Agency (USIA). His speech, one of the
most eloquent from his three-year tenure as director, focused on the
adverse impact of racism. He cautioned the assembly of attorneys that,
within the context of the Cold War, the United States had become the
most scrutinized nation on earth. "Ours is now the fishbowl world,"
he explained, "where we become the focus of many men's attention
and curiosity."[1] With greater access to media coverage of American
society and communist propaganda criticizing Western capitalism,
foreign observers, particularly in the developing world, wondered

increasingly whether the United States offered a more alluring path to modernity than the one advocated by the Soviet Union and the People's Republic of China.

This work explores Murrow's performance at the USIA in advancing the interests of the United States to those peering into the fishbowl during the fast-paced years of Kennedy's presidency from 1961 to 1963. Kennedy ran for office advocating a "New Frontier," and the campaign slogan initially used to inspire the American people to vote for him came to identify his administration's domestic and foreign policies. Responsibility for defending the rationale behind these programs to a global audience fell to the USIA to accomplish through seven modes of communication: radio, television, motion pictures, press, book publishing, exhibits, and personal contact at agency-operated venues across the world.[2] While Voice of America (VOA) became the most far-reaching and best-known arm of the agency, information officers also ran libraries in foreign countries; published a variety of magazines in nearly forty languages from three regional printing plants in Mexico City, Beirut, and Manila; produced their own cinematographic documentaries; and constructed multimillion-dollar exhibits at World Fairs. On a weekly basis, it provided the White House and State Department with assessments of foreign opinions of the United States. In crass terminology, the USIA served as the propaganda ministry of the United States throughout the Cold War.

Notwithstanding the negative connotations often associated with the word today, U.S. policymakers spoke of their information campaigns as "propaganda" until Edmund Gullion, dean of the Fletcher School of Law and Diplomacy at Tufts University, defined the term "public diplomacy" in 1965.[3] Today, public diplomacy specialists would shirk at being called propagandists, but during the Kennedy administration the term did not always have a negative connotation. As Murrow told a reporter in 1962, "I don't mind being called a propagandist, so long as the propaganda is based on the truth."[4] Donald Wilson, Murrow's deputy director at the USIA, argued that despite the way Joseph Goebbels contorted the term "propaganda" in Nazi Germany, the word did not have as much of a pejorative connotation in other languages as it had for English-speaking Americans. "Among many western Europeans," he discovered, "it has no more connotations of mistruth or evil than 'publicity,' 'promotion,' and 'advertising.'"[5]

In *The Cold War and the United States Information Agency: American Propaganda and Public Diplomacy, 1945–1989*, Nicholas Cull defines public diplomacy more specifically as "an international actor's attempt to conduct its foreign policy by engaging with foreign publics" through five core components: listening, advocacy, cultural diplomacy, exchange diplomacy, and international broadcasting.[6] While traditional diplomacy centered on government-to-government relationships typically conducted in secret, public diplomacy emerged as a government-to-people mode of communication that necessitated a level of transparency unprecedented for diplomats prior to the twentieth century.

Acknowledging that it is anachronistic to apply the term *public diplomacy* to USIA operations from 1961 to 1964, the term still appears throughout this text. For contemporary readers Gullion and Cull's conceptualization of public diplomacy provides an invaluable point of reference for understanding Kennedy's USIA. Murrow and his agency did not use the term, but a study of their operations illustrates that they sought the same goals that practitioners of public diplomacy seek today for advancing U.S. international interests. The term does not appear in the following chapters to praise or condemn the USIA's doctrinal application of Cull's five core components, since that would not be historically authentic. However, while most readers share a negative connotation of the term propaganda, they think immediately of public diplomacy as describing more positive, informational, cultural, and educational forms of engagement with foreign populations.

Throughout history, governments have sought to establish favorable links with foreign populations. In *The First Resort of Kings: American Cultural Diplomacy in the Twentieth Century*, retired USIA public affairs officer Richard Arndt begins his study in antiquity, observing that the Greeks dispatched poets and philosophers as ambassadors, while the Romans donated books to the Egyptian library in Alexandria.[7] By sending the colorful and esteemed Benjamin Franklin to Paris in 1776, the Continental Congress selected a commissioner who would persuade the French public, as much as the Court of Versailles, to forge a military alliance with the United States.[8]

If national leaders did not make at least some of their international affairs public, they risked allowing foreigners to define their own version of a desirable outcome to a legal dispute or lethal conflict. Joseph Nye Jr., former dean of Harvard's Kennedy School of Government, introduced the term "soft power" to define an alternative method for achieving foreign policy, besides the two "hard powers" of military and economic might. Whereas hard powers rely on coercion, states can apply soft power to co-opt others toward a desired direction. For Nye, soft power is a "co-optive power" that depends upon the attraction of one's culture, political values, foreign policies, and international prestige.[9] Understanding how to apply and assess soft power requires deftness because it rarely achieves short-term or tactical advantages. Its value can only be assessed over the long term, based on the diffuse effect that it has in shaping public attitudes and behavior. It also demands recognizing how the evolution of media technology has influenced international engagement.

Shortly before the First World War, technological achievements enabled government leaders, journalists, and commentators to communicate with the masses by use of radio, thereby allowing them to inform and influence populations that previously had limited access to current information beyond newspapers, magazines, local gossip, or the occasional social or political rally. During this conflict, however, the U.S. Committee on Public Information (CPI) did not call its radio programming propaganda because the office associated that label specifically with the "deceit and corruption" of the German government's information campaign.[10] Edward Bernays, who served in the CPI during the agency's twenty-eight-month existence, from 1917 to 1919, wrote one of the earliest studies on this topic in his 1928 work *Propaganda*. He sought to explain how the techniques developed by the federal government to elicit popular support for wartime mobilization could be adopted by corporate America to improve its sales or by politicians to gain votes. Bernays explains the value of an information campaign: "In theory, every citizen makes up his mind on public questions and matters of private conduct. In practice, if all men had to study for themselves the abstruse, economic, political, and ethical data involved in every question, they would find it impossible to come to a conclusion about anything."[11]

Less than a generation later, the U.S. government resurrected the CPI in the form of the Office of War Information (OWI) in order to unite the country in a second global war and to project an American voice into Axis-controlled lands. Throughout World War II, newsreels shown before movies in domestic cinema houses provided people with imagery that further shaped their attitudes toward government policies and world events and the behavior of other nations. With its establishment in February 1942, Voice of America began to broadcast similar messages to the world.

Although the government inactivated the OWI in September 1945, the gradual formation of the Cold War led to the emergence of new modes of public diplomacy. Radio remained a mainstay, with Voice of America staying on the air, and the Central Intelligence Agency (CIA) creating Radio Free Europe and Radio Liberty to target audiences behind the Iron Curtain. The next most monumental technological advancement occurred a year after Murrow's arrival in Washington with the launch of the Telstar 1 satellite on July 10, 1962, which made real-time television and telephone signals increasingly available beyond America's shores. As the sophistication of the modes of communication developed, so too did the forms of public diplomacy.

Regardless of the advancing technological capabilities, many American policymakers doubted that a democratic country should continue to maintain a robust propaganda effort after World War II. Some liberals feared that, like Nazis and Japanese fascists, U.S. government officials might begin to direct propaganda toward American citizens. With the military playing a major role in developing information campaigns during World War II and the occupation of Germany and Japan, propaganda further appeared as an uncivilized and coercive tool. Others on both the political right and left believed that the postwar stature of the United States alone would entice the rest of the world to reject communism, without the government spending a single taxpayer's dollar to explain its policies. Many influential policymakers believed that everyone would want to emulate the United

States based on the freedoms, social mobility, and superior quality of life enjoyed by those pursuing the American dream.

William Benton, assistant secretary of state for public affairs from 1945 to 1947, faced an uphill battle preserving his meager operational budget in 1947 from a Congress intent on slashing the vestiges of the federal government's wartime operations. Not only did he find senators skeptical of the potential value of his division, but senior officials within the State Department looked scornfully at public affairs, hoping to return to the good old days of confidential negotiations handled in regal salons by the personal emissaries of heads of state. However, intelligence reports about robust Soviet propaganda efforts throughout Europe alarmed Benton, shaping his conviction about the need for formal American efforts to counter the communists' global misinformation campaign. Benton shared his concern with Nelson Rockefeller, in a letter on March 21, 1947, encouraging Rockefeller to testify in favor of public affairs before the House appropriations subcommittee on foreign affairs: "The odd fact is that I have run into no one in the State Department with an understanding of this problem comparable to that already shown by General [George] Marshall, as well as by [Generals Dwight] Eisenhower and [Walter] Bedell Smith."[12] Diplomats needed to take ownership of public diplomacy, not the Pentagon, and Benton understood that the task could not be relegated to the international marketing practices of American entrepreneurs. "Coca-colonization," a term coined by Austrian historian Reinhold Wagnleitner, would not approximate what the government could and needed to do to win hearts and minds tempted to experiment with communism after 1945.[13] Messages needed to be carefully scripted for specific demographics and polities and simultaneously delivered through multiple media.

In 1948 Senator Howard Alexander Smith (R-NJ) and Representative Karl Mundt (R-SD) coauthored a bill that authorized government psychological and propaganda operations while forbidding them from being directed toward the United States. The U.S. Information and Education Exchange Act, more commonly known as the Smith-Mundt Act, restricted State Department (and later USIA) officials involved with public diplomacy from engaging in strategic communications or information operations within the United States or its territories. The three generals whom Benton cited as adept propagandists, Eisenhower, Marshall, and Smith, all endorsed the legislation. They stated publicly that it would be insufficient to provide relief aid overseas without explaining the motives of the American people for doing so.[14]

Messages articulated through public diplomacy, such as those authorized by the Smith-Mundt Act, can help researchers understand how a government sought to shape international relations during a particular period. Some diplomatic historians dismiss propaganda as a primary source for uncovering the mentalities of a society, since lofty rhetoric often ignores or dilutes the negative aspects of the collective's culture, mentalities, and policies. Michael Hunt disagrees, arguing in *Ideology and U.S. Foreign Policy* that public rhetoric offers historians a trove of material that reveals the recurrent themes and values shared by the society responsible for crafting the messages, even if its members fail to live up to them.[15] Certainly the most recognizable forms of propaganda—Nazi, North Korean, or even "Baghdad Bob"—seem outlandish or comical.[16] However, twentieth-century U.S. propagandists often believed in what they said, even when they knew that the America they presented to a global audience remained only an aspiration because domestic strife, national limitations, or international communist activities prevented their vision from becoming reality. One significant challenge for the historian of public diplomacy, therefore, is to isolate the kernels of truth found within platitudes and to identify occasions when deliberate deception occurs.

Creation of the USIA in 1953 as the government's principal agency for public diplomacy provided the United States with the capacity to minimize "the danger of inadequate definition" of its policies and actions until the agency's closure in 1999.[17] The agency went by U.S. Information Service (USIS) overseas, but used USIA within the United States so as not to be confused with the U.S. Immigration Service. To limit the number of acronyms used throughout this text, then, the agency is referred to as the USIA. Thomas Sorensen, Murrow's assistant director for plans and policy, and brother of Kennedy's counselor, Theodore, believed that the agency countered communist propaganda by articulating America's philosophy: "In freedom we can find the system best for each, and together evolve the larger systems in which a community of free nations can live in peace."[18] For U.S. policies to succeed, they needed to be understood and supported throughout the world. Cull considers the USIA to be the first global agency with the capacity to disseminate information before any private company could afford to do so on its own, as witnessed now in the age of twenty-four-hour satellite news cycles and Internet social media.[19] Although it could be argued that the British Broadcasting Corporation (BBC) provided this already, the British service only included radio and television broadcasts while, in addition to those two modes, the USIA designed traveling exhibits, built libraries, sponsored cultural programs, and published a variety of print material in dozens of languages.

Beyond carrying the message to local audiences, the USIA participated in the federal interagency operations responsible for developing and executing U.S. foreign policy. The research arm of the agency collected and analyzed public opinions that public affairs officers could share with their country team at embassies that needed to respond to host-nation inquiries and demonstrations. In Washington the USIA director carried studies published by his regional and global analysts to the Cabinet Room for National Security Council (NSC) meetings. The material could be factored into the State Department, Defense Department, and presidential decision-making process. To manage these projects, the USIA attracted an eclectic group of employees, including career civil servants, commissioned Foreign Service officers, and young idealists looking to see the world. A handful of men joined the USIA with considerable professional achievements already under their belts: a television network president, a producer for Warner Brothers, a college dean, a university president, and a *Newsweek* editor.[20]

Effective public diplomacy requires more than the propagation of messages: it must be followed by an assessment of their influence. Political scientist Jarol Manheim believes that strategic public diplomacy can be informed through "an applied transnational science of human behavior," such as polling analysis, in order to gauge the efficacy of communications in shaping foreign opinion or action.[21] The USIA sought to accomplish this for the White House through its Office of Research and Analysis, which collected feedback on its messages and conducted surveys to assess international opinions of the United States. In order to expand the overseas survey pool, the office cooperated with the CIA, private pollsters, and foreign universities. Occasionally the tabulated results of these studies convinced members of presidential administrations to respond more aggressively to domestic ills, such as segregation, cited by foreign critics as the source of their disillusion with the United States.[22] In addition to the directed regional and topical studies conducted by this office, Murrow carefully combed the analytical data in the research division's studies before submitting his personal weekly report to Kennedy on international public opinion.[23]

On January 20, 1961, when Kennedy stirred the consciousness of the world's citizens by asking in his inaugural address what they could do "for the freedom of man," he set the tone for rejuvenating America's transnational role.[24] David Bell, Kennedy's director of the U.S. Agency for International Development (USAID), thought that the new president arrived in the Oval Office with a deeper interest in international affairs than domestic concerns because offshore challenges seemed "more worthy of attention," since America enjoyed relative economic prosperity in the early 1960s.[25] White House adviser and former Harvard history professor Arthur M. Schlesinger Jr. encouraged Kennedy to promote the formation of democratic parties in countries with growing communist movements. Not only could communist governments in "red" countries propagate to the rest of the world, but they could leverage the "unofficial" apparatus of the international Communist Party, which spoke a common language and shared a universal ideology. "One of our basic weaknesses in the competition with the USSR is the absence of any organized mass movement willing to be identified with U.S. ideals," he wrote in 1961.[26] Certainly the USIA would be expected to play a vital role in this environment, but in early 1961 the agency faced two challenges to its credibility, one at home and another abroad.

Many Americans found the agency ineffectual at the close of the

Eisenhower administration, particularly because of incriminating charges posed by Senator McCarthy during the height of the Red Scare against "subversive" VOA broadcasters as well as "pro-Communist" books and employees in overseas libraries managed by the International Information Agency of the State Department, the precursor to USIA.[27] Regardless of the Senate's 1954 censure of McCarthy, the perception of the USIA seven years later remained poor, evidenced by the trivialization of its public image and the unapologetic slashing of its budget by Congress. With agency morale low and appropriations modest, Nikita Khrushchev and Mao Zedong elevated their voices for worldwide revolution with comparatively limited American competition. For example, international communist broadcasts, such as Radio Moscow, dwarfed Voice of America at the beginning of the Kennedy administration, and in 1961 Soviet and Chinese broadcasting into the Third World increased 8 percent from the year prior. While the Soviets provided 1,067 hours a week and the Chinese 734 hours, Voice of America provided only 632 hours.[28] To put the USIA's size into perspective with other American Cold War priorities, the agency's annual budget equated to less than the cost of one Polaris submarine when Murrow arrived in Washington.[29]

The second challenge stemmed from the increasing hollowness of the agency's messages during the Eisenhower administration. In *The Truth Is Our Weapon*, State Department historian Chris Tudda contrasts Eisenhower's public diplomacy with his confidential foreign policy objectives. While the president and his secretary of state, John Foster Dulles, accepted a divided Germany and communist sphere of influence in Eastern Europe for the foreseeable future, and they agreed that the United States and Soviet Union could coexist, their rhetorical messages suggested otherwise.[30] Public speeches by administration officials, and communications directed toward Europe via myriad USIA and CIA media, advocated for a "dynamic" containment policy and encouraged the "rollback" of communism through the remilitarization of West Germany, enhancement of North Atlantic collective security, and support for Eastern European liberation movements. This backfired on the administration because it only incited greater fear in the American population by portraying the Soviets as a larger threat while also emboldening Khrushchev to act more abrasively as soon as he realized that Ike would not confront him, evidenced by the Soviet invasion to crush the 1956 Hungarian Uprising.[31] At the close of his second administration, Eisenhower voiced disappointment in not realizing his foreign policy goals vis-à-vis the Soviet Union, but, as Tudda observes, "when it came time to bite the bullet and *implement* their confidential strategies of competitive coexistence with the Soviet Union and alliance management with their allies, they could not break out of the public, rhetorical traps they had created."[32]

While the Eisenhower administration focused on winning the Cold War in Europe, the USIA's messages to the decolonizing world during the 1950s remained disappointing. In the spring of 1960, the president authorized the formation of a committee to evaluate the efficacy of the USIA and consider its incorporation into the State Department. Led by Mansfield Sprague, former assistant secretary of defense for international affairs, the committee submitted a report on December 23, 1960. Although it did not endorse eliminating the USIA, it recommended that the agency reorient its focus. Sprague called attention to the U.S. deficit in Asia, Latin America, and Africa, where "the pace of political developments has outstripped our informational preparations."[33] To achieve its desired influence in the developing world, the report urged the administration to invest in a new form of "total diplomacy" by expanding its funding for educational, person-to-person, and cultural exchange initiatives.[34]

Senator George Smathers (D-FL), a close friend of Kennedy's who managed his presidential campaign in the southeastern United States, found the USIA to be ineffectual in its production of news and cultural programming.[35] Shortly before Kennedy's inauguration, Smathers sent the president-elect a personal assessment of the agency titled "Need for New Type of Leadership and Reorientation for the United States Information Agency." He argued that the agency's "impotency" originated from espousing broad-based platitudes. New leadership might "cut away the excess fat," which the senator identified as educational programs, such as square dancing classes in Nairobi and the translation of "do-it-yourself" books into Arabic. Smathers encouraged

Kennedy to select a new director who would counter anti-American propaganda by defending the country's policy record and national achievements.[36]

The media joined Smathers in lambasting the USIA in 1961. A week after Chief Justice Earl Warren swore Kennedy into office, the *New York Times* assessed the agency's service to America's international image as deplorable: "No country ever had a better story to tell or failed so lamentably to tell it well as the United States in the sixteen years since the end of the war. . . . [The USIA] has been a spectacular disappointment from beginning to end." Journalist James Reston speculated that the failures may not have rested with the directors of the agency but, rather, with Eisenhower and Dulles, for failing to include the USIA directors in formulating foreign policy. "This separation of policy and propaganda is the heart of the problem," Reston argued, before suggesting that Kennedy could rectify the problem by making his USIA director a member of the National Security Council.[37] Another editorial published widely on February 7, 1961, observed that the American story could be no better than the policies pursued by the government. To increase the likelihood that policy would be palatable to a foreign audience, the author called for the USIA's involvement in White House and State Department deliberations: "When the policies are framed, an expert in the molding and shaping of world opinion should be sitting in, and not merely as an observer."[38]

Awaiting his Senate confirmation to become deputy director of the USIA, Donald Wilson, a former *Time* magazine correspondent and member of the Kennedy transition team, responded to Smathers's critique of the agency in a letter to the president. He took exception to what the senator referred to as "fat," arguing that "all these programs exist only to further the achievement of U.S. foreign policy objectives." Specifically, he cited the USIA libraries as being the heart of the agency's overseas program. Wilson conceded to Smathers's call for new leadership: "The appointment of Murrow should kindle an enthusiasm within the Agency (and without) that can prove more valuable than any other single element. This value will lie in Murrow's ability to attract talent to the Agency and to make the most of the talent already in USIA."[39]

Kennedy shared Wilson's optimism in Murrow's potential. In a personal letter to William Benton, who had left the State Department to become the head of Encyclopedia Britannica, Kennedy expressed his excitement about Murrow's imminent arrival in Washington: "We are looking for great things from him and the USIA."[40] When Kennedy's press secretary, Pierre Salinger, confirmed on January 28, 1961, that Murrow had accepted the president's nomination as USIA director, most national newspapers hailed Murrow as an excellent choice for "this sort of interpretative, even evangelistic assignment."[41] Many journalists speculated in their columns that Murrow, acclaimed for his moral courage, would carry this quality to the USIA, lending international credibility to American foreign policy.[42] Influential members within the administration also approved of the selection. Undersecretary of State Chester Bowles, one of the administration's prominent liberals, eagerly anticipated Murrow's arrival in Washington. He wrote a congratulatory note to Murrow to assure him that he would "make an enormous contribution to our foreign policy in these next few years."[43]

After a twenty-five-year career at CBS that had brought celebrity status, fortune, and numerous honors, it is not entirely clear why Murrow chose to leave his $300,000 annual salary in New York City to serve as the chief bureaucrat of a government agency with lackluster approval ratings.[44] His biographers agree that he had grown disenchanted with what he saw as the CBS executives' obsession with profits and their tolerance for sensationalism that encroached upon the integrity of their news division.[45] Murrow's former editorial adviser at CBS, journalist Raymond Swing, joined Voice of America prior to Murrow's arrival at the USIA, and he observed that in 1960 Murrow had had a "thoroughly unhappy" year professionally.[46] Quiz shows and situational comedies attracted the wealthiest sponsors, and Murrow faced cuts in available airtime and resources to produce the caliber of journalism that he aspired to provide for the network. Scholars Betty Winfield and Lois DeFleur contend that Murrow's personal values served as his journalistic standards, indicating that his departure from CBS for the USIA symbolized his disillusion with the television industry.[47] Shortly before accepting Kennedy's offer, Murrow confided to former *Time* correspondent Wilmott Ragsdale: "I am afraid I have never shared the view that we [in American journalism] have the best news coverage in the world. It is true that we throw at the public more unasserted, more undigested, more unevaluated information than is true in the case of other countries, but that doesn't necessarily mean that the public is well informed."[48] Perhaps the USIA appealed to Murrow because he thought that he would be able to sort, digest, and evaluate the information presented through the agency's varied mediums with a level of authority no longer afforded to him in New York.

Uncovering Murrow the man is difficult; he did not write diaries, and his personal correspondence remained scant in expressing personal moods or reflections. His single attempt to maintain a meticulous written account of his experiences occurred in London during World War II, but when a German Luftwaffe bomb exploded in the building housing his office and destroyed his papers, he terminated the endeavor. Date books available in archives are few and empty, suggesting that people removed pages of interest prior to donating them. Those who considered themselves Murrow's friends, and who were interviewed after his death, realized only in retrospect how elusive Murrow had been beneath his public persona.

Murrow came across as glum or morose with his head down in conversations, but as soon as he began talking, he sounded eloquent and engaged. His son, Charles Casey Murrow, thought of his father's reserved appearance as his way of holding back while he formed his thoughts.[49] In the most comprehensive of the three major Murrow biographies, Ann Sperber offers this explanation for his stoicism: "He was a distinct American type, the product of an older social order, preindustrial, Calvinistic, with heavy overtones of guilt, a stern morality, and a sense of right and wrong that owed more to the Bible—'doing the right thing'—than to any set political doctrine."[50] Tufts University archivist Susanne Belovari provides another theory for why few handwritten letters exist: Murrow was somewhat dyslexic and not a very good writer. After BBC colleagues introduced him to the Dictaphone during the Blitz, he began to dictate extensively, even entire scripts for CBS, in an effort to make the script sound more natural.[51]

For other correspondence, he relied on secretaries and in retirement his wife to type his dictations.

In contrast to their exploration of his tenure at CBS, biographies on Murrow provide scant analysis of his three-year tenure at the USIA. As Richard Arndt commented, "We have only begun to pin down the Murrow myth" at the agency.[52] Certainly the bulk of any life history of the celebrated journalist should focus on Murrow's twenty-five-year career with CBS, particularly his formation of the "Murrow Boys" in Europe during World War II and his efforts to challenge McCarthy's legitimacy on his television program, *See It Now*, in 1954. Nevertheless, none of the three major works on Murrow's life that have appeared since 1969 seriously examines his USIA director files at the National Archives, the Kennedy Presidential Library, or the Tufts University archive, which houses his personal and professional papers.

Shortly after Murrow's death in 1965, Little, Brown and Company publishers approached Thomas Sorensen, Murrow's assistant director for plans and policy, encouraging him to write an appropriate "companion piece" to his brother Theodore's book, *Kennedy*. Tom declined the offer because he was only intimate with Murrow's time as agency director and felt that Murrow's life as a journalist should be the primary focus of such a work.[53] However, the view of an agency insider and close associate of Murrow's during his time in Washington might have improved the thoroughness of the chapters pertaining to his directorship in the volumes written by others. Three years after Murrow's death, Tom did write a book about the development of American public diplomacy from World War I through the first Johnson administration, *The Word War*, which includes three chapters on the USIA during the Kennedy years.[54] Compared to the rest of Sorensen's book, these chapters read like a memoir by providing a unique window into Murrow's office. Unfortunately, his notes are few and offer little help for scholars attempting to navigate the USIA record group at the National Archives.

Little, Brown found their author in Alexander Kendrick, releasing *Prime Time* in 1969. With so much USIA material still classified at the time, Kendrick could not access most records and relied heavily on interviews. Ann Sperber and Joseph Persico authored weighty works on Murrow in the 1980s. Although Sperber relied on Murrow's personal papers housed at Tufts University, she did not examine his extensive director files maintained by the National Archives. By 1988, Persico had access to the most declassified documents, but he only devoted twenty pages of his book to Murrow's directorship and opted to rely on interviews in lieu of archival material.

Historians focused on Cold War public diplomacy have peered around the Kennedy administration in much of their work without giving it the attention paid to other presidencies. In addition to Tudda's study of the Eisenhower administration, Laura Belmonte authored *Selling the American Way: U.S. Propaganda and the Cold War*, yet despite the subtitle she only explores the Truman and Eisenhower administrations.[55] Walter Hixson also covers the Truman and Eisenhower years in *Parting the Curtain* by exploring American "cultural infiltration" through the construction of U.S. exhibition pavilions in Eastern Europe and the Soviet Union.[56] Insightful books on Cold War radio broadcasting, especially Alan Heil Jr.'s *Voice of America: A History* and Michael Nelson's *War of the Black Heavens*, only provide a handful of assessments of Murrow's impact on VOA.[57] Although Richard Arndt provides a chapter on the New Frontier in *The First Resort of Kings*, he relies nearly entirely on Murrow biographies as sources.[58]

The best research of Kennedy's public diplomacy appears in a single chapter of Cull's *The Cold War and the United States Information Agency* and several chapters that he authored for anthologies. Cull is somewhat critical of Murrow's tenure with the USIA, opining that he cared more about the appearance of truth in agency programming than the substance of truth. The chapter title "Inventing Truth" indicates his disapproval of Murrow's leadership, and Cull focuses especially on the "growing incompatibility between USIA and VOA" during his directorship.[59] Nonetheless, Cull credits Murrow with influencing Kennedy to bring the USIA into the foreign policy planning process so that agency messages could better complement the operations of other federal entities responsible for executing foreign policy. Cull further recognizes Murrow's efforts to advance civil rights by setting the standard for other government agencies to emulate by hiring more African Americans than any other, and by promoting so many that blacks occupied one in every ten senior and mid-grade USIA positions.[60] Cull sees Murrow's influence in foreign policy to be minimal, however, because Kennedy formulated many of his decisions outside of the National Security Council. Kennedy's preference for executive committees and impromptu consultations left policymaking to a handful of confidants, thereby excluding experts in a variety of fields, including public diplomacy.

As a senior government official, Murrow struggled to deal with Kennedy's minimalist legislative agenda amid the international tensions exacerbated by Khrushchev, crises in Berlin and Cuba, and the emergence of dozens of newly independent states in the Third World. This study relies heavily on USIA documents, dispatches from U.S. embassies around the world, hundreds of oral histories, and Murrow's personal papers to examine one of the most internationally visible arms of the U.S. government that deserves greater scrutiny by scholars of Murrow and Cold War public diplomacy. The first two chapters trace Murrow's decision to leave CBS after his twenty-five-year affiliation and his adjustment to the work of a political appointee in Washington DC. Subsequent chapters examine major foreign policy challenges of the Kennedy administration through the lens of the USIA to assess how Murrow's leadership shaped the execution of public diplomacy and how effectively the agency helped to advance the president's vision. The concluding chapter examines the most likely reason for Murrow's resignation in January 1964—his deteriorating health—and provides a final evaluation of his impact on the USIA.

Murrow believed that the agency served two roles for the United States, both of which departed from the USIA's focus during the Eisenhower administration. First, the agency needed not merely to inform but to persuade foreign audiences about the merits of the American way of life and its policies. Second, it needed to provide expert advice to the president on how his policies influenced foreign opinion. Murrow wanted the USIA to establish long-term strategic objectives and resist living in the present in the way that a traditional news agency operates. In an internal USIA memo written two months into his directorship, Murrow emphasized that the agency "[needs] long-range planning with a full recognition that the principle of flexibility must always apply." While the agency would constantly need to react to explosive stories and counter communist propaganda, Murrow knew that effective international engagements also required the delivery of a dynamic message. Flexibility, coupled with an established strategic end state, would improve the chances of success. "We must be able to take the broad general outlines of foreign policy," he continued, "resolve the inconsistencies to the point that they are explainable, and then proceed in a thoughtful but flexible manner to pursue the aims and objectives which we seek."[61] Murrow's memo championed the feelings of other USIA employees. One public affairs officer, who had served with the agency since its inception, told an Associated Press reporter, "We've got to quit jumping from crisis to crisis, and concentrate on getting our story across to people who count. That's more important than bragging about how many hours a day we broadcast in Cuba."[62]

Despite attending White House meetings regularly, Murrow was not an outspoken member of the administration. Still, Murrow communicated regularly with Kennedy and senior policymakers. He personally submitted the USIA's weekly roll-up on world opinion to the president, attended weekly meetings with Secretary of State Dean Rusk at Foggy Bottom, and interacted with National Security Adviser McGeorge Bundy several times a week. Casey Murrow said that his father thought it a "real coup" to have acquired a seat in the NSC, so perhaps he feared that off-the-cuff comments would jeopardize his attendance.[63] Other insiders believed that Murrow's quiet participation stemmed from a feeling that his advice was not welcomed. However, Murrow carefully selected his opportunities to lend input and kept his points succinct in order to achieve maximum effect. This approach gained him Kennedy's highest confidence, and the president listened to his advice on the occasions when he spoke.[64] Edward Kennedy recalled that his brother relied upon Murrow "implicitly."[65] Biographer Alexander Kendrick explains the Kennedy-Murrow relationship as "a cordial one, based on mutual respect, though in their private characters both men had an instinctive reserve and a kind of scrutiny that precluded any real openhandedness."[66]

Although a liberal, Murrow's journalism background made him

more of a political realist than other administration liberals, such as Arthur Schlesinger Jr. and Chester Bowles, who grew frustrated with what they perceived as Kennedy's reluctance to advance progressive policies at home and abroad. Murrow accepted what he could not influence within the administration. On a few occasions, he spoke up passionately when he believed that his view needed to be heard, such as his plea for the president to take the moral high ground by not resuming nuclear testing, and his personal cables to Kennedy urging him to demonstrate solidarity with West Berlin quickly after the construction of the Berlin Wall. When the president chose a different path or acted slowly to correct a problem, as with his civil rights record, Murrow did not disparage the president but directed the USIA to explain the administration's position to an international audience as clearly as possible. Within his agency, Murrow brought aboard three young and imaginative deputies—Donald Wilson, his principal deputy, Thomas Sorensen, his assistant director for policy and plans, and George Stevens Jr., his Motion Picture Service director—who developed a more sophisticated public diplomacy operation than that of their predecessors.

Murrow expected message guidance and administrative priorities to drive what Voice of America reported and what public affairs officers discussed from outposts around the world. Above all, Murrow felt strongly about the credibility of U.S. information. He found the Soviets' storyline about everything being rosy on their side of the Iron Curtain as "comical," and in contrast he wanted the world to find the USIA's accounts to be believable.[67] Nevertheless, the agency needed to strike a balance so that it did not appear to be disparaging the United States, and seeking that balance consumed Murrow during his years in Washington. Murrow knew that the U.S. Information Agency would not succeed in its mission without engaging its international audience in the "delicate, difficult art of human persuasion" by explaining "why we do what we do" as Americans.[68]

ABBREVIATIONS

AFN	Armed Forces Network
CIA	Central Intelligence Agency
CORE	Congress of Racial Equality
CPI	U.S. Committee on Public Information
FCC	Federal Communications Commission
FRG	Federal Republic of Germany
GDR	German Democratic Republic
HUAC	House Un-American Activities Committee
NAACP	National Association for the Advancement of Colored People
NASA	National Aeronautics and Space Administration
NATO	North Atlantic Treaty Organization
NIE	National Intelligence Estimate
NSC	National Security Council
NSFA	National Student Federation of America
OAS	Organization of American States
OWI	Office of War Information
RIAS	Rundfunk im amerikanischen Sektor (Broadcasting in the American Sector)
USAID	U.S. Agency for International Development
USIA	U.S. Information Agency
USIS	U.S. Information Service
VOA	Voice of America

MURROW'S COLD WAR

1

Good Night, CBS

Right now I suffer from a great sense
of frustration and loss of time.
—EDWARD R. MURROW, March 1, 1960

Few individuals would balk at a yearlong, all-expenses-paid sabbatical to circle the globe, but for Edward R. Murrow, who embarked on just such an adventure, thanks to the largesse of CBS in 1959, boredom set in by the third month. Perhaps the entire idea had been a mistake; perhaps it was time to sever professional ties with the network that had been his sole employer for the past quarter century. Fortunately for Murrow, he did not lack options. As arguably the most recognized and respected journalist in the United States, Murrow received numerous offers to teach in schools of journalism or serve as a college president; however, these remained less enticing than offers to remain a reporter, his true passion. Quietly, the Ford Foundation engaged Murrow about the possibility of helping to create a national public broadcasting network. Murrow's son, Casey, speculates that, given his father's challenges with CBS, he may have preferred to join a nonprofit network where executives focused more on programming content than the size of profit margins.[1]

CBS executives proposed the sabbatical as a cooling-off period and an opportunity to mend a public relations disaster. Tensions between

Murrow and his superiors had developed in the late 1950s over corporate influence in the newsroom. In Murrow's view, their willingness to pander to advertisers who preferred the mundane to provocative content directly hindered the news division's ability to provide viewers with substantive journalism. Dissatisfied with his ability to persuade executives behind the doors of the CBS boardroom at 485 Madison Avenue, Murrow began to vent his frustrations publicly. Beginning his travels in London, where he delivered a lecture in October 1959, Murrow acknowledged to James Seward, a personal confidant and CBS executive vice president, that his differences with network president Frank Stanton seemed irreconcilable. He vented to Seward that he would sorely like to testify before Congress in order to save the dwindling credibility of television journalism or even have a "thorough-going public row."[2]

Stanton did not seem eager to make amends, choosing instead to fight back a week later by insinuating that Murrow rehearsed celebrity interviews for his *Person to Person* television program. Similar allegations about the quiz shows had become a national scandal earlier that same year. The accusation backfired on Stanton, since many in Murrow's audience were incredulous that the network would compare Murrow's meticulous work to the shenanigans of television game shows. It also directly contradicted an official CBS statement from October 24: "As Dr. Stanton has attempted to make quite clear on several occasions, none of us at CBS has the slightest objection to the way 'Person to Person' has been produced. Indeed, we have always been very proud of the program and those who have participated in it."[3] Within days Stanton backtracked, explaining at a New Orleans engagement that he had only cited *Person to Person* as an example of how absurd it was to suggest seriously that CBS canned any of its real-time shows.[4]

From London, Murrow traveled to Switzerland in late November with his wife, Janet—his son already enrolled in a Swiss boarding school—where they remained for the rest of the year.[5] Murrow even arranged for Seward to ship his Ford Thunderbird to Europe from New York so that he and Janet would have the liberty to travel wherever they wished on the continent. Murrow told one confidant

Good Night, CBS

that he sought "no public row" with Stanton and hoped that his employer would discontinue provoking media inquiries into CBS interview shows. However, Murrow remained defensive: "I am still determined that if there is a break they must fire me[;] after all they hired my services not my silence."[6] Reading about Stanton's accusation from Geneva, Murrow cabled his mother to reassure her that she should not worry about the public criticism: "Hope you haven't been concerned about my small row with CBS. . . . They panicked over the quiz show business and thought to throw me to the lions."[7] In another telegram to her on January 5, 1960, he promised her that he would be fine: "Stanton in particular doesn't like people who are not afraid of him and I am not and he knows it. I have become something of a controversial character but that is nothing new."[8]

Despite his confidence in being exonerated, by mid-January Murrow indicated his dislike for the extended European retreat, suggesting that he really did want to get back to journalism. He felt more exhausted on the vacation than he did prior to the trip, and he complained about the poor weather in Switzerland. He felt "very disappointed" by a recent CBS news report on Iran, but he lacked the motivation to write a critique to his longtime producer, Fred Friendly. Murrow also terminated a report of his own that he had begun on the future of television. Evidently restless, he decided to ship his Thunderbird to Israel, where he and Janet traveled by air, to begin a documentary on the Holy Land. Over the winter he read the Bible as a history book and expressed some interest in its narrative but little else in January's frosty gloom.[9]

Despite the biblical project, Israel did not make him any happier: "I have been reading much Plato which doesn't contribute to peace of mind. . . . [and] am being driven mad by well meaning Hebrews."[10] While in the Middle East, he stopped in Iran, spending two weeks on a program for CBS. He elicited the help of Burnett Anderson, the Tehran U.S. Information Agency public affairs officer, who worked closely with him for the duration of the filming. Little did either know at the time, but Anderson would work for Murrow the following year.[11] News arrived of Stanton's testimony before Congress about network production rigging, tempting Murrow once again to respond, but he reconsidered and held his tongue. Frustrated by what he could not mend, he confided in a telegram to CBS radio broadcaster Edward Morgan, "I am tired beyond endurance and wish myself in some far place but know not where . . . enough of this."[12]

Part of his stress stemmed from not knowing what he would be returning to in New York. The network canceled his major television program, the investigative journalism *See It Now*, in the summer of 1958. Since 1953, he had hosted *Person to Person*, a much lighter show where he pioneered the celebrity interview; however, the network replaced him as host with Charles Collingwood, in 1959, prior to Murrow's departure for London. A new show that year, *Small World*, allowed him to serve as moderator for a broad range of guests to discuss current events, but it did not enjoy a regular time slot, which made it challenging to build a loyal audience.[13] Despite his yearlong hiatus, a CBS official told the *New York Times* that Murrow would return to the air on July 1, 1960, without specifying what show he would host. The *Times* reporter noted that Murrow "lived in a shadow of speculation" since leaving the country in July 1959.[14] Still, Seward remained optimistic that Stanton would agree to give Murrow a weekly radio program on Sundays at a minimum.[15]

The Murrows' journey continued across Asia in the spring, but this region also failed to buoy his spirits. In March he remained tired, turning down Friendly's invitation to travel to the Republic of China for a month to cover the Quemoy Matsu crisis because "[I] simply haven't the energy." However, he agreed to record a weekly half-hour radio piece. This did not make him happy either, as he explained morosely to Morgan from India, "Right now I suffer from a great sense of frustration and loss of time."[16] His mood continued to darken toward the end of the month, and in referring to Stanton's most recent public announcement about the future of news on his network, Murrow said, "[It] made me want to vomit." Murrow seemed totally exasperated and ready to terminate his relationship with CBS. Writing to Seward from Hong Kong, he said, "This whole expedition just hasn't worked out. . . . Unless I hear from someone in authority at CBS I am likely to say that the last contact I had with the company was when they sent a man to London to tell me I was fired."[17]

CBS executives continued to debate what to do with Murrow. While lodging at Tokyo's Imperial Hotel, Murrow received a letter from Seward on March 26, 1960, explaining that the television division "wavered" about whether or not to air Murrow's *Small World* on a more regular basis. The network announced publicly that when Murrow returned on July 1 he would do a weekly radio series titled *Background*, in addition to participating in election and political convention coverage. Seward encouraged Murrow to respond to media inquiries about his feud with Stanton by clarifying that it had been grossly exaggerated, and that he understood that the CBS president had used *Person to Person* as an example of upholding media standards, rather than to associate it nefariously with the scandalous quiz shows. Further, Seward suggested that Murrow explain his more recent negativity in the press as a natural response to attacks against his integrity or his commitment to journalistic excellence.[18]

Murrow responded to Seward's recommendations by explaining why he could not agree to regurgitate the corporate talking points. In the last phone conversation he had with Stanton in London the previous October, the network president told him, "We haven't been able to solve this matter." Therefore, Murrow said that "under no circumstances will I say that my belated comment was extreme or unwarranted. . . . I can think of nothing less important than what Dr. Stanton thinks of me unless it's what I think of him." Nonetheless, to assure Seward that he did not seek to exacerbate the situation further, Murrow reminded Seward that, as "an old enough hand," he knew how to keep from being provoked by sensational reporters. He remained on the defensive, emphasizing that he would not tolerate CBS insinuating that he created the rift: "If my conscience wherever it resides summons me to make public comment on the state of TV or radio I shall certainly do so and be prepared to suffer the consequences . . . this sounds pompous as hell, but you will know what I mean . . . right now the whole bloody business seems too juvenile to bother with."[19] Seward sympathized with Murrow's position with one exception: he instructed his friend never to disclose publicly how little he thought of Stanton.[20]

The exile of Edward R. Murrow would have surprised most of his admirers if they had had access to the cables and letters crossing the Atlantic and Pacific Oceans between October 1959 and April 1960. Since 1937, when he began acquiring his CBS audience from London, where he tried to make sense of the disintegration of European civilization, Murrow's name had become synonymous with integrity and honesty. He took his work seriously, sought to illuminate complex issues, both foreign and domestic, and provided eloquent analysis in his commentaries. Further, his listeners would have found his depression alarming, since he always exuded confidence on television, whether interviewing heads of state or reporting on sensitive topics such as civil rights or communist infiltration in the United States. Throughout his life, however, Murrow's family and closest associates knew of his moodiness, even his nervousness prior to going on the air, but he managed successfully to keep this from the public's eye the moment that a microphone activated or a camera began to roll.

His humble origins did not make his rise to international fame inevitable, but the resoluteness that he demonstrated throughout his life helps explain his stubborn unwillingness to compromise his ethics with CBS over programming content. Perhaps he gained this sense of commitment from his Quaker parents, Roscoe C. and Ethel F. (née Lamb) Murrow.[21] Egbert Roscoe Murrow was born at Polecat Creek, near Greensboro, North Carolina, on April 8, 1908, the youngest of three sons. Murrow's father struggled to support the family by selling corn and hay from their modest farm.[22] When Egbert was six—he did not change his name to Edward until his second year of college, after already adopting the nickname Ed—his parents trekked across country for a fresh start in Blanchard, Washington, seventy miles north of Seattle. Although a seemingly risky move, Roscoe decided to uproot his family after hearing promising stories from Ethel's cousin about Washington's logging camps and sawmills. Fortunately Roscoe found employment as a lumberjack and eventually a locomotive engineer for the Samish Bay Logging Company.[23]

Throughout his childhood, Murrow seemed determined to keep up with his older siblings. Murrow looks downright dour as a little boy in a photo of him posing beside his two older brothers, Lacey and Dewey, and some biographers consider this an indication of his stoicism. However, the background of the photo is much more humorous. On the first day of a new school year for his brothers, Murrow threw a temper tantrum because he was not old enough to go to school himself. Since his mother wanted a picture of her three boys, she handed her youngest son a book to settle him down. While he is not crying in the photo, he displays the classic morose stare that many have confused for Murrow being glum when in fact he was focused on a project or deep in thought.[24]

At Edison High School, Murrow completed his academic work, but his real education came from delving into extracurricular activities "as though discovering a buffet" after attending first through eighth grades in Blanchard's two-room grammar school.[25] Voted "most popular" among his classmates, they elected him senior class and student body president. He competed in school debates and baseball and participated in the school's orchestra and glee club.[26] From the age of fourteen until completing college, Murrow spent his summers learning from lumberjacks how to rough it in the wilderness, smoke cigarettes, and incorporate "the exquisite expressiveness" of profanity into his language.[27]

Although he aspired to study law at the University of Virginia, his family's financial means limited him to Washington State College (now University) where he majored in speech. As with high school, Murrow completed his homework but took greater interest outside of the classroom in the Kappa Sigma fraternity and student government, to include serving as president of both the student body and the intercollegiate Pacific Student Presidents Association, and cadet battalion commander of the school's Reserve Officer Training Corps. However, he learned to take his academics more seriously under the tutelage and mentorship of his speech professor, Ida Lou Anderson, a crippled woman only eight years his senior. Murrow became her star pupil by taking every class she offered, and she not only honed his unique delivery style, but she later sent him letters with recommendations on how to improve his broadcasts during his early years at CBS.[28]

With his grades on the rise and finding a passion for debate, Murrow convinced his college to send him to the National Student Federation of America's (NSFA) national convention at Stanford University in

December 1929 where he delivered a speech encouraging his peers to take greater interest in national and international affairs. The speech received such high praise from the audience that they elected him president of the federation, the largest collegiate student organization in the country. His prose and maturity impressed the organization's administrators so much that, upon his college graduation in 1930, they asked Murrow to take a position with the NSFA main office in New York. Accepting the offer, Murrow busied himself with the administration of the federation, a job that came with no salary but a modest living allowance of twenty-five dollars a week.[29]

Over the next seven years, Murrow used the cross-country move as an occasion to navigate his way into the field of journalism, albeit unintentionally. In 1930 he did not know what career to pursue, but the federation offered him the one opportunity that he definitely wanted after graduating from college: a ticket away from the sawmills of Washington. As one of forty country members of the International Confederation of Students, the NSFA afforded Murrow the opportunity to travel to Europe. International conferences allowed him to engage foreign students in political debates, which broadened his worldview. Returning to New York, he learned that producers from the fledgling two-year-old CBS radio network had invited the NSFA to fill a portion of their midday schedule that lacked sponsors so that it would not have dead air. This is how the organization brought Murrow to the microphone and provided him with the chance to utilize the communication skills developed under Professor Anderson. On September 15, 1930, he hosted Robert Kelly, executive secretary of the Association of American Colleges, for an on-air discussion titled "Looking Forward with Students." After the interview, the producers told Murrow that they approved of his performance, but they would only invite him back if he could find bigger names. Amazingly, the twenty-two-year-old succeeded, bringing on international heavyweights such as Paul von Hindenburg and Mahatma Gandhi.[30]

In addition to foreign travel and radio airtime, Murrow participated in a number of student conferences across the United States, including one at Mount Holyoke College in Western Massachusetts, for the International Student Service. Due to a bad case of poison ivy, sophomore Janet Huntington Brewster observed conference proceedings from the balcony, and she found it "repulsive" that Murrow seemed to enjoy a bit too much being the center of attention on the stage of the all-girl school's auditorium. Murrow returned to New York from the conference without meeting Janet, his future wife. In 1933 he left the NSFA after two years as its president, but the director of the Institute of International Education enticed Murrow to join him as his deputy. Best of all, it was a salaried job for someone who had been subsisting on twenty-five dollars a week in Manhattan. While traveling to New Orleans for another student conference, he ran into Janet as he boarded a train in Greensboro, North Carolina. Not only did the pair begin conversing on the rail, but while in Louisiana Murrow focused more of his attention on Janet than he did on the conference.[31] She projected a "quiet, pervading warmth of personality" to complement Murrow's.[32] The two continued to deepen their relationship through the exchange of letters until Janet graduated from Mount Holyoke in the summer of 1933, and Murrow proposed to her that September. After teaching English and commercial law during their yearlong engagement, she married Ed and moved into his Manhattan apartment.

The newlyweds did not remain in New York for long. In September 1935, Murrow gained employment with CBS, a network that still lacked a robust newsroom but had just announced the creation of a new position called director of talks. Even with his respected affiliation with the network, from his time with the NSFA, he worried that his credentials would be unimpressive. He tacked five years to his age on his résumé and wrote that he had double-majored in political science and international relations and earned a master's degree from Stanford University. National Public Radio host Bob Edwards has pointed out the irony: "He was lying again to get a job at CBS, where he would establish a reputation for integrity and become a champion of truth."[33]

Murrow probably did not need to exaggerate his accomplishments to impress Edward Klauber, the vice president who hired him, or William Paley, the network's founder and president. Shortly after Murrow received the position of director of talks, Paley took a personal interest in the mature and zealous abilities of the young man, and the two developed a professional partnership that grew into a friendship that would last a lifetime.[34] From his earliest days with CBS, the twenty-seven-year-old devoted long hours to ensure the perfection of every radio broadcast.

Less than two years into his employment, Murrow traveled to New Orleans in February 1937 to cover a conference where, once again, he experienced a significant life-altering event in the Big Easy. Reminiscing about the earliest days of their courtship at the student conference in New Orleans in the spring of 1933, Janet joined him for the business trip. During their stay, Klauber unexpectedly telephoned Murrow's hotel to offer him a new position as the network's European director. Although Klauber did not share his motive over the phone, network executives were worried about CBS's ability to compete with NBC, due to their rival recently dispatching a reporter to Europe to provide "special events" broadcasts. Caesar Saerchinger—who during his seven-year stint in Europe for CBS broke the story that Edward VIII would abdicate the throne—wanted to come home to do something else for the network. Murrow stayed up all night with Janet debating the reassignment. Although he silently feared that leaving New York would hurt his chances for climbing the corporate ladder, Murrow accepted the offer because of the allure of reporting from overseas. On April 1, 1937, the Murrows sailed for England to set up shop in London, although Murrow regularly traveled to the European continent to cover major stories.[35] His timing could not have been more fortuitous, and the assignment would catapult him onto the world stage.

While England's economy and mood seemed as dreary as its weather in the spring of 1937, the euphoria emanating from Germany, under Adolf Hitler's populist leadership, indicated that the next year might not be as dull for the Europeans. In the late 1930s, most Americans tuning in to listen to one of the three daily CBS news reports wanted to understand how President Franklin D. Roosevelt's New Deal would ameliorate the effects of the Great Depression. Analysis about German rearmament or the propaganda of Joseph Goebbels did not interest the majority. Regardless, Murrow realized through his travels on the continent that it would not be in the interest of the United States for Hitler's worldview to come to fruition. From the summer of 1937 until the U.S. Congress declared war on Germany, on December 8, 1941, Murrow sought to influence the American people to be less apathetic about the Nazis' bullying of their neighbors. On March 12, 1938, for example, Murrow chartered a plane from Berlin to Vienna in order to land prior to Hitler's arrival so that he could report on the Austrian response to the Anschluss before it became official. Working to get around his Nazi censor three days later in a studio in Vienna to comment on the locals' reaction to the animated speech of the Führer, Murrow stressed that, despite the German propaganda praising the annexation of Austria into the Third Reich, he did not find everyone in the city as ebullient. While he could not label the takeover a tragedy without losing his privilege to broadcast, he cagily described the masses' applause beneath Hitler's balcony as "either wholehearted . . . or complete silence," earning himself the icy stare of his Nazi censor.[36]

Despite his youth, Murrow managed to interview many senior British leaders about foreign policy because they needed his help more than he needed theirs. Important individuals, such as outspoken Liberal Member of Parliament Winston Churchill, who ascended to prime minister in 1940, took Murrow's phone calls—probably because Murrow possessed the ability to shape American public opinion in favor of direct support for the Western Allies. A U.S. alliance would become especially vital to British national security after the surrender of Paris, the embarrassing withdrawal of British forces from Dunkirk, and the daily horror of the German Blitz against the people of Great Britain.

The quality of Murrow's broadcasts enabled radio journalism to compete with newspapers and magazines as a serious news medium. Murrow's accomplishments in covering and analyzing the incubation and eruption of World War II belong not only to him but also to an eclectic and celebrated group of journalists whom Murrow hired to cover the continent for CBS. The "Murrow Boys," a label that they did not acquire until the late 1940s, became journalistic legends for both the quality of their reports and the colorful stories behind how many of them captured their scoops in front of and behind enemy lines.[37] Prior to the Blitz and well before the Japanese attack on Pearl

Harbor, this group, which included one woman, called American attention to the dangers of fascism.

This is not to suggest that Murrow only served as a newsroom director. For the nine years that he served as European director for CBS, he relentlessly investigated, interviewed, reported, and editorialized. Murrow had a natural ability to report the news without sounding flat or sensationalizing the story. He made the material accessible to most Americans and added vivid, small details that made the nightmare unfolding across the Atlantic sound believable. Providing instructions to the sole female among the Murrow Boys, he told Mary Marvin Breckinridge to "give the *human* side of the news . . . be honest; talk like yourself."[38] Listening and appraising from Washington State College, Professor Anderson continued to offer Murrow speech advice, including the recommendation that Murrow take a half-second pause between the first two words of his opening phrase: "This . . . is London."[39]

When the Blitz erupted in 1940, Murrow meandered through the streets of London to capture the sounds of the destruction and sorrow in the city as well as the resoluteness of its residents. Reluctantly, the British government relented to his persistent requests to report live from rooftops during the bombings.[40] President Roosevelt, who recognized the inevitability of U.S. entry into the war, but keenly aware of the lack of public support for intervention, appreciated how effectively Murrow's broadcasts captivated and sometimes galvanized the American people.

By the winter of 1941–42, Murrow had become the most popular journalist in America, and he returned home for a brief respite that included a dinner in his honor at the Waldorf-Astoria on December 2. After a series of speakers lauded his bravery and journalism, Murrow took the dais to admonish the guests for failing to assist Western Europe in stopping Hitler.[41] The president wanted to hear firsthand Murrow's assessment of the situation in Europe and invited the Murrows to dinner five days later in the family dining room of the White House. While playing golf at the Burning Tree course in Bethesda, Maryland, on December 7, Murrow learned of the Japanese attack on Pearl Harbor. Naturally, he and Janet expected their dinner invitation to be canceled. However, Eleanor Roosevelt told Janet over the phone, "We still have to eat. We want you to come."[42] The president did not join them for the light fare of scrambled eggs, pudding, and milk, but the first lady told Murrow that her husband still wanted to see him. While he waited on a bench outside of Roosevelt's study until nearly midnight, Murrow smoked and spoke with a number of senior aides as they came in and out of the office. When the president finally beckoned forth the journalist, he offered beer and sandwiches, asked about British morale, and disclosed an honest account of the U.S. military losses in Hawaii.[43]

Another journalist might have run with the story the next day, but Murrow took Roosevelt's words from their thirty-minute discussion in the strictest confidence. He spent the rest of the night pacing his hotel room and told Janet, "I can't make up my mind whether it's my duty to tell it, or to forget it," before ultimately deciding that a troubled president had used him as a sounding board, not as a press secretary.[44] Murrow remained in the States for three months to travel cross-country on a lecture junket, appearing before auditoriums packed with Americans anxious to hear firsthand about the Nazi threat. In a Christmas Eve radio broadcast, he introduced his American audience to a saying that would become his trademark sendoff from his 1950s television programs: "Merry Christmas is somehow ill-timed and out of place, so I shall just use the current London phrase—so long and good luck."[45] He later adapted this into "Good night, and good luck."

With American entrance into the war, Murrow's voice became all the more important back home where parents and wives wondered where their sons and husbands were fighting overseas. *Scribner's* magazine described Murrow as having "more influence upon America's reaction to foreign news than a shipful of newspapermen."[46] Murrow wondered if he too should join the twelve million Americans in uniform. He had registered for the draft in Alabama and Washington DC, but he received a deferral without asking due to his high-profile role in covering World War II from England.[47] Many American policymakers told Murrow that he provided a critical wartime service in the position that he already held. However, Murrow felt guilty about the relative security of living in London, and he hitched a ride on over a dozen U.S. and British bombers that conducted bombing raids over Germany to report the daily hazards faced by the Allied air forces. During a late-night social affair and sendoff in 1942 to one of his "boys," Charles Collingwood, who departed the next morning for North Africa, Murrow exclaimed, "By God, I envy you for going off! I wish I could go along with you!"[48] However, Paley repeatedly emphasized that CBS could not risk losing him on the battlefield.

Murrow remained in Europe for months after World War II ended. He made his last broadcast from London on March 8, 1946, after CBS announced that he would be returning to New York to serve as vice president and director of public affairs.[49] Unfortunately, the life of an executive did not sit well with Murrow. While he created several new programs and organized a documentary unit from his office on Madison Avenue, CBS accepted his resignation from management on July 19, 1947, so that he could return to what he loved: broadcast journalism. As he settled into hosting *Edward R. Murrow with the News* and a nightly fifteen-minute radio broadcast at 7:45 p.m., the Murrow family made a home for themselves in a comfortable apartment at 580 Park Avenue. With his generous salary, he also purchased a country home called Rumblewood, on Quaker Hill Road, in Pawling, seventy miles upstate from New York City, in 1948. Six years later, he sold the property to purchase a larger Pawling estate, Glen Arden Farm.[50] In an interview he called his farm his one "extravagance" in life. [51] His son, Casey, recalls that his father absolutely loved the land and may have been happy simply to have a couple hundred acres in the lush area on the Connecticut border, but Murrow also took great pride in knowing how to operate the machinery and keeping the farm functioning with fulltime employees.[52]

By 1948 network executives began expanding their programming on the increasingly affordable and accessible media of television. Some of the Murrow Boys resisted making the transition, insisting that in-depth reporting needed to be conducted on the radio.[53] It sounded like the same argument made by those in the newspaper business who once scoffed at 1930s-era CBS and NBC broadcasts, seeing radio more for its entertainment value than journalism potential. Murrow did not seek the anchor position for the CBS television news; rather, he preferred to be in the field. During the 1948 presidential campaign season, he reported from both parties' convention floors, weighed down with state-of-the-art, albeit bulky, communications equipment. On November 18, 1951, Murrow hosted his first television show, *See It Now*, which began the year prior as the radio program, *Hear It Now*. Murrow developed both programs with producer Fred Friendly, and until the cancelation of *See It Now* in 1958, the duo championed the use of television to influence viewers to "learn about the nation and the world and thereby citizenship and democracy."[54] The austere set—simply the naked control room of CBS's Studio 41—served as Murrow's forum for in-depth analysis on critical issues of the day, such as the Korean War. While the network's evening news provided headlines for fifteen minutes, Murrow's program contained the substance that critics said had been lacking in television. Murrow's regular presence, according to Bob Edwards, proved as pivotal for television in the 1950s as it had for radio in the 1930s: "Finally, educated people would admit without shame that they owned a TV set."[55]

Despite an increasingly hectic television schedule, including his regular series and special documentaries, Murrow would not give up his fifteen-minute, daily radio news broadcast in the evening. "He just loved radio," Casey recalled about his father.[56] Larry LeSueur, one of the Murrow Boys, tried to explain what drove his former boss to work so hard: "It's his Puritan side. Murrow believes that idleness is a sin."[57] He did, however, take time off every summer, mostly in Pawling, where he consciously set aside his work. The one exception proved to be the occasional phone call to coordinate for an upcoming interview, and his teenage son got a kick out of placing calls for his father, especially the international calls that sometimes meant being patched through several operators in different countries.[58]

In many ways Murrow was the "Voice of America" for the decade prior to his arriving in Washington. Demonstrating the same unflinching resolve that he had demonstrated during World War II, he never backed away from raising controversial issues on his programs when he believed that they needed to be considered more seriously in national discourse. When CBS sponsors refused to advertise on an episode of *See It Now* that accompanied the African American vocalist Marian

Anderson on a tour of Asia, due to its "controversial" nature, Murrow and Friendly found private sponsors, including Eleanor Roosevelt.[59] However, nothing would gain him higher accolades—or more grief—than his decision to enlist in what historian Ellen Schrecker considers the "home front" of the Cold War.[60] The anticommunist antics of Senator Joseph McCarthy just happened to be reaching its apex as *See It Now* became a regular CBS television program.

For Murrow, the second American Red Scare since the Bolshevik Revolution became personal as he saw colleagues lose their jobs because the industry blacklisted them after dubious charges of communist sympathies surfaced. In his television analysis of McCarthy, the chairman of the Senate Committee on Government Operations, Murrow suggested that President Dwight Eisenhower would inevitably have to confront him, even though he had been reluctant to do so.[61] In the meantime, Murrow began his own methodical counter-argument to McCarthyism on *See It Now* in 1954, beginning with a piece on February 12 that called attention to the absurdities of some of the claims made by the senator and his assistants. Identifying Scott McLeod of the State Department's Bureau of Security and Consular Affairs by name, as one of McCarthy's accomplices, Murrow called McLeod's list of 2,200 alleged subversives at the State Department "an inexcusable misrepresentation" given that few of the suspects proved to be guilty. Murrow followed up on February 23 with an examination of the trumped-up charges made against an active-duty army dentist falsely accused by McCarthy's investigators. On air, Murrow reviewed highlights from the transcript of the Senate hearing and discovered that, despite all of his bombastic attacks, McCarthy failed to provide evidence of what the dentist had done. "It is a familiar stratagem," Murrow explained, "to strengthen an accusation without strengthening the evidence."[62]

On March 9, Murrow and Friendly created a montage of McCarthy sound bites and devoted nearly the entire half hour of *See It Now* to playing the senator's own voice. In the final minutes of the program, Murrow provided his own commentary in which he upheld the value of congressional committees but questioned the motives of the House Un-American Activities (HUAC) Committee and the Senate's Internal

Security Subcommittee.[63] He explained: "We must not confuse dissent with disloyalty. . . . We will not be driven by fear into an age of unreason if we dig deep in our history and our doctrine and remember that we are not descended from fearful men, not from men who feared to write, to speak, to associate and to defend causes which were for the moment unpopular." Two days later Murrow focused on how Senator Karl Mundt threw out the evidence that McCarthy's key aid, Roy Cohn, had introduced against Lee Moss, an African American civil servant working for the Army Corps of Engineers.[64]

Exactly one month after Murrow's first direct commentary on the senator from Wisconsin, McCarthy attacked the CBS journalist in a radio interview on March 12, saying that Murrow once served as an "American Adviser" to a summer session at Moscow University. Murrow used his next 7:45 p.m. radio show to address McCarthy's accusation by acknowledging that he had, in fact, visited Moscow in 1935, but that he had been serving as the assistant director of the Institute of International Education, an entity with a governing board that included Secretary of State John Foster Dulles and a number of prominent Republicans.[65] Murrow's rejoinder provides valuable insight into how he sought to confront McCarthy. Rather than make his attacks personal, the journalist focused on the unsubstantiated nature of the senator's evidence as well as on how McCarthy's callousness contributed to the loss of the same individual rights that he ostensibly sought to protect from being subverted by American communists. Meanwhile, McCarthy argued that Murrow made their public dispute personal by portraying him as a bumbling buffoon through smart editing tricks. Murrow insisted that by playing parts of committee hearings and naming the individuals whom special panels scrutinized, including prominent physicist J. Robert Oppenheimer, the format allowed the senator to speak for himself.[66]

Although some historians give credit to Murrow's *See It Now* for McCarthy's downfall, the most important catalyst for the Senate's censure of the "Red Crusader" took place on Capitol Hill and not in a New York television studio. Nevertheless, were it not for television, millions of Americans would not have seen the Army-McCarthy hearings that precipitated McCarthy's admonishment. The evening prior to the now infamous Army-McCarthy hearings, Murrow reviewed the senator's accusations against the army leadership in his April 21 broadcast. Of all the declarations made by McCarthy or his aides, these were no less bizarre, with Roy Cohn threatening "to cause the discharge" of Secretary of the Army Robert Stevens for deliberately preventing exposure of the "Communist infiltration of the Army." Murrow believed that the public hearing would serve the American people well, and he seemed confident that the army would present a sound case for how irresponsible McCarthy and his staff had become. Neither did Murrow seem concerned that this public debate would make a mockery of the democratic system: "The public will have been well served, although at considerable cost in national unity and international prestige as the leader of the free world."[67] For Murrow, the truth might be uncomfortable, but the country would be strengthened by hearing it so that citizens would understand how to place national security threats into perspective.

A month later, when McCarthy called upon federal employees to inform his committee about communist subversion, regardless of directives to the contrary from their supervisors within the executive branch, the White House finally responded directly to McCarthy. On May 28, Eisenhower's press secretary released a statement on behalf of the president and attorney general that reaffirmed the executive branch's responsibility for national security and warned against any citizen seeking to "set himself above the laws of our land, or to override orders of the President of the United States to Federal employees of the Executive Branch of the government."[68] Speaking to his audience that evening, Murrow announced that Eisenhower had finally chosen his ground for confronting McCarthy, and he voiced his approval: "What is here involved is whether a single senator shall publicly recruit and legalize what might be called a private Gestapo within the ranks of those employed by the federal government."[69]

The culmination of the Army-McCarthy hearings occurred on June 10, 1954, when army counsel Joseph N. Welch, on the verge of tears, asked if the senator "had no sense of decency," after accusing a younger colleague of serving under the legal arm of the American Communist Party.[70] Murrow opined that this high-profile debate

Good Night, CBS

encouraged Americans to consider the ramifications of McCarthyism personally: "It seems to this reporter that there is a widespread tendency on the part of all human beings to believe that because a thing happens to a stranger, or to someone far away, it doesn't happen at all."[71] For Murrow, Welch's reaction had been genuinely human, and he seemed hopeful that more Americans would respond similarly when considering McCarthy's behavior. Just as he had in his reporting on the effects of the Germans' daily bombing of the British people in 1940, Murrow sought to use the media as a way to connect his American audience with a seemingly abstract horror by reminding them of its very tangible toll on individual citizens.

Murrow's approach resonated with many in his national audience, and in 1954 scores of organizations showered him with awards. The citation on the annual Freedom House Award presented to him read, "Free men were heartened by his courage in exposing those who would divide us by exploiting our fear."[72] In his acceptance address for the Freedom House Award, Murrow articulated his concern for how McCarthyism had hurt America: "One of the pitfalls into which freedom can fall is in thinking that any national or world emergency justifies putting curbs on freedom."[73]

Throughout his head-on confrontation with McCarthy, from February until June 1954, Murrow never made his attacks against McCarthy personal. Up until the senator's death, he remained primarily focused on explaining to his viewers the issue of losing individual rights under the auspices of protecting national security. On May 2, 1957, when Murrow announced McCarthy's death at the Bethesda Naval Hospital, at age forty-seven, due to hepatitis, the reporter provided a terse, seven-line obituary without commenting on the senator's performance on Capitol Hill.[74] This self-restraint would serve him well in the early 1960s when he would moderate the tone of Kennedy's public diplomacy during periods of heated tension between the United States and the Soviet Union over Berlin, Cuba, and nuclear testing, or the lack of progress in advancing America's civil rights record.

While publicly celebrated for his unapologetic and relentless pursuit of McCarthy, CBS executives worried about whether Murrow's program would cost the network lucrative sponsors who would not want to be affiliated with his provocative reporting. In 1955, *See It Now* lost its fixed time slot, leading some to call the program's irregular appearance *See It Now and Then*. The same year, the *$64,000 Question* quiz show premiered, earning the highest audience rating in its first six weeks, much to Murrow's dismay.[75] He might earn critical acclaim, but Murrow's serious journalism did not enjoy the ratings of the network's game shows, which corporate sponsors much preferred because of their larger audiences. As the interests of America's viewers shifted, so too did CBS advertisers, and the cancellation of *See It Now* indicated that Murrow's star at CBS had begun to fade. Reporting the news remained a core component of network television in the late 1950s; however, executives favored the format of an anchor reviewing headlines to that of a television-magazine program.

Murrow articulated his frustrations with the corporate greed of his industry during an address to radio and television news directors in Chicago on October 15, 1958. It is considered by many journalists to be his finest speech and emblematic of his professional integrity and pursuit of the truth. As depicted in the 2005 film *Good Night, and Good Luck*, Murrow dampened a festive affair by opening with, "This just might do nobody any good," then explained how the relationship between network executives and corporate sponsors hurt the quality of journalism in America. He included his own network, CBS, in this cohort, and he went out of his way to assume personal responsibility for his comments. In the "intellectual ghetto" that he called Sunday afternoons, he could only find "fleeting and spasmodic" references to the critical domestic and foreign issues facing America. Although entertainment television "insulates" citizens from the "realities of the world," he reaffirmed his faith in the American people's ability to reason, so long as networks would begin to risk temporary drops in their profits in order to provide quality programming. This could also be accomplished, Murrow argued, without making television a "twenty-seven-inch wailing wall." He closed by emphasizing the need for Americans to be informed in an age of racial tensions at home and a Cold War abroad: "The trouble with television is that it is rusting in the scabbard—during a battle for survival."[76]

Tensions between Murrow and his network continued to simmer

until 1959, when Murrow sought to escape the stress of New York with his sabbatical. Upon returning to the United States in April 1960, several months earlier than originally planned, relations clearly remained strained at CBS. However, he still retained his fifteen-minute radio slot, and during the first broadcast on July 3, 1960, he discussed how the rest of the world saw the United States based on his recent expedition. Murrow believed that most European countries wanted to opt out of their "contract" with the United States in its Cold War power struggle with the Soviet Union. Although Western European governments and American diplomats continued to provide joint communiqués reaffirming their partnership, Murrow did not believe that you had to scratch too far beneath the surface to discover the skepticism of Europeans who preferred to spend money on their domestic economies rather than on armaments. With respect to the Middle East and Asia, he observed that the lack of modern elements found in the American consumer market meant that emerging nations should not be expected to transform quickly into U.S.-style capitalist economies. Calling for greater tolerance for countries not identical to the United States, Murrow offered, "We should give up the idea that anyone who criticizes our country or its policies is automatically a communist." In his view, tolerance and flexibility in foreign economic and political policy could gain the United States greater admiration in the world. He concluded, "Our example may be more important than our dollars."[77] It almost sounded as if he was auditioning for a broadcaster's billet at the Voice of America.

While the network negotiated with Murrow and his agent over new program possibilities, such as taking over Sunday morning's *Face the Nation*, Friendly suggested that Murrow consider the plight of migrant farmworkers for an installment of CBS *Reports*. In August 1960, Murrow threw himself into the production of this documentary, and *Harvest of Shame*, a "1960 *Grapes of Wrath*," aired on CBS on Thanksgiving Day. Following migrant workers, who seasonally traveled from state to state to pick crops in the land of the "best-fed" people on the globe, reporter David Lowe revealed severe poverty and primitive living conditions. Pointing to a pile of straw, a woman explained that the farm owner had purchased it for the workers to sleep on. When Lowe asked how many bathrooms were available, the woman said there were not any. Lowe asked one farm owner if his employees were happy, to which he responded, "Well, I guess they got a little gypsy in their blood. They just like it. . . . They don't have a worry in the world. They're happier than we are."[78]

Appearing on the program himself, Murrow reminded viewers that this plight did not only exist in the Deep South or California, and he spoke about a camp just a few miles away from Princeton, New Jersey, that only provided two water taps and two outhouses for dozens of workers and their families. By drawing attention to this group, which he said occupied "the lowest level of any major group in the American economy," Murrow hoped to encourage a national dialogue by explaining how migrants slipped under the radar of unions and other labor organizations.[79] It proved to be a critically acclaimed documentary that led to Murrow receiving his fourth Peabody Award in 1960.[80] However, network executives squirmed upon learning of the defensive congressional reaction to the program and the outrage voiced by agricultural interest groups, who called *Harvest of Shame* a gross exaggeration of the situation experienced by migrant workers. CBS executives wanted Murrow gone.

Fortunately for Frank Stanton, he found his opportunity to convince Murrow to leave without having to fire him publicly, thanks to the election of John F. Kennedy to become the thirty-fifth president of the United States. On December 15, the president-elect invited Stanton to his Georgetown home where he offered him the position of USIA director. When Stanton demurred, Kennedy pressed for an alternative. Stanton offered Murrow's name, and Kennedy asked him to discuss the possibility further with Dean Rusk, the incoming secretary of state.[81]

Kennedy's transition team organized an external task force to study the USIA that December, with members including the pollster George Gallup and Murrow, who was unaware of Stanton's conversation with Kennedy. The president-elect wanted to know whether the agency remained a viable entity or if it should be subsumed into the State Department. The task force submitted its report on New Year's Eve 1960, advocating for keeping the USIA independent and reporting directly to the president. It recommended inviting the agency's director to cabinet meetings and serving as an ex officio member of the National Security Council. Reversing America's declining prestige abroad could "be arrested only by more dynamic Presidential leadership, a much clearer sense of our national purposes, sound substantive policies and better coordinated programs for accomplishing them." Kennedy did not approve of all of the report's recommendations, such as one to change the USIA's name to either the International Exchange Agency or U.S. Cultural Exchange Agency. He also rejected the suggestion to absorb all foreign education programs into the USIA, since many programs aligned closely with the mission of other departments and agencies, such as the Defense Department. However, Kennedy did embrace the idea of involving the USIA director in the National Security Council as a way to enhance the quality of the agency's information campaign.[82]

Although Stanton told Murrow biographer Ann Sperber that he planted the seed with Kennedy for Murrow to take the USIA directorship, former Connecticut governor Chester Bowles also claimed credit for bringing Murrow on board, hailing it as "the quickest recruitment venture I think I've ever been in on." According to Bowles's account, while working with Kennedy and Dean Rusk to fill appointments, he told them that Murrow would be ideal to head the USIA. While both agreed with him, neither seemed to take Bowles seriously, saying that the CBS reporter would never leave the lucrative world of journalism for the bureaucracy of Washington. Bowles insisted that the invitation be extended: "Well, if I can get him, will you agree?" Kennedy and Rusk said they would "be delighted" to have him for the New Frontier, but the available records make it impossible to know for certain whether this happened before or after Stanton's visit to Kennedy's home on December 15. As a personal friend of Murrow's, Bowles invited him to Washington for talks, and during their meeting Murrow responded to the job offer: "Of course I'll take it. When do I start?" An excited Bowles shared the news with the transition team, marveling that Murrow accepted the position "without hesitation."[83] Thomas Sorensen, a mid-level USIA officer helping with the agency's transition team and the brother of Kennedy's most trusted assistant, Theodore Sorensen, also credits Bowles with enlisting Murrow.[84]

Casey Murrow recalls that his father asked for advice from a number of friends prior to accepting the offer. Despite falling out with other CBS executives, Bill Paley, now the network's chairman, remained Murrow's friend, and he was one of the first people whom Murrow called.[85] Although Murrow devoted considerable time to analyzing the public and foreign policies of the United States, he never seriously considered leaving journalism for public office prior to 1961. During the Eisenhower administration, he complained about the lack of dynamic political engagement or policies generated by senior policymakers: "The city of Washington lives, calculates and talks politics. Its primary export is waste paper."[86] However, Casey believes that his father accepted the offer to serve in the Kennedy administration for two reasons. First, Kennedy's presidential campaign platform served as a "major lure." Second, Murrow told his son that if any citizen was ever asked to serve their country, "they ought to say, yes." Casey acknowledges that his father's work at CBS had become "certainly less enticing" than in previous years, which also made a professional transition in 1961 attractive.[87] A fresh start might provide him with an escape from the depression and constant disappointments that had clearly plagued the past three years of his professional life, as evidenced by his private telegrams, radio broadcasts, and public addresses.

Another transition team member, Donald Wilson, believed that Murrow would provide a boost to the USIA. A former *Life* reporter, the president-elect's team most likely enlisted Wilson's services because of his close relationship with Robert Kennedy. About the same age, their friendship developed in large part because Wilson's wife, Susan, was a childhood friend of Robert's wife, Ethel.[88] Wilson told John Kennedy that the appointment of Murrow as director would "prove more valuable than any other single element" in improving the capabilities and legitimacy of the agency because Murrow would attract talent and "make the most" of the faculties already found within the agency.[89] Kennedy not only agreed with Wilson's assessment, he also offered Wilson an invitation to serve in his administration as Murrow's deputy director.

Kennedy's selection of Murrow is a bit surprising, given the Kennedy family's history with the CBS reporter. As the head of CBS's European operations, Murrow publicly called for the replacement of Joseph Kennedy as U.S. ambassador to Great Britain because the elder Kennedy advocated for appeasement with Germany as late as 1941.[90] Additionally, Murrow and Robert Kennedy had experienced a run-in over Senator McCarthy. In 1952, the Kennedy patriarch convinced McCarthy to appoint his son Robert, only one year out of law school, to the position of assistant counsel for the Senate's Permanent Subcommittee on Investigations. Although Robert resigned from the position the following year, he continued to voice his admiration for what he saw as McCarthy's meaningful work to protect the United States from communism. In 1954, Robert received one of the Junior Chamber of Commerce's Ten Outstanding Young Men awards, ostensibly given to him for his superior work on Capitol Hill. However, Robert chose to leave the awards ceremony early to protest the keynote speaker, Edward R. Murrow. As Murrow began his address, Robert called attention to himself by standing up from his table and walking out of the banquet hall.[91]

Despite the family history, Murrow may have found Kennedy's offer alluring because he thought that he could shape the direction in which the USIA would proceed. He certainly did not take the job for the money: the director earned twenty-one thousand dollars annually, only five hundred dollars a year more than the agency's deputy director and a far cry from his annual salary of three hundred thousand dollars with CBS.[92] As he prepared to depart from CBS, Murrow used his final speaking engagements and broadcasts to indicate how he hoped the USIA and, more broadly, Kennedy's foreign policy would advance a meaningful transnational dialogue as a compelling component of its Cold War public diplomacy.

In his final speech as a broadcaster, on January 12, 1961, Murrow addressed the Radio-Television Executives Society's Newsmakers luncheon in New York, and several of his observations of the media industry in America would parallel his concerns about how some politicians wanted to conduct U.S. public diplomacy. Mere visual stimulation, Murrow suggested, characterized by the popular quiz shows, failed to stimulate the American mind, and the polling used by networks to gauge their popularity missed the mark in assessing the value of their programming. He warned the executives, "We are so busy *doing* that we have neither the time nor the interest to study the *effect* of what we do, except in purely economic terms."[93] In bringing up economic considerations, Murrow targeted their obsession with generating maximum revenue from advertisers, and he challenged them to realize how they could more meaningfully use their mediums of radio and television.

Ten days later, Murrow's last newscast aired on Sunday, January 22, 1961. More than half of the radio broadcast focused on Eisenhower's farewell address, with little editorializing by Murrow. He approved of Kennedy's inaugural address for its brevity and optimistic tone without sounding arrogant. Assessing the presidency in general terms, Murrow cautioned against thinking that any one man could force his policies down the throats of Congress or the people of a democratic country: "His actual power is less than it is generally believed to be, and most of that power rests on his ability to persuade." However, all presidents have help in articulating their messages, and Kennedy's need to persuade an international audience would soon become Murrow's responsibility. Murrow signed off, "This is Ed Murrow. We shall be back at this time next week."[94] The closing CBS promo reminded listeners to tune in the following Sunday for Murrow's next report, but by then Kennedy had already appointed him director of the U.S. Information Agency.

2

1776 Pennsylvania Avenue

I don't mind being called a propagandist, so long
as the propaganda is based on the truth.
—EDWARD R. MURROW, April 29, 1962

At 10:05 in the morning on March 14, 1961, Edward R. Murrow appeared before the Senate Foreign Relations Committee in room 4221 of the New Senate Office Building for his confirmation hearing to become director of the U.S. Information Agency. While he answered each question confidently and in a measured voice, the former broadcaster appeared visibly nervous throughout the two-hour ordeal due to an assumption that he could not smoke in the committee chamber.[1] As someone who cared a great deal about Western broadcasting and information programs, West Berlin mayor Willy Brandt sat in the visitors' gallery. Although Murrow had lived in New York since returning from Europe in 1946, Senator Henry M. Jackson (D-WA) introduced him because he remained a Washington State resident. After reviewing Murrow's résumé, Jackson told the committee, "One of the real problems that we face in the cold war is to bring to Government men of the caliber of Mr. Murrow."[2]

In his opening statement, Murrow sought to identify himself immediately with the USIA. "All of us in the Agency," he explained, "recognize that in spite of electronic developments, the best form of communications is still face-to-face." He opposed the use of heavy-handed propaganda along the lines used by the Soviets and Chinese, advocating for skillfully persuading an international audience to appreciate America's policies and values instead. "Freedom cannot be imposed," he opined, "it must be sought for, and frequently fought for."[3] Senator J. William Fulbright (D-AR), the committee chair, asked Murrow if he could outline his plan to improve the agency. Murrow identified three points: support the unique information requirements of specific country posts, as opposed to creating blanket regional directives; improve the signal strength of its broadcasting arm, Voice of America; and involve the research division to assist with the production of USIA documentary films. Given the anticipated costs associated with these priorities, Murrow told the committee that he planned to request an increase in agency funding.[4]

Not all of the committee members shared Jackson's enthusiasm for Murrow. In light of *Harvest of Shame*—Murrow's last CBS documentary, which exposed the plight of migrant workers in the United States—some of the committee members voiced concern that, as USIA director, Murrow would focus on controversial aspects of American society rather than highlighting its strengths. Murrow reminded the committee that CBS produced investigative stories for a domestic audience, and in targeting a foreign one, he intended for the USIA to emphasize the desirable and progressive aspects of America. However, he noted that controversial national debates needed to be interwoven into the discussion, so long as the agency found "editorial balance" in its presentation of the truth.

Senator Bourke B. Hickenlooper (R-IA), whom Arthur Schlesinger Jr. found to exude "a tight, self-righteous, mistrustful quality and must be pathological in his suspicion of all liberals and bureaucrats," expressed his concern that such an approach defied good salesmanship.[5] Who, he wondered, would try to sell a machine by drawing attention to its deficiencies? When Hickenlooper pointed to the success of communist propaganda in the Third World, which completely omitted the abject failures of its own system, Murrow resisted the temptation to whitewash America's narrative:

HICKENLOOPER: When we go out and emphasize to the world the deficiencies of our system and do not sufficiently emphasize the overpowering strengths of our system, how can we have success in convincing people that we do have a good system?

MURROW: May I suggest that one of our dilemmas arises from the fact that we are operating a different system, an open pluralistic society, where we cannot conceal our difficulties or our controversies, even though we would like, and if we do not report them responsibly and accurately, they will be reported by other sources and, perhaps, distorted.[6]

During his tenure as director, this remained one of Murrow's primary rebuttals to congressional and domestic criticism against his agency incorporating provocative issues into its programming. If a USIA film or VOA broadcast did not consider something like the civil rights movement, then the agency would cede to independent journalists and foreign propagandists to present a distorted picture without a U.S. rebuttal. Murrow maintained that addressing unsavory aspects of American society worked toward enhancing the USIA's credibility. No longer a journalist, Murrow now had to determine how best to preserve the balance between his agency's presentation of news and its championing of America, since the USIA could not opt out of either.

Fulbright closed the hearing by cautioning Murrow that, despite the bipartisan support for his appointment, presenting the truth would remain an incessant challenge. Fulbright remarked, "I find it very difficult to find out what the truth is. . . . It is very easy to say we are going to spread the truth, but I predict you will have a very difficult time finding out what the truth is."[7] Over the next thirty-four months and several major international crises, Murrow discovered that, indeed, presenting the truth in government propaganda would be no less challenging than preparing a CBS documentary. Not only did he face a skeptical global audience that scrutinized USIA messages against the propaganda of communist governments, but also a Congress suspicious that the USIA would embarrass the United States by presenting too much American truth.

The day after the hearing, many national journalists acclaimed Murrow for his moral courage, speculating in their columns that he would carry this quality to the USIA, thereby lending international credibility to American foreign policy.[8] Murrow's nomination as director was not without its critics, however. Although in the minority, a vocal group of right-wing Americans voiced their objection to Murrow's selection by labeling him a communist for his liberal views—given his "attacks" on Senator Joseph McCarthy in 1954 and his more recent "sensationalism" of the plight of migrant workers in *Harvest of Shame*.[9] Overall, however, endorsements for President John F. Kennedy's nomination of Murrow eclipsed the detractions.

Kennedy arrived in office two months prior to Murrow's confirmation, shortly after Soviet premier Nikita Khrushchev announced his intention to sponsor "wars of national liberation" around the world.[10] Since his campaign for the White House, the president had focused on bolstering America's image and strength in the world, telling Secretary of State Dean Rusk, "Domestic policy can only defeat us, but foreign policy can kill us."[11] Kennedy believed that "American civilization had come of age" in 1961 and that American ideals, not just military and economic might, should shape the global role of the United States. According to Caroline Kennedy, both of her parents hoped to use key components of soft power, including a celebration of American art and culture, to enhance its international appeal. Indeed, the Kennedy administration sought to leverage the First Lady's fashion sense, class, and beauty, by making her an international "sensation" and one of Kennedy's greatest public diplomacy assets.[12]

The president intended to breathe new life into what he perceived as the stale format of the former administration's foreign policy. Kennedy departed from President Dwight Eisenhower's strategic focus on European security by frequently speaking about emerging African countries to his friends and advisers. Referring to the regions south of the equator, the president explained, "Those are so much more the important places to be now as a diplomat." Kennedy believed that he could pick up a phone in order to maintain good relations with friends in Europe; but for the developing world, dynamic men and women representing America needed to be on the ground: "It's those far-out places in Africa that are, you know, the exciting places for a diplomat to be, and where you can do the most."[13]

The British Foreign Office agreed, stressing the need for Western allies to target members of the expanding Non-Aligned Movement. British diplomats identified commonalities among most neutralist Third World states: pride in independence, fear of war, anti-Western sentiment, dislike of a foreign presence within their realm, regional loyalties, moral and cultural inspiration, and economic discontent. For a prodemocracy and capitalist information campaign to work, Americans and Europeans needed to explain their desire to respect the independence of these states and not involve them in the Cold War's East-West struggle. An adequate message, a Foreign Office study argued, would be for the British and Americans repeatedly to remind neutrals that they would enjoy zero economic or political independence in a communist-dominated world.[14]

Kennedy wanted the USIA to focus more attention on Africa and Latin America. Low literacy rates made pamphlets and libraries less useful there than in Europe, and inadequate electrification made radio broadcasts less accessible south of the equator.[15] The president called for an $11 million increase to the USIA's budget early in his administration, which Boston's *Daily Record* also supported: "Otherwise we forfeit the game to Communism—and this is a game we cannot afford to lose."[16] One indication of the president's interest in the agency's value is that, in addition to intelligence estimates from the Central Intelligence Agency, he read the USIA's daily digest of world editorials.[17]

At 3:15 p.m., on March 21, 1961, Kennedy administered the oath of office to Murrow in the Oval Office, while Murrow's wife, Janet, held the Bible and son, Casey, observed.[18] The proposal for an executive-mansion ceremony came from USIA deputy director–designee Donald Wilson, who suggested to one of Kennedy's aides that the president would send a clear message about his confidence in the agency and its new director. Wilson believed that this symbolic measure would help bolster agency morale, which remained bruised since McCarthy's earlier attacks.[19] Some legislators and officials within the new administration continued to recommend that the agency be incorporated into the State Department to provide better oversight of public diplomacy. The agency itself had been without a director since early November 1960, because Eisenhower's director, George

Allen, tendered his resignation immediately after the general presidential election.[20]

As a senior federal executive, Murrow received an annual salary of twenty-one thousand dollars and would not receive a raise for three years.[21] He and Janet purchased the house at 5171 Manning Place, Northwest, Washington DC, from American University president Hurst R. Anderson.[22] Casey, who in the fall of 1960 entered the Milton Academy in Massachusetts, considered himself a "visitor" who only joined his parents during holidays.[23] For the first time in their lives, the Murrows lived in a suburban setting. The house appealed to them, and they considered it comfortable and appropriate for small dinner parties; however, neither Ed nor Janet saw Washington as more than a temporary home. In an effort to achieve the effect of "Arizona sunshine," Janet kept the house airy by letting in plenty of light. The Murrows acquired brightly colored contemporary furniture and decorated with a large collection of modern art. Visitors recognized Murrow's connection to broadcasting quickly by the four radios and two televisions within the residence, an unusually high number in 1961.[24]

Murrow's new job demanded long hours at the office and frequent travel, yet this did not appear to bother Janet who traveled a great deal on her own independently. While she participated in diplomatic functions with visiting dignitaries in Washington, she remained devoted to her established charities. As the new national chair of the Fund for the Future of Mount Holyoke College, her alma mater, she toured the country to solicit fellow alumni in an effort to raise $17 million.[25] She also continued her leadership with the Henry Street Settlement House in New York. These commitments did not make Janet aloof from the USIA. Shortly after arriving in Washington, she began hosting luncheons at her home for female Foreign Service officers and civil servants working in her husband's agency. Not only did it help Janet understand how the USIA functioned, but many of the women met one another for the first time in her home. While most knew of each other by name, they worked in separate divisions and had not previously met. The gatherings allowed the women to network in an era where discrimination against women in the workplace made it helpful for them to be able to support one another. Mildred March, who ran the USIA's Women's Activities Advisory, lauded Janet: "She is the only Agency Director's wife that I've known who had the sensitivity and the foresight to do something like that."[26]

The Murrows rarely participated in the raucous New Frontier social scene nor did they host large parties of their own.[27] Ten years senior to the average member of the Kennedy administration, Murrow did not pay much attention to the colorful Georgetown scene of swanky dinner parties that society columnists reconstructed the next morning in Washington papers. While attending obligatory official functions, Murrow seemed out of place. Observing Murrow mingle among the crowd at a Laotian embassy dinner, the *World-Telegram* noted, "The Murrow on the Washington scene seems to be a far more subdued man at all times than the smile-flashing Murrow of the Person-to-Person program."[28] After visiting Murrow for an interview at his home in Northwest Washington, Dorothy McCrandle of the *Washington Post* said, "Forget hobbies and get back to ideas, and you have Ed Murrow with you." He did not count calories but expressed little interest in either food or wine. Only a few times a year did he escape his routine for golf or hunting.[29]

Murrow considered many journalists in Washington as long-time friends, but he knew that he had to be careful about socializing with them now as a public official. Instead, the USIA's assistant directors and public affairs officers visiting from overseas became favored houseguests for supper and conversations that lasted into the early morning. The Wilsons became good friends, as well as former "Murrow Boy" Larry LeSueur, whom Murrow had recruited for Voice of America, and LeSueur's wife. Another reason for Murrow's decision to maintain a low profile while residing in Washington had to do with his celebrity status. While having people constantly rushing up to say hello might be gratifying at one level, Casey recalls this aggravating his father. Beyond the refuge of his own home, Murrow visited friends who lived outside the Beltway, particularly those on farms who remained away from the watchful eye of gossip columnists and the general public.[30] Voice of America director Henry Loomis often hosted the Murrows at his Middelburg, Virginia, farm where they rarely talked business during hunting excursions.[31] Infrequently, Murrow returned to his working farm in Pawling; Janet and Casey spent most of their summers there, with Ed managing to reunite with them for a few of the weekends.[32]

Murrow commuted six days a week from his home by chauffeured car to USIA headquarters at 1776 Pennsylvania Avenue, just two blocks from the White House.[33] The address was not a coincidence; the building number for the headquarters served as a form of public diplomacy. Waking at 6:30 a.m., he read six newspapers each day by 8:30, when his driver, Manzy Swiegert, arrived to take him to his office. Murrow told a friend that he got "a kick out of the chauffeured limousine."[34] Swiegert chauffeured Murrow throughout his entire tenure with the USIA, and the Murrow family liked him very much. During Casey's home visits from the Milton Academy, Swiegert occasionally made a detour to drop Casey off somewhere in the city when he was technically supposed to be taking Murrow to the office. On rare occasions, Swiegert drove USIA officials home after late-night dinner soirees at the Murrows' after they had consumed too much scotch to drive themselves safely. However, Murrow thought it "absolutely ridiculous" that he and other officials were driven around in Lincoln Continentals, and he asked for his to be replaced with a Ford sedan. The Government Accounting Office refused to switch because its contract with the Ford Motor Company stipulated that the government would lease Continentals. He did, however, persuade the agency to purchase snow tires for his official car—a rarity for Washington DC— because he thought it absurd that drivers struggled to navigate the roads when the city received a snowfall.[35]

Located in room 432, on the fourth floor of 1776 Pennsylvania Avenue, Murrow's large office resembled the typical senior government executive's abode with its polished walnut desk and small sitting area.[36] Murrow brought in a second desk—a tall, stainless-steel drafter's table—to allow him to stand as he read, just as he had done in his CBS office in New York. "It's really a very useful gadget," he explained. "You can stand one column against another better this way."[37] Although the recipient of dozens of major awards, including four Peabody Awards and an assortment of honorary degrees, his walls and bookshelves remained nearly sterile of personal effects. The two exceptions were a bust of President Franklin D. Roosevelt, given to him by friends at CBS when he departed for Washington, and the large microphone that he had used in London.[38]

While he enjoyed his chauffeured limousine, he did not fall for many of the other trappings of the senior executive service. He refused to use a personal elevator, opting instead for one of the two in the main lobby of his headquarters. One morning, with a particularly long wait and more than a hundred employees queuing, Murrow said, loudly enough for dozens of people to hear, "I think that our only solution is to turn the building over on its side."[39] Lowell Bennett, director of research at the USIA, considered Murrow the "granddad" of televised journalism but voiced his admiration about how down-to-earth Murrow could be in the agency despite his celebrity status.[40] No one had ever called George Allen by his first name in the USIA, but Murrow invited senior members of the agency to call him Ed.[41]

Murrow remained approachable and took genuine interest in the agency's employees, and many recalled how this immediately bolstered agency morale. Robert Lincoln, who served as president of the USIA Alumni Association in the late 1980s, warned against confusing Murrow's quiet nature for either aloofness or insecurity: "Although he often looked morose, Murrow was a superb and lively [director]."[42] Murrow referred to himself as a public servant and severed formal ties with his former profession. Writing to the American Federation of Television and Radio Artists in February 1961, he explained why he needed to terminate his affiliation: "I regret to say that now that I have become a Washington bureaucrat, I feel obliged to resign."[43] Nonetheless, Murrow knew that he could not guarantee that he would be able to remain with the Kennedy administration for its entire duration; he served at the pleasure of the president. "I've never given myself a horizon of more than 90 days," he told a reporter who asked about his public service aspirations.[44]

Murrow did not wait for his Senate confirmation to become familiar with his new responsibilities or to provide the president with recommendations for improving international programming. In February, he forged a warm partnership with his incoming deputy, Donald Wilson, as the two discussed ways to improve the quality of the

USIA's services. A friend of Robert Kennedy's, Wilson took a leave of absence from *Life* magazine in 1960 as Washington bureau chief to serve on Kennedy's presidential campaign press staff. After Kennedy's election, Wilson served as the president-elect's transition team liaison to the USIA prior to Kennedy nominating him for the deputy billet. The president may not have picked Wilson simply because of his friendship with Robert, since Wilson's portfolio included significant international experiences abroad as a journalist. He had traveled to thirty-five countries, many of them multiple times, during his eleven years with *Life*. Born in 1925, while Murrow reported from London, Wilson served as a second lieutenant and navigator in the Army Air Force, earning the Air Medal.[45] Murrow came to appreciate Wilson as another outsider who could breathe new life into the USIA, and he praised Wilson for having "a healthy impatience with muscle-bound bureaucracy."[46]

If Kennedy provided a real sense of purpose to the country, then Murrow gave a sense of excitement to the USIA about the work they had to do. He arrived at 1776 Pennsylvania Avenue with two concerns that he wanted to address aggressively. First, he thought that during the 1950s the White House and State Department had "manipulated" the USIA to provide overly positive messages about the United States. He believed in telling as complete a story as possible—"warts and all"—in order to be more persuasive. Second, Murrow recognized the low morale of the agency staff caused by McCarthy-era scrutiny, congressional criticism about the USIA's lack of effectiveness, and the contempt with which many State Department officials held public affairs officers. Murrow hoped to restore the organization and build confidence among its employees.[47] One tangible way that he improved morale came from his efforts to rehire people forced to leave the agency during the Red Scare. USIA officers uniformly lauded Murrow for reinstating George Reedy, a victim of the McCarthy-era purges, as visible proof that Murrow wanted to help erase the scourge on the agency.[48]

Poking around the agency headquarters, Murrow found hardworking employees, and he was "absolutely stunned" by the lack of recognition that they received for producing around the clock, multilingual programming. His operations included newsroom writers, Voice of America linguists, foreign correspondents, and 1,300 public affairs officers working with 7,000 locals at 239 posts in 106 countries.[49] Even at CBS News, executives gave some credit to engineers and administrators who excelled, not just the premier journalists. However, due to the foreign direction of the agency's message, USIA employees received little credit from the U.S. government or Congress for the tremendous work that they put into their jobs. Murrow discovered many civil servants, in Washington and outposts around the world, who demonstrated a great sense of determination, imagination, and passion to serve their country.[50] Murrow revealed to an audience at the National Press Club that he arrived in Washington expecting to find an office full of "dawdlers," but he found instead "a bounty of capable doers." Regardless, he also cautioned administration officials that his people could not perform any better than the policies of their government and the actions of the American people.[51]

Murrow used the agency's annual Honor Awards Ceremony, less than three months into his directorship, to thank his personnel and challenge them. He added dignity to the affair by inviting the Marine Corps Band from Eighth and I Barracks to perform.[52] In his opening remarks, Murrow told employees that, in addition to the award recipients, many others in the room deserved recognition. He encouraged them to continue finding innovative ways to improve their operations, and he hoped that they would make "big noise" with their suggestions, providing, of course, that they went through proper agency channels.[53]

His admiration for midlevel employees did not mean that the performance of the agency's senior leadership completely pleased him. In particular, Murrow voiced concern about the nine-to-five, stovepipe bureaucratic mentality of some of the career civil servants occupying assistant director positions. Murrow wanted senior leaders to see themselves as being responsible for a foreign policy arm of the U.S. government, not simply another federal bureaucracy. The Postal Service could close for weekends and federal holidays, but the responsibilities of the USIA did not entitle the agency to enjoy similar respites. Shortly after taking office, Murrow phoned his main office on a Saturday and received no answer. The next day he instituted a twenty-four-hour duty officer who occupied 1776 Pennsylvania Avenue the way a watch officer manned the National Military Command Center at the Pentagon.[54] Murrow further insisted that his regional directors spend a good bit of time each year in their respective parts of the world so that they could understand the challenges faced by USIA personnel in the field and assess their working relationship with the rest of the embassy or consulate staff.[55]

Of all his new responsibilities, Murrow understood administrative duties the least. He had not enjoyed his brief stint as CBS vice president, and he had readily returned to the role of journalist in 1947.[56] More than any other culture shock in coming to Washington, Murrow genuinely struggled to understand the convolutions of the bureaucracy. Perhaps he naively thought that he could step into the world of policymaking because he had interviewed many national figures since the 1930s. The overall intricacies of how the federal government operated remained perplexing, however: you could easily offend someone on Capitol Hill, the White House, or another executive department by not seeking their approval on a policy seemingly unrelated to their line of work; or you sought to make a change but could not identify who ultimately had power to authorize it. Wilson admired how Murrow gently mocked the red tape of government bureaucracy without appearing arrogant: "He was interested in learning the job and, in his own words, 'not uttering until I know what I'm uttering about.'"[57]

At CBS a talented journalist could rise to executive levels quickly, regardless of time served with the corporation, and Murrow wanted to break with the traditional civil-service mentality at the USIA, which dictated that only personnel with twenty or more years of service could hold senior positions. The earliest performance evaluations that he read did not provide substantial details about the potential of public affairs officers to assume greater responsibility. He grew disturbed by the number of late personnel evaluations received by the administrative office, particularly for those from overseas posts. In a memo to the entire agency, Murrow stated that he found this "inexcusable," and he reminded them of the importance of evaluations for promotion boards. By his third year as director, he not only issued official reprimands to those supervisors who submitted late evaluations, but also to those who wrote "superficial and meaningless appraisals" of subordinates.[58]

Unfortunately, Murrow did not like to confront people who failed to perform adequately. Although he personally tasked agency personnel, if he found their efforts to be subpar a few months later, he directed another executive to take over the task.[59] Some thought that this made him a poor administrator; they would have preferred counseling, guidance, and a second chance from Murrow to fix a problem, rather than being removed from the project. But Murrow's approach illustrated his quarter-century experience in network broadcasting where executives demonstrated little patience for first-time failures.

Firing an employee proved more difficult in the federal government than at CBS. Six months into his job, it exasperated Murrow that he could not terminate the employment of many civil servants who clearly did not deserve to serve in the federal government due to their ineptitude. "I have concluded," he told a group of assistant directors, "that the only way to fire anyone around here is to catch them over in Lafayette Park with a sheep."[60] Lionel Mosley, the chief of personnel, helped Murrow find a work-around. They created what became known as the "pastureland" for officers who needed to be removed from critical functions, where they could collect a paycheck without obstructing agency operations. Certainly less optimal than firing them, this route at least removed ineffectual personnel from sight and mind, if not the taxpayer's pocket.

On July 7, 1961, Murrow ordered the termination of two-year tours for USIA duty assignments, with the exception of hardship tours, because he believed that the relatively short rotations uprooted employees too early. "The practice makes no sense financially or operationally," he explained in a memo to all Foreign Service officers assigned to the agency.[61] Shortly after making this announcement, he criticized employees who resisted accepting hardship tours. The agency would take personal and family health considerations into account, but it alarmed him that few volunteered to serve in the most challenging corners of the world. While this did not happen with everyone, he observed that it happened too frequently in an agency where its main effort resided in the more austere embassies and USIA libraries of the Third World. Even if they did not hold military commissions, Murrow reminded public affairs officers of their duty to be assigned "anywhere" based on the needs of the USIA and the president.[62]

In addition to personnel reshuffling, Murrow demanded greater cooperation between the various branches of the USIA, including the film, exhibition, and book divisions, and Voice of America. Murrow emphasized in a memorandum to his senior staff the importance of synchronizing their efforts with one another in order to ensure their "maximum effectiveness" as the psychological instrument of U.S. foreign policy.[63] When they spoke on behalf of the U.S. government, he expected them to remember that "truth is the best propaganda."[64] He would not accept generic messages or programs because he understood the need to tailor information for specific audiences across the globe. Murrow wanted Americans to take back the term *revolution* from the communists by celebrating the free will of the original thirteen colonies that led to the American revolution, despite Soviet rhetoric that they invented the "world's revolutions." The instability that people in the Third World were enduring, by being caught in the middle of the Cold War, made the tenets of communism attractive; therefore, the USIA needed to counter the "wares of Communism's deceit and hypocrisy."[65]

The distribution of propaganda, Murrow emphasized, need not be a nefarious pursuit. "I don't mind being called a propagandist," he shared with a reporter from the *Miami Herald*, "so long as the propaganda is based on the truth."[66] Speaking with another journalist, Murrow opined, "We [in the USIA] operate on the assumption that everything we do is subject to comparison. . . . In order to be credible, you've got to be complete."[67] He told *Newsweek* that the USIA would "portray this country as it really is." International understanding of U.S. policy would only come through the presentation of the truth and the dreams of the people of the United States. America might be a work in progress, but as the first of the "great revolutions," it possessed the abilities to show other countries how to mature.[68] Murrow warned USIA employees not to become disheartened if other countries failed to develop just like the United States. During his first speech to USIA personnel, Murrow opined, "We cannot be surprised when nations to which we have acted as both midwife and fairy godmother fail to pursue precisely the policies and practices that we advocate."[69] Speaking to the National Press Club on May 24, 1961, Murrow spoke of the intangibles of his agency's mission: "We seek to persuade others of the rightness of our view and that our actions and our goals are in harmony with theirs."[70]

In addition to Wilson, Murrow leaned heavily on his assistant director for policy and plans to manage the USIA. A career USIA officer, thirty-four-year-old Thomas Sorensen most likely attracted the attention of Kennedy's transition team because of his brother Theodore's close relationship with the president. However, Tom's energy and abilities convinced Murrow to retain his services in Washington in the USIA's number three position. Sorensen initially voiced concern that the appearance of nepotism might cause some embarrassment for the president, since Tom had only served in the USIA for ten years. Murrow, who had already considered this, replied, "I didn't ask the President, but I told him I was going to do it, and he said, 'Fine.'"[71] Murrow defended his decision by explaining that, during the transition period Sorensen was the only one who recognized the USIA's need to reduce the number of priority messages that it disseminated in order to ensure the widest circulation of the most critical information. Murrow addressed agency executives' concerns about Sorensen's lack of seniority when he introduced Sorensen at his first staff meeting in March 1961. He noted in good humor, "I would have appointed Tom Sorensen, even if he'd been my brother."[72] This decision illustrates Murrow's disinterest in abiding by the seniority mentality of the civil service by reaching down into his organization to promote those possessing talent.

Murrow leaned heavily on Sorensen's policy office to help him realize his vision. The director distributed an agency-wide memo calling for the improved integration of all media divisions in order to be "responsive to policy direction and emphasis, and faster and more flexible than heretofore." He directed the film, radio, and print divisions to send scripts for major items to Sorensen's office for review and required the policy office to conduct spot checks of different media.[73] To help create mission-specific messages, Sorensen pressed his small staff to articulate their focus in quarterly, long-term policy papers that they distributed to every USIA division. Not only did this provide direction for the public affairs officers overseas, but it also integrated the efforts of the production services in Washington. As Sorensen explained, "This way, a guy who wanted to make a great film in IMS [Motion Picture Service] wouldn't be doing something totally different from a guy who had this idea for a great commentary in IPS [International Press Service] or somebody who had an idea for a great book program in ICS [International Communication Service]." Murrow told Sorensen that he supported his efforts "100 percent."[74] Further, Murrow believed that this oversight would create the USIA's "fast media"—the compilation of Voice of America, the press service, newsreels, and television—to communicate American policy during international crises.[75]

Despite Murrow's endorsement, some long-term members of the agency resented the selection of Wilson and Sorensen, and they referred to the two principal deputies as "Boy Scouts with tommy guns."[76] John Hutchison, the director of the agency's press service, found himself reassigned overseas inexplicably after reprimanding David McCullough, a Wilson protégé, for signing private contracts for writing magazine articles without following proper government contracting procedures. Hutchison suspected that Wilson personally ordered the move.[77] Administration director Lewis Schmidt believed that Sorensen, as a midlevel officer stationed overseas, lacked the experience in Washington to shape policy adeptly. Schmidt found Sorensen arrogant and overbearing when he told Schmidt how to handle the administration of the agency.[78]

Sorensen worried that the agency's existing mission statement to tell the American story abroad meant "50 things to 49 people," diffusing the myriad efforts of the divisions. He hoped to shift the focus from objective-oriented to media-oriented: "In other words starting with the result you want and working backwards, rather than starting from the product and going out there and looking for a result." VOA officials worried that Sorensen's efforts infringed on their journalistic independence, but Sorensen saw value in USIA oversight for sharpening editorials to reflect the government's views rather than those of the editorialist. Additionally, Sorensen wanted Cultural Affairs, still tucked under the State Department's umbrella, to be integrated with USIA overseas operations. This could only go so far, however, because Senator Fulbright considered Cultural Affairs his pet program, and he staunchly objected to the USIA's influence.[79]

One of the concerns that senior agency officials voiced with Sorensen related to his aggressive efforts to scale back the agency's European operations. Since Murrow supported the president's focus on the Third World, Sorensen appears to have followed orders. The pro-Europe cohort within the agency raised a valid defense for their operations: it remained important to bolster America's image at a time when many Europeans believed that the Soviets had gained military superiority over the United States.[80] The standoff in Berlin made this argument especially valid. However, it is also possible that the older generation wanted to preserve plush public-affairs billets in bustling European capitals. It is easy to see how this point of friction led senior personnel to quip that Sorensen was just a political hack, and for Sorensen to write in his own book in 1968 that Murrow sought to sweep out the archaic behavior of those who were not embracing the New Frontier.[81]

Murrow did not devote all of his time to the Third World. He divided the USSR and Eastern Europe from the agency's European division because he believed that the countries behind the Iron Curtain required a different tone than the messages directed to Western Europe, and he felt that the European division concentrated too much attention on U.S. allies. In addition to establishing a new regional division, Murrow restricted the public affairs billet in Moscow to a Russian-speaking officer with prior service in the Soviet Union. Alexander Barmine, a 1930s Soviet defector and army general, had headed Voice of America's Soviet division since 1948, and he voiced concern over Murrow's interest in his programming. Murrow believed that the Soviet division required fresh blood, but he avoided offending Barmine with his reorganization. Instead of ordering Barmine to retire, Murrow "promoted" him to Soviet adviser to the assistant director for the USSR and Eastern Europe. The move worked beautifully, and

Murrow personally greeted Barmine on the morning that he moved into his new office at 1776 Pennsylvania Avenue.[82]

Voice of America sat on the opposite end of Pennsylvania Avenue from USIA headquarters, and it operated with the most autonomy of the agency's divisions. Nevertheless, Murrow expected the radio service to complement the efforts of the agency's other arms. VOA director Henry Loomis, whose arrival at Voice of America coincided with the inception of the USIA in 1953, considered his relationship with Murrow to be "very close," and he generally felt that Murrow allowed him to operate VOA as he wished. As a former journalist himself, Loomis said that Murrow "understood my position and sympathized with it." However, he felt that Sorensen and Wilson's relationship with the White House influenced Murrow to support policies that were less than optimal for the Voice of America.[83] Although Loomis said that Murrow sided with him more often than not, Sorensen argues just the opposite. Sorensen notes that Loomis exploited Murrow's spirit of journalistic integrity to try to convince him that Voice of America needed to remain above politics, but Murrow also recognized that the agency's mission required using its radio service as a message carrier for the administration.[84]

Aside from tending to internal agency operations, Murrow invested a great deal of attention to his relationship with the administration. Since Kennedy had accepted the recommendation of his external USIA task force in December 1960 to provide the USIA director with an ex officio seat on the National Security Council and cabinet, Murrow sought greater access to the commander in chief than had his predecessors. Kennedy ordered the installation of a direct phone line to Murrow's office from the White House, which, the director told the *Washington Post* six months into the job, the president "uses a lot."[85] Murrow referred to the phone as the "blowtorch" when it rang unexpectedly during an interview for a *Newsweek* cover story in September 1961.[86]

During meetings at the White House, Murrow often remained silent for long periods. His son, Casey, speculates that while waiting for the appropriate moment to contribute, his father subconsciously became the reporter gathering information. Murrow thought it was a "real coup" that he had acquired a seat in the NSC, so perhaps he felt self-conscious about the possibility of jeopardizing his seat with off-the-cuff comments about grave matters of state.[87] Murrow made up for his unobtrusive nature during face-to-face meetings by submitting a weekly report to Kennedy on the status of the USIA and international public opinion. Although Burnett Anderson from his staff drafted the reports, Murrow meticulously edited and added analysis to every memorandum. The president expressed particular interest in public opinion surveys and how the agency thought they might affect foreign affairs. Kennedy enjoyed the reports, and, as a byproduct of Murrow's commentary, he began asking Murrow to provide material for his foreign policy speeches because he was not always happy with the material provided by the State Department.[88]

Murrow joked about his difficulty keeping up with the younger members of the administration. Although a workhorse in his own right, the long hours put in by other senior officials amazed him. Casey thought that his father pushed himself harder there than at CBS due to the steep learning curve of the bureaucracy and the rules of the federal system.[89] Robert Evans, who worked in Murrow's head office, observed, "They work Murrow as if he were two men."[90] In an administration teeming with Ivy League executives, Murrow did not seem self-conscious about his Washington State College education. He did, however, make light of the environment by calling upon "Cousin" Luther Hodges, the secretary of commerce, from Murrow's birth state of North Carolina, to suggest that they form an association of North Carolinians to "stand off" against the Harvard men.[91]

Murrow developed a strong working relationship with McGeorge Bundy, the national security adviser, and they spent significant time together preparing public messages for the administration. Bundy often sent Murrow drafts of policy memos, asking for his assistance in shaping the "publicity" of U.S. policy.[92] At Murrow's request, Bundy distributed a memo to the entire White House staff directing them to avoid referring to countries in the Third World as "undeveloped," "underdeveloped," or "backward." A USIA study also said that locals in those countries did not like being referred to as "emerging" states. Murrow encouraged members of the administration to refer to the Third

World as "developing" or "modernizing," which the indigenous people appreciated.[93] When drafting an international speech for Kennedy, Bundy liked having Tom Sorensen serve as the USIA representative on the interagency committee, not only because of his public diplomacy skills, but, as the brother of the lead speechwriter, Tom could provide a unique assessment. As Bundy explained, Tom "was perfectly prepared to say '[Ted] will fight like hell over this,' or 'I don't think he cares about [that],'" which expedited completion of the final draft.[94]

Murrow encouraged senior administration officials to help improve the USIA's programming. In mid-February 1961, prior to his confirmation, Murrow requested that Kennedy ask members of his cabinet to lend greater authenticity to informative programs designed to advance the "convictions we hold at home" by participating in VOA broadcasts.[95] Murrow also asked the president for greater access to intelligence reports. When Loomis first began working for Voice of America in 1953, the White House denied access to the National Intelligence Estimate (NIE) or other NSC documents because "a bunch of commies" filled the Voice of America studios. Murrow pointed out the absurdity of this accusation to Bundy and Allen Dulles, the CIA director. If there were communists in the offices, then fire them; otherwise, how could they expect the radio service to broadcast to another country without knowing the administration's priorities? The CIA and NSC relented, albeit slowly, to Murrow's request. For several months, only Loomis could review the NIE, but eventually a wider pool of VOA personnel responsible for programming received access to the top-secret material.[96]

Murrow sought to establish cordial relations with the vice president, who was not terribly impressed with the USIA. Lyndon Johnson told Tom Deegan, the owner of *Time* and *Life*, that he knew firsthand of the numerous "soft spots" within the USIA that needed to be fixed by the Kennedy administration.[97] Murrow took the first step in seeking to gain the vice president's favor. Two weeks after his confirmation hearing, Murrow sent Johnson a note saying that he had followed Johnson's advice about "keeping a tight rein on the temper" when Senator Hickenlooper questioned his integrity as a reporter. "This note is to thank you for that counsel," Murrow wrote, "and to express the hope that I may have the benefit of your wisdom and experience in the future."[98] Johnson directed personal assistant George Reedy to prepare a short reply, which the vice president mailed on March 23: "You did a fine job of remembering that it is possible to win an argument and lose the sale, and I congratulate you."[99]

Based on their mutually supporting foreign policy roles, one might have expected close USIA–State Department cooperation; however, Murrow's relationship with Secretary of State Dean Rusk was difficult to understand fully. Murrow thought that Rusk was "sort of ineffectual," and he rarely referred to Rusk in his agency correspondence.[100] Rusk did not mention Murrow or the USIA in his memoir of his time as secretary of state, and Rusk's oral history transcripts housed in the Kennedy Presidential Library remain sealed.[101] However, there is no evidence indicating that Murrow and Rusk disparaged one another, either. Murrow regularly attended the secretary's morning staff meetings on Mondays, Wednesdays, and Fridays. The night prior to these meetings, Murrow tasked his deputies to provide his special assistant with information pertinent to critical issues that he could review prior to arriving at Rusk's office.[102]

Aside from Rusk, Murrow considered three senior State officials to be personal friends. Undersecretary Chester Bowles had offered Murrow the USIA appointment on behalf of Kennedy, and John Kenneth Galbraith exchanged letters with Murrow once he became the U.S. ambassador to India. Ambassador-at-large and later assistant secretary of state for Far Eastern affairs W. Averell Harriman considered Ed a "fast friend" since their mutual experience in the London Blitz.[103]

Murrow encouraged USIA officers to move beyond the confines of embassies and libraries in order to help make America understood in the world, challenging his staff to "wear out more shoe leather and fewer typewriter ribbons."[104] Murrow believed that for public affairs officers to be effective, they needed to speak the host-country language. Working with William Weathersby, his director of personnel, Murrow created language-proficiency standards for specific jobs throughout the USIA outposts. If an officer could not meet the minimum requirements, he returned to the State Department's language school and did not return to his outpost until linguistically qualified.[105]

One of the major obstacles that Murrow encountered to improving the quality of USIA programming concerned the desire by some in the State Department to remove cultural programs from his agency, which would leave the agency strictly responsible for broadcasting and publishing news headlines and policy explanations. Murrow believed that the separation of culture and information represented a false dichotomy, arguing instead that they were mutually essential to U.S. propaganda efforts. In a memo to Bundy, Murrow acknowledged that certain programs, such as People-to-People and student exchanges, would be difficult to transfer from the State Department to the USIA, but he remained adamant that other cultural activities, such as traveling exhibitions, lecture series, and music programs, not be removed from his agency. Murrow could not see how dividing public affairs and cultural officers into two separate divisions of government helped to advance American foreign policy abroad. He clarified his position to Bundy by illustrating the inseparable link between culture and propaganda: "Dissemination of information on American culture through various media to selected audiences is perhaps our most important technique for influencing the political thinking of foreign opinion leaders."[106] Ever since placing his microphone on a London street to capture the chaos of an air raid during the Blitz as a young reporter, Murrow understood the need to grab people's attention prior to delving into heavy news and commentary. However, neither Bundy nor the president would definitively provide exclusive ownership of the cultural initiatives to either State or the USIA.

While navigating the bureaucracy, one unforeseen incident during Murrow's first month in office caused a highly publicized embarrassment for the new director. The BBC planned to broadcast Murrow's *Harvest of Shame* in March 1961. Fearing that the foreign audience would confuse the CBS documentary with a USIA education film, Murrow asked Sir Hugh Carlton Greene, a BBC executive and old friend, to cancel the broadcast. Loomis heard that Murrow intended to request the personal favor and encouraged his new boss not to do it, but Murrow insisted on making the call.[107] When news of Murrow's appeal to London leaked to the U.S. media, editorialists accused him of hypocrisy, since he had vowed to tell the truth, warts and all.

"Boy did I make a stupid mistake," Casey recalls his father's realization, "No longer can you just make a phone call to one of your buddies and try to change something."[108]

In the grand scheme of Murrow's tenure in Washington, the *Harvest of Shame* incident was a "blip," but the director considered it a valuable lesson on how to behave as a government official.[109] Murrow confided in Loomis after the media hype that he did not understand how it had become an embarrassment to ask the BBC not to carry his documentary. Loomis considered this an example of how it took Murrow some time to adjust to government life.[110] However, Murrow did not try to cover up his mistake. He asked to meet with as many USIA employees as possible on March 24, 1961, both to introduce himself and to address questions about *Harvest of Shame*. Speaking before fifteen hundred USIA members, in the Departmental Auditorium at Twelfth Street and Constitution Avenue, in Northwest Washington, Murrow acknowledged that it had been "both foolish and futile" to phone his friend at the BBC. Murrow explained candidly that when he made the call he "was not aware of which hat I was wearing."[111]

A nationally syndicated editorial column appearing in dozens of papers praised Murrow for acknowledging his mistake. Its author hoped that Washington politicians, who so often "prefer to compound error rather than confess it," would learn from Murrow's example of humility.[112] It also turned out that the BBC audience received *Harvest of Shame* positively. One columnist at the *London Daily Mirror* commended Murrow for his journalism and wondered if the Soviet Union would ever dare to allow a private news reporter to present such a documentary and then allow it to be exported. "The answer," wrote the author, "is no and Uncle Sam is stronger by the fact that to these queries he can say 'Yes.'"[113]

If the American people truly wanted to win the Cold War without violence, Murrow believed, they needed to devote more resources to the USIA. He reminded the House Appropriations Subcommittee that funding for his agency went beyond paying for broadcasts: "An information problem must be much more than a compendium of words. It must go to and become part of the people it is trying to reach."[114] When Murrow appeared before Congress, he explained how greater funding would enable the USIA to purchase more powerful transmitters for Voice of America, access commercial satellites for television programming, and hire more journalists to keep up with the demands of emerging electronic media.[115] Murrow hoped that Voice of America could go from being the fourth-largest state-run international radio program to advancing beyond the USSR, China, and the United Arab Republic (Egypt) in both broadcasting hours and wattage. If the country remained content to be a fourth-rate propagandist, Murrow suggested it would "forfeit to the inexorable tide of history our role as the promoters of freedom."[116] Murrow told senators that to counter communist misinformation and ensure the delivery of complex messages required the use of multiple mediums and face-to-face engagements: "The Agency must have personal contacts, the mechanical means, and the substantive knowledge to answer questions and allay skepticism."[117]

Some members of Congress doubted that the USIA required funding for operations in African states that remained underdeveloped. Murrow disagreed, telling the House Subcommittee on Africa Affairs that a USIA library became even more vital to the development of such impoverished countries that lacked their own variety of media sources, bookstores, and libraries. By providing free reading material, movies, news, and Western music, Murrow told members of the subcommittee, the United States would "assume an importance in the country not otherwise possible." Further, he objected to the suggestion that Africa should be treated by the U.S. government as a monolithic region, where the embassy in one country could service several neighboring states as well. "Putting a man down in one country may completely isolate him from neighboring countries," Murrow insisted, as newly independent states emerged in Africa between 1961 and 1963.[118]

Senator Allen Ellender (D-LA) especially despised the USIA. During one of Murrow's appearances, the director told the senator that his agency's information operations could be credited with influencing European public opinion to support Kennedy's recommendation for the North Atlantic Treaty Organization to create a multilateral force to handle nuclear weapons. "Come on, Mr. Murrow," the senator responded, "You don't mean to tell me that we had anything to do with it, USIA had anything to do with acceptance of any policies that the U.S. government was trying to institute in Europe. You just can't make me believe that." This infuriated Murrow but he remained silent for nearly thirty seconds before he responded that he meant exactly what he said. Returning to 1776 Pennsylvania Avenue with Schmidt and another senior agency official, Murrow told them, "Well, gentlemen. I draw one conclusion from my hearings this morning, and that is that the pigs shall inherit the earth."[119]

During annual budget hearings, Murrow made his case before the House Appropriations Subcommittee on Foreign Operations, Export Financing, and Related Programs, chaired by Representative John J. Rooney (D-NY) from Brooklyn.[120] Murrow biographer Joseph Persico colorfully noted that "if the USIA was treated like the bastard at a family reunion, Rooney was the mean-spirited stepfather."[121] The representative's disdain for foreign outreach made him a curious chairman of the committee responsible for the budgets of both the State Department and the USIA. During Murrow's first appearance in March 1961, the two sparred over each proposed expansion to the budget. When Murrow explained that he wanted to open a USIA library in Kuwait, a leading oil supplier to the United States at the time, Rooney stopped the director, asking, "Ku-what?"[122] Rooney reduced the agency's requested budget, appalling Murrow. Rather than a budget increase of nineteen million dollars, Congress authorized one for three million, which the House Appropriations Committee considered "ample" for the agency to fulfill its mission.[123]

Garnering congressional support for the USIA remained the bane of Murrow's directorship. Casey recalled that his father found many members of Congress to be "real jerks," and he often considered their line of questioning during committee hearings to be asinine. He could not compare it with anything from his journalism career.[124] *Think* magazine aptly noted the image challenge that contributed to the USIA's uphill battle to acquire funding: "It has neither the tradition of the State Department, the money of Defense, nor the glamour of the mysterious CIA."[125]

Shortly after his first encounter with Rooney, Murrow assembled his senior staff to announce that, in order to prevent similar appropriation challenges the following year, he intended to become more visible throughout the United States by accepting a variety of speaking engagements in order to educate the populace and media about the purpose of the USIA. Although Murrow possessed considerable print and broadcasting assets, the Smith-Mundt Act of 1948 prevented the USIA from propagating to a domestic audience. This did not inhibit him from conducting public engagements as a representative of the Kennedy administration or national celebrity. If he could gain popular support, Murrow hoped it would be easier to garner congressional approval for his budget requests. Murrow spoke to the American public in order to stress the competence of agency employees and, because of his national credibility from his tenure at CBS, Americans paid attention as he described the capabilities and purpose of the USIA and corrected misconceptions dating from the McCarthy era.

During his first three months in office, USIA stories appeared a striking three times more often in the national news than in all of 1960.[126] Murrow appeared before groups as diverse as the National Bar Association and the Advertising Federation of America. Addressing the Educational Press Association, Murrow identified the root cause for why most Americans seemed unaware of the agency's value: "Our product is invisible. Our goals are intangible. . . . Whatever we do is for export only."[127] In a speech to the National Association of Broadcasters, Murrow presented the agency as a dynamic arm for practicing foreign policy: "USIA is the new dimension of the new diplomacy. We occupy the only battle line that engages this entire land. We seek to explain this country and all it does. Our goal is the minds of men. But the war we wage is not the war to capture men's minds; it is a war to free them."[128] In a newspaper interview, he contrasted the meager federal spending on "advertising" to that of a private company: "One American soap company spends almost as much on advertising as the USIA spends explaining U.S. policy abroad."[129]

Murrow tailored each speech for the specific audience he addressed, and he used the opportunity to persuade his listeners that they shared a vested interest in seeing the USIA succeed in its mission. Speaking before a group of trade and academic journal editors, Murrow asked them to donate material for USIA libraries, as a way to offset the agency's modest publication budget. In return, he offered to run stories on the Voice of America about the technical, medical, and scientific work conducted by the institutions and industries that provided the journals. Murrow told them, "You are exploiting not just appetites for goods and services but appetites for a way of life that makes it possible for people to share in freedom the benefits of industrial progress."[130] In 1962 he convinced the nation's five largest publishing houses to donate book bundles for his overseas libraries.[131]

Murrow humanized agency operations in his speeches by including a variety of anecdotes from the field that left his American audience with an appreciation for the lengths that public affairs officers assigned in obscure countries would go to deliver the message. He also cited the reactions of Soviet diplomats to American success. Speaking to the American Council on Education in October 1961, Murrow noted that when puzzled Soviet cultural attachés in Cairo asked locals why they preferred the USIA library to the Soviet's, the Egyptians flatly told them that the Americans were teaching English. "So the Russians did the obvious—when you can't beat 'em, you join 'em," Murrow explained to a gathering of teachers. "At the Soviet cultural center they began teaching English."[132]

Without exaggerating the capabilities of his agency, Murrow stated frequently that Soviet and Chinese propagandists "out-gunned" the USIA, both in radio broadcasts and book and pamphlet publication. Even when Voice of America broadcasted into the same countries as Chinese and Soviet propagandists, the U.S. programs included fewer hours in the native languages. Murrow told a hundred college presidents that China sold half a million books in Spanish to Cuba, mostly of Mao Zedong's writings. While the USIA could hardly match that number, there remained a tremendous interest in foreign countries for reading material on the United States. In November 1961, he tried to put the viability of USIA services into perspective for a convention of public relations experts in Texas: as many patrons visited the agency library in Calcutta as the Library of Congress in Washington; the Pakistani minister of education used USIA textbooks to develop reading lists for secondary schools; and Southeast Asian ferry operators accepted copies of the USIA magazine *Free World* as currency in exchange for passage fare.[133]

As a former president of the National Student Federation of America, Murrow particularly delighted in delivering lectures and commencement addresses on university campuses, returning to the locales where he first gained experience as a public speaker. Just as Kennedy reached out to the youth of America, Murrow encouraged college students to consider their ability to look beyond national borders. Paraphrasing his boss's inaugural address, Murrow encouraged the 1961 graduating class at the Johns Hopkins University to consider careers in public service.[134] At Bucknell University, Murrow told students that "American affairs are now world affairs, and world affairs are now those of America."[135] Speaking at his own alma mater, Washington State University, Murrow laid out America's stakes in the Cold War by drawing parallels to the country's neutrality during the early years of World War II: "The rules of the game are simple: Play we must. And if we lose, only then in the goodness of time will be known what stake we have lost."[136]

To play on the world stage required both the delivery of information and the analysis of its impact. However, the USIA's ability to assess the influence of its programming in shaping foreign opinions of the United States remained difficult to quantify. During a June 1961 *Meet the Press* interview, host Lawrence E. Spivak asked Murrow if he could cite a specific country where USIA operations directly contributed to winning popular support for the United States. Murrow admitted that he could not provide an exact answer, but he measured success "in terms of good will gained, or sometimes simply in the removal of ill will."[137] Some State Department officials were only too happy to point this out during Senate Foreign Relations Committee hearings because they feared that every dollar given to the USIA would be a dollar lost from their own budget. Coupled with reporting truths that Congress found distasteful, the lack of empirical evidence provided by the agency's research division to quantify the USIA's international influence led to further congressional budget cuts during Murrow's tenure.

If Murrow thought that by accepting Kennedy's offer to work at the USIA he would escape the stress of dealing with executives at CBS, he found that the politics and bureaucracy of Washington could be

1776 Pennsylvania Avenue

equally frustrating. The president's invitation to share a nuanced American story with the world attracted Murrow to national service in 1961, but the administrative duties, interagency dynamics, and congressional lobbying greatly surprised him. The fact that Murrow did not resign within his first year, however, indicates that he did not take the appointment simply as a way to depart gracefully from CBS. Immediately upon his confirmation, Murrow urged career civil servants at the USIA to break from their paradigm of delivering stale messages about American superiority in the Cold War to a developing world where the messages no longer resonated as effectively as they had at the conclusion of World War II. By relying on Don Wilson and Tom Sorensen to help him carry out administrative and policy reforms within the USIA, Murrow focused on bringing his five programming divisions together to speak with one voice in explaining the Kennedy administration's foreign policy. At the same time, he objected to generic messages because he recognized the importance of tailoring each one for a unique audience overseas. He hoped to design a more sophisticated information campaign, and he asked Congress for more funding so that he could compete against communist propagandists through the new technological media available in the 1960s. Early rejection by Congress did not deter Murrow from returning to Capitol Hill routinely to request a larger budget.

If agency operations proved challenging, then the simultaneous responsibility of responding to foreign policy crises only compounded the strain that Murrow endured in Washington. On June 9, 1961, during his first USIA Honor Award ceremony, Murrow reflected on the challenges faced by the United States during World War II and the Korean War. "It is long since this country has suffered or sacrificed," he said, adding, "I suggest that the testing time approaches."[138] Five days before Murrow's speech, Khrushchev had issued Kennedy an ultimatum on Berlin at their Vienna summit. Murrow's knowledge of the private exchange in Austria must have been the unnamed "testing time" of his address, and the Soviet premier's threat only heightened the urgency for the USIA to expand its influence and gain international credibility.

3

From Fiasco to Progress in Latin America

To our sister republics south of our border, we offer a special
pledge—to convert our good words into good deeds—in a
new alliance for progress—to assist free men and free
governments in casting off the chains of poverty.

—JOHN F. KENNEDY, January 20, 1961

President John F. Kennedy was not the only world figure drawing
attention to the Cold War ideological struggle in Latin America when
he delivered his inaugural address in 1961. That same year Soviet premier Nikita Khrushchev hailed the publication of the *Manual on the
Fundamentals of Marxism-Leninism*, a seven-hundred-page tome translated into various languages and distributed globally to inspire world
communist revolution. In one chapter, the authors proclaimed:

> Judging by the nature of the problems now facing the peoples of Latin
> America, it is a question of launching an *anti-imperialist democratic
> revolution*. The events of recent years testify that this new stage of the
> national liberation struggle in Latin America has already begun and
> is successfully developing despite the counterattacks of the reaction-
> ary forces and the open intervention of the United States.[1]

Kennedy wanted to shift the focus of U.S. foreign policy to the
Third World: the economically impoverished and politically volatile regions where he felt the last administration had paid insufficient attention, thereby making them plum targets for communist

insurgencies. President Dwight D. Eisenhower refused to bolster the Third World when it risked fracturing the United States' close relationship with Europe, so he approached postcolonial states tepidly or with clandestine operations to preserve authoritarian regimes, as in the case of Iran in 1953, Guatemala in 1954, and Indonesia in 1958. In contrast, Kennedy believed that the Global South would soon experience radical political change with the demise of the oligarchies and a rise in democratic governments, providing that it received encouragement and aid from the United States.

For those who knew Kennedy well, his newfound interest in Latin America seemed curious. Although he made Latin America a central focus of his foreign policy agenda, his wife did not recall him speaking much about the region prior to his inauguration.[2] On October 18, 1960, just two weeks prior to the presidential election, Kennedy criticized Eisenhower's Latin American record before ten thousand people in Tampa, Florida. Addressing a community with a major Hispanic American population, Kennedy harkened back to President Franklin D. Roosevelt's Good Neighbor program, by calling for economic assistance to preclude another country from succumbing to Cuba's recent fate.[3] Charles Burrows, the U.S. ambassador to Honduras, felt that Kennedy's speech generated "almost electrifying" interest among Latin American leaders about the prospects of cooperating with the United States after Eisenhower's departure.[4]

Kennedy hoped that the Alliance for Progress, which he proposed in his inaugural address, would become more than a slogan. He wanted his counterparts in Latin America to see themselves as economic and security partners with the United States. Richard Goodwin, Kennedy's assistant special counsel and later deputy assistant secretary of state for inter-American affairs, takes credit for coining the phrase.[5] Undersecretary of State Chester Bowles believed that the Alliance for Progress emerged as a response to Kennedy's dislike of Cuba: "I think that one thing [Fidel] Castro deserves credit for is waking us up on the subject of Latin America."[6] White House assistant Arthur M. Schlesinger Jr. considered Latin American assistance to be the only aspect of Kennedy's foreign policy agenda seriously developed during the first six months of the administration.[7] David Bell, who became director of the U.S. Agency for International Development in 1962, believed that Kennedy demonstrated a "very deep" personal commitment to rebuilding relations with Latin America, once ensconced in the White House. In Bell's view, the Alliance for Progress possessed the president's unique "style and flare," which would be necessary to overcome Latin American skepticism of U.S. motives for outreach.[8]

Within the first month of the administration, Kennedy involved Schlesinger in formulating the structure of the alliance. The former Harvard professor offered historical perspective and cautioned the president against assuming a paternal role: "Why did the Good Neighbor Policy succeed? Because FDR brought U.S. policy into accord with Latin American aspirations toward political dignity. New policy must do the same." The president wanted to know more, and he used the Food for Peace mission conference in Buenos Aires, Argentina, as an excuse to send Schlesinger to tour the region. Kennedy tasked him to assess the capabilities of ambassadors and the U.S. Information Agency's public affairs officers to connect with the people and to gauge the prospects of regional leaders' support for his initiative.[9]

During his travels through several countries, from February 12 to March 3, 1961, Schlesinger found "enormous expectancy" from various Latin American political figures that Kennedy would help to solve the region's problems. While in Buenos Aires, Schlesinger met with Arturo Frondizi, the host-nation president who stressed that only economic programs would stem the expansion of communism in the region. "Castro," Frondizi lectured, "is not the fundamental question. The elimination of Castro would not solve the problem. What is required is a basic attack on the conditions which produce the Castros and facilitate their appeal."[10] Schlesinger embraced the primacy of economics in fomenting regional stability, confiding in his journal that, "Unless action takes place to improve living standards, several nations will begin to hit the Castro road."[11]

Kennedy formally announced his desire to establish the Alliance for Progress in a speech to members of Congress and Washington's Latin American diplomatic corps, in the White House East Room on March 13, 1961. The president included several phrases in Spanish, much to the chagrin of interpreter Donald Barnes, who felt that

Kennedy "butchered them up" with his Boston brogue.[12] The president warned his guests that the "despotisms of the Old World" threatened the hemisphere's independence and security. In his view, the most viable form of resistance to communism would be to embrace Simon Bolívar's nineteenth-century dream for the two American continents to forge a close relationship. Kennedy reminded the diplomats of their common heritage of gaining freedom from colonialism, and he assured them that the United States shared their desire to advance economic progress and eliminate social injustice. He acknowledged that some of his own fellow Americans had forgotten their kindred spirits, but he challenged the congressional representatives in attendance: "We must turn from these mistakes—from the failures and the misunderstandings of the past." Progress required the reawakening of revolutionary ideas, and he outlined ten tenants to the Alliance for Progress, with only one directly related to military defense. The other nine identified ways to improve the basic needs of the American people: "for homes, work and land, health and schools—*techo, trabajo y tierra, salud y escuela*."[13]

On March 22, the USIA's Office of Research and Analysis reported on international reactions to Kennedy's Alliance for Progress speech, finding in Latin America that every demographic found something appealing about the president's proposed partnership. Most listeners of the Voice of America Spanish service applauded Kennedy's call for the "active participation" of Latin Americans. One journalist cited in the report hailed the address as "the greatest contribution to Pan Americanism in one hundred years," and newspapers in Mexico, the Caribbean, and South America provided ringing endorsements. Even *El Popular*, an anti-U.S. paper in Mexico that often touted pro-communist sentiment, found the proposal to coincide "with the true progressive and revolutionary thinking in Latin America." The leftist Salvadoran *La República* credited the American people with electing "a man of such wide vision and such profound social feeling."[14] Latin American heads of state expressed mixed reviews of Kennedy's proposal. Venezuelan president Rómulo Betancourt understood that domestic social reform needed to complement American economic aid. However, many of Betancourt's peers did not share this philosophy; for them national industry needed to be built before they could turn their attention to social justice issues, ranging from freedom of speech to eliminating political corruption.[15]

Following Kennedy's alliance speech, Schlesinger disseminated a white paper about Latin American politics throughout the administration to garner support for the alliance. When officials met for an interagency discussion on the paper, the Department of State and Central Intelligence Agency approved the basis of his paper. However, USIA director Murrow voiced concern about Schlesinger injecting policy points that were "too racy and liberal" into the program. For example, Murrow disagreed with the recommendation that the administration criticize ousted Cuban president Fulgencio Batista, despite the widely accepted view that he had led a corrupt and ineffectual government. In lieu of reminding Latin Americans about former U.S. misjudgments in supporting Batista, Murrow wanted to concentrate USIA messages on the potential benefits of the new alliance. Reflecting on the meeting, Schlesinger wrote, "Ed Murrow said very little during the conference but, I think, was heartened by my exhortations to his people to get in cadence with the New Frontier."[16]

Despite his reservation about drawing attention to Batista, Murrow supported Kennedy's interest in improving relationships with Latin America, particularly since the president's approach allowed the USIA to develop meaningful public diplomacy. Two weeks after the president's alliance speech, Murrow told a House appropriations subcommittee that the United States shared a great deal in common with newly emerging nations in the Third World. The USIA needed to encourage emerging nations to have patience in allowing democracy and capitalism to take hold by explaining America's own growing pains since 1776. If Congress increased his agency's budget, Murrow believed that the United States could make this message resonate: "In emphasizing programs in the newly emerging and less-developed areas, the Agency intends to use its information tools and techniques to show the peoples of those areas the parallels between the American revolutionary heritage, American aims and motivations, and their own aspirations."[17] Murrow had clearly paid attention to Ken-

From Fiasco to Progress

nedy's March 16 speech, although he omitted the Spanish phrases from his own testimony.

To influence Latin Americans to accept the Alliance for Progress as a joint enterprise with the United States, Murrow recognized that the USIA needed to reveal the insidious nature behind communist efforts to foment revolutions in the region. The Soviet-Chinese-Cuban propaganda effort in the Third World entailed far more than distributing the *Manual on the Fundamentals of Marxism-Leninism*. Communist radio programming, print publication, and political cadre operations throughout Latin America threatened to drown out Voice of America, USIA magazines, and Department of State cultural events. To counter their adversaries' messages, Murrow sought greater funding from Congress to build stronger broadcasting transmitters, publish more literature, produce new film documentaries, and expand agency libraries.

Beyond enhancing the USIA's own capabilities, Murrow supported Kennedy's creation of the USAID to streamline the vital economic aid and entrepreneurial mentorship programs required to modernize the Third World. Kennedy stressed the need for interagency cooperation in developing foreign aid programs in order to avoid throwing money at a problem without assessing the return on the investment. The USAID's second administrator, David Bell, recalled that Kennedy "wanted a strong and vigorous program, and his staff both in the White House and in the executive agencies of the government put together a program [with] which he was satisfied and which he strongly supported during the legislative process."[18] George Ball, the undersecretary of state for economic affairs, supported the USAID in its infancy, and Secretary of State Dean Rusk provided Ball with total autonomy when it came to developing the department's economic policies.[19]

Similarly, Murrow championed the founding of the Peace Corps as a method for improving the people-to-people dimension of Cold War soft power. In a letter to Sargent Shriver, the first Peace Corps director, on March 14, 1961, Murrow shared his eagerness for its success because of the volunteer organization's close link to the mission of the USIA. He also offered advice to Shriver, based on his read of global opinions. Although the corps planned to deploy its first cohort to the Philippines, Murrow recommended starting in a newly independent African country so that communist propagandists could not equate an American activity in the Philippines with a desperate measure to maintain its hold on an "ex-colony."[20] Shriver apparently heeded Murrow's advice, and the first Peace Corps volunteers departed at the end of August 1961 for Ghana and Tanganyika (now known as Tanzania).[21] While Shriver opposed affiliating the Peace Corps with the USIA, because he did not want communists to accuse the Peace Corps of being a branch of the government's propaganda effort, the volunteer program played a positive public diplomacy role in the Third World, particularly in Latin America.

Turning to a traditional ally to develop Cold War public diplomacy in Latin America, Murrow strengthened cooperation with the British Foreign Office's Information Research Department.[22] Although another USIA director might relegate participation in the semiannual Anglo-American working group on joint information policy to subordinates, Murrow's affinity for England led him to attend personally, beginning with the April 11–13, 1961, conference in Washington. During the Eisenhower administration, the British rated Anglo-American information cooperation in Latin America as a "pathetically small scale" endeavor, in part because of the two countries' competing economic interests in the region. During the April working group, the U.S. and British agencies agreed to marry their efforts to prevent the spread of communism in Latin America by advocating for economic reform and an end to social injustices. Since the British maintained diplomatic relations with Cuba, they offered to "discreetly" assist in explaining U.S. policy to the Cuban people.[23] However, British information officers stopped short of criticizing Castro openly, because the Foreign Office wanted to retain diplomatic relations with his government.[24] More broadly across the region, the British tried to preserve the image on the streets that they were not quite as "Gringo" as the Americans.[25]

During the working group, Murrow learned the difference between anticolonialism and neocolonialism. While the USIA believed that it could champion messages of anticolonialism to win regimes to their side, the British warned that the United States had become Khrushchev's favorite target in his imperialist propaganda, rather than the European powers responsible for carving out the colonies a century earlier. Khrushchev accused the United States of "neo-colonialism," something that Murrow's staff had not considered in their own analysis of communist messages in the region.[26] Following the April working group, the USIA began to deliberately counter the neocolonial label in its messaging, but a covert operation that took place five days after the conference frustrated Murrow's public diplomacy strategy.

Despite Kennedy's eagerness to propel the Alliance for Progress forward, the president suffered a major setback, just one month after earning the respect of many Latin Americans, when he authorized the CIA's ill-fated attempt to deploy a paramilitary brigade of fourteen hundred Cuban exiles to retake their home island. The Bay of Pigs invasion failed to unseat Castro from his dictatorial rule in Cuba, and it damaged the credibility of U.S. messages about treating its southern neighbors as partners. Kennedy had not made the decision to approve the CIA-sponsored invasion without serious deliberation, but he kept many of his advisers out of the decision-making process, which severely diminished the options available to him.

Prior to his inauguration, Kennedy learned of the invasion plan when CIA director Allen Dulles and Richard Bissell Jr., the agency's deputy for plans, flew to Palm Beach, Florida, to spend the better part of November 18, 1960, explaining the operation to the president-elect. Revealing the training program for Cuban refugees who wanted to reclaim their homeland, the CIA officials assured Kennedy that the force would be ready to deploy the following spring. Although not in office, Kennedy provided the agency with the "go-ahead" to continue planning.[27] According to the mission plan, the invasion's success depended upon an island-wide uprising that the CIA anticipated would occur spontaneously once Cubans learned about the fourteen hundred exiles wading ashore. However, the agency seemed more concerned about preparing the exiles for amphibious operations than developing the intelligence estimate needed to determine whether the exiles' landing would indeed incite a revolution.[28]

While cooler heads may have prevailed upon the president to cancel the operation, several experienced officials fervently argued that the invasion would not only succeed but that it was vital to regional security. Eisenhower left his copy of the plan in a White House safe for Kennedy, and Dulles remained at the CIA following Kennedy's inauguration. Adolph Berle, director of Kennedy's interagency Latin American task force, considered Cuba a significant threat to regional stability, as he wrote in his journal on January 24, 1961: "The really serious situation is the civil war in Cuba and our attitudes towards it. The present estimate is that eight governments may go the way of Cuba in the next six months unless something is done."[29] Despite Kennedy's publicly stated desire for the United States to respect Latin American governments, he considered Castro's regime too insidious to tolerate. National Security Adviser McGeorge Bundy also believed that Kennedy felt compelled to support the operation because the Republicans would accuse the administration of being soft on communism if it failed to adopt Eisenhower's plan.[30]

Perhaps Kennedy's trust in the CIA's abilities to execute such a daring mission rested with Dulles's confidence in his agency's invincibility, since it successfully overthrew Iranian prime minister Mohammed Mossadegh in 1953 and Guatemalan president Jacobo Árbenz Guzmán in 1954. It may have also stemmed from the president's faith in the intelligence provided by analysts at Langley over other federal sources. Kennedy initially leaned toward the CIA for information about world affairs over the State Department: "By gosh, I don't care what it is, but if I need some material fast or an idea fast, CIA is the place I have to go to. The State Department is four or five days to answer a simple yes or no."[31] Additionally, Kennedy allowed the CIA to serve as the lead agency for the covert operation, in lieu of the Defense Department. This diminished the Joint Chiefs of Staff's involvement in planning a complex amphibious assault and their ability to advise Kennedy adequately on its associated hazards.[32]

Two White House insiders strongly objected to the plan. Theodore Sorensen, counselor to the president, was not brought into the discussions about the invasion, but he could not help overhearing rumors in the West Wing. When he expressed his concern about having the United States involved, Kennedy told Sorensen that he could not disband the brigade without risking the exiles publicly condemning the administration for being weak on communism.[33] Schlesinger voiced his objections in person and in a memorandum to the president. Kennedy tried to assuage him by explaining that he intended to trim the operation down to a "mass infiltration" and keep U.S. forces away from the island. The president also confided in Schlesinger that he found the mission valuable for dealing with the rowdy crowd of Cuban expatriates: "If we have to get rid of those 800 men, it is much better to dump them in Cuba than in the United States."[34]

Although Murrow served on the National Security Council, Kennedy opted to work outside of this advisory group to handle the top-secret invasion. The president relied upon a small group of advisers that excluded many key members of the council. Remaining outside of Kennedy's inner circle further hindered the USIA once the invasion began, because it lacked sufficient time to develop messages to explain the operation to Latin Americans, anticipate mission failure, or develop appropriate messages to explain Kennedy's support for the invasion.

Including Murrow early on might have also given Kennedy access to a report that would have given him legitimate pause to accept the CIA's analysis about the likelihood of a popular uprising: the last public opinion survey conducted in Cuba by Americans. The USIA maintained a copy of the results of a survey conducted by the Institute for International Social Research at Princeton University in 1960, which reported that Cubans overwhelmingly supported Castro, whom they regarded as a revolutionary hero rather than a communist.[35] Since the USIA remained unaware of the impending invasion, its research division did not bring the study to Murrow's attention. It is difficult to believe that, if he had been aware of the report, Murrow would not have hastened to provide it to the president. Even if Kennedy had read the survey, but still chose to support the invasion, he might have at least pressed the CIA to provide updated intelligence analysis about the likelihood of an island-wide uprising. If the CIA analysts returned with an honest assessment of Cuban sentiment that corroborated the Princeton survey, Kennedy may have ultimately canceled the mission.[36] Given the president's faith in CIA reporting at the time, this data could have provided him with the political ammunition necessary to defend himself from Democratic hawks and Republicans whom he feared would chastise him for disbanding the brigade.

During a meeting with principals on March 15, Kennedy made it clear that U.S. forces would not directly support the invasion. To ensure that Castro could not accuse the United States of supporting the rebels, he directed the military representatives at the meeting to keep U.S. naval vessels away from the Bay of Pigs before dawn on the day of the invasion.[37] Berle observed that no one in the meeting asked the president to reconsider reinforcing the brigade, in the event that the Cuban army overwhelmed them.[38] The president evidently trusted Dulles's claim that the Cuban patriots would reclaim their country, just as Castro had successfully launched his revolution with a modest cadre landing on the island in 1959. The president remained confident about the plan three days prior to the invasion at an April 15 meeting with Rusk, Berle, Bissell, Schlesinger, and Bundy. Bundy observed, "Mr. President, do you realize that you are surrounded by five ex-professors?" The president dubbed the group the "Scarlet Pimpernel," and the academics laughed uproariously.[39] Neither their confidence nor lightheartedness would survive the week.

Deputy Director Donald Wilson became the first senior member of the USIA to learn of the invasion when his friend, New York Times reporter Tad Szulc, invited him to breakfast on April 5.[40] Szulc explained that he had just flown to Washington after a three-day visit to Florida, where he found evidence of preparations for a Cuban invasion. Although Wilson tried to appear unalarmed, he rushed to Murrow's office after the meal to retell Szulc's story. Murrow listened quietly but his face betrayed him "clearly getting madder and madder."[41] Murrow drove to Langley to ask Dulles about the rumor, but the CIA director remained mute. As Murrow returned across the Potomac, Dulles informed Bundy about Murrow's inquiry, and the national security adviser phoned Murrow to invite him to stop by the White House. After receiving confirmation from Bundy, Murrow voiced his objection to the plan because he did not believe that the small band of patriots would overcome Castro's forces. Bundy stated that the president had made up his mind, and he ordered Murrow not to discuss the operation with anyone at the USIA, despite the

From Fiasco to Progress

agency's global responsibility to explain the government's role in the operation once it became public.[42]

The unfolding of the operation is well told in numerous works and does not need to be restated here.[43] The assumption that the invasion force would be warmly welcomed by a local populace eager to overthrow Castro's regime proved to be its fundamental flaw. Even when the CIA and Pentagon reported that the exile brigade's situation had turned dire on April 18—after the Cuban air force sank the invaders' supply ship and destroyed their meager air support—Kennedy refused to deploy U.S. military forces. Fully realizing the consequences of his actions, the president began to agonize over permitting the slaughter of the exiles and imprisonment of the survivors, and his tone changed noticeably from when he told Schlesinger on April 7 that it would be best to "dump" the rebels in Cuba. The president realized that a direct U.S. confrontation with Castro could lead to a much broader Cold War confrontation, such as a retaliatory Soviet invasion of West Berlin. Kennedy wrote a letter to Khrushchev on April 18 to emphasize that refugees, not Americans, had participated in the invasion, and he discouraged the Soviet premier from using the Cuban situation as pretext to "inflame other areas of the world."[44]

The USIA's immediate information problem centered on explaining the government's role in the secret mission. While driving in his car on the morning of April 17, VOA director Henry Loomis heard a news report about a group of Cuban exiles landing ashore on the Bay of Pigs and fighting Castro's military to secure the beach. Loomis knew that the operation could not be taking place without U.S. support. Reaching a phone, Loomis called Murrow to vent his frustration about being left in the dark. Murrow's reaction on the other end of the line made his own anger evident: "Dammit, if they want me in on the crash landing, I'd better damned well be in on the take-off!"[45] Murrow agreed that Voice of America should discuss the operation on the radio, especially the Spanish service, and he voiced his confidence in Loomis by closing with, "Go ahead and do what you want to do."[46]

The information campaign could not be that simple. Even if Voice of America sought to provide an accurate depiction of the situation, it competed against two other broadcasters, neither of whom reported the story accurately. The CIA's Swan Island Spanish radio station explained that "everything is going great" for the exiles, while émigrés from private radio stations in Key West and Miami encouraged the Cuban population to join the side of the freedom fighters. The USIA also maintained a shortwave radio operation dedicated to Cuba, which required news guidance.[47] Loomis wondered, "How could any Cuban know what the hell was going on as far as the U.S. was concerned?"[48]

Murrow wanted to persuade his international audience and not simply inform them through USIA media, but the Bay of Pigs fiasco demonstrated to him how government secrecy and competing media could frustrate his vision for improving American public diplomacy in Latin America. The director grew furious with the White House and State Department for not providing clear guidance on how to explain the crisis because he knew that his agency would lose credibility once journalists and the Cuban government began to provide their own version of the story.[49]

By noon on April 17, the VOA Spanish service began reporting on Cuba at the top of every hour. The next day this increased to nineteen hours of original news, which Voice of America continued to provide for the remainder of the week.[50] For the first day and a half of the invasion, Voice of America rebroadcast statements by Kennedy and Rusk saying that the United States "offered only sympathy for the invaders." Broadcasts erroneously noted that the invasion force included more than five thousand exiles, when in fact it only had fourteen hundred.[51] In an effort to curb outlandish CIA radio broadcasts, Murrow coordinated an agreement with Dulles on April 18 for the two agencies to collaborate on messages related to the Bay of Pigs.[52]

At the United Nations, U.S. ambassador Adlai Stevenson found himself equally unprepared to explain American involvement in the invasion.[53] Meanwhile, Schlesinger, who arrived in Italy on April 19, gained a foreign perspective on the invasion and began to appreciate Murrow's concern about how the Bay of Pigs would adversely affect America's international image. Schlesinger observed, "It is evident that the Cuban affair has done us immense damage. . . . Now Kennedy is reviled as if no more than a continuation of the Eisenhower–[John Foster] Dulles past."[54]

The mood in the White House, so light on April 15, changed dramatically when the invasion turned tragic. As casualty numbers mounted, Jackie observed her husband become very depressed in realization of his mistake. He felt that his staff had failed him, especially those who came from the Eisenhower administration: "Oh, my God, the bunch of advisers that we inherited!"[55] Kennedy held the CIA culpable for the failure, which led to Bissell's immediate resignation and Dulles stepping down as CIA director in November 1961. Additionally, the chairman of the Joint Chiefs gained Kennedy's ire. Not only did the president find General Lyman Lemnitzer's advice "ham-handed" during the invasion, but he was also appalled to learn about the Pentagon's Operation Northwoods, a plan for federal agents to conduct terrorism in Miami, which the government would then blame on Cuba.[56]

Kennedy accepted responsibility for the misadventure but did not dwell on the disaster. Ted Sorensen never heard Kennedy commiserate with his staff about the invasion, except for the first few days after the fiasco. The president confided in his closest White House adviser that he truly believed that the U.S. role in the mission would remain clandestine, and that the brigade would relocate to the mountains to pursue a guerrilla war if a popular uprising did not ensue. Sorensen thought that for Kennedy, it was worth the gamble: "He also felt that, had the invasion succeeded without direct United States military intervention, it would have been hailed as a great move, both in this country and throughout Latin America."[57] Kennedy authorized a press statement on April 20: "President Kennedy has stated from the beginning that as President he bears sole responsibility. . . . The President is strongly opposed to anyone within or without the administration attempting to shift the responsibility."[58] In a speech delivered before the American Society of Newspaper Editors that same day, Kennedy publicly defended his decision not to assist "this small band of gallant Cuban refugees."[59]

The Bay of Pigs operation "shocked, puzzled, and angered" most members of the administration excluded by Kennedy from the decision-making process, a sentiment picked up by the international media.[60]

From Fiasco to Progress

The headline of the April 22, 1961, *Herald Tribune* in London read, "Kennedy is to be regarded as politically and morally defeated."[61] Frankfurt's *Neue Presse* reported, "In one day American prestige collapses lower than in eight years of Eisenhower timidity and lack of determination."[62] In Latin America, violence followed media reports about the America-orchestrated endeavor. Demonstrators broke windows and smashed display cases at eight USIA binational centers and libraries; 250 vandals gutted the center in Morella, Mexico, and Molotov cocktails caused five hundred dollars in damage to the Caracas center.[63]

Castro's victory and negative international reactions to the U.S. role in the operation emboldened the Cuban dictator to expand his propaganda campaign throughout Latin America. On May 1, 1961, his government inaugurated Radio Havana, a shortwave international broadcasting service that transmitted 266.5 hours of weekly programming in Spanish, Portuguese, and English by 1963. The Cuban commentators lambasted the "traitorous governments" of Latin America who had ended diplomatic and economic relations with Cuba after Castro gained power. With the financial assistance of the Soviet Union, hundreds of thousands of copies of Che Guevara's book, *Guerrilla Warfare*, and Mao Zedong's *Tactics of a Guerrilla Fighter* appeared throughout Latin America, compliments of printing presses in Havana.[64] Castro authorized the release of a graphic film depicting the corpses of women and children, with a narrator blaming the United States for their deaths, due to its role in the Bay of Pigs invasion. USIA analysts believed that Castro did not release the documentary publicly but only to Communist Party meetings throughout the region.[65]

In light of the surge in communist propaganda and the tarnish on the Kennedy administration, Murrow had his work cut out for him. By May 1961, only three months after his confirmation, the national media rumored that Murrow considered resigning from his post because he felt ostracized from Kennedy's inner circle. Representative Clarence J. Brown (R-OH) told reporters that Murrow did not believe he was as influential within the administration as he had hoped to be as USIA director. One story purported that Murrow hoped to replace Dulles as CIA director, and the affiliated cartoon depicted Murrow pausing before a shop window to look at a Sherlock Holmes costume

From Fiasco to Progress

on display.[66] Murrow denied the rumors publicly, saying that he had no intention of resigning, although he acknowledged that his position provided him a sense of "fascination, mixed with frustration."[67] Casey Murrow denies that his father considered resigning over the Bay of Pigs, primarily because he was "still trying to figure out what his job was" in April 1961.[68] One indicator of Murrow's commitment to the administration was that he sold his five-story home at 130 East Seventy-fourth Street in New York in early May.[69]

Murrow assured skeptics that the administration invited him to participate in policy meetings and that Kennedy valued his opinion; however, he also noted, "[I have] no illusions that I am the secretary of state."[70] On May 25, he told an audience at the National Press Club that he had "no complaints on the degree or frequency of consultation" he had with the president or his senior advisers. However, in his speech Murrow recommended that Americans spend less time dwelling on outer space and more time thinking about "inner space and near places." The comment could only be construed as a subtle commentary on the president's address that same day before a joint session of Congress that called for landing a man on the moon by the end of the decade.[71]

On May 2, 1961, Voice of America dropped its Spanish service from nineteen hours a day down to six.[72] The decision concerned Kennedy, who directed Murrow to have Voice of America return to its nineteen-hour schedule of daily programming for Cuba in order to counter Castro's broadcasts, which included "a major effort" to subvert the Alliance for Progress.[73] With significant modifications being made to voa formatting by the usia and the White House, Alexander Klieforth, the voa program manager, did not understand the agency's policy for Cuba. He phoned Murrow explaining that he did not care if Voice of America began calling for a revolt or even the assassination of Castro, but the usia needed to be definitive. The director agreed, "You know, we don't have a good policy on Cuba."[74] Klieforth met with several other voa executives, and they drafted a broadcast policy for stimulating a peaceful regime change in Cuba. After circulating the proposal through the usia's policy and Latin America divisions, Murrow approved the plan.

Seeking to regain the momentum that the USIA had briefly enjoyed in Latin America prior to the invasion, Murrow instructed the agency to focus its messages on the peoples' potential to modernize with the United States as their partner. Just as he did not agree with Schlesinger's recommendation that they apologize for supporting ousted Cuban president Batista, Murrow wanted to engage his audience about the future and not dwell on the botched invasion. The USIA developed two messages for the Cuban population: Castro had betrayed "the ideals of the revolution," and the Alliance for Progress offered a "promise" for Latin America.[75]

In addition to informing its radio audience and library visitors about the government-to-government initiative, the USIA continued to assess their opinions about the Alliance for Progress. An agency poll conducted of nearly ten thousand people in seven Latin American countries in the summer of 1961 found that most wanted American aid, rather than support from the Soviet Union. The majority in each country maintained an "overwhelmingly" negative reaction to Castro's revolution, but sizable minorities believed that the United States offered aid to their country for "selfish" reasons. Despite their opposition to communism, only in Columbia and Peru did majorities believe that their governments should help the United States win the Cold War.[76]

To learn more about the functions of the USIA's foreign outposts responsible for explaining the alliance to indigenous populations, Murrow traveled abroad as director. Murrow scheduled two regional conferences in which he met with public affairs officers from embassies and consulates to evaluate the effectiveness of messages in Latin America. Accompanied by his wife, Janet, and Undersecretary of State Chester Bowles, they departed on October 4, 1961, for Lima, Peru, to meet with USIA officers in South America. They followed this conference with an engagement in San Jose, Costa Rica, with officers from Central America.[77] Between the conferences, Murrow toured facilities in several countries, much to the delight of the agency's employees. Murrow cared little for the trappings of diplomatic ceremonies; the veteran reporter wanted to ask people questions and learn from them in lieu of standing in receiving lines or indulging in sumptu-

From Fiasco to Progress

ous meals with dignitaries.[78] Edmund Murphy, the public affairs officer in Haiti, considered Murrow's visit to Port-au-Prince to be one of the high points of his career. Murrow made sure that the atmosphere remained relaxed, leading to frank discussions about improving agency operations.[79]

Despite the Bay of Pigs, the agency's approach in Latin America helped to turn public opinion against communism. The USIA observed that Castro's standing in the region began to wane in the fall of 1961, in part because the agency ceased advocating for the dictator's overthrow, which diminished the communist's ability to play up "Yankee Imperialism." The agency continued to label the Cuban regime's policies as misguided, but it explained that democratic societies tolerate debates that permit the evaluation of alternative solutions to political and economic challenges.[80]

This did not mean that the Kennedy administration no longer hoped that Castro would be removed from power. On November 30, 1961, the president charged U.S. Air Force Brigadier General Edward Lansdale to oversee the top-secret Operation Mongoose. The celebrated counterinsurgency expert and his staff planned sabotage, guerrilla, and propaganda warfare operations against the dictator for the remainder of Kennedy's presidency. As part of Mongoose's propaganda campaign, the CIA's radio station on Swan Island changed its name to Radio Americas in an effort to regain credibility with Cubans who identified Swan Radio with the Bay of Pigs.[81] Murrow personally participated in counterinsurgency meetings, provided staff assistance from the USIA, and integrated his agency into the psychological warfare of discrediting the Castro regime and advocating for a turn toward democracy in Cuba.[82]

The USIA's relationship with the CIA further improved with the arrival of a new director, following Dulles's departure at the end of November. Shortly after taking charge, John McCone told Murrow, "We don't want ever again to get caught by something like the Bay of Pigs, where the CIA believed that the people of Cuba would overthrow Castro when USIA had polls saying the opposite. We're going to start a new relationship."[83] This led to two significant policy changes. Murrow, Donald Wilson, and Tom Sorensen, the assistant director for plans and policy, began receiving a copy of the top-secret CIA daily intelligence update sent to the White House. Due to its sensitivity, the courier sat in their office suite at 1776 Pennsylvania Avenue while the USIA officials read the document. Second, the CIA's deputy director for plans, Richard Helms, began meeting with Sorensen to provide an operational overview of CIA activities with heavy emphasis on its psychological operations.[84] This unprecedented access to intelligence helped to refine the USIA's messages and target audiences, adding measurably to the quality of the analysis formulated by the agency's research division.

On December 1, 1961, Castro delivered a speech to affirm his ideological adherence: "I am a Marxist-Leninist and I will continue to be a Marxist-Leninist until the last day of my life."[85] This public declaration made it easier for the USIA to contrast the dictator's motives with those of a nationalist revolutionary focused on ameliorating domestic hardships and injustice. Murrow assured Congress that his agency could build greater support for the alliance by exposing "the evil nature" of Castro's influence in the region.[86] As an outgrowth of the April 1961 Anglo-American information working group, the British Foreign Office provided talking points to its embassies about Castro's affiliation with worldwide communism that defined Castroism as "indistinguishable in internal and foreign policy from Communism."[87] Further, the British Information Services began to refer to Cuba as another satellite country of the Sino-Soviet bloc, and information officers increased their dissemination of anti-Castro, unattributed material to local journalists.[88]

Beyond messages about communism, Murrow's promotion of the Alliance for Progress in Latin America proved effective. By the end of 1961, the USIA found that 71 percent of the people in Bogota, Rio de Janeiro, Montevideo, and Buenos Aires knew of the alliance, and two-thirds of those aware voiced favorable opinions of the program. Attitudes toward the United States improved, according to a December 1961 survey: "Inception of the Alianza over the past year has been accompanied by increased proportions who believe the U.S. is sympathetic to Latin American wishes and hopes."[89] Mexico remained the one exception in the region, where only 14 percent of the general population knew of the alliance. However, Mexican economic and political elites voiced exceptionally high expectations for improved cooperation with the Kennedy administration.[90] Through the USIA, Kennedy's message resonated significantly higher than had Eisenhower's in the region.

Accompanied by the aid trickling in from the USAID, the public diplomacy improved opinions of the United States in the New Year. However, the challenge remained for the USIA not to exaggerate the future benefits of the alliance to Latin American countries. The agency needed to counter perceptions that the United States should provide most of the money to improve the region's standard of living. The goal of the program focused on improving the capitalist system so that the standard of living in Latin American countries would improve due to revenue generated by their private sector. If the United States built a road or sewer system for a country, but host-nation municipal workers or local businesses could not maintain the new infrastructure on its own, the American investment would be wasted. British ambassador to Washington David Ormsby-Gore thought that Kennedy's greatest challenge with respect to the alliance concerned finding the balance between lavishing financial aid and insisting "on the proper degree of self-help and planning by the recipient countries."[91]

Vice President Lyndon B. Johnson argued that American advisers, in lieu of cash, would go further to ensuring that the United States received a return on its investment. He suggested that Kennedy encourage the fifty largest American companies to lend the government their best corporate vice presidents for a year. These businesses, Johnson believed, could provide direct counsel to governments and companies in the Third World. Kennedy asked Defense Secretary Robert McNamara what he thought of the idea. The former president of Ford Motor Company opined, "Well, about 90 percent of the ones you get won't be any good at all. But out of the remaining 10 percent you will get some excellent people."[92]

Kennedy sought to make a personal connection with the region's inhabitants, making his first official trip south of the equator to Columbia and Venezuela during December 15–18, 1961. Given Vice President Richard Nixon's harrowing experience in the Venezuelan capital of

Caracas in 1958, the White House assumed no small risk in scheduling Kennedy's visit.[93] Despite the apprehension shared by some in the administration, the president met genuine enthusiasm from cheering crowds assembled on the city's narrow streets. Jackie joined her husband, delivering her own speeches in Spanish, which truly excited the Venezuelans. Kennedy laughed after President Betancourt informed him that communist students at the Central University of Caracas carried a sign saying, "Kennedy—*No*; Jacqueline—*Yes*."[94]

The USIA reported enthusiastic coverage of the tour by regional journalists. The communist press did not disparage Kennedy so much as focus on the "brutally repressive police security measures" taken by the Venezuelan government to protect the president's travel route.[95] The USIA's motion picture division produced a sixteen-minute color film of the tour and disseminated copies dubbed in Spanish throughout the region.[96] Prior to the visit, Deputy Director Wilson coordinated with presidential press secretary Pierre Salinger for five USIA personnel to join the White House press pool accompanying the Kennedys. Since Kennedy had recently told Murrow how much he enjoyed the agency's colored films, Wilson emphasized to Salinger that they could not produce good documentaries or newsreels without their own camera operators being granted "maximum coverage opportunities."[97] The USIA newsreel proved exceptionally popular with Latin American audiences. The depiction of the U.S. president surrounded by welcoming crowds and the narration that spoke of the intent behind the Alliance for Progress effectively portrayed the Kennedys as a youthful couple sincere in their friendship with Latin Americans. The USIA showed the film at its libraries and special venues throughout the region, and public affairs officers loaned reels to local movie houses.

The tour proved so successful that the president and Jackie returned to the region in June 1962 for a state visit to Mexico. One unscripted event during the two-day visit to Mexico City became an especially valuable public diplomacy gesture. Kennedy asked to attend Catholic mass in the city's cathedral; however, the Mexican president declined to step foot in the church, a curious political decision given Mexico's overwhelmingly Catholic population. Kennedy replied, "There's no problem. I'll go on my own," which he did with a Mexican military aide.[98] This decision further enhanced the U.S. president's popularity with the Mexican people.

Murrow wanted the USIA to produce an even more polished film of the Kennedys' visit to Mexico than the one made for Venezuela and Columbia. Wilson and George Stevens Jr., the agency's motion picture division director, met with Eric Johnston of the Motion Picture Association of America on July 17, 1962, to discuss how to dynamically reach a Latin American audience. As a commercial producer, Johnston recommended creating a short five-minute film that included the president providing a straightforward two-to-three-minute segment describing the Alliance for Progress. Johnston said that he would include the segment in the newsreels that his association played before their movies in theaters across the region. He estimated that the clip would reach tens of millions of Latin Americans.[99] The USIA also produced a twenty-minute documentary, *Progress through Freedom*, which the agency disseminated throughout Latin America, Africa, and Asia.[100] Jackie, who took a great interest in reviewing USIA documentaries, thoroughly enjoyed the Mexico documentary.[101]

No matter how well the USIA disseminated information about the alliance, however, the lack of quantifiable improvement within the economies of Latin American countries eventually led to a decrease in favorable opinions about the value of the alliance. In March 1962, the slothful pace of aid programs trickling into Latin America muted the administration's celebrations for the alliance's first anniversary. This alarmed administration officials who worried that more countries in the region would reject capitalism and democracy in favor of authoritarian methods. Ambassador Ormsby-Gore told the British Foreign Office that, should the alliance fail, "it will in fact probably be impossible to keep most of Latin America on the side of the West."[102] The Soviet newspaper *Izvestiya* criticized the lack of economic prosperity: "Now that the propaganda hullabaloo around illusionary Punta del Este success is over, things are beginning to be viewed in the United States with a soberer eye. Developments are convincing Washington that there is no Latin American unity under United States aegis at all, that on the contrary, there is a high surging tide of anti-Americanism in Latin America."[103]

Despite Kennedy's strategic vision for the Western Hemisphere, many Latin American leaders worried more about surviving politically at home than supporting the U.S. president's interest in reshaping the neighborhood. If they did not believe that regional cooperation would make a difference before their next national election, then some heads of state continued to prioritize their own protective economic initiatives. Brazilian president João Goulart found the bureaucratic structure that managed the Alliance for Progress to be "a ponderous one," and he suspected that funding would still require the approval of the International Monetary Fund, making the foreign aid packages of little value to his people. Bolivian president Victor Paz Estensorro told Kennedy that the alliance's "machinery" moved too slowly for his satisfaction. He cited the excessive delays between requesting assistance, waiting for the completion of an aid study, and the final decision to provide funding. Paz provided a specific example of the problem with "well meaning" international bureaucrats: they were not invested in his country. If an aid project stalled, investors moved on to another country. The Bolivian president wanted to find foreigners committed to seeing a project through to completion, and if they were incompetent, he wanted the authority to fire them. Kennedy sympathized, but he would not support the construction of "hollow buildings" for the sake of providing political capital to regional heads of state.[104]

Kennedy wanted to expedite the investment of larger sums of money south of the border, and he asked the USAID and Congress for their support. He wanted the bureaucracy to be more flexible in its regulations. Meeting with the president in the Cabinet Room on February 16, 1962, Frank Coffin, deputy director of the USAID, recommended a number of bureaucratic moves to help facilitate faster operations, both on Capitol Hill and within the federal government, to get economic aid into the region. Kennedy personally delved into the administrative minutiae during the meeting by reviewing midlevel moves within the USAID by name, and he considered ordering the agency to contract secretaries through the "Kelly girls" in order to find clerical assistants more competent than those available through civil service channels.[105]

From Fiasco to Progress

The USIA continued to encourage Latin Americans to have faith in the long-term benefits of the alliance, but when they did not see measurable results, their support began to wane. Beyond examining the competency of USAID administrators, Kennedy asked his legislative liaisons why Congress seemed so slow to approve financial aid. Senator J. William Fulbright supported the alliance because he believed that it was a suitable strategy for containing Castro without instigating a military confrontation in the region.[106] However, the chair of the Senate Foreign Relations Committee did not speak for all of his congressional colleagues. John J. Rooney (D-NY), chair of the House Appropriations Subcommittee on Foreign Operations, Export Financing, and Related Programs, who could not locate Kuwait on a map and slashed Murrow's budget request, served as a gatekeeper to greater USAID funding. Vice President Johnson told Schlesinger that the House of Representatives suffered from "a chronic inferiority complex," and its members coveted their power of the purse in the same fashion that presidents prized their veto power.[107] However, even if the Congress opened its purse wider, Latin American development could not be appreciated within a matter of months or even years. Regional leaders required patience to persevere in making necessary reforms without another junta stifling progress.

In late July 1962, the United States hosted an Alliance for Progress conference in Chicago. Schlesinger delivered an optimistic speech, but he privately acknowledged the criticism raised by other attendees. Brazilian ambassador Roberto de Oliveria Campos, for example, applauded the concept of the initiative but cited the lack of performance to match the rhetoric.[108] Adolph Berle, who chaired the president's task force for the region, complained about the sluggish economic growth and spread the blame around Washington. Although the alliance's interagency task force found its home in the State Department, Berle criticized the American Republics Division of the Bureau of Inter-American Affairs. At the bureau, he found twenty men, one for each country, who "didn't like anything" related to the alliance. They lacked familiarity with their respective republic, let alone the region, and only two had served in the country related to their portfolio. Many did not speak Spanish. One Foreign Service officer told

Berle that he should be a diplomat in lieu of working as a bureaucrat. An infuriated Berle responded, "This isn't diplomat's work. This is a damn fool arrangement anyway."[109]

Berle also cited the USIA's inadequate information operations in Latin America for the alliance's lackluster achievements. He argued for the establishment of a "propaganda service" that could compete with the misinformation campaigns sponsored by communists in Latin America. Berle did not believe that the USIA had sufficient capabilities: "I don't think that 'information' quite meets the kind of brute adversary attack which was being financed then by the Soviet Union."[110] Although Berle used the USIA as a scapegoat for the lack of alliance progress, he was correct in calling U.S. propaganda inferior to the communists' information campaign in Latin America.

During an Alliance for Progress update on May 31, 1962, Kennedy expressed his concern about a "book gap" in Latin America and instructed the USIA to commence an "all-out effort" to close it. Murrow instructed his publishing service to see what it could do; however, the service reported that the costs for translating and publishing new books exceeded their budget. In August Murrow brought this to Kennedy's attention, using it as an example of how congressional refusal to expand his agency's annual budget severely limited his ability to achieve the administration's Cold War goal of being more prolific in the developing world than communist propagandists.[111] To put superpower expenditures into perspective, USIA deputy director Wilson pointed to Montevideo, Uruguay, which he called "the southern anchor" for communist literature distribution in Latin American (the northern anchor being Mexico City). Wilson explained to Kennedy that the Soviets spent thirteen thousand dollars a year just to fly printed propaganda to the city, which equated to three times the USIA's annual budget in Uruguay.[112]

Murrow privately acknowledged the "gloomy" challenges of publicizing the Alliance for Progress as more than a series of bilateral agreements between the United States and Latin American countries.[113] Nonetheless, the director defended his agency against Berle's attacks because he knew that public diplomacy only worked when matched by USAID funding and host-nation development. In June 1962, Brit-

From Fiasco to Progress

ish diplomats in the region noted that locals sarcastically joked about the lack of economic development with the program: *"Alianza Sí—Progreso No."* However, the British admitted that much of the difficulty rested with instability in the region, from the unwillingness of national leaders to implement the reforms that jeopardized their own political survival, to existing financial crises. The United States asked the British and Japanese to help provide financial assistance to the region, but their support remained fairly limited.[114] Murrow encouraged British information officers to refer to Western "contributions to a co-operative effort" with the developing world, as opposed to calling themselves "donors." Yet when the British suggested that material aid be labeled with a stamp for the Development Advisory Committee, an international entity that included the United Kingdom, to demonstrate broader Western support for democracy, the USAID demurred, arguing that Congress would only fund material stamped, "Made in U.S.A."[115]

On August 15, 1962, Schlesinger addressed students in Henry Kissinger's International Seminar at Harvard University, hoping to articulate the twin domestic obstacles to advancing the Alliance for Progress: Congress and the federal bureaucracy. Using a historical example, he noted that President James Monroe could declare his doctrine and President Franklin Roosevelt could promulgate the Good Neighbor Policy without the permission of Congress. In contrast, because Kennedy's program entailed a price tag, the appropriations committees could essentially veto Kennedy's foreign policy. The bureaucracy itself became a second obstruction. Without naming the USAID or the State Department, Schlesinger labeled career civil servants as the "great dead weight on executive innovation," due to the self-interests of various agencies that did not always run congruent with the president's priorities. He went so far as to declare the federal bureaucracy a branch of government separate from the Office of the President, because a modern president encountered "as much resistance within the executive branch as he would from Congress or the Supreme Court."[116]

Schlesinger described a frustration shared by Murrow and senior USIA officials. The U.S. government could saturate a foreign country with multiple forms of public diplomacy, but when disseminated by itself, information could not serve as the "magic bullet" to resolve national security challenges.[117] Murrow told John Scali on ABC's *Issues and Answers* television program that he believed his agency had made "headway" in educating Latin Americans about the accomplishments of the alliance.[118] Yet without funding for USAID programs, State Department facilitation of cooperation with host-nation governments, or private sector investments in the region, the USIA's message about building a hemispheric partnership rang hollow in mid-1962 after a year without measurable economic improvements for much of Latin America.

Public diplomacy scholar Nicholas Cull cites advocacy as one of the five core components to public diplomacy, and within the larger realm of national security strategy, public diplomacy is only one element.[119] As problematic as it was for Kennedy to allow the CIA to plan an invasion of Cuba without involving all of the principal members of the NSC, the USIA's advocacy for economic development and ending social injustices proved just as ineffectual in the absence of a whole-of-government approach to fostering a partnership with Latin America. In Murrow's first year as director, his agency demonstrated adeptness in responding late to the Bay of Pigs fiasco and in communicating the intent of the Alliance for Progress to Latin America. While the Kennedy administration had another year and a half to make the alliance a reality, an evaluation of its tepid success from 1961 to 1962 provides a valuable case study of how critical it is for U.S. public diplomacy to match the deeds of its government.

On October 15, 1962, Schlesinger sent a new memo from the White House to the State Department outlining his concern about the lack of progress with the alliance. He argued that the convoluted bureaucracy had stymied advancement and actually reverted to the "neo-Republicanism" of the previous administration.[120] Secretary of State Rusk's office did not have time to respond to Kennedy's special assistant. That same day a CIA photo analyst discovered the construction of Soviet medium-range nuclear missile sites ninety miles off the coast of Florida, and the intelligence agency raced the images to the president. Once again, a crisis over Cuba temporarily derailed the administration's plan for building a social and economic partnership with Latin America.

Fig. I. USIA director Edward R. Murrow
and President John F. Kennedy.

Fig. 2. (*Opposite top*) Murrow introduces his son, Casey, and wife, Janet, to Kennedy at his swearing-in ceremony in the Oval Office, on March 21, 1961.

Fig. 3. (*Opposite bottom*) USIA deputy director Donald M. Wilson. National Archives Collection, Box 37, E1069, RG 306.

Fig. 4. (*Above*) Murrow meets with an agency employee in his USIA office. He preferred standing at the drafter's table seen in the background.

Fig. 5. (*Opposite top*) Murrow discusses the impact of domestic
racism on U.S. foreign policy with Eleanor Roosevelt, on her
television program *Prospects of Mankind*, on May 26, 1961.

Fig. 6. (*Opposite bottom*) Murrow addresses Czechoslovakian
listeners, on the occasion of the Voice of America's twentieth
anniversary in February 1962.

Fig. 7. (*Above*) Murrow administers the oath of office to
George Stevens Jr., who became the director of the USIA's
Motion Picture and Television Services at age twenty-eight.
Lionel Mosley holds the Bible.

Fig. 8. (*Above*) Remaining close to some at CBS, Murrow persuaded the network to donate television shows for the USIA's Television Service. CBS News president Richard Salant and producer Burton Benjamin inspect the master print of *The Burma Surgeon* with Murrow.

Fig. 9. (*Opposite top*) Murrow and Voice of America director Henry Loomis at the dedication ceremony of the Voice's relay station in Greenville, North Carolina, on February 8, 1963. The USIA rededicated the facility in honor of the North Carolina native after Murrow's death.

Fig. 10. (*Opposite bottom*) On January 21, 1964, the day he resigned from the USIA, Murrow shares a laugh with Thomas C. Sorensen (right), his assistant director for plans and policy, and Deputy Director Wilson (left).

Fig. 11. President Lyndon B. Johnson congratulates Murrow after presenting him with the Presidential Medal of Freedom, on September 14, 1964. The citation lauds Murrow's service as "a pioneer in education through mass communications."

Fig. 12. Visitors to the U.S. embassy in Tokyo review a tribute to Murrow created by the embassy staff after his death on April 27, 1965.

4

This . . . Is Berlin

What is in danger of being destroyed here is that
perishable commodity called hope.
—EDWARD R. MURROW, August 16, 1961

For Robert Lochner, returning to Berlin in April 1961 to become director of the U.S.-funded radio station Rundfunk im amerikanischen
Sektor (RIAS) was a homecoming of sorts.[1] From 1924 to 1941 he had
spent his youth in Berlin when his father, Louis, served as head of
the Associated Press office until the United States' entry into World
War II.[2] Lochner's familiarity with the city proved fortuitous since
the precipitous escalation of the Cold War in Berlin during the summer of 1961 did not afford him a leisurely transition into managing
the city's most popular radio station. Following construction of the
Berlin Wall that August, Lochner's German friends harassed him
gently, insisting that the U.S. government knew in advance of the
communists' scheme to isolate the occupied city. If Washington did
not have advance warning, why else had Edward R. Murrow, a man
"known always to be where the action is," arrived in Berlin only a
few short hours prior to the wall's creation? Lochner insisted on the
coincidental timing of the U.S. Information Agency director's visit.[3]
Nonetheless, Murrow's arrival mirrored much of the fortune in his
broadcasting career: being in the right place at the right time.

Murrow enjoyed touring overseas USIA facilities, not for the pomp
and ceremony surrounding an official visit but to learn about other

parts of the world and to engage his agency's employees stationed at embassies, libraries, print plants, and radio stations. "He was anti-formality," his son, Casey, recalled.[4] Throughout his formidable career as a journalist, Murrow rubbed elbows with locals and conducted man-on-the-street interviews to gain a deeper understanding of complex problems. The USIA's public affairs officers stationed overseas interacted daily with their host-nation populations, and Murrow wanted to hear for himself their views, which reports, prepared by the agency's regional directors or the research division in Washington, could dilute.

The USIA director began his trek to Berlin by flying to Paris for a conference hosted by Secretary of State Dean Rusk on August 9, 1961, with thirty-two chiefs of mission from U.S. embassies in Europe. Although Murrow did not work for Rusk, he understood the value of hearing the cabinet secretary articulate his priorities to the president's ambassadors, and it provided Murrow with an opportunity to learn firsthand about the level of integration of the USIA public affairs officers within embassies and consulates. Berlin dominated the discussion because recent rumblings from behind the Iron Curtain suggested that the Soviets might sign a separate treaty with the German Democratic Republic (GDR) that would authorize the East German government to control its own borders. This would terminate the Allied Control Council's agreement permitting the Americans, British, and French from transiting between West Berlin and West Germany.

Murrow told the diplomats that the USIA's message about rising Cold War tensions over Berlin would be "simple and subject to repetition" and place the blame on the Soviet Union. He offered talking points for influencing Europeans to appreciate the international importance of Berlin: "The 1961 crisis is no more a 'Berlin crisis' than that of 1938 was a 'Czech' crisis or that of 1939 a 'Polish' crisis." One message exploited the theme of self-determination: "The plan for a 'Free City' of Berlin ignores the fact that West Berlin is already free and that the Soviet aim is to usurp Western rights." Some talking points used raw statistics to alert Western Europeans: twenty-two Soviet divisions occupied East Germany, the ratio of military personnel to civilians was higher in East Germany than anywhere else in Europe, and in recent days a thousand East Germans fled from the communist realm to the West.[5] For the USIA, articulating a clear message to maintain Western cohesion over protecting West Berlin proved easier to accomplish than the information campaign to elicit Latin American support for the Alliance for Progress.

Murrow departed Paris for the West German capital of Bonn to meet with his Western European public affairs officers to discuss the focus and quality of USIA messages and programming. Topics ranged from library exhibits and film screenings to radio broadcasts and magazine publications. The director emphasized Soviet responsibility for the ongoing Berlin crisis, reiterating the same points articulated to ambassadors in Paris. Nearly all of the officers met Murrow for the first time in Bonn, and many arrived either nervous or in awe of meeting the legendary journalist. The director put them at ease quickly before asking tough questions and requesting their honest opinions.[6]

In addition to evaluating *what* they said, Murrow wanted to talk about *how* they said it. On the director's orders, a team of senior USIA officers had traveled through Europe for six weeks that spring to assess operations. The team agreed unanimously that the agency needed to station its most talented officers in Europe, even if the Kennedy administration wanted to focus on the Third World. Mass saturation, although very appropriate in Africa or Latin America, would not resonate with Europe's sophisticated culture. Only the most capable public affairs officers could meet with press secretaries and journalists or engage academics about the more philosophical tenets of U.S. policy. Murrow agreed with the report and directed that staffing in Germany and France be reduced while scrutinizing selection criteria for key billets.[7]

On August 12, at the conclusion of this fruitful dialogue in Bonn, Murrow asked Joe Phillips, his assistant director for Western Europe, and James Hoofnagle, his assistant director for administration, to accompany him on his flight to West Berlin.[8] Murrow wanted to gain a firsthand appreciation for why Soviet premier Nikita Khrushchev labeled the city the "most dangerous spot in the world."[9] With the exception of Cuba, discussions about Berlin consumed more of President John F. Kennedy's time devoted to foreign affairs than any other issue, to include the Soviet Union and Southeast Asia.[10] According to scholar Frederick Kempe, Kennedy's preoccupation with the divided city did not stem from a desire to roll back communism in Eastern Europe—President Dwight Eisenhower discarded that policy when he refused to assist the Hungarians in their 1956 uprising. Instead, Kennedy wanted to deter the expansion of communism in the Third World.[11] In order to concentrate on strategies like the Alliance for Progress in Latin America and bolstering regimes in Laos and the Republic of Vietnam, Kennedy first needed to maintain the post–World War II status quo in Berlin.

Unfortunately for Kennedy, leaders in the Federal Republic of Germany (FRG) and the GDR did not share his interest in the developing world. The West's Chancellor Konrad Adenauer and the East's General Secretary Walter Ulbricht each desired definitive, albeit contrasting, outcomes for their fatherland. Adenauer envisioned a democratic country integrated into the North Atlantic Treaty Organization (NATO) and the European Economic Community, while Ulbricht sought a communist state isolated from the "fascist" influences of the West and protected by the security umbrella of the Warsaw Pact. Ulbricht lobbied Khrushchev emphatically to defend his communist brethren in Germany by signing a peace treaty with the GDR that would authorize him to close his borders around Berlin. As historian Lawrence Freedman noted, Western influence in Berlin threatened "the viability of a communist state" by enabling the free exchange of ideas about capitalism, individual rights, and democracy, as well as the exodus of a workforce to the Western occupation zones.[12] Regardless of GDR propaganda suggesting the contrary, East Germans who crossed the border on a regular basis realized West Berlin and West Germany's economic progress relative to the East.

In the spring of 1961, the demographics of East German refugees coming into West Berlin changed when thousands of farmers left their lands after Ulbricht's government forcibly made them relinquish ownership of their property and transition to collective farming. For a decade, professionals and academics had sought a new life in West Berlin, but now astonishing numbers of farmers abandoned their fields to escape the regime's control. Migration peaked in May

1961 when three thousand East Germans a day arrived at the Marien-felder refugee camp in the southern part of the American sector.[13]

GDR officials went out of their way to invite Western journalists to a June 15 press conference where Ulbricht publicly lobbied Khrushchev to permit him to seal the border.[14] Observing the exodus of people and the daily reminder of Western influence, the Soviet ambassador in East Berlin, Mikhail Pervukhin, agreed with Ulbricht's bleak fore-cast, telling Moscow that it "could be necessary" to seal the state's borders in order to prevent the economic and political collapse of the GDR.[15] Khrushchev worried about the open city in the heart of East Germany and agreed that the GDR should have the right to control access through its territory.[16]

A decision by the Soviet politburo to sign a treaty that would allow the GDR to prevent the Western occupation forces from trav-eling between Berlin and West Germany could not be made lightly. Its members recalled how their former wartime allies defied Joseph Stalin's ground blockades of the city from 1948 to 1949 with the costly Berlin Airlift. Still, the international prestige that Khrushchev could acquire by taking such a bold move might make the gamble worth-while. Within the context of the global Cold War, Khrushchev vied with China's Mao Zedong to be leader of the communist world, and he needed to protect the interests of those within his sphere of influ-ence, lest he expose himself to Mao's criticism.[17] Supporting Ulbricht's desire for a peace treaty would enable Khrushchev to protect him-self from critics in Moscow and Beijing who saw the Soviet premier as failing to take a hard-line approach toward the United States in the Cold War.

In the wake of the Bay of Pigs fiasco, Khrushchev doubted that Kennedy possessed the resolve to protect West Berlin.[18] Further, the president had failed to impress the Soviet premier during the Vienna summit in June 1961. Despite his reception by enthusiastic Austrian crowds and pep talks by his advisers, the Vienna summit did not go well for Kennedy. It did not help that, throughout the two-day confer-ence, the president suffered from severe back pain instigated in mid-May while shoveling dirt during a tree-planting ceremony in Ottawa, Canada.[19] Kennedy allowed Khrushchev to talk in circles, lecture him about ideology, and threaten to sign a separate treaty with the GDR by the end of the year. Although Kennedy made efforts to rebut the premier, the Soviet leader frequently interrupted him, slammed his fist onto a tabletop, and raised his voice to a booming level.[20] With such irreconcilable differences, Kennedy concluded their last conversation on June 4 by saying somberly that it would be a "cold winter."[21]

Before departing Vienna by train, Khrushchev shared his impressions about Kennedy with Austrian foreign minister Bruno Kreisky: "[W]hen it comes to make a decision he displays no understanding. He doesn't understand the times we're living in and the new balance of forces."[22] Kennedy flew to London to confer with Prime Minister Harold Macmillan, evidently depressed about his encounter with Khrushchev and feeling that he had allowed the older statesman to dominate the discussions.[23] Ambassador Llewellyn Thompson told Hans Tuch, the USIA assistant director for the USSR and Eastern Europe, that Kennedy was "genuinely shocked" by Khrushchev's "crudeness, antagonism, and unfriendliness."[24] Kennedy understood that he could not allow West Berlin to be absorbed into the Soviet sphere of influence, but he expressed no enthusiasm for participating in a standoff over Berlin. National Security Adviser McGeorge Bundy believed that it was for this very reason that the summit in Vienna greatly shook the president: "Khrushchev was not violent in tone but he was violent in content."[25]

Although Kennedy believed that he had performed miserably in Vienna, the Western press did not forecast that the winter would be significantly colder. The British embassy in Washington reported to the Foreign Office that Kennedy had returned home "with an enhanced reputation," and the international press posited that some good might come from the personal dialogue. Journalist Walter Lippmann hailed the meeting in his syndicated *Today and Tomorrow* column as "significant and important because it marked the re-establishment of full diplomatic intercourse" absent since May 1, 1960, when Gary Powers's U-2 spy plane crashed in the Soviet Union.[26] The USIA found that favorable opinions of the United States increased 20 to 30 percent in Great Britain and West Germany after Kennedy's visit to Europe (surprisingly, or not, it only rose by 2 percent in France).[27] Italian prime minister Amintore Fanfani told Kennedy during a private meeting at the White House two weeks after the Vienna summit that the Italian public would not support the Soviets gaining "another yard" in Berlin. Fanfani encouraged Kennedy to pressure European allies to contribute more to the continent's defense: "We must persuade the NATO powers that those who are exposed to the greatest risk must have the greatest role in decision making."[28]

In a nationally televised speech delivered on June 6, Kennedy used the word "sober" five times to describe his talks with Khrushchev, and he revealed that "no spectacular progress was either achieved or pretended." Kennedy recounted how he had explained to Khrushchev the importance of West Berlin to Western European security and that the United States and its wartime Allies remained resolute about fulfilling their obligations to their zones of occupation. Tying the address back to domestic politics, he noted the appropriateness of congressional hearings about foreign military and economic aid coinciding with the Vienna summit.[29] In light of Congress's meager funding for his earlier initiatives in the developing world—not to mention the paltry increase to the USIA's budget in July—perhaps the threat to Berlin might change their attitude.

Voice of America broadcast the speech in English and Russian, and although the Soviets typically jammed 25 percent of Voice of America's broadcasts, they did not obstruct Kennedy's words from reaching the USSR.[30] On June 10, Khrushchev released publicly the aide-mémoire that he had presented to Kennedy in Vienna explaining his reasons for wanting a peace treaty with the GDR. On the fifteenth, he delivered a televised speech to the Soviet people voicing his intent to sign the treaty soon. From East Berlin, Ulbricht publicly considered closing Western access to West Berlin, including Tempelhof Airport in the American sector. Despite the Eastern saber rattling, Kennedy did not respond to the provocations. During a press conference on June 27, he restated America's commitment to West Berlin without labeling the situation a crisis. Pundit Hans Morgenthau commented that Kennedy appeared to be taking the same "half-measures" in Berlin that had contributed to the Bay of Pigs disaster in April.[31]

In early July, Kennedy directed his advisers to formulate a strategy for Berlin, but he rejected recommendations made by the Joint Chiefs of Staff for a military buildup to intimidate the Soviets. Defense Secretary Robert McNamara bemoaned the options offered by his uniformed advisers concerning Berlin: "You have no idea what a problem I have with those generals over there. I feel that some of them can hardly wait to drop the bomb. Their military plans consist of a probe. When I ask what happens if the Communists respond to the probe, they say: we drop the bomb."[32] The president also asked former secretary of state Dean Acheson to fly to Berlin to conduct a strategic assessment and provide a paper on the situation. Upon reading the study, Kennedy considered Acheson's recommendation too bellicose and devoid of thoughtful diplomatic options.[33]

From his USIA office two blocks from the White House, Murrow supported a flexible response that emphasized negotiations over beating war drums, but he did not want his agency to sound indecisive about the administration's position either. The director encouraged the president to remain adamant that the USSR and GDR did not seek a true peace settlement since they sought to ignore three of the four Allied Powers. When Kennedy delivered a nationally televised address on the Berlin crisis on July 25, he borrowed a talking point that Murrow sent him to explain the challenges that stemmed from trying to deal with Khrushchev: "We cannot negotiate with those who say, 'What's mine is mine and what's yours is negotiable.'"[34]

The president's July 25 address outlined his Flexible Response policy, one that called for preparing American defenses for the worst-case scenario while stressing his desire to de-escalate the crisis through diplomacy. Kennedy called for a substantial increase in military spending and greater funding for Civil Defense, in the event that the GDR closed western access to West Berlin. To counter domestic skeptics who considered Berlin an untenable defensive position, the president evoked memories of achieving the impossible in World War II: "And so was Bastogne. And so, in fact, was Stalingrad. Any dangerous spot is tenable if men—brave men—will make it so." Kennedy left room for a diplomatic settlement, by committing himself to finding a peaceful solution on the floor of the United Nations and charging the Atlantic community to join the United States in this dialogue with the USSR.[35]

This . . . Is Berlin

The speech provided an important message for the USIA to amplify in its international information programming. On July 31, the agency distributed a one-reel documentary titled *Promise to History* that contained highlights of Kennedy's July 25 speech on the Berlin situation. The agency's regional print plants in Mexico City, Manila, and Beirut published printed translations of the speech in various languages on August 3. Murrow cabled his overseas outposts: "Urge fullest use all outlets." He directed them to articulate that, if the USSR signed a separate treaty with the GDR, the Soviets would repudiate their international commitment to maintain unhindered access to Berlin since the end of World War II.[36]

During the July 1961 Anglo-American information working group in Washington, British information officers recommended that their U.S. counterparts consider exploiting the differences between Eastern regimes. According to a British intelligence report, "There is considerable evidence of dissatisfaction with the restrictive effects of Soviet control and of economic jealousies within the Bloc, all of which should be exploited."[37] The West's information campaign toward Eastern Europe needed to focus on lambasting Moscow in order to weaken its control over the satellites. Fortunately, information officers on both sides of the Atlantic possessed a trove of examples from which to draw upon to illustrate how Khrushchev curbed the independence of Soviet satellites.

Murrow's priority to project an appropriate message that would support the president's vision for stability in Western Europe and the importance of West Berlin to the United States led him to make his detour to Berlin prior to returning to Washington on August 12 at the completion of the Bonn conference. The USIA director arrived with assistant directors Joe Phillips and James Hoofnagle at Tempelhof Airport at 10:00 p.m. Albert Hemsing, the acting public affairs officer assigned to the U.S. mission in Berlin, welcomed the three and drove them to the army's distinguished visitor's guesthouse in Wannsee, a southwestern suburb that had been home to the mission headquarters since 1945. Despite the late hour, Murrow asked for a briefing on the present situation from Hemsing and RIAS director Bob Lochner before turning in for the night, and discussions centered on the headline-generating refugee situation.[38] When Murrow ran out of questions, Lochner suggested that, with the following day being Sunday, Murrow forego his scheduled visit to the U.S. mission and come to his house instead. The mission brief would probably entail an army major pointing to a city map crowded with arrows and explaining how the Berlin Brigade would respond to a Soviet attack. As an alternative, Lochner offered to host a meeting with an English-speaking East Berlin teacher. Murrow jumped at the opportunity to engage a local over the perfunctory military brief.[39]

Public affairs officer Hemsing drove home around midnight from the guesthouse, but he never went to sleep that night. Arriving home, he received several calls, including one from the *Readers' Digest* European writer who inquired about the unusually high number of East German police in the vicinity of the Brandenburg Gate. Hemsing confirmed with a military colleague in the mission headquarters that they knew of nothing significant in the city, but the calls continued. At one in the morning, Lochner called Hemsing to say that RIAS had picked up an East German radio announcement: "With the backing of the Warsaw Pact, the German Democratic Republic, to thwart the reactionary designs of West Germany and NATO, etc., was taking measures to protect its borders—including the border between East and West Berlin."[40] On the streets, GDR border guards and soldiers constructed expedient barricades with barbed wire and steel tank obstacles.

Phone calls continued but, instead of press inquiries, the journalists began providing spot reports to the public affairs officer. Hemsing used the second telephone line in his home to call E. Allan Lightner Jr., the U.S. minister to Berlin, but he did not answer. He then called the army's duty officer who was reluctant to wake Major General Albert Watson Jr., the Berlin commandant. Only after threatening to phone the general's quarters himself did Hemsing convince the officer to wake the general. Frustrated by the apathy of mission officials, Hemsing chose to notify Washington indirectly about the situation by speaking with a personal friend, Lothar Loewe, who represented West German radio and television in the American capital. Loewe in turn filled in the State Department's Berlin task force more expediently

This . . . Is Berlin

than did mission or army channels.[41] The USIA employee's initiative directly led to Kennedy being notified on his yacht off of Hyannis Port around noon on Sunday about the construction of the Berlin Wall.[42]

RIAS director Lochner did not get to sleep that night either. After receiving calls from his German staff, he jumped into his car with diplomatic license plates at 1:00 a.m. to inspect the barricades. The GDR security forces did not prevent Lochner from crossing into East Berlin because they seemed more interested in their construction duties than checking papers. Lochner collected sounds of the barriers going up with his tape recorder that he provided to RIAS and VOA for their broadcasts. On his third trip into East Berlin, at 10:00 a.m. on Sunday, he entered the Friedrichstrasse train station where he found thousands of exasperated people carrying suitcases and cardboard boxes. The East German transportation police, who reminded Lochner of the Nazi Schutzstaffel in their black uniforms, stood arm-in-arm along the staircase to the elevated train. When an elderly woman asked one officer when the next train to West Berlin would arrive, he sneered, "That is all over—you are all sitting in a mousetrap now." RIAS provided the only live predawn radio coverage in Berlin. GDR stations played their canned recording about the need to offset Western aggression, while other West Berlin stations did not begin providing news until 6:00 a.m. RIAS broadcasted an update every fifteen minutes, which Lochner hoped would encourage more East Germans to escape. [43]

James Hoofnagle also did not get to bed, not because of a ringing telephone but due to jetlag. Turning on the radio at the Wannsee guesthouse, he heard a frantic RIAS reporter. Since he was not very familiar with the city landmarks mentioned in the report, he woke Phillips, who recognized the tension in the reporting. Alerting Murrow, the trio trekked to the U.S. mission headquarters.[44] As they pieced together details of the developing situation from the operations center, Murrow theorized that the barriers might not lead to nuclear war, but they would certainly not gain the GDR or USSR sympathy from the international community. The East German maneuver "absolutely astounded" Murrow, but he remained convinced that it would eventually backfire.[45]

Murrow became so mesmerized by the wall's construction that he elected to remain in Berlin for three days, even though he originally planned for just an overnight trip. He spent his time touring the perimeter of the Western sectors and crossed into East Berlin five times on Sunday in a car mounted with an American flag. Although the East German police yelled, "Halt," Murrow calmly instructed his driver to continue because the Allied Control Council's charter guaranteed officials from all four powers unimpeded access to one another's sectors. Only Soviet soldiers could lawfully stop to check the papers of officials from the other Allied countries. Hoofnagle, who accompanied Murrow, felt very nervous about the crossings, as did the driver, but none of it seemed to rattle the veteran wartime journalist.[46] His small entourage stopped in Hotel Adlon on Pariser Platz, adjacent to the Brandenburg Gate. As they sat sipping warm East German beer in the only wing of the luxury hotel to survive World War II, they listened to press hammers tearing up the street. The Americans watched construction workers—each with an armed soldier watching over him to ensure that he did not defect—create the obstacles. Opposite the iconic gate, hundreds of West Berliners shouted at the East German police, demanding that they remove the barriers.[47]

While Murrow made his way through Berlin, public affairs officer Hemsing sat through the first round of meetings with the three Western commandants. After a long debate, they agreed to issue a protest to the Soviet commandant for the "incidents" occurring along the city's sector borders. Tasked with finalizing the statement for the generals, Hemsing stopped writing when Lightner received a call from Assistant Secretary of State Foy Kohler. Kohler explained that Rusk vetoed the idea of the commandants issuing a statement; the only official response to the GDR's action would come from Washington. However, the president's response did not come quickly. Hemsing clocked fifty-six hours between when the GDR sealed the border and when Kennedy issued his formal protest. West Berliners, already perplexed by the weak American response to Khrushchev's bombastic threats since June, greeted the U.S. response with "dismay and anger."[48]

Western intelligence analysts suspected that the East Germans would need to do something to stop hemorrhaging its citizenry, but they were clearly unprepared for the rise of barriers on August 13.[49] When news reached the White House about the initial wire barricades, McGeorge Bundy turned to Robert Amory Jr., the deputy CIA director to ask, "What the hell do we do now?" Amory seemed energized by the drama, encouraging Bundy to "vividly enhance your commitment to Berlin" by deploying mechanized troops via the GDR's autobahn.[50] Willy Brandt, the lord mayor of West Berlin, cabled Kennedy: "It would be welcomed if American garrison were to be demonstratively strengthened."[51] General Maxwell Taylor, whom Kennedy recalled to active duty as his military adviser, cautioned against such a brash approach, fearing high casualties within the first hours and a good chance for escalation.[52]

The morale of West Berlin residents plummeted because they expected a decisive response from the Western powers, and Murrow acutely understood that the silence of the U.S. government failed to assuage local fears.[53] During his three-day visit, Murrow dropped in regularly on the RIAS station, taking great interest in how it reported developments. During a reception hosted in his honor by Lightner, Murrow questioned Lochner at length about how RIAS explained the situation to its German audience. Lochner enjoyed more freedom than the VOA language services in Washington, a critical element to effective broadcasting in Berlin, due to the time delay that caused policy guidance from the USIA to arrive too late for responding to a crisis. In mid-August RIAS staff worked day and night, and the visiting USIA executives told them that they were doing a "marvelous job" of explaining the situation to Berlin residents.[54]

The president's slow response may have stemmed from all three Western heads of government being on furlough for the weekend: Kennedy in Hyannis Port, Macmillan in Northern England, and Charles de Gaulle at his country home of Colombey-les-deux-Eglises.[55] Despite receiving reports at his Cape Cod home, the president refused to return to Washington earlier than Monday morning. On August 14 he sent a short note to Rusk that provided no orders to conduct diplomacy but only to consider the propaganda value of the GDR's actions: "The question we must decide is how far we should push this. It offers us a very good propaganda stick which if the situation were reversed would be well used in beating us."[56] While Kennedy seemed to believe that time was on his side, many West Germans considered his slow response to indicate that he did not appreciate the gravity of the situation. Nor did the noticeable increase in the "cockiness, smugness and jubilation" of East German security forces help to reassure the West Berliners.[57]

After three days of observing firsthand how the administration's slow response contributed to a precipitous decline of morale in West Berlin, Murrow felt compelled to contact Washington. From the Wannsee guesthouse on August 16, Joe Phillips captured Murrow's concerns about a potential "crisis of confidence" onto paper, before the USIA director reworked the draft on a typewriter for another hour himself. Hemsing carried the message to the mission's code room, ostensibly to direct the cable to the USIA's deputy director Donald Wilson, but Murrow fully intended for Kennedy and Rusk to read it.[58] Citing his personal interviews with Mayor Brandt and German journalists, Murrow warned U.S. policymakers that their efforts to remain unnerved by the rise of the wall greatly frustrated West Germans. The president's inaction appeared to them as a "letdown." The "psychological climate" urgently required mending that the USIA could not achieve without the administration first making more assertive protests and demonstrations of power. Although the U.S. government submitted a letter of protest on August 15, Murrow believed that the Germans considered it "belated and tepid." While not recommending military action—Murrow emphasized in the cable that no one in Berlin equated the wall to "Hitler takes over Rhineland"—he called for Kennedy to bolster West Berlin confidence before its citizens emptied their local bank accounts and vacated their homes for the refuge of West Germany. Murrow eloquently qualified the psychological impact of the wall: "What is in danger of being destroyed here is that perishable commodity called hope."[59]

The *Washington Post* speculated that Murrow's cable motivated Kennedy to deploy an army column to West Berlin and send Vice President Lyndon Johnson to welcome its arrival.[60] Years later Hemsing remained convinced that Murrow's detailed cable helped prompt the president to appear more resolute.[61] Lochner agreed and credits

This . . . Is Berlin

Murrow's decision to reach out to the president for improving the West Berliners' opinion of the United States: "From my own participation I know that that was very effective indeed in sort of stopping the erosion of morale."[62]

Murrow's advice influenced the actions that Kennedy chose to take after meeting with the Berlin Steering Group on August 17, a day after receiving Murrow's cable.[63] The attorney general urged his brother in a formal memorandum written the same day to respond more vocally about the wall's construction: "We have been handed a propaganda victory of tremendous dimensions on a silver platter and we are just not taking advantage of it." Robert Kennedy did not worry about the messaging from the USIA or Voice of America, which he considered to be "undoubtedly in good hands under Murrow." He wanted to exploit nongovernment efforts, including American students, professors, and labor and business leaders involved in Europe.[64] Mobilizing this base required Kennedy to articulate a policy that they could incorporate into their informal public diplomacy.

After Murrow cabled Washington, Hoofnagle worried that Murrow was missing his opportunity to shape USIA messages by remaining in Berlin. Summoning up a bit of courage, he told his boss, "Mr. Murrow, you're not a journalist anymore—you've got a job in Washington." Hoofnagle did not think that Murrow liked hearing that, but the director returned to the United States the next day.[65] The world's largest public diplomacy organization would benefit from the return of its director, but his principal deputies had not sat idle waiting for his return. In Murrow's absence, Deputy Director Donald Wilson energized the agency to aggressively inform the world about "Khrushchev's crisis" in Berlin through the publication of pamphlets and by beginning the production of a thirty-minute film, *Journey Across Berlin*, both available in thirty languages. Voice of America provided recordings to non-U.S. radio stations around the world, which included the sound clips made available by Lochner, and the USIA distributed fifteen articles for use in foreign newspapers and magazines.[66]

Murrow later referred to Berlin as "a living public relations laboratory."[67] Khrushchev's decision to allow Ulbricht to construct the wall on August 13, 1961, provided a fantastic public diplomacy opportunity. To expedite the dissemination of information in the weeks after it rose, the USIA relied heavily on the "Potomac Cable," an unclassified commentary cleared by the State Department as "an authoritative policy statement" that served dually as guidance to embassy staffs and material for public affairs officers to place in host-nation newspapers and on radio stations.[68] Murrow insisted that the USIA refer to the "Khrushchev crisis" and explain how Soviet intransigence in Germany endangered free people across the globe. Voice of America aired a three-part program titled *The Manufactured Crisis*, and it rebroadcast Kennedy's July 25 Berlin speech in thirty-five languages, which an estimated twenty million people heard. The agency's Motion Picture Service distributed nine hundred reels of the president's two addresses to ninety-five countries. USIA library managers reported "very heavy local usage" of an illustrated pamphlet containing fifteen articles related to the crisis, and overseas information centers mounted window displays containing photos, charts, and captions about the divided German capital. By November, public affairs officers assisted the West German government in bringing over seven hundred and fifty foreign correspondents to Berlin, to include thirty-five journalists from Africa and Asia. In Washington the USIA chaired a quadripartite working group of information ministers from Germany, France, and the United Kingdom to develop broadcast guidance.[69] In Murrow's view, "the Communists have stubbed their toes, and badly."[70]

Journalist Joseph Alsop believed that Kennedy looked at the Berlin Wall with "some relief" because, despite the psychological shock, it contained the "genuinely insolvable" problem of Berlin.[71] Khrushchev's reputation in the communist world depended, in no small part, on his bolstering of the East German regime. He knew that an East German or Soviet invasion of West Berlin would lead to a serious international conflict, but he could not allow the GDR to continue to lose its most educated and ambitious citizens to illegal immigration to West Berlin. In his own memoirs, Khrushchev acknowledged that a physical wall enabled him to demonstrate support for Ulbricht without personally inciting a war with the West.[72]

Influenced by Murrow's calls for a psychological response, Kennedy chose to send a military convoy on the autobahns through GDR territory to West Berlin to enhance the U.S. Berlin Brigade. The soldiers would be welcomed by Vice President Johnson, whom Kennedy sent in advance. To further strengthen the symbolism of American resoluteness, the White House asked retired Army General Lucius Clay, military governor during the Berlin Airlift, to accompany Johnson.[73] City residents stood in an uninterrupted drizzle for two hours to greet Johnson's motorcade, with some "weeping with joy." Johnson and Brandt, who accompanied the vice president in his car, walked part of the way to city hall so that the vice president could shake hands with a few from the estimated one million-strong crowd. Along the route, Johnson's entourage noticed the number of recent billboards, many in English, calling for Western solidarity.[74]

Arriving at city hall, Johnson addressed a massive crowd whom he called his "brothers in the east," and he affirmed that communist actions had united the Western allies "more firmly than ever."[75] Roused by the throngs, Johnson deviated from his White House–approved speech to pledge "our lives, our fortunes and our sacred honor" to defending West Berlin. Public affairs officer Hemsing, who coordinated international press coverage of the vice president's visit, grimaced at the remark, and he was not the only skeptic among U.S. personnel in attendance.[76] While he remained affable in public, privately Johnson told Brandt that the mayor's public letter to Kennedy complaining about his hesitancy to respond made the West look weak.[77] The United States could not practically prevent the wall from rising, and Brandt knew that too, as he later confided in Arthur Schlesinger Jr.: "No one proposed that we try and stop the erection of the Wall. We all supposed that such action would run the risk of war."[78]

Touring in the city, Johnson believed that the "single most important element" of success for his mission would be the arrival of American soldiers.[79] The drive through East Germany to Berlin should have only taken six to eight hours for a military convoy, but the troops arrived in West Berlin behind schedule looking tired, slightly dirty, and unshaven. This worked in their favor: They were not on parade; they were "real fighting men." Their march through the city boosted the morale of the residents, according to surveys conducted by the USIA in West Berlin.[80] Together Johnson and Clay stood before another massive crowd to welcome the American battle group driving in from the West. The vice president delivered a speech explaining how the communists built the wall out of frustration that West Germany and West Berlin had been a post–World War II success story, a historical fact that eclipsed the meager economic growth of East Germany. The convoy commander, a veteran of World War II, noted that not since the liberation of France had American soldiers received such a grand reception.[81] Lightner, the head of the U.S. mission, assessed the vice president's visit to Berlin as the most important event in the city's recent memory since Stalin's lifting of the blockade in 1949.[82]

Soviet and East German media covered Johnson's visit with their own unique spin. Responding to RIAS broadcasts, Eastern propagandists disparaged the station for its "lies, spies, and packrats." Murrow considered the communist response to be "a tribute to the power of truth but also a measure of the gulf that divides our two ways of life."[83] The GDR's lead newspaper equated U.S. support for Brandt to its commitment to Third World authoritarian leaders:

> On arriving, Mr. Johnson said: "Now I can examine with [my] own eyes consequences [of] this tragic situation . . ." Do exactly that, mister, since you have great experience with tragic situations. First Laos, then Cuba. Was it not you who visited also Mr. Diem in South Vietnam and Mr. Chang Kai Shek in Taiwan? In this case, it was quite appropriate that precisely you should come to Mr. Brandt. As collector of forlorn U.S. creatures, don't fly next to Helgoland [northern German island], but rather to commander of Bizerte [Tunisia].[84]

Although Brandt served as Johnson's escort, the U.S. government deliberately did not invite Chancellor Adenauer to accompany the vice president from Bonn. Johnson needed to solidify Western cohesion to guarantee Allied access to West Berlin. Adenauer's presence could threaten to detract from this focus by discussing Berlin as a component of West German politics. Adenauer perplexed Kennedy, who confided in his counselor, Ted Sorensen, after meeting the chancellor at the White House in April 1961, that he was talking to "a man who had lived in another world."[85] For the president, this made it very difficult to discuss realistic solutions for pressing German problems.

This . . . Is Berlin

Johnson did not want Adenauer there, either, but he provided a different interpretation for why the chancellor's presence would not help: Adenauer's political standing was weak in West Berlin.[86]

Despite the strange quirks that seemed to be trademark embarrassments of Johnson's international trips, the U.S. mission staff in Berlin appreciated the impact of the vice president's visit.[87] The Texan seemed immediately to grasp the importance of showmanship, but he also realized the gravity of the situation. The entire experience must have been surreal: the wild cheers of the ebullient crowds, the marshal air of the arrival of a U.S. Army motorized column, the international press documenting every step of his visit, and the icy glare of GDR security forces inspecting him from across the barbed wire. In his report to Kennedy, Johnson recounted his experience in a West Berlin refugee camp: "I saw the ruins of a building that had been wrecked by our bombers in the war, and here was a German woman kissing my hand in gratitude."[88]

For Murrow, grandstanding helped to protect the perishable commodity of hope in West Berlin, and he directed the USIA to highlight the vice president's trip in its radio, film, and written media. Unfortunately, Johnson did not fully grasp the value of the information agency in projecting his visit to an international audience. The vice president did not understand why the USIA had sent two personnel with his press pool to Germany because, in his view, it took two seats away from U.S. journalists. The Texas politician seemed more interested in using the trip to win votes at home than to restoring American credibility in Western Europe. Murrow's deputy, Wilson, defended the agency's request to send a photographer and journalist with the entourage. To gain "maximum propaganda mileage," the USIA could not rely solely on commercial sources to prepare real-time, dynamic broadcasts. During Johnson's stay in Berlin, Yoichi Okamoto, the agency's best photographer, snapped shots while reporter William McMenamin frequently filed stories on the Wireless File to seventy-seven countries for newspaper placement.[89] Johnson did not seem to appreciate that the USIA's efforts proved more influential for advancing U.S. public diplomacy than a front-page headline in the *New York Times* or *Chicago Tribune*.

On August 25, the agency's Motion Picture Service released *Journey across Berlin* and shipped thirty-five-millimeter and sixteen-millimeter prints to outposts by air. The film examined the closing of the Berlin border, the construction of barricades, the city residents' sad reaction, and the vice president's trip to welcome American troops. Murrow instructed USIA outposts to show the film as widely as possible.[90] The USIA published a color magazine on the impact of the wall but stopped short of printing mass quantities for distribution. Murrow convinced the ardent anticommunist German journalist Axel Springer to pay for his press, the Ullstein publishing house, to print three million copies in eleven non-English languages. This proved an effective work-around to the financial burden the USIA would otherwise incur, because the U.S. Air Force would only transport the magazines if the agency reimbursed it for the strategic lift.[91] The National Security Council decided that the USIA needed to pay for the air freight after staff assistant Kenneth Hansen questioned the urgency in getting the pamphlets to Europe so quickly. In his note to Bundy, Hansen argued, "Berlin is not fleeting and will probably remain a problem for some time."[92] For Murrow, time was fleeting and Springer agreed.

In early October, RIAS increased its broadcasts to East Berlin fivefold thanks to the construction of additional antennas in West Berlin and by borrowing Voice of America's million-watt tower in Munich for four hours a day.[93] The USIA also coordinated with the Armed Forces Network (AFN) station in West Berlin to read USIA commentaries because Murrow's staff knew that thousands of Germans listened to the broadcasts meant for American service members and their families living in Europe. Jack Jurey, an editorialist for Washington DC's radio station WTOP, called this illegal since it equated to propagandizing American citizens, AFN's primary audience. Donald Wilson defended the USIA's use of the AFN: as representatives of the United States living abroad, service members constantly received inquiries from host-nation people interested in understanding U.S. policy.[94]

Seeking additional messages to encourage international protests against the GDR and USSR, Murrow recognized that the USIA could capitalize on the humanitarian story in Berlin.[95] In one of the agency's posters intentionally vying for emotional appeal, a German bride is seen being propped over the wall so that her mother can briefly hold her hand from the other side after her wedding. In the second picture, the tearful bride clutches her new husband and both look into the distance, presumably toward the wall. The caption reads, "Sometimes one can shake hands across the wall, but usually onlookers can only gaze or wave at the bride on her day of days as she says goodbye to her mother with binoculars."[96] Feedback collected by the USIA's research division indicated that the messages resonated around the world. The public affairs officer in Usumbura, Burundi, reported that the two films, *Journey across Berlin* and *Promise to History*, drew thousands to commercial theaters.[97]

USIA officials continued to confer with their Western European counterparts about the Berlin crisis. The British Foreign Office applauded the USIA's publication of the pamphlet *Berlin 1961*, which complemented the British Information Service's own booklet, *Khrushchev's Crisis*. British information officers credited Murrow with making "wise use" of the message that Khrushchev could de-escalate tensions at any time.[98] John Peck, the British representative to the Council of Europe in Strasbourg, France, wrote to Leslie Glass, Murrow's assistant director for Western Europe, to encourage the USIA to emphasize economic and social ties rather than the NATO military alliance in its messages. Peck thought that many more Europeans, on both sides of the Iron Curtain, identified themselves with the European common market but not necessarily as members of the Atlantic community.[99]

Many of the Europeans less enthused about a military alliance resided in Western Europe. In the United States, the Berlin crisis enabled Kennedy to gain the public support required to move forward more aggressively with his Flexible Response policy by developing greater conventional military strength in lieu of relying primarily on the nation's nuclear arsenal. However, Kennedy remained skeptical that Europeans fully agreed with his approach to Berlin. Conferring with advisers in the Oval Office on September 5, 1961, Kennedy complained, "There is a great amount of residual anti-German feeling in Europe, and Khrushchev is playing it out with great skill."[100] Murrow warned Kennedy that only 24 percent of the British populace supported the proposition of fighting to defend West Berlin in late September.[101] A month after the wall's construction, the president wondered if it made the USSR look worse or if it only added to what he considered a lackluster foreign policy record.

Kennedy had a legitimate reason to be concerned. On October 19, 1961, USIA deputy director Wilson sent the president a memo reporting that majorities in Western European countries questioned the military supremacy of the United States and thought that it lagged further than the Soviet Union in the space race.[102] Murrow, however, did not see Berlin as a disaster, and he hoped that the administration would remain unflinching in the face of Khrushchev's provocations in Berlin coupled with his resumption of nuclear testing on September 10, 1961. Addressing the Poor Richard's Club in Philadelphia, the director explained: "What is at stake is not Berlin but the world and the manner in which its people shall live, whether fear will cause them to flinch or falter when the next payment for freedom falls due."[103] Under Murrow's guidance, the USIA adjusted its information campaign in Western Europe to counter low opinions of America's ability to achieve its international goals.

In an event well publicized by the press in October 1961, Murrow presented that year's Freedom House Award to Mayor Brandt at the organization's twentieth-anniversary luncheon in New York City. Not only did the USIA director effusively praise Brandt, he hailed the city residents whom the mayor represented: "For by so recognizing you we give currency to our concern over your fate and the fate of those who live in your city. Theirs is the residence of the brave, for they dwell in the shadow of tyranny." Speaking about the recent construction of the "wall of Ulbricht," Murrow speculated that it would be no more enduring than the wall that took Roman emperors 150 years to construct but only lasted "a pitiful handful of years" against the northern hordes. Although Murrow did not suggest that the West would be the barbarians storming the communists' wall, he emphasized American unity with the West Berliners, stating that both peoples shared an "ultimate destiny."[104]

Meanwhile in Berlin, where Clay remained after the vice president's visit, the retired general initiated his own public diplomacy to impress the Germans on both sides of the wall. Although he did not serve in an official diplomatic or military capacity, Clay began to push his right to have American military personnel in official cars cross into East Berlin without showing identification cards. GDR officials insisted on stopping them for identification, and Clay made a great noise arguing for his right, as a member of the Allied Powers, to travel freely throughout the city. The State Department disagreed and said that Clay's actions exacerbated tensions. The British military commandant agreed with the American diplomats, and the foreign minister asked Secretary of State Rusk to convey to the president, "We do not consider that the Western Powers have any right to send armed forces to exercise authority in the Soviet Sector any more than the Russians have the right to exercise similar authority in the Western Sectors."[105]

In addition to the diplomats, Clay aggravated the U.S. Army chain of command because, as the president's personal representative, he delivered orders to the Berlin Brigade without asking for approval from the generals who commanded the forward-deployed American forces. In his own mind, Clay wanted to impress one message on the people of Berlin and the Soviet commandant: the Soviets remained responsible for the security of East Berlin, and they, not the East German government, remained responsible for the wall. Although dangerous, his actions served as much a public diplomacy purpose as did the USIA's messages.

On October 22, the USIA possessed a passenger seat in another of the most memorable scenes of the Berlin crisis. Mission administrator Lightner and his wife sought to cross into the Soviet sector, but the East German police refused to permit them to enter without showing their identification. Since the car had U.S. Army plates, the mission administrator refused to show his diplomatic passport. When the East Germans would not let him enter, Lightner phoned the mission headquarters from the Check Point Charlie guard station. Public affairs officer Hemsing raced to the scene, arriving in time not only to witness but to participate in Clay's latest test. Clay instructed armed U.S. Army military policemen with fixed bayonets to escort Lightner's car across the intracity checkpoint. Hemsing pleaded with Lightner's wife to get out of the car, but she insisted on staying with her husband, so the USIA employee scrunched into the backseat of the Volkswagen with them. Together they defied the East Germans twice.[106]

While this made for a sensational news story, it worried many officials in Washington and led directly to the tank standoff at the checkpoint on October 27. When, once again, East German police denied a U.S. diplomat passage into their sector, Clay ordered tanks to the checkpoint. Tanks with GDR Army insignia appeared; however, reporters observing the activity noted that the crews spoke Russian and not German. Clay seemed satisfied that he had proven his point to the Soviet commandant. During the standoff, Hemsing observed an elderly East German take advantage of the military confrontation to run across the sector boundary shouting in German, "I am free, I am free!"[107]

In a counterpropaganda campaign of their own, when the East Germans began reinforcing the wall on November 19, 1961, Ulbricht's government explained its need to reinforce against a possible Western armored invasion. As East German security forces placed anti-tank obstacles around the widest avenues and intersections along the border, loudspeaker vans drove through neighborhoods to explain that the barriers would "frustrate Western aggression." The British speculated another motive: the new obstacles would enable the Soviets to withdraw their tanks with the confidence that they would not need to be recalled to repel a Western invasion.[108] Although an Allied offensive into the East remained unlikely, the plausibility of armored "escorts" by the U.S. Berlin Brigade of American officials posed a potential eyesore for the East Germans and Soviets.

In early December 1961, Murrow flew to Paris to meet with his British and French counterparts responsible for their own countries' public diplomacy. Murrow told Kennedy that he hoped the visit would continue to "harmonize our activities."[109] The British understood why the United States took a hard-line stance on Berlin, but they did not want to take such an aggressive approach in their own messages. They believed that defending Berlin at all costs would be unthinkable to an "uncommitted world" that still questioned the need to risk World War III with the Soviets over Germany, the nation responsible for World War II.[110]

This . . . Is Berlin

In late December, the USIA produced a ninety-minute television program for the people of Berlin with a special Christmas message from the United States that appeared on December 25. Murrow asked Kennedy to personally provide a two-minute message for inclusion, which the president accepted by asking the agency for a draft message. The show's message reaffirmed the U.S., British, and French commitment to the defense of West Berlin. Live portions of the program filmed in Berlin included Francis Cardinal Spellman, the archbishop of New York, celebrating mass for American military personnel and their families, and African American singer Marian Anderson making a personal appearance.[111]

In his annual report to the British foreign ministry, Ambassador David Ormsby-Gore assessed the first year of the Kennedy administration with mixed results: "After the first flourish of enthusiasm President Kennedy has settled for a more conservative policy, thereby disappointing some of his liberal friends. Contrary to expectations he has been more successful in the field of Foreign Policy than in Home Affairs."[112] To a great extent Kennedy's management of the Berlin crisis earned him this favorable mark in international relations. He prevented hawks like Dean Acheson and Lucius Clay from exacerbating the situation with unnecessarily hostile gestures toward the Soviets. Following Murrow's advice, albeit slowly, the president directed his administration's methods for showcasing the immoral and desperate measures taken by the GDR to stop the hemorrhaging of its populace seeking freedom in the West. By bolstering West Berlin with marshal displays and stump speeches, and amplifying it through public diplomacy, the United States preserved the three Western sectors as, in Murrow's words, "a sentinel beacon against the gutted shell of life that contaminates the land around it."[113]

Robert and Ethel Kennedy joined in the public diplomacy campaign, arriving in West Berlin in late February 1962, a dreary time to visit northern Germany. Arthur Schlesinger Jr. accompanied the attorney general, describing the wall as "an obscenity" in great detail in his journal: "Not only is its conception barbaric but its execution— the crude, gray concrete blocks, the bricked-in windows of apartment houses along the sector line, the vicious tank traps, the tall picket fences effected to prevent East Berliners from waving to sons or fathers in West Berlin—is repellent and hateful."[114] Regardless of the weather, nearly one hundred thousand residents gathered before the city hall to hear the president's brother deliver an address. The East Germans staged a propaganda gimmick by releasing red flags strung on balloons from their side of the wall. To the delight of the crowd, Kennedy noted, "They will let their balloons come over— but not their people."[115]

By August 1962, it would have been premature to accept Murrow's forecast that the wall would completely backfire on the communists. However, one year after construction began Khrushchev had not signed a separate peace treaty with East Germany, either. American analysts attributed this to the GDR's dismal economic situation, a breakdown in the distribution of basic foodstuffs, and rising discontent among the East German population, particularly over compulsory military service. Until Ulbricht successfully created a self-sustaining nation, the Kennedy administration seemed confident that Khrushchev would not turn over certain policy and defense functions to the GDR.[116] While Khrushchev proved cavalier at the Vienna Conference and in permitting Ulbricht to build his wall, he did not want to lose control of East-West relations by empowering the GDR to drag the USSR into direct conflict with the United States by unilaterally declaring war on the American sector of Berlin. Perhaps Berlin was not actually a "bone in his throat," as Khrushchev complained, but "a cancer," as Murrow opined.[117]

On June 26, 1963, Kennedy went to see the wall for himself. The itinerary for the president's final European trip did not initially include West Berlin, but his advisers prevailed upon him to add the city.[118] Kennedy intended to personally reaffirm America's commitment to the security of Europe during his ten-day trip.[119] His briefing book focused on the visit's public diplomacy potential. Broad objectives included furnishing "tangible evidence of American good will toward the German people," and providing "graphic emphasis to the continuing American presence in and responsibility for Europe."[120]

The visit to Berlin became iconic in Camelot lore. Kennedy invited General and Mrs. Clay to accompany him to Berlin, but Clay did not wish to draw attention away from the president. In lieu of traveling with Kennedy on Air Force One, the general joined the president at the U.S. air base in Wiesbaden, West Germany. When Kennedy told Clay that he had enjoyed his time in Germany thus far, Clay responded, "You haven't had any reception yet, you just wait until you get to Berlin, you're going to see something that you've never really seen before."[121] Indeed, 60 percent of the West Berlin population gathered to greet the president. After he visited the wall by car, Kennedy delivered an address before city hall. Angier Biddle Duke, the State Department's chief of protocol, recalled a great number of people fainting during the president's speech, and Duke admired the speed with which police bearing stretchers appeared to haul the unconscious people away.[122]

RIAS director Robert Lochner served as Kennedy's translator in Berlin. During the tour of the city, but prior to the delivery of his speech, the president told Lochner, "I want you to write out for me on a slip of paper 'I am a Berliner' in German." The radioman wrote out "ICH BIN EIN BERLINER" on Kennedy's copy of the speech.[123] Kennedy used the phrase twice before his attentive audience at Rudolph Wilde Platz in a speech that reaffirmed America's commitment and honored the city's residents for their service on "freedom's frontier." He encouraged advocates of the communist system to visit Berlin to understand the stark truth behind the socialist utopian mirage. Acknowledging that the West still had room for improvement, Kennedy reminded his audience that at least free countries "never had to put a wall up to keep our people in, to prevent them from leaving us." The president believed that the wall and greater Cold War divide would eventually collapse, but until that time, he encouraged the residents of the "defended island of freedom" to remain stalwart and optimistic.[124]

Murrow's deputy director for policy and plans, Thomas Sorensen, said that "Kennedy's visit to Western Europe did what no amount of USIA propaganda could ever do."[125] Kennedy biographer Robert Dallek labeled the tour "a grand triumph of public diplomacy."[126] The USIA's research service reported that Western European media considered Kennedy's visit as "an overwhelming personal but rather limited political success."[127] Despite the wide European coverage, the Soviet bloc devoted less than 2 percent of its total radio commentary to the president's visit, but its news services did note that Kennedy's appearance by the Berlin Wall furthered the Americans' "slanderous campaign against East Germany."[128]

Many residents in the GDR heard other accounts of Kennedy's visit, thanks to RIAS, VOA, AFN, and Radio Free Europe. To a great extent, the USIA contributed directly not only to the formation of this information campaign, but also in convincing the administration of the need to urgently respond to the construction of the wall. From Murrow's cable to the White House on August 16, 1961, to public affairs officer Hemsing's decision to circumvent proper command channels to inform the State Department about the developing situation in real time, the USIA served a vital purpose in convincing the administration to expose the wall as a desperate effort by the GDR to force its people to embrace communism when they would rather live under the social and political systems enjoyed by the other half of their countrymen in the West.

Compared to the frustrations that Murrow and his staff experienced in April 1961 when responding to the Bay of Pigs fiasco, the Berlin crisis afforded the USIA a golden opportunity to synchronize its assets in explaining the Kennedy administration's position. When Murrow referred to Berlin as "a living public relations laboratory," he could have cited the USIA's role as a textbook example for how the agency could enhance the foreign policy objectives of the U.S. government when permitted to be fully integrated into the national security apparatus.[129] On August 13, Murrow just happened to be in the right place at the right time, and the experience of driving back and forth between Berlin's occupied zones during the earliest phase of the wall's construction enthralled him. Murrow's decision to delay his return to Washington and remain in the city for three days probably had more to do with the rekindling of the journalist's sense of adventure and nostalgia for racing to Vienna to report the Anschluss or summoning the courage to tag along on an Allied bomber.

Murrow did not interfere with public affairs officer Hemsing's work, Lochner's management of RIAS, or Lightner's role as chief dip-

This . . . Is Berlin

lomat. Rather than complain to mission staff about what he believed to be a lethargic response from the White House, he chose to write a sharp cable to alert administration leaders at a critical moment. This quiet approach, a hallmark of Murrow's leadership style, proved effective on both sides of the Atlantic. In Washington Kennedy responded to the perceived "crisis of confidence" by dispatching the vice president, General Clay, and a military convoy. In Berlin, Lightner and Clay came to appreciate Hemsing's value to the mission and kept their public affairs officer involved in the day-to-day challenges that festered in the "most dangerous spot in the world."

Throughout the Kennedy administration, the USIA urged Western Europeans to remain united in the Cold War, and it used the Berlin Wall as a symbol within its information campaign to expose to the world the absurd contradictions of communist ideology versus practice. Other global challenges tested the Kennedy administration, but under Murrow's leadership the USIA consistently amplified a message about America's commitment to Berlin, thus making it harder for Khrushchev to sign a separate treaty with the GDR or to win the affection of international observers surveying the ninety-six-mile cement wall surrounding West Berlin.

5

Mr. Murrow Goes to Hollywood

This agency has spearheaded the intelligent use of the motion
picture in the national interest to a degree unprecedented in the
United States with the possible exception of World War II.

—EDWARD R. MURROW, June 19, 1963

Although John and Jacqueline Kennedy rarely escaped from the White
House to take in a movie, they indulged in viewing films from the
mansion's family theater. The First Family liked musicals, and Jackie
made her husband's affinity for *Camelot* legendary after his death.[1]
The president also enjoyed viewing USIA documentaries produced
to educate international audiences about the United States and its
international policies. When Edward R. Murrow stepped down as
director of the USIA in January 1964, Jackie wrote a note in his farewell album describing how, after dinner in the residence, Kennedy
often suggested that they head downstairs to watch another "film of
Ed Murrow's."[2]

The value of motion pictures as a form of Cold War public diplomacy predates the Kennedy administration.[3] By the mid-twentieth
century, the broad international availability of newsreels, films, and,
to a lesser extent, television, made this medium an inevitable exten-
sion of the "ancient platform tradition."[4] Tracing American popular
culture from 1947 until 1960, Stephen Whitfield argued in *The Culture of the Cold War* that many U.S. officials felt compelled to expand
their anticommunist messages beyond the formation of national pol-

icies and projections of military power by incorporating them into art, entertainment, and pastimes. Many influential American elites privately acknowledged that few true Stalinists resided in the United States; however, they remained alarmed about the subversive nature of communist ideology on American society.[5] Among those outside of Washington who embraced ardent anticommunism were movie stars and film executives "conscripted" into supporting the House Un-American Activities Committee. Beginning in 1947, the Motion Picture Alliance for the Preservation of American Ideals invited the HUAC to Los Angeles. The alliance's conservative leaders pledged to help fight communism through their selection of pro-American scripts and by maintaining unofficial blacklists of actors, writers, directors, and producers scourged by the HUAC.[6]

As Tony Shaw noted in *Hollywood's Cold War*, since the presidency of Harry Truman, "Washington regarded film as an indispensable means of projecting what it saw as the superiority of capitalism within and beyond its own immediate sphere of influence."[7] Shaw's comment speaks to something more subtle than the obvious Cold War themes popularized in blockbusters of the era, from the espionage of the James Bond series to psycho-thrillers such as *The Manchurian Candidate*. Ordinary dramas and comedies set in American cities and suburbs provided foreigners with an idealized portrayal of a free and prosperous society that made the United States appear more enticing than any World War II epic, such as *The Longest Day* or *Sands of Iwo Jima*. Historian Reinhold Wagnleitner referred to the psychological benefits of Hollywood's glamour as the "Marilyn Monroe Doctrine."[8]

Executives in Washington and Hollywood expended considerable energy and money developing propagandistic films to overtly celebrate the American way of life.[9] From the late 1940s through the end of the Kennedy administration, Shaw argues that Hollywood "declared full-scale war" on communism, and, until the quagmire of Vietnam during the Johnson administration, film producers trumpeted such messages enthusiastically and voluntarily.[10] With the increasingly widespread accessibility of color films and the advent of satellite communications during the Kennedy administration, Murrow joined the USIA fully aware of the importance of motion pictures as a component of his agency's overseas information campaign. This included news-reels shown before movies in commercial theaters, USIA-produced documentaries made available free or at a nominal cost, and, with the cooperation of Hollywood, American movies screened at international film festivals.

The Soviets and Chinese entered into the global film competition with the United States by the early 1960s. Concerned by the mass appeal of American "cultural imperialism," Nikita Khrushchev and Mao Zedong's propagandists worked diligently to pull back the veneer of Hollywood to expose the realities of poverty, racism, and "Western decadence." During the Kennedy administration, the Soviets and Chinese invested heavily in cinema on the African continent, where dozens of countries had recently gained their independence from European powers and debated whether to align with the West, the East, or the Non-Aligned Movement. In 1961, for example, communists provided film vans, projectors, and film studies scholarships in Ghana, Guinea, Mali, and Tunisia. The Soviets built a new six-hundred-person theater in Guinea and refurbished several others with air conditioning.[11] In light of these initiatives, film professor Richard MacCann partially credits Khrushchev for convincing Congress to fund the USIA's Motion Picture Service.[12]

Murrow arrived in Washington in 1961 with considerable appreciation for motion pictures as a means of conveying information. He may not have appeared in the movies, but Murrow understood television, a medium he considered "potentially more important than the development of the zipper."[13] Returning to New York from London after World War II, Murrow and producer Fred Friendly developed a weekly, half-hour television-news magazine, *See It Now*, for CBS. MacCann hailed Murrow's contribution to the revolutionary medium that began to eclipse radio: "Television's whole approach to news and public affairs was largely formed by this wise and worried man."[14] Murrow's assistant director at the USIA for plans and policy, Thomas Sorensen, argued that Murrow "had been more responsible than any other man for setting the tone and direction of American radio and TV public affairs programs," and in 1961 Murrow sought to do the same with government media.[15]

Mr. Murrow Goes to Hollywood

Drawing upon his twenty-five-year CBS career, Murrow contributed in three unique ways at the USIA in the realm of film and television. Leveraging his celebrity status and journalism credentials, he reached out to former network colleagues and Hollywood acquaintances to challenge them to improve the quality of their productions and donate programs for the USIA's use. Although many American movies and television shows promoted Wagnleitner's "Monroe Doctrine," an increasing number celebrated crime, sexuality, and juvenile delinquency, which Murrow worried would tarnish the American image abroad. Murrow's efforts along this line achieved mixed results, just as his first postsabbatical radio address had on July 3, 1960, when he opined, "Our example may be more important than our dollars."[16] Murrow also created the agency's first satellite usage policies in 1962, after NASA launched Telstar 1, the first television communications satellite.[17] While rejuvenating the television capabilities of the USIA, he remained cautious about expecting too much public diplomacy value from beaming programs around the world. Murrow understood that in the early 1960s it would be very tempting to spend millions of dollars on television programming but reach far fewer people than could be influenced through radio broadcasts and films for a fraction of the price. Finally, and most enduring, Murrow found a Hollywood producer, George Stevens Jr., to take the helm of the USIA's Motion Picture Service. Stevens would receive international acclaim for producing public diplomacy documentaries that resonated with audiences around the world.

While preparing for his confirmation hearings in February 1961, Murrow began considering how to improve the relationship between the USIA and the country's film and television industries. He planned to use his substantial personal contacts to garner the support of businesses and private citizens to assist in furthering public diplomacy. Nurturing such relationships would require individual contact, and Murrow looked for additional funds to host official and informal events of his own as agency director. However, the USIA was not CBS, and federal executives did not receive expense accounts comparable to corporate presidents. After discovering that the USIA "representation fund" covering such expenses contained a meager five hundred dollars a year, he contacted the Carnegie Endowment for International Peace to request a grant of a few thousand dollars a year to foster relationships that he believed would improve America's image abroad.[18]

Murrow believed that Kennedy could convince American media executives to assist the USIA. In July 1961, he recommended that the president host a lunch with executives from the three major television networks in order to gain their permission to use some of their programs for USIA television and film screenings free of charge. This, Murrow argued, would enable his agency to distribute a larger quantity of popular shows than its budget would permit them to purchase.[19] For democracy to thrive in a world of competing ideologies and a cacophony of media, Murrow recognized that television, much like radio had done three decades earlier, needed to be used by policymakers to better inform the public about political discourse. Despite his less than ideal departure from CBS, Murrow assessed his relationship with the top executives from all three major networks as "excellent" in 1961, and in September he sent the head of USIA's Television Service to New York to discuss expanding their cooperation on a worldwide basis.[20]

On October 5, 1961, Kennedy took Murrow's advice and met with the chairs of CBS, NBC, and ABC. The president of the National Association of Broadcasters and Murrow joined them at the White House luncheon. Beyond securing program rights, Murrow encouraged Kennedy to ask the network presidents to consider America's image when producing new shows. The sensationalism and violence in television detracted from the more wholesome image that the agency sought to present. In his read-ahead memorandum to the president, Murrow suggested that "a few words from you might cause them to scrutinize their export in terms of impact as well as income."[21] The luncheon's collegial atmosphere and the president's good nature succeeded in gaining the USIA access to free or low-cost programming; however, Kennedy proved less persuasive in steering networks toward more wholesome shows.

Beyond the television networks, Murrow set his sights on fostering a better relationship with Hollywood for the same rationale. He recalled the closeness of Washington-Hollywood relations in the early

Mr. Murrow Goes to Hollywood

Cold War and thought that, by engaging film executives directly, he could rekindle some of the warmth seen with the former Motion Picture Export Association.[22] Kennedy asked Murrow to target more of the Third World's youth and labor leaders by introducing them to American entertainment. In lieu of serious news programming, the president believed that messages found in music and movies would gain greater attention from younger and less-educated demographics.[23] Murrow's contacts in the film business included scores of celebrities whom he had interviewed on the CBS television program *Person-to-Person*, which he hosted from 1953 to 1959.[24] In addition, Murrow's public debate with Senator Joseph McCarthy in 1954 had endeared him to many actors who willingly agreed to represent the United States at international film festivals as a personal favor to Murrow.[25]

Among others, Charlton Heston volunteered to attend the 1961 Berlin International Film Festival, and he stopped in USIA headquarters at 1776 Pennsylvania Avenue prior to departing.[26] Heston returned from Germany so impressed with the experience that he wanted to form a pool of celebrities who would make themselves available to the USIA for future international exchanges.[27] Murrow contacted performer Danny Kaye personally, convincing him to appear in Moscow for an agency exhibit. Hans Tuch, the USIA's assistant director for USSR and Eastern Europe, cited Kaye's support as a prime example of how Murrow's dynamism advanced the USIA's information campaign behind the Iron Curtain.[28]

Murrow lobbied Hollywood executives to improve the wholesome content of their scripts. Since the mid-1950s, the quality of American films making their way across the globe did not always sit well with diplomats and public affairs officers, who shirked at the increasing amounts of violent and sexual content. The USIA bemoaned its inability to co-opt Hollywood's depiction of American life in a 1960 internal assessment: "On these matters the industry prefers to be guided largely by its own domestic code and by moral standards established by importing countries."[29] The federal government could not prohibit the sale of Hollywood films, but Murrow hoped that movie executives would follow his logic and curb some of the vulgarity in future productions. For those movies that the agency did endorse, Murrow understood that the USIA needed to be careful not to advertise them, lest someone criticize the films as government propaganda.[30]

In the early 1960s, about 70 percent of cinemas around the world projected Hollywood movies, but despite their dominance, international film critics often disparaged the cultural value of American films. Turner Shelton, who headed the USIA's Motion Picture Service for the first year of Murrow's directorship, pointed out the hypocrisy: When it came to content, foreign critics downgraded American movies while celebrating numerous foreign films containing many more "morally objectionable" scenes. In Shelton's view, foreign critics considered movies a form of national image, and many European elites resented the booming success of American popular culture in their own countries while European movies lacked similar ticket sales. Shelton cautioned USIA executives not to be too anxious to shape Hollywood's image because the industry generated a decent degree of admiration for the United States, without the heavy editorial hand of a Washington bureaucrat. Further, he remained optimistic that producers would take the necessary precautions on their own initiative to present a favorable image.[31]

Murrow disagreed with Shelton's interpretation of how international audiences viewed American films, and he did not trust Hollywood executives to adopt a more tasteful approach. Murrow could validate his argument in March 1961, when Universal Pictures asked the Defense Department for assistance in filming *The Ugly American*, a story about an abrasive and condescending U.S. ambassador to the fictitious Southeast Asian country of Sarkan. The Pentagon sent the script to Shelton for review, and he was shocked to find that a key supporting character, Joe Bing, served as the USIA public affairs officer in Sarkan's capital. During earlier discussions, the studio representative assured Shelton that Bing would be a "special assistant" at the embassy. Shelton insisted that, if Bing's position did not change from the public affairs officer, the Defense Department should not provide military assistance. The Pentagon agreed with Shelton's reservations.[32] Learning of the debacle, Murrow considered sending a USIA liaison to California, in order to prevent future embarrassments.

Murrow explained to the White House that, short of censorship,

Mr. Murrow Goes to Hollywood

the USIA could not guarantee that the image of America in Hollywood films would be favorable, but he continued to engage studio executives. The agency possessed limited Informational Media Guaranty funds to pay for commercial films distributed overseas, and in October 1961, Murrow narrowed eligibility for the funds to those making "a positive contribution in support of U.S. policy objectives, or must reflect favorably on the United States."[33] While commercial studios did not rely on these funds, they did like to have Defense Department support for military films, but such cooperation would evaporate if scripts did not follow USIA guidelines.

In June 1961, Attorney General Robert Kennedy recommended to Murrow that he recruit movie stars to make public statements about the unique freedoms enjoyed in America. Murrow liked the idea and flew to Hollywood with Eric Johnston, president of the Motion Picture Association of America, in November 1961 to meet with movie stars willing to record radio messages for Voice of America.[34] Sending Murrow out West made sense, not only because of his position, but also because he was the most recognizable member of the administration, after the president.

In addition to soliciting the support of actors, Murrow used the trip as an opportunity to address film executives en masse. On November 5, Murrow spoke before the senior executives of the largest production studios in Hollywood at a dinner sponsored by the Motion Picture Association. With tens of millions of people around the world viewing American films every week, Hollywood had the opportunity to help the USIA improve America's position in the world vis-à-vis the Soviet Union. In his address, Murrow invited the executives to pause for a moment and consider that much of the world learned about America through the cinema. Murrow explained the USIA's quandary: "There are many people abroad who think that beyond the Mississippi lie lands still periled by warring Indians and that all other Americans live in penthouse apartments, drive limousine-dimension convertibles and wear tailored furs."[35] Murrow shared with them his idea of dispatching a USIA officer to California to help film studios select the most appropriate scripts that presented America in the best light—not as a censor, but as an adviser.

Unsurprisingly, Murrow found much more success in California convincing actors to participate in international film festivals and public service clips than in eliciting studio executives to produce movies with positive messages. According to the *New York Times*, the industry responded generally negatively to his November 1961 speech. After all, one of the elements making movies so popular in America and throughout the world was the fantastic escape it provided from the drudgery of ordinary life.[36] The *Motion Picture Herald* wrote, "Mr. Murrow knows little about the film medium." Martin Quigley, the paper's editor in chief, opined that if Murrow wanted a particular image of America portrayed in film, it would be Washington's prerogative: "The Hollywood film is a story-telling, entertainment medium. When it does that job well, it serves not only audiences in America but throughout the world."[37] Political satirist Art Buchwald wrote in his *New York Herald-Tribune* column another viewpoint. "The big problem as I see it, Ed," he penned from Paris, "is not that the world has the wrong image of Americans but that pretty soon it won't have any image at all." Buchwald's concern stemmed from the growth of the European Common Market, which he believed would continue to grow and turn inward, not because they disliked America, but because they chose to ignore it.[38]

Perhaps Murrow had an inkling that the executives would not embrace his call when he observed that Johnston only begrudgingly agreed to accompany him to Hollywood.[39] Even though he served as Murrow's escort, Johnston publicly objected to Murrow's advice to the executives, telling reporters after the speech that producers should be able to use their own discretion and artistic vision. Prior to Murrow's arrival, the Academy of Motion Pictures said that the press would not be invited to the dinner because its leaders worried that the academy's prestige would suffer greatly if Murrow "even lightly castigated" their work. This lack of transparency perplexed the USIA's Motion Picture Service director, since Murrow's address advocated for the free flow of information.[40]

Despite the bad press following his speech, several filmmakers agreed to support the production of a series of propaganda films that *Newsweek* called "soft policy," decades before political scientist Joseph

Mr. Murrow Goes to Hollywood

Nye coined the term "soft power."[41] United States Pictures owner Milton Sperling praised Murrow for leaving his $300,000-a-year job to become a civil servant and speak on behalf of the president of the United States in Hollywood: "We do need advice on what kind of pictures would help. That advice must come from the government or Murrow."[42] The legendary producer Samuel Goldwyn, a friend of Murrow's, told him in a note the following year, "As you know, I am always ready to cooperate."[43] Murrow encouraged Kennedy to meet with a number of film executives to elicit rights to their movies for USIA programming, and Murrow offered to prepare a list of leaders in the film industry.[44] Arthur B. Krim, president of the United Artists Corporation, wrote to Kennedy's secretary, Evelyn Lincoln, to endorse Murrow's recommendation: "There is much that private enterprise in this industry can and should be doing in cooperation with our Government and in furtherance of its objectives, over and above the single objective of private profit."[45] The president eventually followed up on this recommendation in the fall of 1962.[46]

For the remainder of his time at the USIA, Murrow continued to prod Hollywood to help him with his international mission. In September 1963, Murrow proposed to create five project groups with the assistance of the motion-picture industry, in order to leverage Hollywood in advocating public diplomacy. Each group would develop plans for a specific task: the acquisition of African theaters by major American film companies; selection of the best American films for an overseas tour; a scholarship program for foreign students to study cinematography with American filmmakers; a project to coordinate the preservation of American films; and the use of personalities abroad, much like the celebrated "jazz ambassadors."[47] Executives who promised to help Murrow in this endeavor included the presidents and heads of the boards of eight major studios—among them Roy Disney—as well as leaders of actors and writers guilds.[48]

At the same time that he reached out to the private sector, Murrow did not forget to challenge his own Motion Picture Service to provide intriguing documentaries to complement Hollywood's output. Lighthearted commercial entertainment would not sufficiently persuade a foreign audience of America's superiority over the Soviets.

Neither, in Murrow's mind, would the USIA documentaries produced during the Eisenhower administration, when the Motion Picture Service focused on communist oppression behind the Iron Curtain, the testimonies of successful defectors, and the Soviet response to the 1956 Hungarian Uprising.[49] Instead, he wanted the agency's film division to showcase American individualism, ingenuity, and optimism in its own documentaries. His background as a journalist influenced his guidance to the Motion Picture Service, evidenced by his directive to use human-interest stories as the narrative for films.[50] Speaking as a television reporter in 1959, Murrow emphasized the irreplaceable value of "the individual who has conviction, and who can in some mysterious manner convey that conviction to the viewer."[51] Themes of individuality would be anathema to the core message of communist films propagated to the developing world that celebrated the collectivization of societies and economies.

In addition to their information value, documentaries provided cultural benefits that helped counter the foreign film critics' charge that the United States provided nothing of substance in their movies. In the 1930s, British documentarian John Grierson considered the documentary genre as "the creative treatment of actuality," and USIA productions during the Kennedy administration appeared in two forms.[52] The first offered windows into the lives of typical Americans, while the latter approached provocative topics by presenting or criticizing the status quo. During Murrow's tenure, civil rights, poverty, and international relations elicited great interest, and Hollywood films often skirted these topics, making them appropriate for USIA documentaries.

USIA officers in the field agreed about the value of documentaries and encouraged Murrow to bolster the Motion Picture Service. Public affairs officer Leon Poullada cabled Murrow from the West African capital of Lomé: "Films are an excellent vehicle for getting our message across in countries like Togo."[53] Historian Tony Shaw agreed, referring to the hundreds of documentaries and newsreels produced by the USIA during Murrow's tenure as "white propaganda" that did not attack their Cold War adversary nor convey blatant messages about American socioeconomic superiority.[54]

Mr. Murrow Goes to Hollywood

Motion Picture Service director Shelton appeared a bit more skeptical about the global value of documentaries: "I have serious doubts that we would ever be able to find a common denominator which would serve our purposes in all countries."[55] This marked a significant point of departure between Murrow and many of the older members of the agency who had spent their careers in the federal bureaucracy. Murrow argued that a well-crafted and broadly themed message could have mass appeal and influence. If the USIA tried to produce a film for every regional demographic, then the agency would not be speaking with one voice. As he had instructed his staff shortly after his arrival, Murrow wanted the agency to slim down the number of messages, perhaps just to five at any one time, and to say them dynamically and repetitively.[56]

Murrow tasked his overseas posts to provide footage for the film division. In the fall of 1961, the Motion Picture Service began a series of weekly African film magazines titled *Today*. Most outposts supported the initiative by regularly submitting footage, but this became a double-edged sword. Soon the service became overwhelmed with the volume of footage, and the agency began to ask outposts to be more selective and descriptive of each reel mailed to Washington.[57] The other unforeseen problem emerged when African outposts voiced concern about showing the weekly program when it did not include coverage of its own nation. Public affairs officers worried that locals might infer U.S. favoritism toward other African countries.[58] This provided some validity to Shelton's concern that a general information program might not be suitable for every region, let alone the globe.

When it came to human-interest stories, arguably no other American captivated international attention more than did John F. Kennedy. Returning from his first overseas travel in April 1961, Vice President Lyndon Johnson urged the administration not to leave the president's portrayal entirely up to the media.[59] The USIA responded by producing *The Task Begun: President Kennedy in Europe, 1961*. Kennedy appealed to Europeans directly to consider "how much work we in the Free World have to do" to advance peace and security.[60] In addition to capturing the president's congeniality with heads of state, the color film showcased enthusiastic crowds pressing against police lines to catch a glimpse of the Kennedys in Paris, Vienna, and London.[61]

Murrow also recognized the First Lady's popular appeal, evidenced by the international media often providing more details about Jackie's fashion sense than the contents of her husband's speeches. Public diplomacy scholar Nicholas Cull considered Jackie's participation in her husband's visit to Europe in June 1961 as "one of the year's few unqualified propaganda successes."[62] After learning of CBS's partnership with the White House to produce the First Lady's televised tour of restoration efforts at the mansion, Murrow contacted Kennedy's press secretary, Pierre Salinger, to suggest that Jackie add a couple of lines about her home being the "People's Home" in both French and Spanish. The USIA spliced the lines into appropriate reels of *White House Tour with Mrs. John F. Kennedy* distributed by the agency to sixteen countries.[63] For fifty minutes, Jackie showcased the nineteenth-century American art and furniture that her committee had acquired as part of its effort to restore the mansion to its pre–1902 glory. As she explained on camera, she wanted the White House to represent the best of America: "We have such a great civilization, but most foreigners don't realize it."[64] International reactions proved overwhelmingly positive, with critics calling Jackie sophisticated and charming. A writer for London's *Daily Mirror* shared that the First Lady "almost made me feel ashamed that the British burned the House in 1814," but followed this lighthearted remark more seriously by wondering if British television would ever air a tour of Buckingham Palace.[65]

In addition to the White House, the USIA successfully built partnerships with various other components of the federal government to prepare documentaries. Throughout the 1960s, the Interdepartmental Committee on Visual and Auditory Materials for Distribution Abroad met monthly on the third floor of 1776 Pennsylvania Avenue. Although chaired by USIA's Motion Picture Service, the list of participants reflected the interest in information films throughout the federal government. Eight cabinet departments created their own audiovisual service, as did NASA, the Atomic Energy Commission, the Library of Congress, the Federal Aviation Agency, and the National Science Foundation.[66] Each agency provided technical expertise in producing educational films about a broad swath of topics ranging from American art to the effects of radioactive fallout.

The group vetted film scripts based on their suitability for foreign audiences. For example, when the air force representative presented the group with *Highway Mortality* and urged it to be shown by the USIA, the group resoundingly said that high-speed automobile accidents would not resonate in the developing world. Murrow suggested to Arthur Sylvester, the assistant secretary of defense for public affairs, that his department provide movies pertaining to the Pentagon's scientific weapons research as a way to impress other countries about American scientific capabilities. Specific recommendations to Sylvester included explaining the "fail-safe" mechanism as a way to reassure people about the U.S. government's nuclear safeguards, and describing how military assistance improved the readiness of foreign militaries.[67]

Ten months into his job, Murrow confided in friends that he found himself "frustrated but fascinated" by his responsibilities. He worked fifteen hours a day to improve the quality of a broad assortment of programs and services yet sometimes wondered if the USIA fully understood his vision.[68] Part of this challenge stemmed from the reticence of senior staff members who were so set in their bureaucratic ways that they passively refused to embrace the policies developed by Murrow and his two principal deputies, Donald Wilson and Thomas Sorensen. Sorensen summed up the agency's shortfall in *The Word War*: "Unfortunately, the service's Washington staff of several hundred included few innovative minds, not excepting the head of the [motion picture] service, and the contractors—mostly old-time newsreel producers—were equally uninspiring."[69] When it came to the Motion Picture Service, Shelton did not fully embrace the approach of senior leadership to revolutionizing their methodology.

During his visit to Hollywood in November 1961, Murrow stopped in the home of Samuel Goldwyn, a friend with forty-nine years of experience as a Hollywood producer. Murrow discussed his frustration with the limits of his Motion Picture Service staff and his desire to strengthen USIA-Hollywood relations, particularly in an effort to produce better documentaries. Murrow wondered aloud if he could entice a career producer to serve as head of his film division. Goldwyn suggested his own son, Sam Jr., who had worked for General Dwight Eisenhower in Paris as a documentary producer. However, the younger Goldwyn wanted to remain in Hollywood. Goldwyn then suggested George Stevens Jr., the son of a respected filmmaker, who could call upon his father's contacts in an effort to attract talent to the USIA.[70]

Stevens initially demurred when Goldwyn encouraged him to consider the job, but he did not want to pass on an opportunity to meet the famed Edward R. Murrow. Stevens and Murrow met in Hollywood for two hours on November 5. During their discussion, Stevens did not seem terribly interested in taking the government job, but he wanted to discuss producing a documentary on Jackie Kennedy's upcoming trip to India and Pakistan. His artistic recommendations for both content and themes confirmed for Murrow what a Hollywood producer could do for his Motion Picture Service by rejecting the stark, anticommunist genre favored by the Eisenhower administration. Murrow encouraged Stevens to visit him in his Washington office to discuss the matter further. While in the national capital, Stevens began to take Murrow's offer more seriously. He liked the idea of joining the New Frontier: "Here were all these young men who had given up jobs to get behind JFK. It was an exciting atmosphere of fresh thought and action, of energy, of youth. I was young, and I thought I could fit in with that atmosphere."[71] Stevens greatly respected Murrow, especially his tremendous "capacity to arouse a dormant enterprise," and he found that employees throughout the agency proudly stated, "I work for Ed Murrow."[72]

Murrow felt "very excited" when Stevens accepted the position as director of the Motion Picture Service because he believed that Stevens would greatly improve the quality of their documentaries.[73] Shortly after Stevens began his job, Murrow sent Goldwyn a letter of thanks for making the recommendation.[74] As Nicholas Cull observed, Murrow found in Stevens a "unique combination of youth, energy, and film production."[75] Stevens was certainly young; he arrived in Washington to begin work at the age of twenty-eight, in February 1962. Many veteran USIA officers, including Shelton, remained skep-

Mr. Murrow Goes to Hollywood

tical of Stevens, but his creativity in producing the films of the First Lady's tour of Central Asia earned him international acclaim and the respect of colleagues in the agency and throughout the presidential administration.

Central Asia intrigued Jackie, and although the president seemed indifferent to allowing his wife to travel there on her own, he authorized the USIA to make two documentaries, one covering her tour of India and the other of Pakistan.[76] Stevens recommended producing films that revealed the "moment-to-moment" reactions and expressions of Jackie during her travels.[77] Senior USIA officers doubted that films of her visit would generate international interest, and Stevens privately confided in Murrow, "We will see how much we achieve."[78]

Stevens and director Leo Seltzer set out to create a film that blended the fantastic settings, exotic clothing, and closeups of the indigenous people. *Invitation to India* opens with scenes of traditionally dressed Indians and ancient palaces, but the narrator reminds viewers how the five-thousand-year-old civilization had transformed to join the "contemporary world of today." In Delhi and throughout her travels through the Indian provinces, the First Lady warmly engages every crowd, and her broad smile captures her delight. The narrator never mentions the Cold War or the threat of communism; however, he remarks on India's peaceful elections, as the world's largest democracy, and five-year economic plans designed to further modernize the country. Jackie's voice closes the film, by thanking the people of India for their hospitality and affirming the "confident vision of the future" shared by Indians and Americans alike.[79]

In a similar approach, *Invitation to Pakistan* opens with Punjabi music and a shot of men wearing long tunics gazing at a magnificent temple. Pakistan appears more rustic than India, but Jackie's interaction with the people and her genuine delight in the visit illustrate the simple pleasures that come from sharing one's culture, friendship, and a common desire for peace and security. The First Lady embodied the friendship between Pakistan and the United States, and in her voice-over she reaffirmed her desire to understand more about this country, rather than to extol American virtues.[80]

U.S. ambassador to India John Kenneth Galbraith, whose lanky frame appeared in several scenes with Jackie, watched the documentaries with the Kennedys at their weekend getaway at Glen Ora, Virginia, on April 1, 1962. Galbraith found them "quite good but somewhat deficient in editing"; but the president appeared "visibly impressed" by his wife's performance.[81] The combined $73,000 production cost for *Invitation to Pakistan* and *Invitation to India* led a handful of American journalists and congressional representatives to criticize the USIA for wasting taxpayer dollars on a film glorifying Jackie.[82] Sitting in Washington's DuPont Circle, after reading a particularly scathing domestic review of his work, Stevens worried that he had only hurt the administration and the USIA. Nevertheless, the criticism only piqued the interest of the American public, already great fans of the First Lady, who wanted to see the films for themselves.[83] Because federal law prohibited propagandizing to a domestic audience, release of the USIA productions required a joint resolution of Congress. Following the successful vote on Capitol Hill, United Artists bought the editing rights from the USIA, cut the two films into a half-hour program, and distributed *Jacqueline Kennedy's Asian Journey* with the Christmas 1962 release of *Taras Bulba* starring Yul Brynner and Tony Curtis.[84]

The overwhelmingly positive response to the film may have helped Stevens convince others, besides Murrow, that he belonged in an executive position at the agency. In February 1962, Kennedy personally asked Stevens to join an ad hoc committee to advise Warner Brothers Studios on the production of *PT 109*, a dramatization of Kennedy's wartime naval service in the Pacific, as commander of a PT boat sunk by a Japanese destroyer.[85] Still, Stevens looked more broadly. While Jackie's film set an upbeat tone for the Motion Picture Service, Stevens knew that, if he hoped to achieve long-term success, he had to evaluate and improve the division's operating procedures. He set out to remove the obstacles that required the USIA to accept the lowest bid for production contracts. American taxpayers did not need to waste money on extravagant movies, but neither would they be receiving a return on their investment if the USIA produced B-rated films that lacked public diplomacy value. Stevens explained, "I knew we couldn't get the picture we wanted if we were restricted to the mentality and methods of low-budget newsreel production."[86]

Stevens exhibited little patience for the Washington bureaucracy, and he brought "new life and greater professionalism" into the Motion Picture Service, according to Tom Sorensen. The assistant director for policy and plans occasionally argued with Stevens over film topics and content, but Sorensen later acknowledged that Stevens made valid points more often than not.[87] Stevens wanted USIA officials and the Motion Picture Service staff to understand his business, and he invited them to premieres hosted by the Motion Picture Association in Washington.[88] In lieu of contracting with a film studio, Stevens hired specific producers to develop each film. While he deferred to the artistic license of individual directors, Stevens served as executive producer for all USIA documentaries, which enabled him to step in to shape their public diplomacy messages.[89] Stevens proved more judicious than Shelton in what he allowed his division to release. After reviewing a labor union documentary in August 1963, Stevens said that it would not be appropriate for foreign audiences, since it focused on U.S. union leaders who would be unknown to "overseas rank and file trade unionists."[90]

As Stevens educated USIA personnel about filmmaking, they taught him about the nuances of international public diplomacy. Alan Fisher served as chief of foreign productions under Stevens, and he approved of Stevens's cinematic creativity and credited him with the production of "a great many good, good films" for the agency. However, Fisher did not believe that Stevens initially appreciated the importance of creating a documentary for a target audience or articulating a national message. For Stevens the film technique took precedence over the message, so Fisher occasionally circumvented Stevens quietly, in order to make more of an information film than merely a documentary.[91] Just like the tension between Murrow and Shelton, not everyone agreed on how overt or focused a message should be, but USIA surveys confirmed that Stevens's international audience approved overwhelmingly of his films. When Stevens screened a film on Somali prime minister Abdirashid Ali Shermarke's visit to the United States with the Somali ambassador in Washington, the diplomat told Stevens that the documentary would be very popular in his country because its "theatre" feel made it more interesting than a newsreel.[92]

For Stevens, good documentaries required less narration. This offered economic value too, since it decreased the amount of time and money spent on dubbing films into thirty-plus languages. From an artistic viewpoint, he sought to elicit emotional responses through camera angles and music rather than from a narrated script. Stevens explained his approach in a 1965 interview: "If we can get people moved to tears about Kennedy, for example, they will be more likely to hear the things we say at other levels." This did not mean that Stevens sought to create sappy films, which he knew that his foremost champion and critic would not condone: "Ed Murrow saw most of our films in the rough cut stage. We couldn't show anything corny to him!"[93] Despite his interest, Murrow did not seek control of either the microphone or camera, and he declined Stevens's invitation to narrate *America Presents America.*[94]

As the vice president suggested, the U.S. government could exploit the popularity of the president in its public diplomacy. In February 1963, Stevens gained permission from the White House Communications Agency to distribute reels of the filmed interview *After Two Years: A Conversation with the President.* Seated in his Oval Office rocking chair, Kennedy spent an hour conversing with the ABC, CBS, and NBC White House correspondents about how he assessed his performance as president. Kennedy spoke candidly about his relationship with his advisers, called the Bay of Pigs invasion a "disaster," and voiced optimism about continuing to foster cooperation between the United States and the developing world.[95] The USIA's release of the interview received rave reviews from foreign television broadcasters, U.S. ambassadors, and public affairs officers, who contacted USIA libraries to request copies for additional showings. A Dutch newspaper considered it "by far the most important TV program of the year, thanks to the President's open-hearted and stone-hard arguments." In Kenya, a *Daily Nation* editorial found Kennedy's interview a compelling demonstration of the "unbeatable" value of film for presenting an individual's humanity and personality."[96]

Stevens proved successful in recruiting commercial producers to create USIA documentaries, just as Murrow had hoped. He contracted St. Louis–based film producer Charles Guggenheim to create a thirty-minute color documentary on Central America called *United in Progress*, which depicted the tangible benefits of the Alliance for Progress for average people in the region.[97] Guggenheim's work, which covered Kennedy's visit to Costa Rica in March 1962, provides an excellent example of framing a pro-democracy and free-market capitalism film without specifically mentioning communism or dwelling on the consequences of living under a totalitarian regime.

Speaking over scenes from a vibrant marketplace, the narrator describes the efforts of Latin American governments to forge a common economic market as their most "important step forward since their independence from Spain." During the March economic summit in Costa Rica, Kennedy had congratulated America's neighbors for their collaboration and pledged the continued support of the U.S. government for the Alliance for Progress. The narrator reminds viewers that such an initiative would have been impossible five years earlier when the countries were dependent upon the United States and Europe for manufactured goods. Through the emerging common market, Latin America had begun to develop industry, and images of trucks, railroads, small factories, and the Bank of Central America replaces scenes from the farmers market. While a group of children read books in one of the three thousand schools built with alliance funding, another bunch runs toward a riverbank to greet a boat carrying an American doctor to a remote area. Guggenheim ties the three themes of industrial modernization, education, and medicine together in the final scene with Kennedy addressing thousands at a Costa Rican university. The president praises the benefits of the alliance for protecting the region from "the remnants of dictatorship" and defending against "those who seek to impose a new tyranny in this hemisphere." The president boards Marine One, and as the helicopter rises over the banana trees, the narrator encourages viewers to take heart in the alliance: "The revolution has not been wasted; it has only begun."[98]

The film appeared throughout the Western Hemisphere, as well as in Africa, where viewers expressed great interest in the film's message about American interests in assisting the developing world. When asked for reactions in Accra, one Ghanaian hailed it as the "finest

Agency production on record." Another stated that if America could help South America, then perhaps it could help Africa too. Viewers in Europe hailed its "imaginative camera work," "intelligent buildup," and "lively supporting sound track."[99]

Murrow asked Stevens to provide greater attention to African Americans in documentaries, not only to address the civil rights movement but to explore the lives of average African Americans as well. The next major documentary described the August 1963 March on Washington for Jobs and Freedom, culminating with Martin Luther King Jr.'s speech on the steps of the Lincoln Memorial. Conservatives in Congress and the USIA objected to drawing attention to American segregation; nevertheless, Stevens assured Murrow that the picture would be a "film of value" for the agency's effort to explain the civil rights movement in the Third World.[100] Stevens hired James Blue, an Oregon producer whom he first met at the Cannes Film Festival, to produce *The March*, which the USIA distributed in 1964.[101]

Stevens insisted on creating a documentary of the president's June–July 1963 visit to Europe. He contracted with Los Angeles–based producer Bruce Herschensohn, with whom he had collaborated on documentaries about the U.S. space program and the Alliance for Progress. Not only did Stevens admire Herschensohn's work, he appreciated his ability to write, direct, edit, and even compose a soundtrack for a film.[102] Given the modest USIA film budget, Herschensohn proved ideal for helping Stevens economize production costs. Kennedy only appeared in the last of the five cities shown in the documentary, and three of the cities he visited on his European tour are never mentioned. However, Stevens believed that Herschensohn's approach would achieve two public diplomacy goals: effectively incorporate psychological messages and create an appealing picture for audiences beyond the four countries of the president's trip.[103]

The USIA released *Five Cities in June* in the summer of 1963, narrated by Charlton Heston. The first act centers on Vatican City, with the colorful pageantry of the coronation of Pope Paul IV. The documentary shifts to grainy black-and-white film from an undisclosed Soviet city, unknown because the Soviet government secretly launched a two-manned rocket into space in June without releasing footage until after the event. Heston contrasts the secrecy of the Soviet space program to the American one covered extensively by the international press. In the third "city," a village in the Republic of Vietnam, South Vietnamese soldiers arrive by air, ground, and river to expel the Viet Cong. Although the film only shows Vietnamese soldiers entering the village, the Huey helicopters and armored personnel carriers remind viewers of the U.S. role there as well. The film turns next to Tuscaloosa, Alabama, where the first two African American students enter the University of Alabama in June. Violence does not erupt, but federal marshals and army Green Berets appear on site, before Governor George Wallace permits the students to enter. Heston acknowledges that racism remains a problem in the United States, but he affirms the government's determination to allow all citizens to enjoy civil liberties. Finally, to place America's legal challenges into perspective, the film turns to Berlin. Desolate streets, crudely constructed cement walls, and bricked window frames stand in stark contrast against the ebullience of crowds welcoming the president of the United Sates. Standing on a platform before city hall, Kennedy connects the meaning of the five cities selected by the USIA: for those who do not understand the difference between the communist and free world, "Let them come to Berlin!"[104]

Beyond his rolodex of accomplished film producers, Stevens encouraged recent graduates of film schools to apply for USIA contracts, internships, and fulltime employment. Inviting those demonstrating the most potential to visit him at 1776 Pennsylvania Avenue, Stevens offered contracts through the Young America series to the top few.[105] Murrow wanted a Motion Picture Service director capable of networking in Hollywood, and Stevens succeeded in attracting commercial talent to the USIA. Stevens convinced Terry Sanders from the University of California, Los Angeles, the first student to win an Oscar for a documentary, to produce a film on American political conventions.[106] He contracted Kent Mackenzie from the University of Southern California, whose college project on Bunker Hill earned him a Silver Award from the Screen Producers' Guild, to produce a documentary on U.S. government vocational training programs.[107] In 2006, Gerald Krell, one of Stevens's first interns, directed *Three Faiths*, a documentary for the Department of State explaining commonalities between Christianity, Judaism, and Islam.[108]

Stevens continued to look for ways to improve the propagation of his division's work through the USIA's overseas posts. He advocated for updating decaying systems from the past decade with modern technology and ensuring that agency employees understood how to operate the expensive equipment. Steadily, Stevens made quantitative progress in this endeavor. By 1963 the USIA owned 7,574 projectors throughout the world, having purchased 787 new ones that year. To maintain them, the agency deployed three regional motion-picture technicians to make periodic maintenance visits and teach local employees how to correctly operate the equipment.[109] The USIA increased the number of traveling technicians by 1964, explaining the investment in a cable to outposts around the world: "The importance of such visual media as motion pictures . . . is such that the overall effectiveness of USIS operations can be impaired if post personnel are not able to make the most effective use of motion pictures for influencing priority audiences."[110]

Stevens also concerned himself with the physical infrastructure for projecting his films overseas. He wanted the U.S. government to build cinema houses in the developing world to ensure wider dissemination of American films. By July 1963, Stevens coordinated with the U.S. Agency for International Development and Arnold Picker, vice president of United Artists, to discuss funding for constructing overseas theaters. The USAID's deputy administrator for private enterprise and development financing supported the plan, since it would support local business interests.[111]

Stevens's efforts to improve the Motion Picture Service did not disappoint Murrow, who was eager to showcase these productions to senior administration officials, some of whom continued to question the value of USIA cinema. On February 5, 1963, Murrow invited his friend Assistant Secretary of State W. Averell Harriman to attend a film screening of recent agency productions at the Motion Pictures of America's Washington office. "I think you will enjoy seeing this selection of new films," he wrote in a personal letter, encouraging Harriman to bring his wife.[112] The following month, he invited Pierre Salinger and his wife to another viewing.[113]

Making documentaries and newsreels would only matter if international audiences voiced approval of them and increased their support for the United States and its foreign policies. To assess their success, the Motion Picture Service requested that public affairs officers assigned to embassies provide an annual statistical report on the films' impact. In 1962 Murrow increased this requirement to a semi-annual report, and he personally cabled those outposts who failed to provide their report on time. He considered the report the "most important single document" providing the agency with data for refining its film program and urging Congress to provide more money for the most costly arm of his agency.[114] In addition to interest in the reception of their own films, the Motion Picture Service asked public affairs officers to report on any Sino-Soviet film activities, including their themes, quality, and local reception.[115]

By 1963 relations between the USIA and Hollywood had improved measurably since Murrow's visit in November 1961. Murrow confessed to television news correspondent John Scali, "I have learned that government officials should not give advice to commercial media."[116] A dozen movie stars traveled to the Moscow International Film Festival that summer, including Sidney Poitier and Danny Kaye, who left on short notice as a favor to Murrow.[117] Kaye offered to provide entertainment on July 4 at the American embassy and to any children's groups Murrow recommended.[118] Universal Studios sent Tony Curtis to Moscow, and Murrow thanked Curtis for helping to make the American delegation a "wonderful success."[119]

The Hollywood Guilds Festival Committee selected U.S. entries for international film festivals, but its members consulted with the USIA for guidance on appropriateness. For the 1963 Moscow International Film Festival, the committee selected *The Great Escape* about a group of Allied prisoners of war who successfully break out of a German army prison camp. The German officers and soldiers are portrayed as buffoonish and incapable of matching or anticipating the ingenuity of the prisoners. State Department and USIA officials screened the movie, and they particularly liked the World War II movie because it "gave counterpoint to the image of Nazi Germany military leadership set forth in present Communist propaganda." Since the 1940s, the Soviet government cited Nazi trickery for their ability to surprise Joseph Stalin and gain an initial advantage in World War II. Indeed, Russians commented at the festival that the portrayal of German officers as susceptible to the prisoners' escape ploy was "not understandable" based on their wartime experience.[120]

Stevens served as chair of the U.S. delegation to Moscow, although previous heads came from Hollywood, rather than the government.[121] Foy Kohler, the U.S. ambassador to the Soviet Union, wrote to Murrow praising Stevens for working carefully through tedious details and forming a superb delegation. Stevens choreographed the appearance of every delegate and movie in the most favorable light for the United States. "I am happy to see that you have been able to find such an able and industrious young executive," Kohler wrote, "to fill one of your most important positions."[122] Replying to the ambassador, Murrow credited Stevens with doing "a remarkable job" in overhauling the Motion Picture Service.[123]

The USIA had a television service, which Nicholas Cull dubbed the "poor sister" to the agency's film department.[124] Murrow understood television journalism, but as agency director he grappled with the advent of a new medium: satellite communications. In August 1962, international headlines reported the successful launch of the Soviet's Vostok III and IV satellites. The USIA reported that many commentators around the world suspected that Khrushchev could use the Soviet lead in the space race to pressure the United States into accommodating his demands over Berlin or terms for a nuclear test ban treaty.[125] Murrow mentioned in several of his early public speaking engagements that Americans should not be so fixated on the space race and, even if the Soviets put a man on the moon prior to the United States, it would have little effect on American priorities: "The future of those who inhabit this minor planet is not on the moon, it is here on the ground where street lights are more important than stars, as those lights illuminate the path to the courtroom where justice is served."[126] However, he believed that, once the American people chose to sacrifice and make the space race a priority, they would supersede the Soviets' recent technological achievements.[127]

Murrow worried less about "weaponizing" space than the potential for the Soviets to use satellites to beam television signals around the world. Given how expensive the technology remained for both space transmission and ground reception, he did not see it as a significant threat for the remainder of the 1960s. Speaking on a panel at the First National Conference on Peaceful Uses of Space in May 1961, Murrow cautioned the conference participants not to expect too much from satellite television: "In the end we still deal with the base element of human communication . . . satellites will not make it any better; it will simply diffuse it over a wider area."[128] Two years later, at an Anglo-American information working group in London, Murrow told his British counterparts that he did not think that satellite television would be effective for another fifteen years and speculated that it would probably remain a private monopoly due to its high cost.[129]

Although Murrow completely supported the privatization of satellite television, he still wanted his agency to use the emerging media to some degree. In 1962 the USIA doubled its television budget to $3.7 million, but prohibitive production costs led Murrow to focus more on the acquisition of documentaries and English language-learning programs, rather than developing programs in agency studios. The agency created an Arabic-dubbing facility in Cairo where television signals could be beamed and edited for distribution across the region.[130] Murrow told the House Committee on Space and Astronautics that his agency could only improve their satellite broadcasting further if Congress increased the USIA's budget. Based on existing appropriations, he told representatives that his agency could not afford to "squander millions for the novelty" on nascent satellite systems. The Television Service's budget, staffing, programming, and signal strength considerations had to be address first. Murrow reminded the committee that technology alone would not guarantee more effective public diplomacy: "Space satellites will neither solve our dilemmas nor salve our consciences."[131] Above all else, the USIA needed to develop unique, honest, and attractive messages to ensure its credibility.

Murrow's selection of Romney Wheeler, a former NBC vice president, as director of the Television Service did not prove as innovative as his selection of Stevens. Murrow replaced Wheeler in 1962 with Chuck Hill, a colleague from CBS. Chester Opal, a career USIA officer with recent experience in Saigon, served as Hill's deputy. Although an earnest bureaucrat, Opal confessed to knowing very little about television. Fortunately, Hill found Stevens to be extremely gracious and generous with his time, coming over from the Motion Picture Service frequently to provide advice. Most of the agency's television programming involved documentaries and newscasts, with some of the earliest shows covering the construction of the Berlin Wall and John Glenn's space orbital. In-house writers prepared the scripts and storyboards, but the service contracted outside expertise for filming and editing. The service worked with commercial television specialists in New York; and Ricardo Montalban's brother, Carlos, narrated Spanish programs.[132]

Stevens found himself increasingly involved with the Television Service. Averell Harriman invited Stevens to visit his Foggy Bottom office to strategize about how to target Africa through television.[133] The State Department estimated that at least five hundred thousand Africans watched 132,000 television sets on the continent (excluding Egypt).[134] USIA television programming in Africa concentrated on Nigeria, the country that Murrow considered the "key" to the region. To illustrate the advantages of American modernity, the agency produced a series of ten fifteen-minute programs featuring a Nigerian commentator examining topics such as higher education, vocational training, and the Tennessee Valley Authority. Another program, *Let's Learn English,* not only provided an educational benefit but also showcased U.S.-African cooperation, by reporting on the visits of African leaders to Kennedy's White House. Since the USIA did not own a television network, it provided material to foreign stations. To ensure that state-owned stations included USIA programming, the Television Service skirted potentially divisive policy issues like Berlin, Cuba, and nuclear testing.[135] The absence of critical information messages supported Murrow's concern about the USIA's inability to saturate a locale through television, as opposed to newspaper, radio, or film.

Besides television, the USIA explored using satellite communications to improve their broadcasting of Voice of America. On August 23, 1963, Murrow met with Vice President Johnson, whom Kennedy tapped to head the country's space program, at VOA headquarters in

Washington to participate in a conversation via satellite with Nigerian foreign minister Jaja Wachuku. For the first time, Voice of America used the synchronous communication (SYNCOM) satellite, a simultaneous telephone call and radio broadcasting system that permitted Johnson to speak with Wachuku on a phone in Lagos. For the inaugural use of the system, Voice of America could have selected a major European power, but instead chose Nigeria, given Kennedy's interest in the developing world. The vice president emphasized in his remarks the historic significance of the radio program and his pleasure that the United States continued to improve communications with Africa.[136] For Murrow, the call demonstrated how the space age could improve the quality of life for mankind. This had nothing to do with military capabilities; it concerned improving the dialogue between diverse peoples.

In satellite communications, television broadcasts, and film distribution, the USIA achieved measurable public diplomacy results between 1961 and 1963. Murrow argued in a speech to the Advertising Federation of America on June 19, 1963, "This agency has spearheaded the intelligent use of the motion picture in the national interest to a degree unprecedented in the United States with the possible exception of World War II."[137] By the end of 1963, the USIA estimated that six hundred million people a month had viewed one of the agency's films in one of fifty-two languages.[138] Arthur M. Schlesinger Jr., who wrote film reviews for *Show* magazine while serving in the Kennedy administration, said of the Motion Picture Service, "There have not been so many striking films stimulated in Washington since the days of Pare Lorentz and the Department of Agriculture film program a generation ago."[139] By 1963, annual reports submitted by public affairs officers credited Murrow and Stevens's overhaul of the Motion Picture Service for the overwhelmingly positive responses from audiences worldwide who appreciated the new artistic experimentation through creativity and individuality.[140]

During Murrow's tenure, the USIA produced sixty-seven films—thirty-six documentaries and thirty-one major films—in addition to hundreds of newsreels. Cooperation with Hollywood improved, as evidenced by Murrow's enlistment of celebrities to support international film festivals and Stevens convincing accomplished directors to create agency documentaries. Charles Guggenheim enjoyed working with Stevens so much that he moved his production company from St. Louis to Washington DC. Beyond winning contracts for documentaries, Guggenheim helped the USIA produce monthly, television news programs for Latin America.[141] In October 1962, the service instituted the USIA Intern Program to attract graduates of cinematography schools. Through the efforts of the Motion Picture Service, the USIA acquired the rights to sixty-six other films from Hollywood studios for little to no cost, saving the agency roughly $500,000 in 1963 alone. In 1963 the service changed its productions to short, one-reel documentaries that played prior to movies in foreign theaters. Stevens also served as chair of the American delegation to film festivals in Cannes, Venice, and Berlin.[142]

While Stevens's efforts were measurable, quantifying the public diplomacy impact of the USIA's Motion Picture Service remained as difficult as assessing the effects of VOA broadcasts. Nicholas Cull identified three weaknesses with the employment of documentaries by USIA: a time-consuming production process, an expensive enterprise, and "a one-way, top-down" medium.[143] Regardless of Cull's legitimate criticism, Stevens's human-interest approach helped to amplify the administration's messages in a manner that appealed to international audiences. Speaking at the 1965 American Film Festival, Stevens succinctly explained the value of his division of the agency: "Selling is too simple a word for our needs. . . . What is required is understanding . . . [through] a vigorous and unending communication with curious people of other lands. For this task the motion picture is eminently qualified."[144]

Stevens's rejection of the notion that the USIA could "sell" America during the Cold War echoed Murrow's own message to his agency, Congress, and the Kennedy administration. By accepting the complexity of their mission, Murrow and Stevens made memorable documentaries that advanced Kennedy's foreign policy goals. This is not to suggest that the Motion Picture Service achieved all of the goals established by the agency's leaders, since budget constraints and bureaucratic challenges limited its ability to develop as dynamically as they'd hoped. Nevertheless, the innovations of this period led historian Tony Shaw to dub Stevens's tenure with the agency as the "Golden Age" of the Motion Picture Service, proving that the USIA did not seek to supplant Hollywood but, rather, augment Tinseltown's projection of the United States for inquisitive audiences across the globe.[145]

6

The USIA and the Cuban Missile Crisis

Domestic policy can only defeat us, but foreign policy can kill us.
—JOHN F. KENNEDY, in Arthur Schlesinger Jr.'s journal, January 31, 1964

With the possible exception of the assassination of John F. Kennedy on November 22, 1963, no other event from his administration has captivated historians or the public more than the Cuban Missile Crisis of October 1962. Fifty years since the confrontation, insightful primary sources continue to surface, and thoughtful analysis appearing in recent publications challenges the traditional story retold in the memoirs of Kennedy's closest advisers. White House assistant Arthur Schlesinger Jr. called the crisis "the most dangerous moment in human history"; Secretary of State Dean Rusk said that the United States came "eyeball to eyeball" with the Soviets; and Attorney General Robert Kennedy praised his brother's courage in confronting both Nikita Khrushchev in Moscow and hawks around his Cabinet Room table.[1] Regardless of the varying assessments of the administration's performance during the crisis, Kennedy and Khrushchev deserve credit for finding a mutually agreeable solution that de-escalated tensions prior to the superpowers engaging one another on the shores of Cuba or through the nuclear incineration of one another's capital. Ultimately both chiefs of state gained what they sought: Khrushchev agreed to withdraw his nuclear missiles and garrison from Cuba, and Kennedy promised that the United States would not invade the island nation.

Global public awareness of the crisis significantly shaped its outcome, and use of the airwaves prevented either leader from negotiating exclusively in secret. Khrushchev sought to keep the missile deployment classified, yet Kennedy's televised address on October 22 prevented the Soviet leader from leveraging a Caribbean nuclear capability against U.S. aggression toward Cuba.[2] To understand how the Kennedy administration successfully communicated the threat posed by the missiles requires an assessment of the contributions of the U.S. Information Agency. Although Murrow spent the crisis convalescing from pneumonia, it is illuminating to contrast the USIA's role in October 1962 with its absence from the administration's planning and execution of the Bay of Pigs invasion in April 1961. The agency's operations in Washington and around the world during the missile crisis indicate how well USIA officials had internalized Murrow's guidance on how to engage an international audience and support the administration's national security objectives. Through its inclusion in the administration's response process, the USIA directly shaped international opinion in support of Kennedy's demand that Khrushchev withdraw his missiles from Cuba.

In the grand strategy of the Cold War, Khrushchev equated Cuba to Berlin. West Berlin festered like a piece of World War II shrapnel embedded within the Warsaw Pact, providing the United States with a bastion 115 miles deep inside the Soviet's sphere of influence. Khrushchev sought a comparable advantage in the Western Hemisphere and romanticized about a vibrant Marxist government in Cuba serving as a beacon for Latin American communists. After he failed to gain international sympathy, by permitting the German Democratic Republic to barricade West Berlin in August 1961, Khrushchev sought to reaffirm his commitment to world communist revolution by bolstering Fidel Castro's dictatorial regime with offensive Soviet weapons. Khrushchev found it "completely unrealistic" to believe that the United States had ceased its efforts to remove Castro after the Bay of Pigs operation failed, and he chose to construct a substantial nuclear garrison on the island to thwart future efforts.[3] Although Kremlin officials did not seek a nuclear war with the United States, they worried that American hubris might lead to another invasion of Cuba. As historians Vladislav Zubok and Constantine Pleshako explained, politburo members wondered, "What if 'the dark forces' in the Pentagon, CIA, and the State Department drew Kennedy into another Cold War adventure?"[4] By secretly infiltrating surface-to-surface missiles, Khrushchev anticipated completing the launch sites prior to their discovery by U.S. intelligence. Although nuclear missiles ninety miles from the coastline of the United States would certainly not sit well with the American people, Khrushchev doubted that Kennedy would have the gall to risk war with the Soviet Union by attacking the nuclear sites. The missiles would protect Castro from another Bay of Pigs and inspire bourgeoning communist insurgencies in jungles and mountains throughout the region.

The Soviet premier did not base his concern for Castro's security solely on paranoia. Admiral George Anderson, the chief of naval operations, observed Kennedy's "obvious" intent to "get rid of Castro."[5] Despite the botched Bay of Pigs operation, and his personal agony over its senseless loss of life, the president authorized Operation Mongoose on November 30, 1961, a top-secret, interagency effort to overthrow Castro. The Pentagon's counterinsurgency expert, Air Force Brigadier General Edward Lansdale, developed the "Cuban Project" to incite a revolt of the Cuban people.[6] The following month, Lansdale outlined a long-term plan of covert efforts involving the attorney general's office, the CIA, various defense agencies, and the USIA. Their plans included psychological operations, sabotage, and political and economic support for opposition groups in Cuba. CIA assistant director Richard Bissell went so far as to authorize two attempts to assassinate Castro, and Richard Helms authorized a third involving American "underworld figures."[7] While these dubious endeavors failed to unseat Castro, they absorbed a bewildering amount of the administration's intellectual and fiscal capital.

There is no evidence that Murrow endorsed assassination plots considered by the U.S. government. Political scientist Lars Schoultz found that the "closest approximation to a smoking gun" to implicate senior Kennedy administration officials occurred during a Special Group (Augmented) meeting on August 10, 1963.[8] According to William Harvey, a CIA official present at the meeting, Secretary of Defense Robert McNamara suggested that the group "consider the

USIA and Cuban Missile Crisis

elimination or assassination of Fidel."[9] Both Murrow and CIA director John McCone voiced objections to the suggestion. In 1975 McCone testified to the U.S. Senate Select Committee to Study Governmental Operations with Respect to Intelligence Activities (the Church Committee) that "at no time did the suggestion receive serious consideration by the Special Group (Augmented) or by any individual responsible for policy."[10] In his testimony, McCone stated that Murrow emphatically opposed proposed assassination plots: "I was not alone in that. Mr. Murrow took exception. I remember that very clearly."[11]

This did not mean that Murrow opposed U.S. efforts to disrupt Castro's regime. In June 1961, Murrow recommended to Bundy that the White House "plant" a question about the Cuban air force's acquisition of MIG fighters at the president's press conference scheduled just before Kennedy's departure for Latin America.[12] In a May 1962 memorandum to the president on psychological warfare targeting Cuba, Murrow wrote: "Our daily VOA programming maintains a high level of credibility. We feel that this level must be maintained at all cost. We must look to covert or other types of operations for programming of a harder propaganda line."[13] In a memorandum to McCone, written two months after the Cuban Missile Crisis, Murrow suggested that the CIA conduct sabotage operations, by "putting glass and nails on the highways, leaving water running in public buildings, putting sand in machinery, wasting electricity . . . damaging sugar stalks during the harvest."[14]

More overtly than Mongoose, the Defense Department conducted three massive exercises between April and October 1962. Ostensibly the costly maneuvers validated the military's ability to respond to threats posed to national security interests around the world. However, the April and October operations could not be confused with any other contingency than the invasion of Cuba. April's Operation Lantphibex I-62 involved ten thousand marines amphibiously assaulting the beaches of the Puerto Rican island of Vieques. Some seventy-five hundred marines came ashore at the same beaches in mid-October as part of Operation Phibriglex 62, an exercise to liberate a Caribbean island from "Ortsac," a fictitious dictator whose name, when spelled backwards, is Castro.[15] Given the grandiose scale of the training, Khrushchev did not require a mole in the White House to appreciate the depth of Kennedy's dislike for the Cuban regime.

Kennedy worried about the threat that Castro's ideology posed to politically unstable countries in Latin America, and he expected Khrushchev to aid Castro in order to counter the United States' renewed efforts to engage the developing world. Italian prime minister Amintore Fanfani told Kennedy in June 1961, "It is not a matter of fantasy to suppose that Khrushchev will regard Latin America rather than Africa as the great field of combat with the U.S. in the next few years."[16] Castro's celebrated lieutenant, Che Guevara, publicly thanked Kennedy in Uruguay for authorizing the Bay of Pigs invasion: "Before the invasion, the revolution was shaky. Now it is stronger than ever."[17]

Regardless of Che's assessment, Castro's rhetoric failed to entice most Latin Americans. According to survey data collected by the USIA in November 1961 from residents of Mexico City, Rio de Janeiro, Buenos Aires, Montevideo, and Bogota, only 10 percent shared a favorable opinion of Cuban communism. The USIA reported that Mexicans overwhelmingly disliked Castro—citing him as a "menace to the region"—and they hoped to see his influence in the region recede further. Despite this regional sentiment, USIA analysts cautioned the administration against developing an information campaign that overtly called for Castro's overthrow: "Hearing less about Castro from top U.S. officials seems to make people feel that his influence is declining." Additionally, Latin Americans said that they preferred to hear about Cuba from their own journalists.[18]

The USIA chose instead to stress the social and economic potential of the Alliance for Progress in their Latin American information campaign. Between the Bay of Pigs mishap and the discovery of Soviet missiles in Cuba, the USIA did less to malign Castro and more to celebrate the values of democracy and capitalism. Cuban propaganda disseminated throughout the region made it tempting for U.S. public diplomacy officials to respond to every charge from Havana about "Yankee imperialism," no matter how absurd. Instead, the USIA incorporated survey feedback into policy formation, and the agency's radio, print, and film divisions dissuaded Latin Americans from embracing communist promises of utopia without resorting to heavy, monotonous criticism about the economic woes and human rights violations rampant in Castro's police state. Until the missile crisis, the preponderance of the USIA's messages simply ignored Cuba.

Regardless of how they underplayed Castro's influence in the region in their public diplomacy, Kennedy administration officials obsessed over the dictator's military capabilities. National security officials wanted to ascertain the presence of Soviet advisers or weapon systems in Cuba. Beginning in February 1962, Kennedy ordered two U-2 high-altitude reconnaissance flights over the island every month to photograph the terrain. However, upon the discovery of Soviet SA-2 surface-to-air missiles on August 29, 1962—the same air defense system used to shoot down CIA pilot Francis Gary Powers's U-2 over the Soviet Union on May 1, 1960—the administration grew nervous about the vulnerability of their reconnaissance planes. To minimize the newfound threat posed to American pilots, Kennedy ordered flyovers in September to take cautious routes "in-and-out" of central and eastern Cuba. This decision to ignore the western portion of the island led to what scholars David Barrett and Max Holland call the "photo gap."[19] The administration placed fears about creating an international incident over a downed pilot above surveying the very part of Cuba where the Soviets were constructing missile sites that same month.

Prior to the discovery of Soviet missiles, the USIA had developed a variety of messages for the Cuban people to influence them to reject communism. While the agency focused on democracy and capitalism themes throughout the rest of Latin America, as part of its Alliance for Progress information campaign, it did not shy away from criticizing the tangible shortcomings of communism to the Cuban people. But neither did Murrow want the various arms of the USIA to exaggerate stories about agriculture failures, empty government promises, or diplomatic isolation: "It is fundamental that we operate on a basis of truth. Ours is, and must be, a dedication to the factual."[20] When the United States terminated diplomatic relations with Cuba, following Castro's ousting of President Fulgencio Batista in January 1960, the USIA closed its library in Havana and lost direct contact with the populace. Limited to broadcasting from afar, Murrow asked the British embassy in Havana to help transmit U.S. radio into Cuba, which the British agreed to do, so long as the messages did not call for Castro's overthrow.[21]

To ensure that public affairs officers followed his instructions, Murrow relished the opportunity to escape from Washington to evaluate their performance and hear their concerns about USIA policy guidance. On September 26, 1962, Murrow traveled to Paris, a stepping-off point for the beginning of a five-week tour of the Near East and South Asia. Coming down with a serious cold in France, he delayed his departure for Tehran, where he was scheduled to participate in the dedication ceremony of a new USIA binational center. Although colleagues urged him to return home, Murrow insisted on flying to Iran; but shortly after his arrival in Tehran his condition worsened and he collapsed. Iranian doctors misdiagnosed his pneumonia as pleurisy during a weeklong hospital stay. When he regained the strength to fly, he canceled the remainder of his itinerary to return home, much to the disappointment of public affairs officers anxious to meet him in India and South Vietnam. American doctors x-rayed his chest, judging the dark spots on his lungs to be scar tissue from former bouts of pneumonia. Perhaps he already suffered from lung cancer, but it would be another year before physicians issued that prognosis. Discharged from a New York hospital on October 12, Murrow headed to his cherished farm at Pawling for a few more days of recovery.[22]

On the fourth day of Murrow's convalescence in Pawling, Arthur Lundahl, the CIA's chief photo interpreter, stood in the Oval Office, briefing Kennedy on three photographs from a U-2 flyover of western Cuba taken on the morning of October 14. Labels on the photos brought meaning to the obscure objects: "ERECTOR LAUNCHER EQUIPMENT" and "MISSILE TRAILERS."[23] Lundahl confirmed for the president the deployment of Soviet nuclear missiles to Cuba. Had the CIA and Defense Intelligence Agency not received warnings from a handful of informants on the island to canvas the western terrain for suspicious activity a few days earlier, it is unlikely that the United States would have discovered the sites prior to their completion.[24]

The photos upset the president greatly, and Jacqueline Kennedy recalled that her husband took Khrushchev's actions as a personal affront.[25] However, being upset and being impulsive do not necessarily follow from one another, and the president did not use his frustration with the Soviet premier as an excuse to pursue a brash course of action. Kennedy kept the information closely held in order to prevent someone within the government from leaking the news to the press, thereby creating political and public hysteria. Hours after receiving the CIA brief on October 16, Kennedy formed an executive committee, "ExComm," of the National Security Council, to analyze how to eliminate the threat. From the beginning of his presidency, Kennedy and National Security Adviser McGeorge Bundy had agreed that the National Security Council would be "what the President wants it to be," which made it malleable enough to add and drop committees and protocols at the commander in chief's discretion.[26]

The thirteen hand-selected men comprising the initial ExComm, who met at 11:50 a.m. on October 16 to discuss Cuba, did not include a USIA representative because neither Kennedy nor Bundy thought that the agency needed to participate this early in the crisis. The president fully intended to involve the USIA in the *public* crisis, but so long as it remained tightly restricted information, he did not see a reason to read-in his information experts. USIA deputy director Donald Wilson later speculated that Kennedy did not want anyone else to know about the missiles until he had determined how he wanted to respond: "He was naturally concerned that the more people that knew, the more danger there would be of this being revealed."[27]

Following a routine cabinet meeting on October 17 about reducing federal hiring and expenditures, Robert Kennedy asked Wilson if Murrow would return to town by the weekend. When Wilson explained that his boss would still be on sick leave, the attorney general asked Wilson to cancel a family trip to New Jersey and remain available.[28] That afternoon, Thomas Sorensen, the USIA's assistant director for plans and policy, joined his brother, Theodore, for lunch at the White House. Tom observed his brother's anxiety in the West Wing's navy mess, yet Ted would not say what bothered him. After Tom's departure, the presidential counselor asked Kennedy if he could tell his brother once the president broke the news to Wilson, in order to prevent speculation from 1776 Pennsylvania Avenue. The president agreed begrudgingly.[29]

On October 19, the attorney general phoned Wilson, instructing him to see Assistant Secretary of State George Ball for a briefing. That night at Foggy Bottom, Ball outlined the classified situation, recommending to Wilson that he begin thinking about how to explain it to the Cuban people. The next morning Bundy called Wilson to his White House office where he provided greater detail. Kennedy authorized Wilson to begin developing an information campaign, but only with three others in his agency: Tom Sorensen; Hewson Ryan, USIA assistant director for Latin America; and Henry Loomis, director of Voice of America.[30] With this decision, Kennedy brought the USIA into the ExComm before informing his own press secretary, Pierre Salinger, or the State Department's public affairs bureau. Tom Sorensen attributed this to Kennedy's high valuation of the agency: "He wanted this story told abroad in exactly the right way so the U.S. would not be viewed as the aggressor."[31]

Returning to his office, Wilson telephoned Loomis to request his presence, and Loomis arrived from the opposite end of Constitution Avenue to find Sorensen already in Wilson's office. After quickly explaining developments, Wilson established the first priority for the USIA. Since the president had not made any decision regarding the release of the top-secret photographs, their primary concern needed to be figuring out how to get more broadcasting signal into Cuba once the White House gave them a message to transmit. Loomis urged Wilson to convince the CIA to hand over their station on Swan Island in order to prevent the transmission of diverging messages from various government broadcasters, as heard during of the Bay of Pigs. He also recommended that Voice of America assume temporary control of eleven commercial radio stations in the southeastern United States. Although federal use of domestic stations violated the Smith-Mundt Act, they contacted the Federal Communications Commission (FCC) and secured permission to transmit Voice of America's signal via the private stations, providing that they gained the voluntary cooperation of the station owners.[32]

The small meeting at USIA headquarters on October 20 yielded a policy memorandum titled "Radio Propaganda Plan," which Wilson submitted to the White House that night. It recommended amplifying Voice of America throughout Latin America, but especially to Cuba, with the support of private American radio stations. Noting his concern about preventing a tragedy similar to the Hungarian Uprising of 1956—by allowing exaggerated broadcasts of what the U.S. military intended to do—Wilson emphasized the importance of the USIA maintaining control over all government broadcasts. This included incorporating Armed Forces Radio–Guantanamo Bay and the CIA's Radio Swan. Provisionally, this editorial control would not extend to three commercial U.S. stations that provided Cuban refugees with airtime for political commentary. Wilson assured the White House that, if the political commentary did not fall in line with the administration's message, then Voice of America would suspend the exiles' airtime for the remainder of the crisis. In accordance with Kennedy's guidance, the USIA sought to avoid inflammatory programming.[33] Wilson's efforts to maintain a tempered but focused message indicated how well he understood Murrow's intent that the USIA provide coherent information campaigns that avoided a cacophony of conflicting and bombastic American messages that could confuse or repulse its international audience.

Wilson attended his first ExComm meeting on Sunday, October 21, and he participated in every subsequent meeting through November 2, whereupon Murrow rejoined Kennedy's policy circle. During the October 21 conference, the president did not rule out a military strike, but he expressed his desire to provide a public warning to Khrushchev rather than a declaration of war.[34] Kennedy voiced his concern that a U.S. attack on Cuba would incite a Soviet retaliation against West Berlin. He directed Wilson to be prepared to explain that if the United States felt compelled to respond forcefully against the Soviet missiles or naval vessels in the surrounding waters, Western Allies should anticipate a retaliatory strike on Berlin.[35]

The entire world learned about the sites on October 22, when Kennedy delivered a televised speech announcing the discovery and his decision to quarantine Cuba in order to prevent additional Soviet war materiel from reaching the island. The USIA needed to work fast to amplify the president's address, but Wilson could not involve the majority of his staff, let alone the public affairs officers stationed around the globe, until the speech aired. In generic guidance to USIA divisions, Wilson stated, "Fullest possible world coverage must be given to the President's statement." Solidarity within NATO and the Organization of American States (OAS) mattered greatly to the administration, and the USIA needed to clarify the president's security concern before Khrushchev or Castro made their own case public.[36] Sorensen followed Wilson's memorandum to the agency with information policy guidance released after Kennedy's speech. The USIA would ensure that "unmistakable evidence" showed the location of Soviet nuclear weapons in Cuba, that Soviet actions demonstrated their "untrustworthiness," and that Khrushchev lied by calling the missiles purely defensive in nature. Further, Sorensen outlined how to explain American security policy: The quarantine would protect the Western Hemisphere, and Kennedy derived legal justification for objecting to the Soviet deployment from the 1947 OAS Treaty of Rio de Janeiro.[37] Sorensen's memorandum stressed that agency messages avoid overly emotional or inflammatory commentary by highlighting Latin American protests against the Soviet action instead. Concluding the directive, Sorensen wrote, "Do not use any comment, regardless of source, which is not wholly consistent with the lines set forth in the President's speech and this instruction."[38]

Given the extremely sensitive nature of the situation, Wilson made the unprecedented decision to scrutinize VOA broadcasts. Burnett Anderson, USIA deputy assistant director for plans and policy, served on Walt Rostow's working group at the NSC during the crisis until October 21, when Wilson recalled him. The acting director told Anderson to spend the duration of the crisis at Voice of America. "You're personally responsible for every word said on the air," Wilson explained the day prior to the president's national address. Wilson assured Anderson that Loomis already knew of this arrangement and that it did not reflect any doubt on the VOA director's ability. Rather, due to the speed with which the situation was changing, Wilson wanted someone "clued in" and with contacts in the ExComm to sit in the newsroom.[39]

When Anderson arrived at Voice of America and explained his mission to Loomis, the VOA director said, "Well, here's the desk," and began moving toward the door. Anderson told him that he did not want his desk, his secretary, or his job. He intended to take a seat in the newsroom and read every news script, editorial, and commentary before a broadcaster read them on the air. Loomis briefly contemplated resigning, and Anderson spent several minutes convincing him that to do so would be a mistake. Loomis eventually calmed down, and Anderson remained at Voice of America for the next three weeks. Both made the best of a delicate situation, and they sustained their friendship.[40]

The draft of Kennedy's first national address on the missile crisis arrived at the USIA on the morning of October 22. It would be televised that night, and the agency needed to provide simultaneous translations on Voice of America and disseminate transcripts of the speech to media outlets around the world. To reduce the risk of a leak, Wilson ordered several Russian and Spanish linguists to be locked in a room with the draft. Around 2:00 p.m., press secretary Pierre Salinger asked Loomis to come to the White House. Based on Wilson's recommendation, Kennedy agreed to amplify Voice of America via U.S. commercial radio stations in Florida. Salinger asked Loomis to help him contact station managers and convince them to allow the radio service to borrow their transmitters. They had never done anything like this, and both men felt a bit apprehensive about the response that they would receive from the first manager on their list. Loomis watched as the press secretary made the initial call: "This is Pierre Salinger. The President is going to make a very important talk; it's going to be of world-shaking importance. He has asked me to ask you for your help and assistance in this matter. Will you help?" The manager responded, "Yes, what do you want me to do?"[41]

Success! Salinger explained that Kennedy would like to broadcast a VOA program, and he handed the receiver over to Loomis who walked the manager through how to rewire his console to allow Voice of America to retransmit through his station. Salinger did not reach the final station on the list until five minutes prior to the president's speech, but all eleven were operational by 7:00 p.m. Neither Salinger nor Loomis knew how long they would need the stations, and Voice of America ended up monopolizing their signal for the next five days. Loomis phoned the eleven station managers daily, renewing his request for an additional twenty-four hours by pleading: "You know this is the possibility of World War Three, and we've got to do everything we possibly can. We really appreciate your patriotism and self-sacrifice." Only the smaller stations asked to regain control, at least partially, in order to carry local football games that provided a major source of revenue for them. Loomis agreed, and they stopped transmitting Voice of America to Cuba for three hours on game day.[42]

Public diplomacy scholars Nicholas Cull and Alan Heil Jr. argue that Wilson took excessive control over the news and editorial content of Voice of America during the crisis.[43] Murrow biographer Ann Sperber agreed, maintaining that Anderson's presence and Sorensen's directives "exacerbated the tensions inside USIA as Policy took over the Voice" for the duration of the crisis.[44] Tom Sorensen defended this action as "news management" and pointed to the president's expressed desire to keep information precise and to avoid hysteria.[45] Murrow's first biographer, Alexander Kendrick, wrote sympathetically about Wilson and Sorensen's decision to monitor Voice of America closely. As a federal entity, paid for by taxpayers, and chartered to provide public diplomacy on behalf of the U.S. government, Voice of America needed to broadcast specific messages repeatedly to convince the world to reject Khrushchev's decision to deploy nuclear missiles to Cuba.[46] In April 1961, Murrow called for the formation of a single "fist" of the agency's five programming divisions because he wished to rein in independently minded broadcasters, programmers, writers, and producers.[47] Anderson's presence at Voice of America for three weeks helped to assure that the USIA's fist remained tight throughout the emotionally volatile and rapidly changing standoff with the Soviet Union.

On the evening of Kennedy's address, a group of senior USIA officials gathered in the conference room down the hall from Murrow's office. At 7:00 p.m. sharp, they turned on the television but did not see their president. Instead, two attractive women sang about doubling your pleasure with Doublemint Gum. Then the president faded in to explain his decision to stand against Soviet aggression in the Western Hemisphere. Lewis Schmidt, USIA assistant director for administration, sat in the conference room, thinking silently how only in America would an announcement about "possible Doomsday revelations" be preceded by such a frivolous commercial.[48]

In his address, the president described the offensive capabilities of the medium-range ballistic missile sites in Cuba that could reach Washington DC, Mexico City, and the Panama Canal. He reported that the Soviets had begun assembling strategic bombers capable of carrying nuclear payloads from air bases being constructed on the island. Kennedy called Khrushchev's actions reprehensible to all of humankind: "Neither the United States of America nor the world community of nations can tolerate deliberate deception and offensive threats on the part of any nation, large or small." Speaking to his "good neighbors" south of the U.S. border, the president noted that for the first time Latin America faced a potential nuclear threat. To gain the moral high ground in this latest Cold War confrontation, Kennedy emphasized the secrecy of the Soviet operation several times.[49]

The president outlined seven steps that his administration would pursue to protect the United States and its allies. While hoping to resolve the crisis diplomatically through the United Nations, the OAS, or bilaterally with the Soviets, Kennedy stated that he would not discount other options. Until Khrushchev agreed to remove the missiles, the U.S. Navy would establish a quarantine to interdict any vessel transporting military materiel to Cuba, beginning the morning of October 24. Kennedy closed by emphasizing his resolve to protect American interests while leaving Khrushchev with space to de-escalate the situation: "Our goal is not the victory of might, but the vindication of right—not peace at the expense of freedom, but both peace *and* freedom, here in this hemisphere, and we hope, around the world."[50]

Voice of America carried the speech live while the USIA's wireless service transmitted teletypes of the address in multiple languages. Following the talking points issued by Sorensen in his policy guidance, public affairs officers provided news releases and background interviews to foreign journalists. Kennedy's delivery gained some international support, but the photos would be essential to influence skeptics who felt that the president's pronouncement of a quarantine would only heighten tensions with the Soviet Union. The USIA lobbied aggressively to gain access to the U-2 photographs; however, the CIA and the Pentagon objected to releasing the photos because they did not want the Soviets to realize the surveillance capabilities of the U.S. intelligence community. The president initially told Wilson that the USIA could not reproduce the photos.[51]

Kennedy reversed his decision after the White House learned that the USIA's public affairs officer in London had already provided the top-secret photos to the British press on October 23. David Bruce, the U.S. ambassador to the United Kingdom, went to Heathrow Airport himself to pick up film arriving from the United States that the State Department directed him to show to senior British officials. James Pettus, the public affairs officer in London, saw the classified aerial photos shortly after their arrival at the embassy. A member of the embassy staff argued that they needed to be declassified before the ambassador or Pettus could disseminate them to the British. The senior CIA officer resolved the dispute by declassifying the bundle on the spot, and the USIA printed twenty-five sets of the photos.[52]

The ambassador delivered five copies to the British government, including Prime Minister Harold Macmillan and Defense Minister Peter Thorneycroft, while Pettus sent the remaining twenty packets directly to the British press. Some members of the Labour Party dismissed the photos as fakes, but the majority of the British Conservative government and national press accepted the photographs' authenticity.[53] Foreign Minister Lord Hume appeared on British television with blowups of the pictures, pointing to and carefully describing each object. Back in Washington, where the State Department did not expect the London embassy to release the evidence so quickly, a member of the secretarial staff phoned the London press attaché in the middle of the night, "Who the hell gave you permission to turn those pictures loose?" The attaché responded, "The guy that brought 'em."[54]

Wilson considered the mishap "the best thing that ever happened" because it provided his agency with crucial evidence to influence their international audience.[55] The president authorized USIA access to the photos on October 23, and Wilson ordered their reproduction and distribution around the world by the time of Ambassador Adlai Stevenson's UN presentation on October 25. USIA regional print plants in Mexico City, Beirut, and Manila published thousands of copies of Kennedy's speech inside a pamphlet illustrated with pictures of the sites. In Washington the USIA's modest photo lab produced 64,215 photographs of the missile sites, while the Motion Picture Service distributed two hundred reels of Kennedy's address dubbed into several languages.[56]

Over the next several days, the White House continued to monitor the situation in the Caribbean and await Khrushchev's response. Having received advance warning from the White House, access to the photos, and additional broadcasting capabilities, the USIA remained focused on influencing its global audience to believe that the Soviet Union bore responsibility for the standoff. In preparing his policy guidance, Sorensen explained that the "USIA sought to convey the picture of an unpanicked but determined America, unflinching in the face of intimidation but avoiding war unless Moscow made it necessary."[57] The agency carried the message to the Third World that Khrushchev's irresponsible decision to place nuclear missiles in Cuba proved that the Soviet Union served as an inadequate model for developing countries.

Kennedy began his ExComm meeting on October 25 by discussing psychological operations possibilities with Wilson. The president doubted that the average Cuban realized the severity of the crisis because a recent speech by Castro never mentioned the existence of the missiles, only a heightened *yanqui* threat to his government. Wilson offered to conduct a leaflet drop with photographs depicting the location of the missiles. However, the chairman of the Joint Chiefs of Staff, General Maxwell Taylor, cautioned the president against a leaflet drop due to its danger to low-flying aircraft. Given the threat already posed to fast-moving, high-altitude reconnaissance aircraft, Taylor raised a valid point. The president moved to another issue without making a final decision about the leaflet drop, but he tasked Wilson to still produce handouts.[58] The USIA created a leaflet in Spanish, titled "The Truth," calling the Soviet weapons offensive in nature and a threat to the lives of the Cuban population and world peace. The write-up emphasized that neither food nor medicine would be blocked by the quarantine, "only aggressive Russian War materials." On the reverse side of the handout, a labeled photo depicted one of the sites under the heading "THESE BASES ENDANGER CUBAN LIVES."[59] The president approved the handout on October 26, and the USIA coordinated with the Joint Chiefs of Staff for F-105 aircraft to drop them, should Operation Bugle Call (its code name) be initiated. However, Kennedy never authorized the drop.[60]

As part of the public diplomacy campaign, Kennedy asked Ambassador Stevenson to convince other members of the UN Security Council to condemn the Soviets' actions. The White House dispatched Arthur M. Schlesinger Jr. to New York for moral support to Stevenson. Robert Kennedy told Schlesinger: "We're counting on you to watch things in New York. That fellow [Stevenson] is ready to give everything away. We will have to make a deal at the end; but we must stand firm now. Our concessions must come at the end of negotiation, not at the beginning."[61] Schlesinger compared the United Nations to "a permanent political convention" with so many factions, competing ideas, and challenges against unifying behind one leader or message.[62] However, the administration's misgivings about Stevenson proved warrantless. On October 25, when the Soviet ambassador refused to confirm his government's deployment of nuclear missiles to Cuba, Stevenson told him that he stood in "the courtroom of world opinion" and would wait for the ambassador's answer "until hell freezes over." While nervous laughter arose from the Security Council chamber, the Soviet ambassador's equivocating weakened Khrushchev's position for the tens of millions of people who witnessed the exchange on television or heard it on the radio. Watching the exchange from a television set in the Oval Office, Kennedy confided in an aide, "I never knew Adlai had it in him." Referring to Stevenson's presidential race against incumbent Dwight Eisenhower, Kennedy further opined, "Too bad he didn't show some of this steam in the 1956 campaign."[63]

The following morning, October 26, the president returned his attention to psychological operations with the ExComm. With so many moving pieces, Kennedy thought that a leaflet drop had already occurred, but Wilson reminded him that he had not issued an order.

Wilson used the opportunity to discuss the poor quality of the photos in the handbill created by the army's psychological operations unit at Fort Bragg. How could the average Cuban understand the grainy images, even with an explanation in Spanish? Wilson recommended using the photos that Stevenson had presented the day prior to the UN Security Council. National Security Adviser Bundy supported Wilson: "I think the President's good decision is that everything is waived, and you get the one you like best."[64] McNamara also offered Wilson the use of eighteen photos that the Defense Department provided to *Time* magazine. Kennedy voiced his pleasure in the USIA's efforts: "We've got a pretty good message. In any case, you can have all, any of the pictures, and do it whatever way you think best."[65]

Despite Stevenson's televised performance and the photographic evidence, several boisterous peace demonstrations erupted around the world. Many British citizens worried that a superpower stand-off over Cuba would expand to a confrontation in Berlin or, worse, nuclear war over Europe. On October 27, leaders of the far left parties mobilized ten thousand protesters, who filled London's Grosvenor Square in front of the American embassy to voice their opposition to the quarantine. Four rows of bobbies lined the front entrance as police officers on horses watched from the sidelines. In an era before bulletproof glass, the guards placed barbed wire in front of the glass doors and parked buses around the embassy as barricades. Public affairs officer Pettus slipped out the back door to meet his Soviet counterpart for lunch. At the height of the crisis, the two information officers sat down for a drink while the Soviet official told Pettus that the Americans had a problem. Pettus agreed but offered that both countries were "pretty dumb" about Cuba: The United States invaded the Bay of Pigs and the Soviet Union deployed missiles, so the Cubans had managed to get both countries into trouble. After a moment the Soviet agreed, "Yes we got some trouble." The noon lunch turned into a rambling conversation over several more drinks, and Pettus staggered back to the embassy four hours later where the demonstration continued.[66]

Despite protests like the one in London, the Kennedy administration's information campaign persuaded millions of people that the Soviet Union had provoked the United States. The USIA proved least effective in influencing populations in communist countries who did not listen to Voice of America, or the CIA's Radio Liberty or Radio Free Europe. When communist governments referenced the Cold War confrontation, they called it the "Caribbean crisis," deliberately censoring any mention of the missiles.[67] Hans Tuch, the assistant USIA director for the USSR and Eastern Europe, found himself in Leningrad, having volunteered to serve as the USIA–State Department escort officer for the New York Ballet's tour of the Soviet Union. The dancers and audience enjoyed their performance immensely, oblivious to the U.S.-Soviet confrontation. Unbeknownst to Tuch, he was the only U.S. diplomat in the Soviet Union outside of Moscow. At the height of the crisis, on October 27, the embassy phoned Tuch's hotel to inquire about his safety. After he described their warm reception, the embassy staffer pressed Tuch: "Have you been listening to the radio?" When Tuch explained that he was much too busy with the ballet, the stunned staffer ordered him to tune into Voice of America immediately.[68]

As the standoff continued, the hawks' first-strike argument grew more emphatic, and Kennedy began questioning the value of his blockade. During the October 26 meeting of the ExComm, the president hinted at the need for a U.S. military strike against the missile sites: "Even if the quarantine's 100 percent effective, it isn't any good because the missile sites go on being constructed."[69] That evening Kennedy received a timely letter from Khrushchev proposing to remove "our military specialists" in exchange for a public promise by the American president not to invade Cuba.[70] Curiously, Kennedy did not begin his ExComm meeting at ten o'clock the next morning by discussing the letter. Instead, he asked how to improve U.S. reconnaissance over Cuba to verify the status of the Soviet launch sites. He wanted the Pentagon to expand its surveillance flights into the night, with air force planes launching flares to provide illumination for the cameras. Less than fifteen minutes into the discussion, a message arrived from the Associated Press ticker. Growing anxious about preventing a nuclear war over Cuba, Khrushchev had delivered a second letter to Kennedy via Radio Moscow. He upped the ante from

USIA and Cuban Missile Crisis

his private letter, by requiring the United States to remove its Jupiter nuclear missiles from NATO installations in Turkey, in exchange for the removal of Soviet missiles in Cuba.[71]

Although many senior administration members found the public offer dubious, Khrushchev's maneuver proved an effective exploitation of radio broadcasting. The world now knew of his willingness to compromise, which would make any U.S. military attack on Cuba appear reckless. He also reminded a global audience that, since 1959, the Americans had positioned their own missiles along the border of the Soviet Union. As Khrushchev explained to Alexandr Alexiev, his ambassador to Cuba, the United States "should be made to feel the same way we do. . . . They have to swallow the pill like we swallowed the Turkish one."[72] In his speech on October 22, Kennedy had pledged to pursue any diplomatic route available to prevent an escalation in tensions; therefore, he could not ignore Khrushchev's public offer.

As the president deliberated how to respond, tensions escalated further on October 27, when a Soviet air defense battery in Cuba destroyed a U-2 flying over the island, killing its air force pilot, Major Rudolf Anderson. This revelation led Kennedy to question the risk of nighttime surveillance during the afternoon ExComm. Wilson offered to broadcast a message on Voice of America every five to ten minutes during night operations to explain in Spanish to the Cubans the purpose of the lights in the sky, so that they would not confuse the flares with a U.S. aerial attack. The acting USIA director excused himself from the meeting to "make sure that nobody does anything wrong with this one" in the VOA newsroom.[73] This serves as a prime example of both the value of the USIA participating in the ExComm meetings and Anderson's presence in the newsroom to verify that last-minute changes made their way into broadcasts heard by millions of listeners.

Following Wilson's departure from the Cabinet Room, Kennedy focused on how to respond to Khrushchev's proposals. Fully considering the public diplomacy repercussions of his response to Khrushchev's second offer, Kennedy instructed the State Department to soften the language in its draft response. By 7:30 p.m., on October 27, Robert Kennedy and Ted Sorensen merged their own drafts into a final letter for the president's signature. With the wordsmithing assistance of his closest aides, Kennedy chose to respond to the premier's first offer and essentially ignore the second one pertaining to U.S. missiles in Turkey.[74] In private however, Kennedy directed his brother to inform Soviet Ambassador Anatoly Dobrynin that the administration pledged to remove its missiles from Turkey.[75]

Khrushchev accepted Kennedy's pledge quickly in a message over Radio Moscow on October 28, and the international tensions that had mounted so quickly over the past thirteen days seemingly evaporated. Wilson responded emotionally to the outcome:

> I remember on Friday and Saturday nights at home I literally wondered whether I'd come home the next night—and then suddenly it all resolved itself, or became resolved on that Sunday morning, and the attitude was lighthearted in that [Cabinet] room. I mean, all of a sudden this huge burden was lifted and I felt like laughing or yelling or dancing—I was the youngest man there and I'm not saying anyone else felt like dancing, but that's the way I felt.[76]

The United States derived its advantage during the Cuban Missile Crisis from Khrushchev's blunder. Kennedy acknowledged to a reporter following the crisis that he did not think Khrushchev placed the missiles in Cuba because he intended to launch a preemptive nuclear attack. He did, however, expect Khrushchev to publicly gloat about possessing nuclear missiles ninety miles from America's shore once they became operational. This, the president explained, "would have politically changed the balance of power. It would have appeared to, and appearances contribute to reality."[77] By publicly presenting Soviet actions as duplicitous and a threat to world peace, Kennedy gained the initiative and overwhelming global support.[78]

By demonstrating restraint, Kennedy earned Khrushchev's respect, something that he had not enjoyed since their summit in Vienna the year prior. Indeed, the premier's respect for Kennedy strongly influenced his willingness to trust the American president's word to foreswear invading Cuba. Khrushchev's interest in improving communications led to the creation of a Hot Line between the White House and Kremlin the following summer.[79] As scholar Lawrence

Freedman observed, Khrushchev became "an enthusiast" of détente with the United States after the crisis, namely in the form of seriously engaging in diplomatic negotiations over a nuclear test ban treaty that Kennedy had sought since the beginning of his administration.[80] Additionally, Ted Sorensen believed that the favorable outcome of the crisis enabled Kennedy to extend more significant peace overtures to the Soviets than he could have done previously in his administration, and he did just this in his speech about peaceful coexistence, given the following year at American University on June 10, 1963.[81] With the de-escalation of standoffs in Berlin and Cuba, the president could reach out to Khrushchev in pursuit of nuclear disarmament, having proven his foreign policy credentials to domestic critics and Republican rivals.

Although the crisis effectively ended on October 28, the USIA did not precipitously de-escalate its information campaign in Latin America. After all, the missiles had not returned to their shipping containers, let alone the Soviet Union. ExComm meetings continued as well, and on October 30, Wilson informed the president that Cuban exiles in America sought to buy airtime on U.S. radio stations to voice "inflammatory statements" about Castro and Khrushchev. Fearing that this would only fuel domestic anxiety, Kennedy instructed Wilson to talk with the chair of the FCC to find some way to block the broadcasts without appearing to be overtly censoring private radio stations.[82]

On October 31, Kennedy told Wilson that he wanted USIA messages throughout Latin America to stress that the Cuban Missile Crisis remained a hemispheric concern and urge the population to improve their security partnership with the United States through the Organization of American States. The president instructed Wilson to limit derogatory terminology against Castro and explain how the United States justified its continued aerial surveillance of Cuba with an OAS resolution, rather than a unilateral decision.[83] After learning that Castro refused to permit UN inspectors to verify the removal of missile sites in Cuba in early November, Kennedy wanted the USIA to blame Castro only for "obstructing peace." However, he did not want the agency messages to describe Castro as a "Soviet stooge."[84]

Wilson provided Kennedy with a summary of USIA broadcasting

operations targeting Cuba on November 2. Voice of America transmitted on thirty-three separate shortwave frequencies twenty-four hours a day. From 7:00 p.m. until 6:00 a.m. the following morning, eleven medium-wave U.S. commercial radio stations linked to Voice of America to amplify the signal, and the British ambassador in Havana verified reception of the American broadcasts. Wilson recommended introducing "stratovision," an experimental airborne television program provided by the USIA's two specially equipped DC-6 airplanes that could transmit to Cuban television sets. However, the system would have limitations, and the agency estimated that, if employed, the Cubans would find a way to jam the television signal within three weeks.[85] At the November 6 meeting of the ExComm, the president ruled out the possible use of the stratovision capability, saying that it should "be saved for an emergency." The chair of the FCC joined Wilson at the ExComm meeting to recommend the alternate use of two fifty-watt, medium-wave radio stations, one from the USIA and the other from the navy, to begin broadcasting directly to Cuba that weekend. Kennedy approved the recommendation.[86]

A reassuring sign for the international community that tensions had de-escalated occurred during a cultural diplomacy event on November 13, 1962. In exchange for the New York Ballet's tour of the Soviet Union, the Bolshoi Theater Ballet Company performed Swan Lake to a packed Capitol Theater in Washington DC, festooned with U.S. and Soviet flags. Both national anthems played prior to the beginning of the performance, and after the show, President and Mrs. Kennedy joined Ambassador and Mrs. Dobrynin backstage to greet the cast. Having returned to work at 1776 Pennsylvania Avenue, Murrow found tremendous value in reporting on the event in forthcoming USIA programming.[87]

Besides disseminating information, the USIA's research division continued to conduct surveys and analyze feedback during and after the crisis. Referencing its division's most recent report, Murrow told the ExComm on November 19 that many Latin Americans believed that the United States was not "doing enough" to hold Castro culpable for the situation.[88] Nonetheless, the president did not want the USIA to focus its messages on Castro, because he did not want to

USIA and Cuban Missile Crisis

invite Khrushchev to point to American instigations as evidence that the United States would not honor its pledge to respect Cuba's sovereignty. Since the focus needed to remain on Soviet activity, Murrow recommended that the USIA "make a louder noise" about the administration's intent to expand aerial surveillance over the island.[89] On December 10, Kennedy acquiesced to Murrow's recommendation by authorizing the CIA to coordinate with the USIA to allow Cuban refugees to broadcast on CIA-contracted transmitters.[90] Although Murrow seemed aggressive in targeting Cuba after his return to work, he continued to advocate for focused messages and refrained from diverting all of the agency's capabilities to targeting Cuba.[91] Murrow endorsed the president's decision not to employ the stratovision DC-6 aircraft, believing it more appropriate for "the most grave and impelling circumstances."[92]

By mid-December, after observing a partial redeployment of Soviet forces, the administration no longer worried that Khrushchev might renege on the agreement. Analysts and pundits alike began writing assessments of the U.S. government's performance during the crisis. In its January 1963 analysis, the U.S. Advisory Commission on Information praised the administration for bringing the USIA into the policy process prior to Kennedy's televised address on October 22. Assessing the interagency cooperation between the NSC, USIA, CIA, and State and Defense Departments, the report noted, "Cuba was a good example of a situation where USIA was properly used by the U.S. Government."[93] Kennedy's inclusion of Wilson, Loomis, and Tom Sorensen enabled VOA broadcasters to prepare news and analysis immediately after the president's speech. This ensured that all of the USIA's media components—radio, film, print, and television— received clearly defined information objectives.

Pulitzer Prize–winning journalist William Randolph Hearst Jr., who had criticized the USIA and Voice of America over the past decade, praised the agency's approach to Cuba. "Uncle Sam never had it so good South of the Border," Hearst wrote. The journalist honed in on Voice of America's use of Cuban refugees who told their story in "the Caribbean's hot war of words."[94] Not only did Hearst think that the exiles provided compelling stories for listeners in Cuba, but their messages alerted Latin America about the perils of communism. After reading Hearst's editorial, Murrow scrolled a note to his staff: "Damn good."[95]

On December 4, the owners of ten of the eleven commercial radio stations, who had lent their transmitters to Voice of America, arrived in Washington at the invitation of the president. During a Rose Garden ceremony, Kennedy emphasized the importance of their role in October, and Murrow assisted him in presenting each owner with a certificate of appreciation.[96] From the White House, Murrow hosted a lunch for the owners at the Metropolitan Club, where he thanked each of them for their service to the nation by "using their transmitters in the interest of truth." Although Loomis's daily phone calls to the station managers during the crisis always entailed entertaining questions about how much they would be reimbursed for the lost airtime, every owner left Washington agreeing that it was "really a patriotic thing" without seeking financial compensation. All of their airtime ultimately cost the USIA the price of lunch at one of Washington's most exclusive clubs.[97]

In the months following the crisis, the USIA studied international reactions to the crisis and its effect on the reputation of the United States. Murrow worried about the Soviets drawing attention to the U.S. missiles in Turkey, even though the president did not pledge publicly to remove them. The director wrote to Kennedy on December 13 to explain that it could pose "real problems," if the Soviets chose to push the message that a base in Cuba and a base in Turkey were equivalent. The USIA found some indications that Soviet propaganda output had begun, albeit slowly, to focus on this message.[98] The president requested examples of the foreign press making this correlation, and Murrow provided the White House with a variety of quotes from several European newspapers. The British *Guardian* noted, "What is sauce for Cuba, is also sauce for Turkey, Berlin and other places." USIA surveys in Africa even indicated considerable support for the United States to return the naval base at Guantanamo Bay.[99]

Despite editorials about superpower quid pro quo, international opinion polls collected in January 1963 clearly illustrated overwhelming support for how the United States had managed the crisis. Traveling

USIA and Cuban Missile Crisis

in Africa just after the crisis, Undersecretary of State Chester Bowles met leaders who voiced their admiration for Kennedy's response, and they recognized the "bare-faced falsehoods" provided by Soviet diplomats during the crisis.[100] The USIA found that Western Europeans overwhelmingly approved of Kennedy's response. With the exception of France, U.S. foreign policy and leadership gained significant boosts in polls collected from every USIA outpost in the region. A USIA poll conducted in the United Kingdom, France, Italy, and West Germany, showed greater confidence in U.S. military strength compared to the Soviets by February 1963. After a year of static European opinions about American military might vis-à-vis the Soviets, this particular change excited USIA officials. The agency's research service pointed out that U.S. foreign policies received their highest approval rating in Europe since 1956. For the first time since Kennedy assumed office, more than 50 percent of West Germans believed that American defenses would deter Soviet aggression in Europe.[101] With the exception of a handful of communists, the Greek population almost unanimously approved of Kennedy's handling of the situation and hailed the withdrawal of Soviet weaponry as a "Communist retreat." For a country that had struggled to maintain its democratic structure and public support for NATO, the positive endorsement energized the public affairs officer in Athens.[102]

During the meeting of the Anglo-American information working group in London, in May 1963, British information officers told their American counterparts that for the first time in two years, they believed that the West had regained the "propaganda initiative" over the Soviets, thanks to Khrushchev's blunder in Cuba.[103] Since the rise of the Berlin Wall in August 1961, the USIA had attempted to persuade Europeans that the Soviet Union did not share nuclear parity with the United States, but surveys continued to reflect Western doubt until after the missile crisis. This renewed faith in American sincerity about pursuing diplomatic solutions to Cold War confrontations would help attract support for the administration's efforts to sign a nuclear test ban treaty with the Soviet Union, as a significant step toward superpower disarmament.

In Latin America, the USIA discovered greater approval for Kennedy and U.S. policies, a welcome response after nearly two years of tepid reactions to the administration's Alliance for Progress. Murrow explained to the host of *Issues and Answers* that his research division found no evidence to suggest that Castro had regained his popularity in Latin America ten months after the Cuban Missile Crisis.[104] Irate with Khrushchev's decisions to redeploy troops and missiles to the Soviet Union, Castro's subsequent rants did not endear him to his neighbors, either. Radio Havana became increasingly hostile toward other Latin American states after the crisis, running a clip of Castro lambasting regional leaders and calling for a renewed communist revolution "because that road is much easier in Latin American countries than it was in Cuba."[105] When the CIA reported evidence of Cuban subversion in Latin America in January 1963, Murrow advocated for the intelligence to be shared with the OAS and heads of government throughout the region.[106]

Sitting out the Cuban Missile Crisis frustrated Murrow greatly, not so much because he missed out on the action, but because he could not report for duty when his country depended on its information agency.[107] Despite his noticeable absence, the USIA adopted his principles about keeping the message clear, focused, and truthful. Murrow spoke with pride about his agency's performance, telling a congressional subcommittee how the USIA framed its message: "The experience of Cuba seems to have demonstrated at that time and place that no nation, not even the most belligerent, the most aggressive, dares risk a direct confrontation with America's nuclear might."[108] Despite the USIA's oversight of his newsroom, Loomis praised Voice of America's broadcasts during the crisis as the best-coordinated operation of his seven-year directorship.[109]

Through the quality of its broadcasting and other forms of information programming, the USIA deserves credit for generating international support for Kennedy's desired resolution to the crisis. Ironically, public diplomacy could instead have worked in Khrushchev's favor, had he announced the missile sites to the world first. If the premier had explained that Soviet missiles in Cuba were no different from U.S. nuclear missiles in Turkey, then the Kennedy administration might have been less successful in portraying Khrushchev as duplicitous and unstable. However, the Soviets' penchant for secrecy, and the discovery of the sites before their completion by U.S. surveillance, enabled the United States to break the news and frame the narrative themselves. The USIA presented the standoff as a concrete example of how the Soviet Union posed a continuing threat to the free world and was a wholly inadequate model for developing countries to emulate. This public diplomacy approach required the careful articulation of messages through an expansion of Voice of America's transmitter capabilities, the inclusion of sensitive reconnaissance photographs in print material, and explicit guidance to public affairs officers engaging journalists and curious onlookers around the world. Just as Adlai Stevenson told his Soviet counterpart that he stood in "the courtroom of world opinion," the success of the USIA's information campaign helped to convince Khrushchev that he would not advance the promulgation of communist revolution in Latin America by escalating tensions with the United States over Cuba.

7

Advocates for a Test Ban

What is to be tested is not so much nuclear
devices as the will of free men to remain free.
—EDWARD R. MURROW, August 31, 1961

Throughout the Kennedy administration, the U.S. Information Agency
relied on its "fast media"—Voice of America, the press service, newsreels from the Motion Picture Service, and the USIA Television Service—to respond rapidly to international audiences clamoring to know
more about American policies related to sensational topics.[1] For brief
periods, crises in Berlin, Birmingham, and Cuba dominated global
headlines, requiring the USIA to clarify U.S. actions before communist propagandists could effectively spin the stories for their own benefit. Other policy priorities did not capture international attention as
easily. Over the course of his presidency, John F. Kennedy sought a
nuclear test ban treaty with the Soviet Union, but the painstakingly
slow diplomatic process failed to remain front-page news. It did not
help that the president's own senior advisers often disagreed on what
U.S. nuclear policy should be. Nonetheless, USIA director Murrow
faced the challenge of keeping foreign audiences interested in Kennedy's efforts to de-escalate Cold War nuclear tensions.

In 1958 the United States and Soviet Union agreed to a voluntary
suspension of nuclear testing, but negotiations in January 1961 in
Geneva, Switzerland, for a permanent test ban treaty remained inconclusive. As he entered the White House, Kennedy did not believe that

the American people wanted their government to reduce its nuclear arsenal. After all, he had spent the 1960 presidential campaign convincing many Americans of a "missile gap" between the United States and the Soviet Union. While no such gap existed, international opinion remained skeptical that the United States truly possessed a preponderance of military force over the Soviets. USIA polling indicated that international opinion considered the U.S. military inferior to that of the Soviets. In a memorandum to Deputy Defense Secretary Roswell Gilpatric, Murrow recommended that, even if areas of inferiority existed, the Pentagon needed to stress that such nuances did not "destroy the validity of our claim of primacy."[2]

Harlan Cleveland, the assistant secretary of state for international organization affairs, did not believe that Kennedy seriously considered a test ban treaty prior to entering the White House. Aboard his yacht, the *Honey Fitz*, the president discussed the upcoming United Nations resolution on general disarmament with Cleveland and Adlai Stevenson, his ambassador to the UN. Offhandedly, Kennedy commented, "Oh, this disarmament. Well, that's really just a propaganda thing, isn't it?" Greatly alarmed by his boss's apathy, Stevenson countered, "Well, now, you know, Jack, you've got to have faith." Cleveland explained to Kennedy that the Soviets were not serious about their public calls for total nuclear disarmament because the United States would reject dismantling its entire nuclear arsenal. The politburo wanted the Western "imperialists" to turn down their offer so their propagandists could blame the United States for escalating the arms race. Cleveland recommended that it would be wise to provide a counter offer, one within the realm of feasibility for the American public and Congress. As the yacht returned to shore, Kennedy came to see a test ban treaty as a legitimate policy objective for his administration.[3]

The president communicated his intentions to Premier Nikita Khrushchev through emissaries and in person during the June 1961 Vienna summit. The following month, Murrow instructed his public affairs officers stationed around the world to make the administration's desire for a test ban treaty their principal information message.[4] It would not be the first time that Murrow championed nuclear arms limitations; Eisenhower's New Look doctrine of mutually assured destruction had alarmed him in the 1950s. In his March 18, 1954, CBS broadcast, he quantified the square-mileage destruction capability of each hydrogen bomb and described how massive retaliation necessitated the production of even more rockets. Murrow created a pun about Eisenhower's security policy: "So we have a new look at an astonishing peril. Even more than other dangers, it has to be faced, thought through, and met. But here is one danger that cannot be met and overcome by creating a greater danger."[5] On September 6, 1954, Murrow welcomed Eisenhower's announcement of the formation of an international atomic agency to advance the peaceful use of nuclear energy. Placing the creation of this entity into Cold War perspective, the journalist opined, "This new agency, if it be pressed forward with vigor, will do more than months of propaganda to persuade millions of non-Communists that our purpose is peace."[6] As USIA director in 1961, Murrow still believed that a test ban would serve as a sagacious step toward reining in what he considered the insanity of the previous administration's nuclear deterrent theory.

Although Murrow voiced his opposition to the Bay of Pigs and urged Kennedy to respond vigorously to the Berlin crisis and American racial segregation, he appeared most vocal during National Security Council meetings in pressing his view for a nuclear test ban treaty. On June 24, 1961, Murrow told Undersecretary of State Chester Bowles that the administration needed to do a better job of persuading allies and nonaligned states about the "rightness" of a U.S. policy to refrain from further nuclear testing. "We believe this issue is a key," he said, referring to a recent USIA study, "conceivably *the* key, to our Cold War posture in the coming year." Without support for the test ban, he feared that the United States might lose support on other issues, including solidarity for the security of West Berlin. For much of the world, nuclear policy remained a volatile issue, and Murrow wanted the USIA to engage them with "patient repetition of reasonable arguments cast in emotional terms."[7] Although an advocate for honest reporting from agency media services, Murrow did not see a contradiction in presenting information in a way that evoked fear about the fallout of a potential nuclear war.

Advocates for a Test Ban

An August 1961 USIA report supported Murrow's argument. With the exception of Great Britain, 70 percent of the people surveyed in Western Europe supported nuclear disarmament. While they doubted the sincerity of Soviet disarmament overtures, a majority of the 70 percent in favor of the initiative also voiced dissatisfaction with Kennedy for failing to pursue a treaty with Khrushchev more aggressively. In France, people held the United States equally culpable with the Soviets for the stalled negotiations. The survey also asked how people would react if the Soviets resumed testing, and the majority of Europeans accepted that the United States would be compelled to resume their own testing in response.[8]

The timing of the survey's last question proved apropos. While diplomats continued their talks in Geneva, Khrushchev unnerved the world by resuming nuclear testing on August 30, 1961, only two weeks after the rise of the Berlin Wall. After 340 meetings, the Geneva Conference on the Discontinuance of Nuclear Weapon Tests recessed indefinitely on September 9.[9] The Soviet premier blamed Kennedy's policies for his decision. As Khrushchev explained in Moscow to John McCloy, the U.S. envoy for disarmament, Kennedy's declaration to close the missile gap, expand the conventional military, and bolster special operations forces worried hardliners in the politburo who compelled Khrushchev to authorize the new testing. The decision may have had less to do with demonstrating Soviet power and more to do with the premier's personal desire to preserve his leadership at home. Over the next three months, the Soviets conducted more than fifty aboveground nuclear tests.[10]

During the National Security Council meeting on the morning of August 31, Kennedy solicited the advice of his foreign policy advisers about how to respond. The Joint Chiefs of Staff advocated for a resumption of U.S. testing, regardless of whether the Soviets ceased their testing. However, other Defense officials, including Secretary of Defense Robert McNamara and his deputy, Roswell Gilpatric, urged Kennedy to continue to seek a test ban treaty, despite their adversary's intransigence.[11] The military's position did not surprise the president, since an ad hoc panel on nuclear testing had argued in July 1961 that so long as the United States mirrored the number of tests conducted by the Soviet Union, it would achieve nuclear parity for the foreseeable future.[12]

Murrow expressed his most vocal opposition to the resumption of U.S. testing during the August 31 NSC meeting by arguing that the administration would be forfeiting "the greatest propaganda gift we have had for a long time."[13] Immediately after the meeting, he sent Kennedy a two-page memorandum outlining his thoughts on how the United States should react to the new Soviet tests. By choosing not to resume U.S. testing, the Kennedy administration would expose Khrushchev's duplicity and help to alleviate international anxiety about the two superpowers ramping up for a violent confrontation, while the rest of the world sat precariously in the middle. He advocated for patience and encouraged American diplomats to explain that the U.S. nuclear arsenal remained adequate to defend the country and its allies. As a demonstration of American confidence, Murrow argued against consulting with allies about how to respond, lest observers see it as a sign of American vacillation. However, he did urge Kennedy to raise the issue of Soviet irresponsibility before the United Nations.[14]

To stress to Kennedy that he had arrived at this decision rationally, Murrow pointed out that no one in the American scientific community or military had warned that waiting a few more weeks to resume testing would endanger national security. Strategic patience, he offered, could even co-opt nuclear disarmament groups: "This [wait] time, if properly employed, can be used to isolate the Communist Bloc, frighten the satellites and the uncommitted, pretty well destroy the Ban the Bomb movement in Britain, and might even induce sanity into the SANE nuclear policy group in this country."[15] In order to advance America's leadership within the free world and provide the USIA with sound bites for its own media, Murrow recommended that Kennedy dispatch senior administration officials to articulate this position on television and radio.[16]

After reading Murrow's memorandum, Kennedy asked him to assist in rewording the White House's response to Khrushchev's latest provocation, drafted by Secretary of State Dean Rusk.[17] The final message that Murrow shaped mentioned nothing about preparations

Advocates for a Test Ban

for future American testing but, instead, concentrated on the world's "disappointment" with the Soviet's decision to "substitute terror for reason." Kennedy assured the American people and their allies that the U.S. nuclear arsenal would more than adequately protect the free world.[18] Given that the news coincided with the Non-Aligned Movement's high-profile conference in Belgrade, the president aimed his remarks toward those international leaders who remained adamant that they did not need to choose a side in the Cold War. USIA analysts thought that Khrushchev deliberately announced his decision to resume nuclear testing on the eve of the Non-Aligned Movement meeting in Belgrade to "awe" Indian prime minister Jawaharlal Nehru and Egyptian president Gamal Abdel Nasser. Information analysts further speculated that the Soviets may have believed that their tests would frighten nonaligned leaders into demanding that Kennedy meet Khrushchev's demands for disarmament before the world collapsed into nuclear war.[19]

Enlivened by the president's stalwart response on August 31, Murrow continued to caution Kennedy against giving into pressures to renew American testing. In an impromptu strategy session in the hallway outside of the president's bedroom on September 1, with Kennedy standing in his bathrobe, McCloy and Rusk spoke as if personally betrayed by the Soviet's intransigence, and they urged the president to resume tests. Murrow and White House adviser Arthur Schlesinger Jr. offered the president their opposing view before Kennedy sent them all away, appearing irritated by the debate. As they descended from the family quarters, Murrow told Schlesinger that he intended to press the issue again with Kennedy. Schlesinger offered to help and followed Murrow back to his office at 1776 Pennsylvania Avenue, where they drafted another memorandum for the president to read prior to his departure for a weekend in Hyannis Port.[20]

Murrow's second letter to the president on the issue argued that time "continues to work for us." Kennedy should pay more attention to the generally favorable domestic-press reaction to the White House's initial response to Soviet testing, rather than to "predictable sources" clamoring for new tests on Capitol Hill and at the Pentagon. So long as the president blamed Khrushchev for instigating fear, the United States could be seen globally as a "repository of hope." If Kennedy had to cave into domestic pressures, Murrow hoped that the president would wait until at least Monday night, when the non-aligned conference concluded in Belgrade. This might at least spare the United States from being lumped with the Soviets in the conference's published resolutions.[21] Murrow included with the memorandum a hastily prepared USIA report documenting that nonaligned leaders viewed Khrushchev's recent decision with "contempt." One Asian delegate to the conference asked: "What do we have left to talk about? A reduction of nuclear armaments had been one of the basic planks of the conference platform, and Khrushchev has torn that out before we can get started."[22]

A detailed, three-page report confirming that world opinion sided with the United States arrived at the White House shortly thereafter. USIA analysts predicted that global protests directed against the Soviets would shift toward the United States if Kennedy chose to resume testing as well. Murrow cited international concerns about nuclear fallout, followed by the potential escalation of hostilities in the Cold War, as the two major objections raised against the resumption of U.S. testing. Although some within the international community might begrudgingly understand the need to defend the West, "the unaligned and neutral countries tend to view all nuclear testing as an unmitigated evil."[23]

Murrow's argument about how the Non-Aligned Movement would respond to an American resumption of nuclear testing led Kennedy to wait until the completion of the Belgrade conference. Public diplomacy scholar Nicholas Cull cites the September 1 memorandum as Murrow's "only decisive contribution" to Kennedy's nuclear policy.[24] However, his August 31 memorandum and remarks during the NSC meeting also contributed to his argument and influenced the president to have the USIA director help shape the White House's official response. The president chose not to resume U.S. testing, at least until the Soviets conducted another test.

It did not take long for Khrushchev to try his patience again. When a third test occurred the first week of September, Kennedy felt compelled to authorize an American test. Prior to going public,

Advocates for a Test Ban

he called Murrow on the "blowtorch"—Murrow's term for the dedicated White House telephone line in his office—requesting Murrow's presence in the Cabinet Room where Kennedy explained his decision to senior administration members.[25] Among those assembled was Adlai Stevenson, who expressed his regrets that the president chose to resume testing. Kennedy asked emotionally, "What choice did we have? They had spit in our eye three times. We couldn't possibly sit back and do nothing at all. We had to do this." When Stevenson argued that the United States continued to win the "propaganda battle" by remaining steadfast, Kennedy looked incredulous and asked why, if that was indeed the case, protesters had not thrown stones through the windows of Soviet embassies around the world. In Schlesinger's opinion, Kennedy believed that a resumption of testing would appeal to neutralists, like Yugoslavia, and he confided in his journal that night, "The fact is that Tito sold out Murrow and Schlesinger."[26]

Kennedy released a public statement at 5:00 p.m. on September 5 to announce that, due to Soviet intransigence, he felt compelled to "take those steps which prudent men find essential." He offered the Soviets one last chance, by encouraging Khrushchev to return to the negotiation table to ban all testing by September 9.[27] When Moscow remained silent, Kennedy ordered the first U.S. test to occur on September 15. Without acknowledging that not a single noncommunist country supported the recent Soviet tests, Soviet international radio reported that Khrushchev enjoyed popular domestic support for his "defensive" measures.[28]

USIA coverage of Kennedy's September 5 message focused on how the United States would resume testing "safely," through experiments in underground laboratories that prevented radioactive fallout from contaminating population centers. Murrow told Tom Sorensen and Henry Loomis that he did not want agency broadcasts to exaggerate the effects of the fallout in its reporting; they needed to be "substantiated by scientific evidence."[29] USIA messages explained the differences between U.S. and Soviet proposals in Geneva, highlighting that Khrushchev had rejected Kennedy's call for the United Nations to inspect its nuclear facilities.[30] While Voice of America broadcast this news around the world, Moscow's TASS omitted the point about American testing being conducted underground.

To emphasize the administration's transparency, Murrow recommended to the president that he permit U.S. and foreign journalists to attend the upcoming nuclear test in Nevada. "This contrast with Soviet secrecy was always profitable for us," Murrow opined in another memorandum to Kennedy, "and should now be even more so."[31] When the president announced the creation of a permanent U.S. disarmament agency on September 26, Murrow shot a cable to public affairs officers overseas about the importance of incorporating this initiative in their outreach with concerned foreigners: "It illustrates the U.S. conviction that new avenues toward peace should be sought unremittingly, in times of tension as well as in times of calm."[32]

The best way to counter bombastic communist propaganda, Murrow argued, was through the art of persuasion: "I for one am persuaded that we have no alternative: we must persuade, or perish in the attempt."[33] In October 1961, Vice President Lyndon Johnson asked Murrow how his agency explained the simmering nuclear tensions through its media services. The USIA's general counsel assured Johnson that the agency engaged international audiences aggressively, "including those behind the Iron and Bamboo Curtains," to understand how the Soviets had escalated the nuclear standoff by resuming testing first, and that they alone would be responsible for any effects from the fallout.[34]

While Murrow dutifully directed the USIA to explain Kennedy's rationale through its broadcasts and programming, he continued to urge the president to suspend U.S. nuclear testing. During the November 2 National Security Council meeting, news of the Soviets' detonation of a fifty-megaton bomb on October 31 dominated the agenda. Despite the magnitude of the explosion, Murrow recommended that the administration clarify its intentions to suspend testing, based on confidence in its ability to protect the United States and its allies with its existing arsenal, and that it did not seek to further torment a world held hostage by the nuclear capabilities of the two superpowers. To add weight to his proposal, Murrow summarized the latest

Advocates for a Test Ban

findings from the USIA's research division documenting the international community's response to the most recent Soviet blast as anger rather than fear. From across the table in the Cabinet Room, Kennedy replied that such a pronouncement was no longer feasible. The president had sided with the hawks, who argued that the United States looked weak by not matching the Soviets test for test.[35]

Kennedy demonstrated remarkable restraint by not relenting to some of the more outlandish pressures to expand the country's nuclear capabilities. As advisers described the strategic value of creating the next megaton bomb that would outclass the mightiest missiles in the Soviet arsenal, Kennedy occasionally asked the group, "How much was the yield of that bomb that was dropped on Hiroshima?" The president already knew the answer—twenty kilotons—and so did his military and science experts, but he used the rhetorical question to remind policymakers that the theoretical destruction offered by an ever-expanding arsenal did not make existing nuclear munitions any less lethal.[36] Kennedy did, however, ask Murrow to remain after the meeting on November 2 to help him craft his public response.[37]

The Soviets' fifty-megaton detonation truly incensed Murrow, and it led him to reach down several levels into his organization to personally edit the VOA special report on the topic. Voice of America had begun developing an hour-long program about the effects of nuclear testing, *Have You Been Told?* The writers worked deliberately to keep coverage of the world's reaction to the testing as deadpanned as possible. When Loomis and two of the VOA writers showed the script to Murrow, the director complained that he did not like it. "Juice it up some," Murrow directed. "Really hit them." The writers struggled to find new material before their deadline. They included the sounds of explosions and a gruesome headline from Cairo's *Al Gomhuriya* lamenting how "We're all going to die" from the poisons of Soviet testing. Claude Groce, from Voice of America's Central Program Services, thought that *Have You Been Told?* sounded more like a spoof than a news story when it aired.[38] Murrow voiced his approval of the program and ordered all VOA transmitters to be massed, in order to broadcast to the widest audience possible behind the Iron Curtain.[39] He coordinated with the CIA and Defense Department to have the program transmitted simultaneously on Radio Free Europe, Radio Liberty, and the Armed Forces Network.[40]

Murrow's personal management of the VOA program frustrated Loomis, who felt that he should have been given the opportunity to oversee production himself.[41] Perhaps Murrow believed that emotionalism would break the Eastern Europeans' tolerance of the Kremlin's reckless policy decisions. However, the USIA later confirmed that the program did not influence Soviet listeners significantly. The most reputable feedback arrived in a cable from the public affairs officer in Moscow: "For a Soviet audience it would have been better to have it done in a more matter-of-fact, straightforward style."[42] Murrow's involvement with *Have You Been Told?* was one of the few occasions where emotion muddled his ability to assess the recommendations of regional specialists objectively and trust his media services to follow his intent.

In addition to targeting the Soviet bloc, European public affairs officers knew that they needed to influence NATO allies who worried that the United States lagged behind the Soviet Union's military capabilities. British information officers encouraged their American counterparts to clarify that an agreement to meet to discuss disarmament did not equate to an agreement between the United States and Soviet Union to dismantle their nuclear arsenals. The USIA needed to stress to Western Europeans that the United States would not abandon its defense obligations to the alliance.[43] Part of European perception of U.S. military readiness stemmed from the Hollywood image of Americans being self-absorbed and disinterested in global affairs. A USIA survey found that the majority of Western Europeans believed that Soviet scientific achievements outpaced the United States. They equated Americans' pursuit of a comfortable standard of living to disinterest in science and assumed that fewer American students sought scientific and engineering degrees than in the Soviet Union.[44]

In lieu of saber rattling, Murrow favored using the space race to counter prevailing European opinion, through a form of competition much safer than nuclear fission. The president concurred that the space program would help to unify the American people while strengthening the country's position in the world. He appointed Vice

Advocates for a Test Ban

President Johnson to head the Space Council overseeing NASA, as a way to indicate the level of importance placed on this costly initiative. Kennedy cared little for the potential medical or scientific benefits of space exploration, but he did make the American space program a pillar of his presidential campaign because he believed in the symbolism of surpassing the Soviets in reaching the heavens. Without the Cold War, historian James Giglio argued, there would never have been a race to the moon.[45]

In Kennedy's view, President Eisenhower's space program had lacked "imagination, vitality, and vision," and he voiced his determination to provide all three.[46] Since Yuri Gagarin's orbital around the world on April 12, 1961, the Senate had supported Kennedy's request for a larger budget for NASA, and the USIA capitalized on Alan Shepard's successful suborbital flight on May 5, 1961, in its worldwide programming and exhibits.[47] On May 25, Kennedy spoke before a joint session of Congress to commit the United States to landing a man on the moon before the end of the decade.[48] The president's speech enthralled audiences at home and abroad, but the sluggish pace of the program's development prevented NASA from dominating international headlines. Despite Kennedy and Murrow's desire to counter unfavorable opinions of U.S. defense and scientific capabilities by exploiting the space race, the USIA's information campaign could not adequately offset the global anxiety fomented by Khrushchev's nuclear testing.

During White House policy discussions in February 1962, Murrow persisted in asking the president to consider the public diplomacy value of taking a less hawkish approach in his nuclear policy. While Europeans considered the Soviets to be ahead of the United States in terms of scientific, space, and military capabilities, they still believed that the United States possessed greater industrial capacity, excellent agribusiness, and a superior standard of living. Since 1960, the USIA found that most Europeans believed that the United States had "arrested" the widening gap between the Soviet Union and themselves, even if it had not completely closed.[49]

Rusk, McNamara, Chairman of the Joint Chiefs of Staff General Lyman Lemnitzer, and Dr. Glen Seaborg, the head of the Atomic Energy Commission, dismissed Murrow's line of reasoning and voiced unanimous support for the resumption of nuclear testing for political and security reasons. This time they called for atmospheric testing, in addition to underground testing.[50] General Lemnitzer argued that testing would provide the United States with more advanced nuclear weapons, a better understanding of the effects of the weaponry, and analysis of their employment in "operational environments."[51] Murrow disagreed with the weight that State and Defense leaders placed on the value of such risky experimentation. During an NSC meeting on February 27, Rusk encouraged Kennedy to resume testing, based on the absence of serious international backlash against the series of Soviet tests. Murrow immediately corrected the secretary of state's understanding of world opinion toward Khrushchev, citing a USIA poll. However, Murrow conceded that, by this point, the world was "somewhat prepared and conditioned" for the United States to resume testing in response to Soviet bullying.[52] Once again, the advocates for testing won over the president, and the United States planned to resume atmospheric testing for the first time since the 1950s. In a national address on March 2, Kennedy explained that, if the Soviets would not cease their testing, he saw no alternative than to resume atmospheric testing over the Pacific Ocean in April. He closed his lengthy address by voicing his sincere hope that Khrushchev would compromise, but his obligation to defend "the freedom of the American people" required him to take this measure.[53]

Curiously, the Soviets did not jam Kennedy's March 2 speech during Voice of America's first Russian broadcast, but Murrow told Kennedy that, "following a policy decision," they began to block the American transmissions the next day.[54] International reactions to Kennedy's announcement did not surprise Murrow. Latin Americans strongly supported the president's decision to resume testing, but the rest of the Third World generally opposed the decision. Europeans did not seem pleased with the news either, but most acknowledged that, within in the context of the Cold War, it seemed "tactically correct." A USIA study completed the week following Kennedy's address found one nuance: "Even the more critical comment was in no way comparable to the severe criticism leveled against the Soviet Union when it broke the moratorium on testing."[55]

Fortunately for the Kennedy administration, a recent breakthrough in the space race helped to draw international attention away from nuclear testing. On February 20, a week before the final NSC decision to announce atmospheric testing, John Glenn's space capsule splashed safely into the Atlantic Ocean after successfully orbiting Earth three times. In a deliberate effort to show his confidence in American technological capabilities, Kennedy used the occasion publicly to invite the Soviet Union to participate in joint space exploration endeavors, beginning with the launch of a weather satellite. Khrushchev demurred, arguing that such an enterprise would be inappropriate prior to a resolution concerning nuclear disarmament.[56] The USIA heralded Glenn's success widely and quickly: seventy-two hours of film footage to thirty countries, radio coverage in thirty-seven languages, and colorful, seven-panel displays for dozens of information centers and libraries. By emphasizing how Glenn controlled his own space craft, which cosmonauts had not done up until this point, the USIA's message convinced many that the United States had not only closed the "space gap" but had exceeded Soviet capabilities.[57]

The USIA received overwhelmingly positive feedback from outposts around the world. The public affairs officer in Usumbura (since renamed Bujumbura) reported that news of the orbital captivated Burundian audiences who flocked to private theaters where the USIA made its documentary available. Noting the locals' enthusiasm, the officer promised to continue distributing photos and stories to Burundian newspapers because "we cannot help but score points with local audiences."[58] The public affairs officer in Athens noted that the agency's ability to publicize American space achievements in 1962 enabled the post to significantly "redress the psychological balance" since the launch of Sputnik.[59] Murrow recognized the public diplomacy value of the physical spacecraft in influencing foreigners to accept U.S. space superiority. The USIA director believed that the United States could "make a terrific impact abroad" by showing off Glenn's *Friendship 7* in Moscow, Belgrade, Cairo, New Delhi, and Jakarta.[60] Indeed, for the next decade, space exhibits remained the most popular attraction for visitors to the USIA's overseas libraries. Complementing the space capsules, USIA exhibits contained information on and models of U.S. satellites. Murrow also believed that the 1962 launch of the Telstar communications satellite improved America's "public position" in the space race.[61]

By the summer of 1962, despite the successful exploitation of America's position in the space race, USIA officials did not believe that they were making headway in their information campaign about the administration's policy on nuclear nonproliferation. An agency study revealed that, between August 1961 and August 1962, Western European confidence in America's ability to "provide wise leadership for the west in dealing with present world problems" had dropped by 10 percent.[62] Murrow believed that this drop originated, in part, from the lack of a clear message by the administration on its nuclear policy. While Kennedy spoke about his interest in signing a test ban treaty with the Soviets, many senior national security officials continued to speak as if they did not want a treaty, in order to look stronger by conducting more testing. During a National Security Council meeting on May 31, Murrow said that, until all U.S. government agencies could agree on what its position would be, the USIA should not discuss internal Washington debates because it would make international negotiations appear "futile."[63]

During the June 1962 meeting of the Anglo-American information working group, British representatives recommended that the USIA publish a pamphlet-sized copy of Kennedy's treaty proposal, which they would be willing to distribute. The Foreign Office noted that world interest in the disarmament discussion between the United States and Soviet Union was "not very lively," and the Soviets sounded more appealing in propaganda that boasted "bigger promises" than the Americans' offer. The British hoped that the USIA would step up its efforts to explain how the Kennedy administration's proposal would provide greater international security than Khrushchev's counterproposal.[64]

Communist propaganda offered "bigger promises" but also flagrant misinformation. Following the launch of the Soviet's Vostok II and IV in August 1962, USIA polling found significant numbers of people around the world fearful of the potential use of space as a new dimension of warfare. Pollsters found that many people believed the

Advocates for a Test Ban

United States had recently suspended planned atmospheric nuclear testing on account of Khrushchev's demand that the United States not endanger the cosmonauts. As bizarre as the story sounded, it served as an excellent example of the influence of communist propaganda, especially in the developing world. Murrow partially blamed the State Department for failing to say expressly that the U.S. decision not to conduct high-altitude testing had nothing to do with Khrushchev. He also hoped that the Defense Department would articulate that the Soviet space launches had no impact on America's defensive capabilities. Murrow recommended to the president that the administration issue a "string of statements" that would leave no room for conjecture by the foreign press.[65]

Kennedy attributed his frustrations with stalled nuclear negotiations in Geneva to Soviet grandstanding. Ambassador Anatoly Dobrynin told Chester Bowles that his country resisted an atmospheric testing treaty because the Soviet Union lacked large underground caves, similar to those available beneath the United States, where scientists could conduct comparable explosions. To dig such caves would be costly and not worth the investment, in Khrushchev's opinion.[66] However, the brinksmanship of the Cuban Missile Crisis helped to foster a more tempered dialogue between the two superpowers by the winter of 1962. For the first time since the Soviets walked away from the negotiation table in January 1961, the specter of drafting a nuclear test ban treaty reappeared. An agreement could not be accomplished overnight, but Khrushchev indicated his willingness to participate in rational diplomacy, but he expected the United States to make the initial offer.

Seeking to break the impasse, Kennedy used his commencement address at American University on June 10, 1963, as an occasion to deliver a major foreign policy speech on peaceful coexistence. Days earlier, Ted Sorensen had invited his brother, Tom, to help him draft the speech in which the president would articulate to the world his interest in easing the Cold War, in the wake of the Cuban Missile Crisis.[67] Kennedy spoke of the West and Communist bloc's mutual interest in "genuine peace." The superpowers' capabilities, he explained, had made warfare unthinkable "in an age when a single nuclear weapon contains almost ten times the explosive force delivered by all of the allied air forces in the Second World War." Just as the problems were manmade, the president believed that the nuclear impasse could be "solved by man," if those on both sides of the Iron Curtain examined their attitude toward peace. As a first step, Kennedy stated that a test ban would eliminate the environmental hazards of continued nuclear testing and contribute tangibly to limiting nuclear proliferation.[68]

Tom Sorensen called Kennedy's speech "the most useful Presidential pronouncement in years" for U.S. public diplomacy.[69] Given his involvement in drafting the speech, Sorensen prepared the USIA's policy guidance in advance and expected every USIA media service to give it immediate attention. Unsurprisingly, he "raised holy hell" the day after the speech when he learned that copyeditors at Voice of America had failed to make it their top story and addressed other issues in their daily commentary instead. Illustrative of the episodic tension between the policy and broadcasting arms of the USIA, Murrow called Loomis and Sorensen into his office for a meeting. Loomis stood his ground, but Sorensen objected, arguing that Voice of America's decision contributed to the speech failing to have the immediate global impact that the White House expected.[70] Murrow agreed with Sorensen. Although he did not reprimand Loomis, Murrow made the point that Voice of America's number one customer resided at 1600 Pennsylvania Avenue, and everyone at the USIA needed to be sensitive to the president's policy priorities. After the meeting, Voice of America replayed the speech, while USIA's regional print plants published handbills and the Motion Picture Service distributed newsreels with speech highlights.[71]

Kennedy's address influenced Khrushchev to return seriously to the negotiating table over the test ban treaty because the president provided him with a face-saving reason to reach across the Iron Curtain without appearing humiliated by the Cuban Missile Crisis. Moscow's TASS published Kennedy's June 10 speech in its entirety and interviewed Khrushchev for his reaction. The premier described the speech as a step in the right direction, reminding readers that "the Soviet Government in its foreign policy has always proceeded from the Leninist principle of the peaceful coexistence between states with differing social systems."[72] His comments reflected a remarkable shift in tone since meeting with Kennedy at the Vienna summit in June 1961.

Polish diplomat Marian Dobrosielski credited Kennedy's American University speech with "breaking the log jam" over nuclear diplomacy.[73] By the end of July, negotiators finalized a settlement agreeable to both superpowers, and Kennedy sent Assistant Secretary of State W. Averell Harriman to Moscow, as the government's representative for the ceremonial signing. Marking the twilight of Harriman's distinguished diplomatic career, which included service as America's ambassador to the Soviet Union throughout World War II, the president commented, "That's really quite a crown."[74] Following the ceremony, Khrushchev walked Harriman across the Kremlin's square for dinner at Catherine the Great's Palace. Introducing him as "Gaspodin Garriman" to a crowd of Russian onlookers, the premier said, "He has just signed a test ban treaty and I am going to take him to dinner. Do you think that he deserves dinner?" The group cheered, and Harriman silently noted the contrast between how Khrushchev and Stalin interacted with the Soviet population.[75]

The USIA's printing service rushed photos of the signing ceremony to posts around the world, where public affairs officers observed cautiously optimistic reactions to the treaty. While small countries unanimously supported the treaty, skepticism remained in Western states uncertain of Khrushchev's sincerity in honoring the treaty.[76] Some commentators warned Western policymakers not to let their guard down. Alarmed by domestic critics urging the Senate not to ratify the treaty, Murrow appeared on ABC's *Issues and Answers* to counter the hardliners. "I do not believe that we would recover from the sense of disappointment, indeed of betrayal that would be felt around the world," he told host John Scali, "if, having pressed so hard and so long for this treaty, we now refused to ratify it."[77]

While many officials in Washington patted themselves on the back and millions around the world sighed in relief when Khrushchev finally affixed his signature to the nuclear test ban treaty, Murrow reminded Americans that this did not end the Cold War. The agreement made the possibility of disarmament more likely, but the struggle to win hearts and minds would continue: "I see no indication whatsoever of a let-up in the ideological cold war." Bearing in mind that American civil rights violence had just reached a crescendo in the summer of 1963, Murrow told a reporter that Soviet and Chinese propagandists would now concentrate on other issues that defiled America's image. Referring to foreign media coverage of the racial violence in Birmingham in May 1963, Murrow lamented that over the past three months the USIA suffered "more of a beating in public than it has experienced at any time in its history."[78] It was not a coincidence that Murrow delivered this warning just days after the House of Representatives slashed $4 million from his agency's budget. The USIA needed to address a myriad of other misperceptions propagated by the communists as well, including American defense and space capabilities. The research department conducted its most comprehensive security survey to date in June and July 1963, finding that across the globe, people voiced admiration for Americans but still believed that they trailed the Soviets militarily and scientifically.[79]

In an effort to counter these perceptions, USIA officials persisted in developing new methods to trumpet the space program, since it remained the most captivating scientific topic and more appealing to the public than focusing on U.S. military strengths. When Murrow learned that Kennedy planned to wait until 1965 to launch a new Gemini spacecraft, he urged the president to send another flight of the existing Mercury model before the end of 1963. The Soviets planned to launch a two-man spaceflight that winter, and Murrow worried that the psychological value of this news, without a reciprocal U.S. space flight, would hurt international opinion further. Murrow appreciated the showmanship involved: "I understand the great risk of failure, but we must accept this or call off our space program."[80] To commemorate NASA's fifth anniversary, the USIA director invited Vice President Johnson, as head of the Space Council, to prepare an article for an August 1963 media packet. Johnson obliged, congratulating the space agency for putting 145 payloads into space compared to the Soviets' 43. The vice president emphasized the government's commitment to space exploration for peaceful purposes by lauding the value of American weather and communication satellites, while

Advocates for a Test Ban

pointing out that Soviet satellites did not provide any direct services for the people of the Socialist Republics.[81]

Until the abrupt termination to the Kennedy administration, the USIA's information campaign to counter perceptions of Soviet technological superiority had achieved mixed results. Nonetheless, the agency helped to gain international respect for U.S. security policies through programs explaining the value of a nuclear test ban treaty, thereby making it increasingly difficult for communist propagandists to label the United States as an irresponsible nuclear power. The USIA would not have proved as effective in this pursuit had Murrow not personally invested so much time in persuading Kennedy to resist the temptation of matching the Soviets test for test.

Beyond its public diplomacy value, Murrow understood that the country's nuclear strategy would be the most consequential aspect of its Cold War policy. As a longtime advocate for disarmament, he championed restraint in responding to Khrushchev's saber rattling and advocated that Americans and their allies trust in existing U.S. defense capabilities. When Kennedy deferred to hawkish advisers and resumed nuclear testing, Murrow dutifully fell into line to defend the president's decisions. Nonetheless, while public affairs officers engaged library visitors, and VOA broadcasters commented on U.S. policy, Murrow continued to offer Kennedy legitimate reasons to halt testing and pursue a ban. Ultimately, the president achieved his goal, and throughout the grueling process of securing a treaty banning further nuclear testing, the USIA provided a compelling narrative that helped the rest of the world to delineate between Soviet rhetoric and Soviet recklessness.

8

Birmingham, the Story Heard 'Round the World

We cannot do good propaganda unless we have
something good on which to base it.
—ELEANOR ROOSEVELT, May 26, 1961

As dusk settled over Montgomery, Alabama, on Sunday, May 21, 1961, a rowdy group of white supremacists, clenching rocks and Molotov cocktails, surrounded the city's First Baptist Church (Colored). Hollering racial obscenities, their voices rose quickly over those singing hymns inside the house of worship. Assembled within the sanctuary were a group of "Freedom Riders," sponsored by the Congress of Racial Equality (CORE), who had paused on their bus ride through the South to meet with the Reverend Martin Luther King Jr. and nearly a thousand members of his congregation.[1] Although window glass shattered across the floor and smoke thickened the air, the beleaguered occupants did not dare risk fleeing from the protection of the church's brick walls. Outside, a small band of overwhelmed federal marshals waited anxiously for the arrival of an Alabama National Guard battalion, and they struggled until the following morning to disperse the crowd. Montgomery police commissioner L. B. Sullivan remained indignant and disparaged the marshals' arrival to a television reporter: "We did not invite them here. We have no intention of turning our city over to them."[2]

Four days later, in his first public address as director of the U.S. Information Agency, Murrow drew attention to the detrimental impact of domestic racism on the country's ability to champion freedom and democracy internationally. Speaking at the National Press Club in Washington DC, to a group that until January he would have referred to simply as colleagues, Murrow warned all Americans against dismissing foreign media coverage of anti–civil rights activities as exaggerated communist propaganda. "To some of us the picture of a burning bus in Alabama may merely represent the speed and competence of a photographer," he explained, "but to those of us in the U.S. Information Agency it means that picture will be front-paged tomorrow all the way from Manila to Rabat." Turning next to a more local issue, Murrow reminded the Washingtonians about the pervasive discrimination faced by African diplomats in the city. "It is bad enough that they read headlines of . . . bus burnings and beatings," he suggested, but "it is even worse that they find it near impossible to live in the capital of our nation." Murrow closed his speech by provoking further national discourse: "This is not something the Communists did to us. We do it ourselves. . . . Is it possible that we concern ourselves too much with outer space and far places, and too little with inner space and near places?"[3]

The national media carried this debate into its headlines and editorials the following week. A reporter for the *Des Moines Register* opined, "Americans must realize that they are in as much danger of losing the cold war in Alabama (or Iowa) as in the Congo or Laos."[4] The British embassy considered Murrow's speech "admirable" and cabled select quotes to the Foreign Office.[5] Increasingly in the early 1960s, Americans began to understand that domestic policy and foreign policy could not be as neatly isolated from one another as the policymakers and legislators—who favored maintaining the racial status quo—were arguing. Fifteen years earlier, with the advent of the Cold War, President Harry Truman recognized the hollowness of "Leader of the Free World" platitudes, if his administration did not confront civil rights at home, and he referred to racism as "America's Achilles' heel."[6] However, neither Truman nor Eisenhower actively sought to pursue the reforms desired by civil rights leaders. Their only deliberate responses stemmed from the explosion of the most scandalous events that demanded some sort of executive action to ameliorate.[7]

Communist propagandists sought to discredit America's self-proclaimed title as the leader of the free world by emphasizing its racial inequality and legalized forms of segregation. As the divide between East and West widened in Europe, and emerging Third World nations contrasted the benefits of capitalism against communism, civil rights became a favored topic for communists to exploit, since they "could shine a glaring spotlight on their chief adversary and, with little effort, point out U.S. hypocrisy for the world to see."[8] Most acutely in the early 1960s, the postcolonial spasm of national liberation movements in the Global South concerned President John F. Kennedy gravely. By 1961 the African continent had begun to transform rapidly into a collage of nation-states. Independence did not guarantee that emerging African nations would join the anticommunist bloc, and failure to promote tolerance at home threatened to turn emerging African states away from aligning with the West in the Cold War.

Although several nascent countries claimed a position of nonalignment, many analysts at the CIA and State Department remained convinced that if the United States failed to support and nurture newly independent states, then surely the Soviets or Chinese would establish communist governments there. If the U.S. government did not foster relationships with these states, Secretary of State Dean Rusk anticipated that Moscow would "make the most of its opportunity to develop divisions within the free world and to be the champion of the colored races—the same old game."[9] Kennedy sought to prevent the formation of "new centers of Cold War" in postcolonial Africa through U.S. outreach.[10] He supported African nationalism and voiced frustration when he felt that the U.S. Agency for International Development or State Department bureaucracy moved too lethargically to assist fledgling governments. The president extended personal gestures, including inviting African heads of state up to the White House residence following official functions to meet Jackie and his children.[11]

In *Cold War Civil Rights: Race and the Image of American Democracy*, Mary Dudziak argues that U.S. civil rights reform occurred for a myriad of reasons, but during the Cold War, a desire to lend credence to platitudes about racial tolerance and an inclusive democracy at home instigated the movement's advancement. By focusing on the civil rights events that captivated international audiences during this era, she illuminates how many federal reforms occurred as components of the government's Cold War strategy. Dudziak affirms that although Kennedy developed a civil rights agenda, "its priorities were not always the priorities of the movement."[12] The dramatic actions taken by civil rights activists and the heinous counteractions of their opponents generated global headlines and commentary that forced the Kennedy administration and, to a lesser extent, Congress to confront institutional racism as a moral injustice.

Between 1961 and 1963, policymakers could not escape the dominating issue of race in public diplomacy. During an office call in Dakar on April 5, 1961, the Senegalese prime minister warned Vice President Lyndon Johnson that racial discrimination in the United States was a "black spot" on America's image.[13] Nevertheless, Kennedy resisted pressuring Congress to pass civil rights legislation for the first two years of his presidency. In *The Cold War and the Color Line: American Race Relations in the Global Arena*, Thomas Borstelmann labels John and Robert Kennedy as "cool-headed pragmatists," who remained wary of the moral idealism of many of their liberal friends in the Democratic Party.[14] During his presidential campaign, Kennedy neither inspired nor gained the confidence of many African American civil rights leaders. Speaking at a National Association for the Advancement of Colored People (NAACP) rally during the primaries on July 10, 1960, Kennedy received boos at the beginning of his speech.[15] His brother convened a meeting of Democratic delegates the following day, providing them with a characteristically direct order on how to respond to inquiries about his older sibling's position:

> Now I want to say a few words about civil rights. We have the best civil rights plank the Democratic party ever had. . . . Those of you who are dealing with southern delegations, make it absolutely clear how we stand on civil rights. Don't fuzz it up. Tell the southern states that we hope they will see other reasons why we are united as Democrats and why they should support Kennedy.[16]

Berl Bernhard served as staff director of the U.S. Commission on Civil Rights from 1958 to 1963, and after spending two years with the Eisenhower administration, he expected Kennedy to move decisively to address African American concerns. However, he grew disheartened even before Inauguration Day. Bernhard described talks between Kennedy's transition team and his office as "informal and very fleeting," and the White House did not contact the commission again until late March 1961. Presidential adviser Theodore Sorensen explained to Bernhard that the legislative climate was not right to bring civil rights to Capitol Hill, but the president intended to leverage the Justice Department to address issues such as housing and federal employment.[17] After Kennedy announced that his brother would serve as the attorney general, Martin Luther King Jr. told associates, "As the head of Justice, he's our No. 1 target for all things we will have to do in our quest for freedom in this country."[18]

Harris Wofford, special assistant to the president for civil rights from 1961 to 1962, believed that Kennedy did not seriously attempt to address civil rights injustice until the violence of 1963 "brought the matter to a head so forcefully that he could not put it aside."[19] Prior to that, on occasions where Kennedy advocated for ending discrimination, Wofford remained critical, arguing that the president delivered public pronouncements or issued executive orders in response to specific embarrassing occurrences in the South, rather than charting a long-term strategy for fundamental change to social and political mentalities. Even outsiders, such as the British consul general in New Orleans, argued that reform depended upon the commitment of the nation's chief executive.[20]

Two of Kennedy's greatest champions, Arthur M. Schlesinger Jr. and Ted Sorensen, conceded that the president considered civil rights a political issue rather than a moral one until witnessing the 1963 brutality in Birmingham. However, they also defended Kennedy's record by arguing that he stood little chance of convincing a majority in Congress to support such legislation. Having observed the failure of a civil rights bill to pass the Senate in 1957, Kennedy "had read the arithmetic" in Congress and decided to rely on executive orders as the only viable alternative to doing nothing at all.[21] Kennedy defended his conservative policy agenda during the first two years of his administration by reminding his liberal critics that he did not receive a mandate in 1960 to pursue an aggressive social agenda, as evidenced by the House of Representative's rejection of his bills to introduce public health insurance and create an Urban Affairs Department.[22]

While Kennedy utilized his executive power selectively to address aspects of American racism, Murrow faced the challenge of explaining the civil rights movement to the world. Despite the important relationship between public diplomacy and Cold War foreign policy, studies on Murrow, Kennedy, and the civil rights movement have largely overlooked the USIA's role. Dudziak's *Cold War Civil Rights* never mentions Murrow in the chapter on Kennedy, and Borstelmann does not examine the contributions of the USIA in *The Cold War and the Color Line*. Nevertheless, accepting Dudziak and Borstelmann's arguments about the centrality of Cold War pressures on propelling domestic civil rights reform invites a more critical examination of how Murrow's contributions to the formation of American public diplomacy shaped world opinion of Kennedy's civil rights record.

Murrow personally believed in ending segregation, making his opinion very clear to the American public and presidents well before joining the Kennedy administration. One of his earliest demonstrations in support of racial tolerance occurred in December 1930 when, as the president of the National Student Federation of America, he organized a desegregated conference for college students in Atlanta, Georgia. Murrow convinced white delegates to allow black delegates to join them at the Biltmore Hotel by warning them that to do otherwise would tarnish the name of their organization in the *New York Times*. Since hotel policy prohibited serving African Americans in the dining room, white students passed the plates served to them, by African American waiters, to their black colleagues.[23]

In his May 18, 1954, television broadcast on CBS, Murrow lauded the Supreme Court ruling in *Brown v. Board of Education*. Not only did he call the decision an example of African Americans gaining equal rights as citizens, albeit slowly, but he placed it into the perspective of the Cold War: "Students of world opinion can testify that this decision will add power to the United States' influence in the world. . . .

The ethical pieces in the armor of American defense aren't comparable with the other pieces, but they are no less essential, and they may be even more important."[24] During the 1957 Central High School standoff, Murrow reported live from Little Rock and explained to his national audience how Arkansas governor Orval Faubus's refusal to integrate students cost the United States "dearly in world prestige." In a moment when U.S. officials outspokenly criticized the Soviet subjugation of Hungarians, following the 1956 uprising in Budapest, "Communists could not have asked for more timely and effective anti-American propaganda than our own dispatches about Governor Faubus." Murrow proposed that the creation and enforcement of a meaningful civil rights act would "do us more good abroad perhaps than any measure since the Marshall Plan."[25]

A few weeks prior to joining the Kennedy administration, Murrow visited Birmingham in January 1961 to evaluate the severity of Southern segregation and participate in a discussion with the Birmingham Council. Rev. C. Herbert Oliver of the council lauded Murrow's address to the organization, which had "stirred up the dregs of many hardened consciences." Oliver wrote to Murrow to thank him for his appearance: "Our appeals so often go unheard, but somehow your coming brought to the forefront that fear of the light which haunts creatures of darkness."[26]

As a political realist, Murrow understood that American public opinion, reflected by the intransigence of Congress and Southern governors, would not support an abrupt termination to the legal and cultural obstacles faced by African Americans in 1961. Casey Murrow does not recall his father being overly critical of the president for the pace of his civil rights reform because Murrow recognized that Kennedy "couldn't do everything at once," given the political climate in America at the time.[27] As USIA director, Murrow provided message guidance to his media divisions to report, analyze, and explain domestic violence, grassroots demonstrations, and the legal efforts made by those involved in the civil rights movement. This information campaign provided a more honest portrayal of American challenges to a foreign audience too sophisticated to accept platitudes that whitewashed the plight of African Americans.

From 1946 through 1960, the U.S. government explained the slow pace of civil rights reform as reflecting a "natural" American process that should not be rushed or condemned: "Democratic change, however slow and gradual, was superior to dictatorial imposition."[28] Early USIA publications wrote starkly about slavery, not to shock foreign readers about how such an evil institution once thrived in the United States, but to indicate the country's progress. As a seasoned journalist, Murrow understood how this approach had failed to foster credibility, especially with audiences in Africa. Not everyone in Washington agreed. Just as Murrow witnessed apathy, if not downright contempt, from Congress when it came to increasing his agency's appropriations, the Democratic Congress did not support robust civil rights legislation and worried that the USIA's focus on the topic diminished America's image further.

Due to the absence of a coherent civil rights platform, it did not take Kennedy long to complain that administration officials were "flying off in several directions" with respect to explaining his position.[29] Still, his tepid leadership on the matter did little to synchronize the administration's approach. During a cabinet meeting on February 16, 1961, the president tasked department secretaries to conduct surveys to see how many minorities they employed so that the administration could consider giving blacks more opportunities for career advancement.[30] The vice president recommended sending African American diplomats to Africa early in their diplomatic careers. The State Department needed more black Foreign Service officers, and Johnson called for an end to the "'Jim Crow' consular service situation."[31] By addressing equal employment opportunities within the federal government, the president hoped to set a standard for the private sector.

The USIA could not rely on incremental, equal employment opportunities within the federal government to persuade Africans to ally with the United States. Murrow encouraged USIA broadcasters and public affairs officers to discuss the challenges central to the civil rights debate in their international discourse. In a February 1961 *Redbook* magazine interview, Murrow argued that enhancing national security required a frank discussion about unpleasant issues, to include racism.[32] He made film production a priority given the medium's accessibility in the developing world. In his first month on the job, the director instructed the Motion Picture Service to produce documentaries on the lives of typical African Americans, after discovering that the USIA had not produced such films prior to his arrival.[33] In June 1961, Murrow told the film division to produce a documentary on the work of the Civil Rights Commission, a bipartisan congressional organization.[34] When providing films or magazines to African countries, the agency debated what the ratio should be for pictures depicting African Americans versus whites. Murrow objected to a ratio, and, like his reluctance for seeking to quantify the success of USIA programs, he preferred a more amorphous equation. Speaking before the House Subcommittee on African Affairs, Murrow stated, "The answer plainly lies not in numbers or formulae but in an attitude and an impression. The attitude must be one of awareness of a need to reflect the role of Negroes in American life. The impression must be that we accomplish a success in sincerity in reflecting that attitude."[35]

In August 1961, Murrow approved production for a second documentary focused on African Americans, titled *The Negro American—A Progress Report*. In lieu of celebrating enormously successful African Americans, Murrow wanted to depict average citizens and avoid mentioning hot spots in the civil rights movement. He believed the removal of references or images from Little Rock or Birmingham would present an "exciting picture but . . . a more or less calm presentation of the facts as they exist regarding the progress of the American Negro."[36] Murrow did not wish to fuel policy fires that Kennedy sought to avoid, but he believed that the USIA could provide a balanced approach to engaging global audiences on the high-profile issue. He continued to value the jazz ambassadors and cultural performances that enjoyed tremendous success during the 1950s, and he reminded the president that only the United States could claim to "export its underprivileged" to celebrate its national culture.[37]

Murrow made effective use of his national celebrity status by using his domestic speaking engagements to explain the consequences of not improving the situation. Addressing the Missouri State Legislature on May 1, 1961, Murrow cited a principal cause for the U.S. government's inability to deter some nations from adopting communism, despite earnest efforts to inform them about the advantages of American capitalism and democracy. "We cannot successfully extol the virtues of the American way of life abroad," Murrow stated, "when we cannot provide and insure it for several million Americans living in this land." He pointed to the contradiction between meeting diplomatically with African leaders as peers and treating African Americans as second-class citizens.[38] The USIA could parade space capsules around the world without convincing a single foreigner of the practical advantages of the American lifestyle. Murrow encouraged a national debate and grassroots demonstrations as coveted aspects of a free society, and he defended the USIA's examination of such activities publicly.

A complementary threat to the USIA's credibility emerged with the flagrant discrimination against African diplomats assigned to Washington DC.[39] An alarmed Murrow warned that a refusal to rent a house to diplomats or permit them to use highway rest stops between Washington and New York City could "lose us as much influence as anything the Soviets might do."[40] He explained in his speech at the National Press Club on May 24, 1961, how the behavior of average Americans contradicted the messages of American diplomats in Africa: "We would have them join our company of honorable men in defending against encroachment of our dedication to dignity and freedom. But it is a dignity to which we will not fully admit them."[41]

Murrow raised the issue of discrimination against African diplomats while appearing on Eleanor Roosevelt's television program, *Prospects of Mankind*, on May 26, 1961. Without reform at home, he argued before a national audience, "we are not going to be able to convince people abroad that we in this country are by example doing what we are urging them to do." Murrow rejected the suggestion made by another guest that racial discussions by the USIA hurt the United States. He insisted that telling the truth caused less damage than obfuscating the critical domestic issue in his agency's news and commentaries. The former First Lady agreed in her closing remarks to the program: "Out of this comes to me a great sense of responsibility for the individual. We cannot do good propaganda unless we have something good on which to base it."[42]

Examples abound of the discrimination experienced by representatives of the developing world. Habib Bourguiba, the Algerian ambassador to the United States, speculated that 80 percent of the African diplomats started wearing their national dress in lieu of business suits as "a kind of little protection" against the discrimination they encountered in Washington and New York.[43] When the Nigerian second secretary ordered breakfast in a DC restaurant, the waitress handed him a paper bag and instructed him to eat elsewhere. Drawing attention to the issue, Undersecretary of State Chester Bowles cited the *Lagos Daily Times* coverage of the incident: "By this disgraceful act of racial discrimination, the U.S. forfeits its claim to world leadership."[44] A *Life* reporter asked a waitress working at a Washington diner why she had refused to serve the Chad ambassador. She responded frankly: "He looked like just an ordinary run of the mill nigger to me. I couldn't tell he was an ambassador."[45] Some African diplomats classified Washington as a "hardship post," as if they had received orders for the capital of a war-torn country, and family members began to return home to escape the harassment.[46] The administration established the Special Protocol Service Section within the Department of State Chief of Protocol's office to assist African diplomats in finding suitable housing and embassy sites, while Ambassador Adlai Stevenson worked quietly to persuade Manhattan landlords to rent to the influx of African diplomats arriving at the United Nations.[47]

An *American Evening Sunday* editorial labeled the treatment of African diplomats as an "astonishing display of national childishness," and called upon Southern congressional representatives to look beyond their provincial racism and make the federal capital a more hospitable city.[48] Another editorial argued that treating African diplomats differently from African Americans would not improve America's reputation, but reinforce the hypocrisy instead. The author observed that diplomats could not wander around Washington wearing an "I'm a foreigner" sign, and that the only practical solution would be popular support for civil rights.[49]

Surprisingly, some of Kennedy's ambassadors to African countries did not appreciate the sensitivity of the issue about how white Americans treated blacks. Two newly appointed ambassadors arrived at the

White House prior to their departure for Africa wearing a "slave brace-let" inspired by Nigerian slave traders who laced together ornamen-tal Portuguese coins as jewelry. An exasperated president instructed Rusk "to send out a memo to everyone in the Foreign Service that not one of them can wear a slave bracelet anymore."[50] Even for the 1960s, it seems incredible that the president of the United States needed to point out the offensive nature of their accoutrements to his emissar-ies to the African continent.

International media coverage of the Washington embarrassment challenged the credibility of USIA personnel serving in Africa. Fol-lowing a lecture to a group of African students about opportunities in America, one audience member told the USIA-sponsored professor that he missed the larger point: "It is more important to us that one of our diplomats was refused service in a Virginia restaurant than any of this talk."[51] Murrow appreciated the damning effect of racial vio-lence on his agency's programming. Worldwide headlines presenting a "stark picture" of Freedom Riders being jailed and assaults against African Americans frustrated the efforts of public affairs officers to place stories within their proper context.[52] Even when USIA media personnel attempted to highlight national objections to local inci-dents of violence, the shocking photos that preceded the headlines eclipsed the details of the story. USIA researchers found that Soviet and Chinese broadcasts directed to the Third World devoted consid-erable time to editorials on America's "rampant racism."[53]

Beyond the Cold War urgency for correcting the racial divide in the United States, Murrow made it clear that he hoped to see improve-ments for moral reasons. He explained his stance to the House Edu-cation and Labor Committee: "I think it would be a mistake to base our action against discrimination mainly on the ground that our image abroad is being hurt. We should attack this problem because it is right that we do so. To do otherwise, whatever the overseas reac-tion might be, would violate the very essence of what our country stands for."[54] On October 20, 1961, Murrow assisted Jewish American writer Harry Golden in drafting the "Kennedy Declaration," a proc-lamation of the president's commitment to making the U.S. Consti-tution accessible to all American citizens. The authors intended to reach an international audience with the document as well, by calling for patience abroad until Americans committed themselves to the cause. The narrative captured the central theme adopted by the USIA: "Neither the President nor any of his cabinet members nor any Federal official can change the hearts of men. The individual alone, abetted by his belief in God, can change his heart. But the President and his cabinet and the officers of government can say, 'Obey the law.'"[55] Kennedy approved the declaration for worldwide distribution by his information agency.[56]

Murrow released an internal USIA memorandum in November 1961 detailing a new strategy for developing civil rights messages. He believed that the agency could apply tactics from his sparring with Senator Joseph McCarthy in 1954. This entailed speaking directly to the criticism raised by the opposition without name-calling or becoming defensive. Murrow recommended that Kennedy conduct a series of television talks akin to President Franklin D. Roosevelt's Fireside Chats, since the public responded positively to Kennedy. The USIA would amplify Kennedy's message by distributing newsreels and translated transcripts of the address. The memo encouraged cabinet members to reiterate Kennedy's messages in their own addresses: "Frequent backgrounders should be given by top officials who can offer intelligent evaluations of world events." The memo also advised public affairs officers not to regard their host-nation media as an adversary but as an enabler to spreading the message.[57]

Assessing the efficacy of the USIA's approach to discussing civil rights in December 1961, Murrow acknowledged that most accomplishments remained intangible. Nonetheless, he lauded the agency for working more seamlessly as a single unit, which he likened to a "wrist" for the fingers represented by the five media departments.[58] In January 1962, Murrow embarked on a three-week tour of Africa so that he could see for himself how country programs contributed toward advancing the government's political and psychological objectives. The assistant director for Africa released Murrow's travel plan to public affairs officers in African embassies, reminding them that Murrow disliked pomp and ceremonies, preferring instead to concentrate on understanding field operations. Of the nine countries he visited, he devoted five days to Nigeria, which he considered a "key" country in the region.[59] He returned from his tour energized by the work he witnessed his officers performing and the dynamism of the indigenous people, referring to Africa as a "continent marked by new-born countries wrapped in the swaddling clothes of enthusiasm." When the USIA opened libraries in newly independent countries, the ribbon-cutting ceremony often became an affair of state, with cabinet ministers in attendance.[60]

Returning to Washington, Murrow spoke to the Lincoln Group at a celebration for the hundredth anniversary of the Emancipation Proclamation on February 10, 1962. He connected the Civil War to the contemporary civil rights movement: "Underlying the issues of slavery was a relationship of status between black and white. The nation one century later is still engrossed in realigning that relationship."[61] A month later, Murrow directed the distribution of copies of the five-volume report recently published by the U.S. Commission on Civil Rights to every USIA library. He also enlisted the help of African American celebrities to visit African countries to speak with common people and the press. Poet Langston Hughes accepted Murrow's offer in the summer of 1962, cutting the ribbon at the new USIA library in Accra, Ghana.[62]

Kennedy recognized the challenge faced by the USIA in finding the elusive balance between presenting dark truths and optimistic ideology. During an address to Voice of America employees celebrating the twentieth anniversary of their broadcast service on February 26, 1962, the president charged the agency to present credible information:

> This is an extremely difficult and sensitive task. On the one hand as an arm of the government and therefore an arm of the nation . . . it is its task to bring our story around the world in its most favorable light. But on the other hand, as part of the cause of freedom, and the arm of freedom, we are obliged to tell our story in a truthful way, to tell it, as Oliver Cromwell said about his portrait, "Paint us with all our blemishes and warts, all those things about us that may not be so immediately attractive."[63]

Despite Murrow's fervent efforts to draw domestic attention to civil rights and reframe USIA messages, African Americans remained frustrated with the pace of change. The administration focused on other policy priorities, often overseas, such as Southeast Asia, Cuba, and the resumption of Soviet nuclear testing. Assessing American civil rights progress a year into the Kennedy presidency, Ambassador David Ormsby-Gore informed the British Foreign Ministry that Kennedy had made "steady if unspectacular progress." He did credit the president with responding to hate crimes and discouraging extremism from either side of the civil rights movement.[64] Still, the administration's record remained spotty, and federal suits and judicial actions to force compliance did not address the most elementary forms of discrimination. Southern leaders continued to ignore Supreme Court rulings. For example, although the Supreme Court declared the 1956 Louisiana state law prohibiting white and black college students from playing on the same sports team to be unconstitutional in 1958, the state school system continued to segregate teams in 1962.[65]

In October 1962, civil rights returned to the foreground of the Cold War, when Kennedy was confronted with the first major race riots of his presidency. On October 1, international interest in the American South spiked over riots in Oxford, Mississippi, after segregationists tried to prevent air force veteran James Meredith from enrolling in "Ole Miss," the University of Mississippi. Governor Ross Barnett asked Robert Kennedy why he would not persuade Meredith to attend another university. In some twisted logic, Barnett offered to provide Meredith with a state-sponsored fellowship to any university *outside* of Mississippi.[66] The violence injured 166 federal marshals and led to the death of a British reporter from London's *Daily Telegraph*. For the first time in his presidency, Kennedy followed Eisenhower's precedent from Little Rock and deployed five thousand soldiers to restore order.[67]

The USIA's senior leaders worked deliberately to shape the public diplomacy response to this high-profile incident. Murrow invited NAACP and CORE leaders and Robert Kennedy to speak on Voice of America about the federal response. The attorney general tried to explain the limits of federal authority: "What the world saw in Mississippi was a democratic nation putting its house in order. It was proof

Birmingham

of our intent to live not by rule of men but by rule of law."[68] USIA deputy director Donald Wilson directed overseas posts to report back to Washington on the steps they had taken to put the James Meredith incident into perspective.[69] The Usumbura, Burundi, outpost cabled about its publication of several positive stories about African American activities that occurred that same week, including the Negro Poet Festival and an African-sponsored charity in New York.[70] Wilson must have recognized immediately, however, that these human-interest pieces would never detract interest away from Ole Miss.

Once the president intervened to enforce Meredith's enrollment, foreign media coverage of the violence precipitously diminished. According to the USIA's research department, those surveyed in Africa, South Asia, and the Middle East hailed the president's decision to use troops. While media coverage may have ended, the USIA's year-and-a-half-long effort to provide an upbeat view of civil rights progress since Kennedy's inauguration lost momentum. Public opinion polls conducted by the USIA in Africa found that the majority of people believed that education and not laws or punishment would eradicate racism. Citizens in communist and allied countries alike ranked racial prejudice as the "chief blemish on the image of the American people." Buried in the report, USIA analysts identified an international media trend that would continue to resurface with each major confrontation between a Southern state and the federal government: "Despite the factual nature of news coverage based primarily on Western wire services, the vivid portrayal in news reports and wire photos of the more sensational aspects of the incident—such as the rioting and bloodshed—may well have left a more lasting impression on the less palatable aspects of the racial situation in the U.S."[71]

In its own coverage of the Ole Miss standoff, the USIA did not ignore the casualty numbers but concentrated on explaining the federal response to one state's intransigence. Speaking to an audience in North Carolina, Murrow defended the necessity for his agency to draw attention to the violence, in part to place the story within the proper context that the foreign press often sensationalized. In its own broadcasts, Voice of America had the capacity "to show the positive virtues of a bad vice, to indicate that its very isolation highlights the progress this land is making."[72] The USIA attempted to clarify the separation of powers between state and federal governments. Compared to the centralized systems adopted by most new countries in Africa, the autonomy of American states seemed incomprehensible. Under Murrow's guidance, informational pamphlets and VOA broadcasts attempted to convince foreign audiences that the executive branch of the U.S. government worked as earnestly as it could within the limits of its power.

Undersecretary of State Bowles happened to be on an official visit to Africa during the Oxford violence. Assessing the deftness of USIA personnel whom he met, Bowles wrote, "By and large, our information efforts in Africa are being conducted with skill." The high quality of Foreign Service Officers assigned to missions and the "excellent impact" of the Peace Corps helped to refute Soviet and Chinese propaganda. However, Bowles worried that the bureaucratic red tape delaying the arrival of promised economic aid—much like in Latin America—threatened to mitigate the effects of public diplomacy. In some cases, a two- to three-year lag existed between the promise of aid and its arrival.[73]

In the aftermath of the Meredith incident, Kennedy was still not prepared to call for civil rights legislation. In 1962 Kennedy proposed thirty-one major pieces of legislation, none of which specifically addressed the issue.[74] In the absence of legislation, Murrow looked for tangible ways for the USIA to improve race relations. Within his own agency, Murrow sought to correct discrimination in hiring and promotion policies, and, by 1963, the USIA had doubled the number of blacks in its career civil service.[75] As the only federal agency to bring its foreign-national employees to the United States for training, the USIA created first-hand witnesses of life in America. Four times a year, fifteen foreign-national trainees arrived in Washington for two weeks of training, followed by six weeks of traveling across the country to become familiar with America's diverse cultures. Murrow encouraged Kennedy to meet with one of these groups of trainees so that he could articulate his philosophy on civil rights, but the White House staff said that the demands of the president's schedule would not permit it.[76]

The USIA looked for opportunities to contrast American racial difficulties with those experienced by the Soviets. Despite their claims of international unity with all communist societies, Bulgaria embarrassed the Eastern bloc in February 1963 when the preponderance of African students attending universities in Sophia departed due to "intolerable racial discrimination and abuse." Voice of America reporters interviewed dozens of the students and informed listeners across Africa about communist doublespeak.[77] However, the agency had to tread delicately so as not to appear hypocritical. One month earlier, an official U.S. government study recognized the poor treatment suffered by African students in the United States. Among the challenges to improving views of the United States in Africa, the *Eightieth Report of the U.S. Advisory Commission on Information* cited the reception, training, and hospitality of foreign students, which, the report revealed, left "much to be desired."[78] Voice of America's broadcasts about the disenchantment of Africans living behind the Iron Curtain did not impress African students in Europe. In a survey conducted by the USIA of 298 African students studying in West Germany, 61 percent rated U.S. race relations as poor or very poor, while only one in ten criticized the treatment of minorities in the Soviet Union.[79]

In early 1963, the USIA showcased the life of average African Americans through the distribution of a pamphlet titled *Success Stories from America*, which heralded the lives of individual blacks who would not typically gain notoriety in the press. Its pages examined a few of the nineteen million African Americans whose families were, allegedly, fully integrated into U.S. society. The agency continued to distribute movies and documentaries to Africa aimed at illiterate and educated audiences alike. Murrow told the House Subcommittee on African Affairs on March 5, 1963, that the USIA had produced eight documentaries on African Americans and anticipated jumping to twenty-two the following year.[80] Defending his focus on the topic, Murrow told skeptical congressional representatives: "To be persuasive we must be believable; to be believable we must be credible; to be credible we must be truthful."[81] Persuasiveness would come from explaining racism within the larger context of American life. Two months later, the greatest incident of racial violence during Kennedy's presidency exploded onto the headlines of the international press, threatening the very credibility that Murrow's USIA sought to achieve.

On May 3, 1963, more than three thousand African Americans, including nearly a thousand children and teenagers, organized a civil rights march through Birmingham, Alabama. Police chief Theophilus "Bull" Connor ordered his officers to disperse the peaceful crowd through intimidation and assault. Riveting photographs of police dogs snarling at children and fire hoses pummeling teenagers appeared on the covers of international newspapers and communist propaganda. The most poignant element of the coverage stemmed from a new media: live television coverage. Historian James Patterson credits this unique factor as the reason for Birmingham becoming the "pivotal" point in the civil rights movement at home and abroad.[82] A wave of protests across the United States followed the violence in Birmingham, reflecting African American discontent beyond the South. The Justice Department tallied forty-three demonstrations in fifteen states, including sizeable protests in Chicago and Philadelphia. An NAACP spokesperson announced that Los Angeles would be the next "target of a Birmingham style campaign."[83]

Observing the coverage for themselves, elites in many decolonized African states reexamined the promises of the American system over that of the communists. With images from Birmingham fresh in their minds, the heads of state from members of the Organization of African Unity met in Addis Ababa, Ethiopia, on May 22 to debate affiliating with the Non-Aligned Movement.[84] It is unlikely that any form of U.S. public diplomacy would have provided an effective countermeasure for these nascent African states that continued to question the wisdom of integrating into Western economic and security alliances.

The State Department's Bureau of Intelligence and Research reported that Soviet broadcasting related to the Birmingham civil rights violence multiplied seven-fold compared to the Ole Miss standoff, nine times greater than the Freedom Riders' ordeal in May 1961, and eleven times greater than the Little Rock crisis of 1957. Soviet propaganda centered on four points: racism is an inevitable part of the capitalist system; the lethargy of the U.S. federal government to respond to segregation indicated national support for the status quo; it is hypocritical of the United States to call itself the leader of the free world; and the treatment of domestic minorities is indicative of what Americans think of Asians, Africans, and Latin Americans in their native lands. Curiously, the report noted that while wildly exaggerated stories appeared in communist Third World newspapers and radio programs, the tone of domestic Soviet editorials remained surprisingly tame. USIA analysts found that *Pravda* presented facts from Birmingham selectively and made no mention of differences between state and federal governments. The analysts hypothesized that rising tensions within the Soviet bloc about the treatment of their own ethnic minorities in 1963 may have led to this somewhat gentler treatment.[85]

Regardless of the underlying motive, Soviet exploitation of American racial prejudices in its own propaganda ensured that the subject remained a major consideration in Cold War foreign policy. For some U.S. policymakers, their inability to control the media eventually caused them to support civil rights reform. Indeed, the extensive international coverage of the Birmingham violence necessitated a more decisive response from Kennedy. Domestically, the visceral nationwide reaction jarred the administration, whose senior officials could no longer point to the efforts of the Justice Department as sufficient for advancing civil rights. One African American leader in the movement, invited by Robert Kennedy to his New York City apartment, lambasted the attorney general: "If this is the best you can do, the best is not enough. The record of the Justice Department is totally inadequate."[86]

Kennedy recognized that he needed to pursue a new direction with his civil rights policy after Birmingham. More importantly, he now understood the need to declare racism a moral blight and introduce legislation to end institutional forms of segregation. The president dispatched key members of his cabinet to lay the groundwork for his own national speech on civil rights. Speaking before representatives from a variety of nongovernmental organizations on May 27, Rusk likened the challenge of countering communism abroad while racial problems simmered at home to running a race "with one of our legs in a cast." He explained: "Our voice is muted, our friends are embarrassed, our enemies are gleeful because we have not really put our hands fully and effectively to this problem at every level of our life, beginning with the local community." Murrow appeared on the CBS talk show *Washington Report* to call racism "the real handicap" confronting the USIA's overseas mission. Standing at Gettysburg cemetery on Memorial Day, the administration's senior Southerner, Vice President Johnson, delivered a national plea to end segregation: "One hundred years ago the slave was freed. One hundred years later the Negro remains in bondage to the color of his skin. The Negro today asks for justice. We do not answer him, we do not answer those who lie beneath this soil, when we reply to the Negro by asking for patience."[87]

Kennedy tasked Ted Sorensen to draft a speech for him to deliver live on national television on June 11, where, for the first time, he called upon Congress and the American people to support civil rights legislation. The speech would also be directed toward an inquisitive international audience skeptical of Kennedy's resolve to correct the domestic scourge. Sorensen recounted the significance of Birmingham in his first memoir: "And President John Fitzgerald Kennedy, recognizing that the American conscience was at last beginning to stir, began laying his own plans for awakening that conscience of the need for further action."[88] The week prior to the historic address, the president flew to Hawaii to set the scene in one of the most ethnically diverse states in the union. From Honolulu, Kennedy stated that, when considering peaceful coexistence, "there is no place from where it is more appropriately said and understood than in this part of the United States here on this island."[89]

In his speech on June 11, Kennedy defined the advancement of civil rights as a moral issue, one "as old as the Scriptures and as clear as the American Constitution." The president reminded his fellow Americans of their engagement in a worldwide struggle to "promote and protect the rights of all who wish to be free." When he deployed troops to Berlin or Vietnam, he did not only send white soldiers. "It ought to be possible, therefore," he argued, "for American students of any color to attend any public institution they select without having to be backed up by troops." He wanted Americans to stop considering this as a sectional or partisan issue; African Americans faced discrimination in every city from San Francisco to New York. As in his inaugural address, Kennedy once again challenged Americans to do more for their country. On June 11 he specified one of their civic responsibilities: "A great change is at hand, and our task, our obligation, is to make that revolution, that change, peaceful and constructive for all. Those who do nothing are inviting shame as well as violence. Those who act boldly are recognizing rights as well as reality."[90]

The USIA set out deliberately to explain the president's new focus to the international community. Voice of America broadcast the address live worldwide, and USIA radio-teletyped it to 111 posts for distribution to local media outlets. The three regional printing plants, located in Mexico City, Manila, and Beirut, produced leaflets with translations of the speech for rapid distribution. USIA's Motion Pictures Service created a newsreel with speech excerpts that the agency transported by air to USIA libraries.[91] The State Department required U.S. embassies to assess reactions to the president's address, and ambassadors to African countries met with presidents and prime ministers to explain Kennedy's new policy agenda.[92] President Grégoire Kayibanda of Rwanda responded to a briefing from the American ambassador by suggesting that it would be "highly regrettable" if Kennedy continued to "play into the hands of anti-American propagandists especially Soviets and CHICOMS [Chinese communists]" by failing to terminate segregation.[93]

On June 14, Murrow reported to the president that the international press "almost unanimously" approved of his charge to the American Congress and people. The Nigerian *Morning Star* hailed Kennedy as the president who "will go down in history as one of the greatest champions of the rights of man that ever lived," and the Algerian *La Republique* anticipated that "it is certain that segregation will be vanquished finally." The USIA discovered that the peaceful resolution of the Cuban Missile Crisis in 1962 lent credibility to the president's June 11 speech. The Soviets paid little attention to Kennedy's national address about civil rights, but Moscow Radio continued to use Birmingham in its propaganda: "Many of the methods used by U.S. Fascists and racists resemble those of Hitler's time. . . . The fascist swastika can be seen more and more clearly against the background of the burning crosses of racism."[94]

On June 19, civil rights legislation appeared as a cabinet-meeting agenda item for the first time during the Kennedy administration, and the president tapped his brother to oversee the drafting of the legislation.[95] Kennedy wanted the bill to require all public establishments to serve people regardless of race, authorize the federal government to participate more aggressively in lawsuits to end school segregation, and offer greater protection for voters.

That afternoon, Kennedy dispatched Rusk to Capitol Hill to introduce the administration's plan to submit a civil rights act later that year. The unorthodox selection of the secretary of state to discuss domestic politics with senators indicates the broader Cold War implications of the bill. Rusk outlined the national security interests to the Senate committee: "In their efforts to enhance their influences among nonwhite peoples and to alienate them from us, the Communists clearly regard racial discrimination in the United States as one of their most valuable assets."[96] Murrow also spoke about the topic in Atlanta before an Advertisers Federation of America convention, insisting that the USIA explain U.S. policy to Africans in terms they would comprehend.[97] Kennedy told African American leaders that "this issue could cost me the election, but we're not turning back."[98]

The outreach of senior administration officials did not convince all Americans of the need for reform, and Congress would not pass the Civil Rights Act until 1964. Commenting on Rusk's speech about the risk racism posed to defeating communism, a pundit at Washington's *Evening Star* opined, "If there is some truth to this, we still remain unimpressed." The editorialist pointed to the "rampant injustices and tyrannies" that ravaged the same Asian and African states that Rusk argued were criticizing the United States. Until the Third World conducted its own housekeeping, the *Star* writer did not believe it had a stone to throw.[99] This simplistic rendering of international relations remained popular with many Americans who continued to believe that they maintained the finest society in the world, and the developing world would reject the empty promises of communism.

While the cabinet convened on June 19, the USIA's Research and

Reference Service released a report on the *Recent Worldwide Comment on the U.S. Racial Problem*. Polls identified Kennedy's June 11 address as decisively turning popular opinion in Africa in favor of the United States, instilling a belief in the administration's determination to address a moral issue. The researchers wrote, "The Administration has established firmly the impression that it is dedicated to achieving racial equality in the U.S." African media highlighted the president's "courage" and "firmness in the face of political risks." Some African journalists went so far as to compare Kennedy to Lincoln. However, analysts pointed to a "strong note of skepticism" indicating that if permanent corrections to segregation did not occur soon, the favorable views toward the administration would reverse. African reactions toward U.S. racial violence remained largely emotional and displayed little interest in or understanding of the legal questions and constitutional system. Engaged Africans did not care about statutory separations of power between the federal and state governments; they only cared about ameliorating the plight of their "dark brothers" in the United States.[100]

The USIA continued to come under scrutiny in the United States for explaining too much in the wake of Birmingham. Two weeks after the president's address, the *Utica Observer Dispatch* claimed that the "racial conflict had run away with the USIA" because it exposed too much in the documentary *The Negro American*. One agency official complained in a background interview with reporter James Canan, "We can't possibly begin to tell the story with one film. We can't even keep up with the story . . . if we leave out too much of it someone overseas is going to say we're slanting it."[101] Murrow reasserted to the *Philadelphia Enquirer* that the USIA did not obscure the ugliness of the situation in Birmingham, and he blamed Alabama officials for their lethargic response to Bull Connor's abuse of power.[102]

While demonstrating a willingness to be forthcoming in addressing major incidents of racial violence, Murrow did not encourage his agency to draw attention to every single act of racial violence. He wanted the USIA to discuss what other overseas sources discussed in their papers and programs. A limited "official use" memo, prepared by John Pauker from Tom Sorensen's plans and policy staff on July

26, 1963, described how Voice of America and other agency news sources would report these incidents: "Local disturbances which are not likely to be exploited abroad should not be reported. Our positive emphases are intended to keep the national goal in sight—even when other sources of information, however motivated in their reporting of developments, tend to obscure that goal." If too much attention focused on the violence—even if the USIA spent equal time describing the legal process—most foreign observers would be captivated by the vivid images of the physical abuse and ignore the "dull reading" of judicial actions. Murrow approved circulation of the memo, scrawling in longhand on his personal copy, "John Pauker—This is *very* good paper. ERM."[103]

Pauker's memo reveals how the USIA defined the impact of the civil rights movement and race relations on its ability to garner international support for U.S. foreign policy. The author cited three specific challenges: a "genuine misunderstanding" by foreigners of the complexities of American society; commercial media dwelling on "sensational developments" while overlooking the nonviolent, legal aspects of the movement; and "deliberate distortion by our enemies [to promote] an impression of pervasive injustice and intolerance in the United States." The USIA's emphasis on progress concerning racial issues would not "gloss over negative developments" but would counter or put into context the misinformation that skewed foreigners' views of the United States. In lieu of apologizing for incidents where state or local authorities frustrated the efforts of civil rights leaders, Pauker wanted the journalists to explain the protests, sit-ins, and demonstrations as "inevitable by-products" of a democratic society learning to become more tolerant and supportive of equal rights for all its citizens. To depict it as a broader social alliance, the agency needed to highlight the involvement of state legislatures, white activists, church groups, professional associations, and women's groups in the movement.[104]

The long-term strategy for the USIA, which Murrow first outlined in May 1961, heavily influenced Pauker's memo. The policy paper addressed the agency's perpetual challenge of balancing the truthful presentation of news events with the ideals of U.S. society in its propaganda. If Murrow had permitted his personnel to continue presenting information as they had during the 1950s, they would not have established the rapport with their international audience necessary to make their presentation of Kennedy's June 11 speech sound credible. In lieu of simply stating that racism is bad and not representative of the country at large, Murrow required his agency to acknowledge that tension existed in the United States and then detail the limitations of federal democracy to correct institutionalized segregation. When discrimination against African diplomats and the riots in Oxford, Mississippi, headlined international media, the various information arms of the USIA explained the steps taken by the Kennedy administration without exaggerating their effects. Subsequently, when the violence in Birmingham captivated international observers, the USIA's foreign audience continued listening to Voice of America and frequenting agency libraries, where they could discuss this topic with public affairs officers.

The domestic struggle continued, and the USIA stood ready to carry the dialogue overseas. On August 28, 1963, nearly two hundred thousand Americans participated in the March on Washington for Jobs and Freedom to express their solidarity for the civil rights movement and to call upon Congress to vote for Kennedy's legislation. The day culminated with Martin Luther King Jr. delivering his poetic "I Have a Dream" speech from the steps of the Lincoln Monument. The USIA distributed copies of King's press conference following the historic gathering on the National Mall with hopes that the newsreel would provide "exceptional value" in explaining the civil rights movement.[105] Murrow directed the Motion Picture Service to produce a documentary titled *The March*, which the USIA released in 1964.

The half-hour film opens with an introduction by Carl Rowan, the most senior-ranking African American in the Johnson administration, who succeeded Murrow as USIA director in January 1964. Rowan tells viewers that the march illustrated the "procedures unfettered men use to broaden the horizons of freedom and deepen the meaning of personal liberty." The documentary emphasizes the national unity behind the demonstration: a bus convoy from Los Angeles, Chicago teachers carrying placards calling for integrated schools, and volunteers in a New York warehouse making eighty thousand cheese sandwiches for lunch. Clips of organizers and participants conspicuously include white men, women, and children standing in solidarity with black citizens. Noticeably absent from the film is the voice of a narrator, who speaks sparingly at the beginning and end, allowing the sounds and voices of the march to convey the message to the USIA's audience. Viewers could not miss the spiritual undertones of the march either, with groups praying in churches before the march, demonstrators singing hymns throughout the film, and the sermonlike address delivered by King. Indeed, the documentary's presentation of the entire event remained upbeat, with its music, the smiles and fellowship of the marchers, and the absence of vitriolic rhetoric in the speeches.[106]

Tom Sorensen hailed *The March* as a "master propaganda stroke" that showed the world hundreds of thousands of citizens peaceably demonstrating for improved civil rights in their nation's capital.[107] However, Stanley Plesent, the USIA's general counsel, warned Murrow prior to the film's overseas distribution that many in Congress remained uncomfortable with the agency drawing attention to King, particularly in light of scandalous material possessed by the Federal Bureau of Investigation. Murrow tersely responded, "Tell 'em to go to hell."[108] He recognized the importance of screening the documentary in the developing world, just as he had wanted Americans to watch *Harvest of Shame* on CBS, on Thanksgiving Day, 1960.

Although not released until March 1964, two months after Murrow's resignation from the USIA, *The March* did not gain many supporters from within the administration. Wilson confided in Murrow that Robert Kennedy and Rusk felt that it did not provide a "balanced" picture of what had occurred in Washington. During a screening for the Senate Foreign Relations Committee, only Senator J. William Fulbright appeared "absolutely intrigued." Without Murrow available to convince the Johnson administration of its value, the USIA did not distribute it to all of its posts, but only those where the country team "digs it." Despite the lack of official endorsements, *The March* enjoyed a broad international reception and received honors from film festivals in the Netherlands, the Philippines, Australia, and at Cannes, France.[109]

In his retirement, Murrow told Wilson that he remained "unrepentant" about the importance of *The March* in explaining the civil rights movement. As for those demanding balance, Murrow argued that they knew "nothing about either balance or pictures." The debate reflected the continued trepidation of policymakers and legislators about how much truth to present in overseas information campaigns. Tom Sorensen told Murrow that one senator reiterated his belief that USIA documentaries should only represent "the good side of America." He objected to the overseas release of *The March* while, ironically, saying that he had no issue with the film being shown in the United States.[110]

Between July and November 1963, Murrow continued to make public appearances across the United States in his capacity as USIA director, where he raised awareness about the importance of civil rights. He recognized that regardless of the number of Hollywood films screened or space-travel exhibitions displayed overseas, audiences consistently returned to the topic of race relations when interacting with the USIA's public affairs officers. Speaking at a Federal Bar Association's convention on September 26, 1963, Murrow noted that Americans should not be surprised by the tremendous foreign interest in U.S. segregation. "While America's space sensations rise and fall in world attention," Murrow explained, "America's race relations seem to remain in the undiminished spotlight." The director lauded USIA employees for dynamically engaging the sensitive topic, but he believed that the country needed to correct its social ills for more reasons than to ease his agency's burden of advancing the administration's foreign policy. Just as he had confronted McCarthy and addressed the plight of migrant workers as a CBS journalist, Murrow, as USIA director, believed that America would be a better country for confronting its domestic ills: "The reason we attempt racial progress is not the opinion of people overseas. It is at base the conscience of ourselves here at home, the conscience of the deniers and the denied. We do this because we demand it of ourselves. We do it because it is right."[111]

Tom Sorensen argued that the USIA had given little thought to American racism until Murrow assumed the directorship. Murrow understood the correlation between the credibility of America's leadership in Africa and Asia and its treatment of African Americans at home. As assistant director for policy and plans, Sorensen enforced the director's three-pronged guidance for discussing civil rights: face the problem head on; report race relations in depth; and treat African Americans as equal participants in a multiethnic society, in lieu of constantly comparing them to freed slaves.[112] Murrow argued with Southern senators who objected to the USIA taking American racism head on in its informational programs by pointing out that people will be more receptive to positive information when they hear bad news from the same source. Near the end of his tenure, Murrow still considered race relations the "number one handicap" for trying to tell the American story overseas.[113]

Although racism remained too entrenched in American society for Murrow to modify through his domestic public engagements, his approach to conducting public diplomacy proved more genuine than his predecessor's. Critics may argue that Murrow should have resigned after witnessing Kennedy's disinterest in using the bully pulpit of the White House to push for civil rights legislation in 1961. However, Murrow did not sacrifice his liberal principles by continuing to serve at the USIA. As the country's most respected journalist before moving to Washington, he understood American opinion better than most career politicians in Kennedy's cabinet. As a political realist, Murrow understood that he could do more to help foster domestic debate and inform the global discussion of American civil rights from within the administration than by resigning in disgust. As Murrow reaffirmed after leaving office in 1964, "We cannot be effective in telling the American story abroad if we tell it only in superlatives."[114] Indeed, the public diplomacy provided by the USIA during the Kennedy administration helped to foster the transnational dialogue that enabled foreign pressures to influence domestic civil rights policy during the Cold War.

9

Counterinsurgency Propaganda in Southeast Asia

I am convinced that we cannot persuade the
world—particularly that large part of it which does not
get enough to eat—that defoliation "is good for you."
—EDWARD R. MURROW, August 16, 1962

After the failed Bay of Pigs invasion, three months into his administration, President John F. Kennedy grew more cautious in his approach to winning the Cold War, telling one of his closest advisers, "There will be no more disasters. I've got to be very careful about what I do; I have to appear very strong and very determined."[1] Indeed, Kennedy deserves credit for preventing the Berlin crisis from leading to direct conflict with the Soviet Union, for de-escalating the Cuban Missile Crisis, and for securing a nuclear test ban treaty. However, the president's response to these confrontations should not be confused with him resigning to the inevitability of world communist revolution. Evidence of Kennedy's steadfast commitment to preventing the expansion of communism can be found in his involvement in Southeast Asia where, between 1961 and 1963, the United States entrenched itself, despite the questionable behavior of the South Vietnamese government. As historian James Giglio noted, "Kennedy became a victim of his own rhetoric."[2] The lofty magniloquence of his inaugural address, his desire to counter Republican criticism that Democrats were "soft" on communism, his decision to increase defense appropriations by 15 percent, and the formation of the army's Special Warfare Center at Fort Bragg, North Carolina, may have actually limited Kennedy's options for responding to the growing popularity of communism in Southeast Asia.

Kennedy's interest in the region began with his concern for the independence of Laos where, after a military coup in August 1960, a fledgling regime claimed neutrality while struggling to subdue an indigenous communist insurgency, the Pathet Lao. Lao army captain Kong Le, who orchestrated the coup, did not see himself as a politician, and he asked Prince Souvanna Phouma to head the government. Souvanna stressed to U.S. ambassador Winthrop Brown his desire for Laos to remain neutral in the Cold War. If given autonomy and the respect of the international community, he promised that his government would remain anticommunist. The prince found little value in a military alliance offered by the United States because he feared that it would attract reprisals from his communist neighbors in China and Vietnam. Brown did not doubt Souvanna's commitment to neutrality, but he doubted that the prince would have the political clout to deter the communists from gaining headway within the kingdom.[3]

The day prior to his inauguration, Kennedy spent more time discussing Laos with outgoing President Dwight Eisenhower than any other issue.[4] War studies professor Lawrence Freedmen noted that Laos "was hardly of great strategic importance in itself, except that it had long borders with China, North Vietnam, and South Vietnam, and so provided a route through which communists might travel to noncommunist areas."[5] The incoming president considered the Pathet Lao to be the greatest challenge to Souvanna's government, and he labeled it a puppet of the Soviet Union, rather than a grassroots social movement. Kennedy cited the conspicuousness of Soviet military aircraft over Laos as evidence of external support for the Pathet Lao. In his correspondence with Premier Nikita Khrushchev, as well as in his public statements, Kennedy sought to convince the Soviets to honor Souvanna's desire to remain neutral, by ceasing their financial and material support to the Pathet Lao.[6]

During a luncheon on March 20, 1961, with journalist Walter Lippmann, Kennedy stated, "We cannot and will not accept any visible humiliation over Laos." When Lippmann questioned the infallibility of the domino theory in Southeast Asia, the president responded by voicing his concern for the fragility of pro-Western regimes in the region.[7] That same month, when a multinational conference opened in Geneva, Switzerland, to negotiate Laos's political future, the president dispatched W. Averell Harriman, the seasoned diplomat who knew Khrushchev. Kennedy emphasized to Harriman the importance of securing Souvanna's cooperation for a neutral government and opposition to Soviet assistance.[8] Although confident in his own abilities, the elder American statesman's autonomy frustrated members of the Laos country team, who felt removed from the negotiations, and Ambassador Brown referred sarcastically to Harriman as "Secretary of State for Laos."[9]

Kennedy proved cautious about throwing the military might of the United States into the jungles of Laos. A month after Harriman's arrival in Geneva, the failed Cuban invasion taught Kennedy that he could not implicitly trust his intelligence and military advisers, and this kept him from plunging the country into war over the security of Laos.[10] Kennedy confided in White House assistant Arthur Schlesinger Jr., in May 1961, "If it hadn't been for Cuba, we might be about to intervene in Laos now."[11] Harriman agreed with the need to resist the temptation of charging into Indochina, but he remained adamant about the importance of U.S. involvement in the country. As he told Ambassador Brown, "We must never face the President with the choice of abandoning Laos or sending troops."[12]

Developing a viable policy for Laos, let alone all of Southeast Asia, required a comprehensive interagency study that, unfortunately, Kennedy did not direct. To formulate foreign policy, Kennedy balked at utilizing the formal National Security Council, which he found cumbersome. National Security Adviser McGeorge Bundy recalled that the president disliked three words: "Cold War" and "strategy." Instead, Kennedy preferred ad hoc executive committees, special groups, and even discussions in his bedroom. He arrived at the White House convinced that he could develop a fresh look at the world without getting bogged down in the academic theories of grand strategy, or worse, the stale recommendations of the federal bureaucracy. After the fiasco of the Bay of Pigs, Kennedy began to second-guess executive departments and grew wary of hawks from the Pentagon and within his own party. Bundy watched the president tear up "bad papers" from Chairman of the Joint Chiefs of Staff General Lyman Lemnitzer, something that he did not believe that his boss would have done prior to the failed invasion.[13] The president also placed less value on recommendations from the State Department. According to Jacqueline Kennedy, her husband thought that Secretary of State Dean Rusk seemed "terribly scared to make a decision," which drove him "crazy." Kennedy did not dislike Rusk, but he believed that the entire Foreign Service worked too slowly, and he occasionally quipped, "Bundy and I do more work in the White House in one day than they do over there [at Foggy Bottom] in six months."[14]

The president preferred the counsel of Secretary of Defense Robert McNamara to Rusk for developing courses of action for Southeast Asia. The former president of the Ford Motor Company initiated a rigorous review of existing defense projects, in order to establish a "controlled, flexible response tailored to the level of the political or military aggression to which it was responding."[15] He shared Kennedy's penchant for developing special operations and psychological warfare capabilities and argued that these assets would enable the United States to gain friends and prop up dominoes without involving conventional military forces. In theory, this flexibility would prevent regional turmoil from expanding into a global confrontation. Addressing colleagues at the White House, McNamara told them that it was "absolutely indispensable that we go down this road" to secure Southeast Asia, beginning with bolstering Laos against the Pathet Lao.[16]

Roger Hilsman, director of the State Department's Bureau of Intelligence and Research, considered Laos to be, above all, a psychological confrontation between the communists and the "outside world."[17] As a psychological problem, Kennedy expected the U.S. Information Agency to help the United States gain international support for Lao neutrality. Long before his arrival at 1776 Pennsylvania Avenue, Murrow had accepted the need for the United States to bolster Southeast Asia. In his CBS radio broadcast on February 9, 1954, Murrow had strongly advocated for U.S. involvement in the remote region during

Counterinsurgency Propaganda

France's struggle to maintain possession of Vietnam. From his perspective, the formation of just one communist state would threaten more than the French: "And if Indo-China is lost, all Southeast Asia will be lost in time, and with it, all hope of the survival of Western power and ideas on the Asian mainland. . . . Compromise in Indo-China could be a defeat for this country of immeasurable magnitude."[18]

As USIA director, Murrow took serious interest in the administration's counterinsurgency planning related to Laos, and he received permission to join some of the president's ad hoc advisory committees. He participated in the Special Group (Counterinsurgency), a fifteen-member group chaired by General Maxwell Taylor, which Kennedy created in January 1962. Although Bundy did not formally add Murrow as a regular member of the group until August 13, 1962, his involvement began months earlier.[19] When Murrow could not attend, he sent Burnett Anderson, his deputy assistant director for plans and policy, to represent the USIA. An advocate for interagency cooperation, Murrow believed that the committee would improve the quality of the analysis provided to the president.[20]

Murrow searched throughout the USIA for officers with field experience in counterinsurgency to support the president's strategy. In December 1961, he found his lead planner when he learned that John Anspacher had completed his public affairs assignment in Saigon. As Anspacher prepared to board a ship in Hong Kong for a leisurely return home, a courier approached him with a message that the USIA director wanted him to telephone immediately. When he returned the call, Murrow asked him to return to Washington as soon as possible to help with a new project. This meant foregoing the cruise and boarding a plane, but Anspacher believed that if Murrow "asked you to do something you turned yourself inside out to do it and you didn't press him for a reason why." Arriving in Washington, Murrow sent him directly to the Special Group (Counterinsurgency) in January 1962.[21]

In addition to attending interagency meetings, Anspacher designed the USIA's counterinsurgency training program and organized a speakers' series that nearly every agency member in Washington, Murrow included, attended in 1962. An assortment of experts from the State Department, sociologists from Ivy League schools, and foreign media correspondents delivered lectures.[22] To facilitate greater cooperation between agencies, the CIA invited Murrow to send two senior officers to the Counterinsurgency Program Planning course offered periodically throughout the year to discuss how members of a country team could work together to diminish "communist subversion."[23] Attorney General Robert Kennedy expressed personal interest in the advancement of counterinsurgency training across the federal government, and he advocated for Foreign Service Officers and USIA personnel to receive training on how to respond to insurgencies early in their careers.[24] He asked Murrow and Rusk detailed questions about a six-week counterinsurgency program created by the State Department and the USIA, and he dropped in to listen to speakers and occasionally lectured himself.[25] Murrow also ensured that the USIA supported the diplomats responsible for negotiating over Laos by dispatching veteran public affairs officer James Markey to assist Harriman in Geneva. Harriman thanked Murrow and praised Markey for providing the U.S. delegation with extremely valuable assistance in formulating responses to media inquiries.[26]

Murrow encouraged his employees to attend training provided by other agencies, and dozens of USIA personnel attended the military's war colleges where, during the Kennedy years, they received a block of instruction on limited warfare. However, the information officers agreed that the military did not see insurgencies in the same way that the newly formed State-USIA counterinsurgency school taught its students. Keith Adamson, who served as a public affairs officer in Vietnam in the 1960s, considered the counterinsurgency views of his classmates at the Army War College at Carlisle Barracks, Pennsylvania, to be rather ill conceived and heavy-handed:

> They didn't talk about insurgency as being anything strange; they felt it was somebody who wanted to fight, and they were going to fight it the way they thought the fight ought to be conducted. Some members of the class wanted a few more megatons of nuclear weapons, and others wanted a few more tanks, and so on. They all had their own solutions to it. In the psychological warfare side, in PSYOPS, most of the proposals that came out were dirty tricks.[27]

Counterinsurgency Propaganda

Evidently the colonels had not sat through the Robert Kennedy lecture series about developing political and economic stability and training local security forces.

In the realm of psychological warfare, Murrow established a cordial relationship with McNamara, and he welcomed military commanders to his office to discuss overseas operations.[28] The agency also created a liaison officer attached to the army's Special Warfare School.[29] Such cooperation made sense, given that the Defense Department possessed a variety of information capabilities directed toward Southeast Asia.[30] Murrow and McNamara arranged for a USIA representative to serve on the personal staff of each combatant commander to provide public diplomacy expertise, much like the political adviser already dispatched by the State Department, who offered diplomatic counsel to the senior generals and admirals in Europe and the Pacific.[31] By forging a professional relationship with McNamara, Murrow did not seek to circumvent Rusk. When it came to the formulation of foreign policy, Undersecretary of State Chester Bowles believed that his department maintained a nonconfrontational relationship with the USIA, thanks to Murrow's cooperation and daily communication with senior diplomats.[32]

Murrow's personal interest in building meaningful connections throughout Washington set the standard for USIA employees who learned from their director that they would not succeed in their mission by broadcasting and engaging other countries in a vacuum. The absence of meaningful dialogue between the key foreign affairs agencies in Washington would ensure that rivalries and bickering would take place within any country team representing the government overseas. Within every American embassy, three people spoke for the United States: the USIA public affairs officer, the State Department cultural affairs officer, and the Defense Department information officer. Because all three hailed from different agencies, an information disaster could erupt if they did not get along. However, as Murrow demonstrated in his relationship with Bundy, McNamara, Rusk, and CIA director John McCone, when officials chose to set aside their egos, they produced meaningful policy. Whether they were willing to acknowledge it or not, they needed to complement one another's efforts by speaking a similar message.

In the Lao capital of Vientiane, the public affairs officer actively looked for culturally appropriate methods to convey the USIA's message: communism would not help the troubled country, nor would it allow the people to preserve their traditional lifestyle. In cooperation with the Royal Lao government in 1961, the USIA leveraged traditional Laotian minstrels, known as Mohlam singers, to influence the populace to support neutrality. An ancient musical art, the Mohlams wrote morality plays about local happenings, and the USIA filmed shows that the singers performed related to the violence caused in the countryside by the Pathet Lao. Distributing the films widely throughout the small country—sometimes by dropping a reel, generator, and projector, by helicopter, into remote areas—Murrow hailed the Mohlams as "town criers" in the jungle.[33]

In an effort to find the most qualified public affairs officers to serve in tumultuous countries like Laos and South Vietnam, Murrow modified the promotion process at the USIA. By December 1961, he had personally approved the selection of officers for Foreign Service (FS)-1 positions, the highest rank before entering the Senior Foreign Service. He instructed the USIA's regional directors to present him with a list of all of their FS-2 officers with recommendations for promotion. In lieu of having a promotion board, Murrow made selections after discussing the recommendations with his closest advisers, Deputy Director Donald Wilson and Tom Sorensen, his assistant director for plans and policy.[34] This approach to selecting the agency's base rung of senior leaders did not conform to the bureaucratic norms of the federal government, but it did prevent some lackluster officers from receiving a promotion solely for time served in grade.

As Murrow considered dynamic methods for improving the USIA's counterinsurgency capabilities, Kennedy sought additional options for responding to the growth of Asian communism. The administration's interest in neutrality for Laos did not serve as a blanket strategy for all of Southeast Asia. While Kennedy believed strongly that the Soviets propped up the Pathet Lao, he considered the Viet Cong a homegrown insurgency inside of the Republic of Vietnam supported by Hanoi and Beijing. The president believed that he needed to increase military support to South Vietnam throughout his presidency because he had pledged in his inaugural address to "meet any hardship, support any friend, oppose any foe, to assure the survival and the success of liberty."[35] Since he doubted that the Soviets would intervene, as they had in Berlin and Laos, Kennedy chose to take a more deliberate approach in Vietnam. He admired Vietnam's victory against the French in 1954 and found it "tragic" that the Vietnamese might lose their independence once again, this time to the communists.[36]

Compared to Laos, Bundy found clear potential for South Vietnam to remain self-sustaining: "It was an entirely different problem in terms of available means of operation because insofar as you had an effective government there you had something you could help, and the Vietnamese had proven themselves quite able."[37] In April 1961, Kennedy's advisers generally agreed about the necessity of increasing the size of the Military Assistance and Advisory Group (MAAG) in South Vietnam.[38] However, Kennedy remained reluctant to deploy conventional troops; he preferred military advisers and skilled Special Forces troops wearing the Green Beret. He explained the potential quandary of relying on large formations to Schlesinger: "But it will be just like Berlin. The troops will march in; the crowds will cheer; and in four days everyone will have forgotten. Then we will be told that we have to send in more troops. It is like taking a drink. The effect wears off, and you have to take another."[39]

In 1961 Bundy argued that the administration did not seriously consider any other options than continuing to bolster South Vietnamese president Ngo Dinh Diem, despite the fact that he remained unpopular with significant demographics within his country.[40] Bundy's brother, William, the deputy assistant secretary of state for international security affairs, succinctly described the drawback to relying on Diem: "He was the greatest bottleneck in the history of human government that I've ever seen." The elder Bundy believed Diem's ego and quest for total control prevented him from using his government efficiently or empowering subordinates.[41] Regardless, the Kennedy administration did not see a viable alternative until the fall of 1963.

Early in the administration, Murrow endorsed Kennedy's strategy for South Vietnam wholeheartedly. He had voiced approval of Diem when the Vietnamese president visited Eisenhower in Washington on May 10, 1957. Murrow seemed pleased with Diem's leadership, observing on his CBS radio broadcast that "Diem is proving to be the classic example of what can be done to stop Communism." He went further in his endorsement: "Not only has Diem probably saved his own country, he *may* have saved Southeast Asia in the process."[42] In the first year of his presidency, Kennedy directed the USIA to improve international support for Diem, and Murrow developed an information campaign through the Special Group (Counterinsurgency). In a special message to Congress in May 1961, Kennedy explained the value of the USIA in supporting American efforts in Southeast Asia: "We are engaged in a worldwide struggle in which we bear a heavy burden to preserve and promote the ideals that we share with all mankind, or have alien ideals forced upon them. That struggle has highlighted the role of our Information Agency."[43]

Kennedy's Vietnam task force published a silver-covered Presidential Program for Vietnam on May 23, 1961, which articulated a campaign plan for dealing with the insurgency. In addition to economic and military priorities, the plan included six psychological tasks, most involving the USIA. Murrow's agency would help Diem's government develop a clearer public information program for its own people to inform them about how they could help their government combat communists. The country team would influence the Vietnamese Ministry of Defense to declassify more information about communist terrorist activities so that it could be compiled and distributed to the international press by USIA public affairs officers. In secret cooperation with the CIA, the USIA increasingly exposed the details about deteriorating conditions in North Vietnam to the press. Turning to cultural diplomacy, Murrow's agency received additional funding to construct an opulent U.S. pavilion at the Saigon Trade Fair in 1962, in order to celebrate the bounty enjoyed by a capitalist society.[44]

In May 1961, Vice President Lyndon Johnson visited Vietnam to conduct what the press began to label as the Texan's unique "shirtsleeve diplomacy."[45] A month after the Bay of Pigs, the administration

Counterinsurgency Propaganda

may have sought to reassure the Vietnamese people that, despite the Cuban debacle, the United States remained committed to the security of the Republic of Vietnam. The embassy in Saigon suspected that with "no place to go except to stick with the U.S.," Diem had become particularly nervous since April that Kennedy might seek a neutralist solution, based on his reluctance to support the exile brigade at the Bay of Pigs.[46] During his stop in Vietnam, Johnson told reporters that he intended to take his "campaign" to the people of South Vietnam, regardless of the threat posed by the Viet Cong. The host-nation population responded enthusiastically to the vice president, particularly to his address before the national assembly. Meanwhile in Hanoi, communists gathered to protest U.S. plans to dispatch "guerrilla warfare experts" to South Vietnam. The media in South Vietnam, Thailand, and Taiwan commented favorably on Johnson's statements and public engagements and found his attitude refreshingly clear compared to U.S. policy about Lao neutrality.[47] Ambassador Frederick Nolting lauded Johnson's superb public diplomacy job: "We are convinced Diem's confidence in [the] U.S. has been greatly increased by [his] visit."[48]

Returning from his visit to the region, Johnson told Kennedy that he found Diem to be "a complex figure beset by many problems" surrounded by advisers "less admirable and capable than he." Still, the vice president believed that the Republic of Vietnam "can be saved," but only with the United States bolstering Diem. One passage from Johnson's report proved a troubling look into the future:

> The battle against Communism must be joined in Southeast Asia with strength and determination to achieve success there—or the United States, inevitably, must surrender the Pacific and take up our defenses on our own shores. Asian Communism is compromised and contained by the maintenance of free nations on the subcontinent. Without this inhibitory influence, the island outposts—Philippines, Japan, Taiwan—have no security and the vast Pacific becomes a Red Sea.[49]

Part of Johnson's concern stemmed from Soviet aid, advisers, and propaganda in the region. From his study of USIA opinion polls, Murrow worried about the appeal of Khrushchev's propaganda in the developing world because it promised a simplistic approach to modernity compared to the more complex system of the West. "We must admit that in competition with the Soviets we are at a disadvantage," he explained to students at the Johns Hopkins University. "To an emerging society shopping for a ready-made philosophy in the market place of ideas, democracy appears difficult to operate."[50] Hosting Murrow on her television show, *Prospects of Mankind*, Eleanor Roosevelt agreed with her old friend about the information challenge they faced, adding that the Soviets always failed to acknowledge their none-too-inconsequential limitations, notably the loss of personal liberties and protection under the law.[51]

For the USIA to be effective in countering communist propaganda, Murrow believed that it had to explain the nuances of U.S. policy as soon as it changed, rather than waiting to respond to new criticisms. Tom Sorensen sought Murrow's support to improve the responsiveness of the agency's media services when policy directives modified information objectives. Sorensen felt that they failed to rewrite scripts or programs when new guidance appeared. Murrow agreed, and in a memo to his staff, he asked for the "unstinting cooperation" of the media chiefs to improve their crosstalk with the policy division.[52] Further, he created the position of director for media content and tasked every regional and department director to prepare two worldwide themes that the agency should espouse. He gave them a week's notice and then met with them in his office on a Saturday morning, April 29, 1961.[53] He considered the creation of a director of media content as the greatest accomplishment of his first year in office, which he described as the "wrist" for the various media that had not been speaking with one voice.[54]

Energized by Murrow's support, Sorensen charged his policy planning staff to be fully aware of National Security Council and State Department developments. Howard Needham, a USIA policy staffer, began his day with a review of the 50 to 150 cables that came in overnight from his particular region. After scanning them for priority issues or requests, he typically walked to C Street to confer with his counterpart at the State Department to see if he shared the same concern. At lunchtime, the USIA convened the informal "noon confer-

Counterinsurgency Propaganda

ence" with regional policy officers and representatives of each of the media divisions. Needham recalled the meetings as being "extraordinarily efficient." Within half an hour, the agency formulated information guidance to disseminate to every USIA outpost relevant for the next twenty-four hours. Long-term guidance proved a bit more strenuous for policy staffers to produce. Written quarterly, Sorensen's assistants normally toiled for several weeks to compose news policy in the form of a memorandum. Formulating psychological objectives required analysis of news and public opinion from each country, in addition to an understanding of agency policy objectives. After a great deal of conferencing and long-distance phone calls, the published guidance helped public affairs officers prepare for their interaction with the local media.[55]

One of the primary themes in USIA programming directed toward Southeast Asia focused on countering communist propaganda about Western imperialism. Agency analysts speculated that communists concentrated on colonialism for three reasons. First, anticolonial fervor made it easy to present the West in a negative light, making it an attention grabber. Second, communist doctrine argued that imperial powers would collapse with the absence of raw materials and markets from its colonies, and the Soviets hoped to weaken the West's economic strength. Finally, communists blamed the "national bourgeois" for the economic challenges suffered by the impoverished masses in the developing world. This message effectively drew the peasantry and urban poor away from supporting the very governments that the West sought to bolster. The USIA countered the claims of American imperialism by reminding its audience that while the 650 million former colonists had gained their independence since World War II, the Soviets and Chinese had subjugated over 700 million. The agency's programs highlighted specific brutal responses to democratic movements from Budapest to Tibet.[56] Opinion polls in 1961 indicated that U.S. messages about bolstering South Vietnam resonated throughout Southeast Asia, due to fears about the threat that a unified, communist Vietnam with a battle-hardened army would pose.[57]

The year 1961 closed without stabilizing Southeast Asia, when the November neutrality agreement for Laos precipitously fell apart in the

New Year. Frustrated, Kennedy wanted to remove his Special Forces advisers from Laos, but his advisers persuaded him only to threaten publicly to do so. This message helped to improve Laos's political situation by the spring of 1962.[58] Seeking to demonstrate quantifiable progress in some aspect of his foreign policy in the region, Kennedy turned greater attention to the Republic of Vietnam. It does not seem that the president renewed his interest in Vietnam due to a strong commitment to Diem's regime; rather, it stemmed from his geostrategic desire to improve his Cold War posture vis-à-vis Asian communists. During the National Security Council meeting on November 15, 1961, Kennedy admitted that the United States could walk away from Vietnam without suffering serious security repercussions, as the official meeting notes make clear: "The President said that he could even make a rather strong case against intervening in an area 10,000 miles away against 16,000 guerrillas with a native army of 200,000, where millions have been spent for years with no success."[59]

Reports by General Maxwell Taylor and Walt Rostow, head of the State Department's Policy Planning Council, shaped Kennedy's ultimate decision to steadily increase U.S. support for Diem. Sent to South Vietnam by Kennedy to assess the security situation firsthand, in June 1961, Rostow and Taylor returned to Washington to argue against continuing the conventional military training that had been provided by the U.S. advisory group since the Eisenhower administration.[60] Instead, the emissaries called for counterinsurgency tactics and the training of small units capable of conducting village security operations, area surveillance, and patrolling against groups of Viet Cong guerrillas, in lieu of anticipating a full-scale invasion by Ho Chi Minh's army across the Demilitarized Zone.[61] This proposal appealed to the president because it would demonstrate his Flexible Response approach without risking heightened tensions among the United States, the Soviet Union, and China.

While Murrow directed the USIA to champion the administration's counterinsurgency efforts to protect the fragile South Vietnamese government from communist aggression, he objected to the technique of chemical defoliation. In November 1961, Diem requested from Kennedy the tactical employment of chemical agents to destroy

Counterinsurgency Propaganda

the vegetation and crops surrounding areas under Viet Cong control. Murrow's assistant director for the Far East, Paul Nielson, alerted Murrow to the fact that the Pentagon had drafted a memorandum for Kennedy's signature to begin using defoliants.[62] A week later, Murrow cautioned Kennedy against giving in to Diem's request because it would create a propaganda boon for the communists. When the White House indicated that it would authorize the U.S. Air Force to conduct defoliation, the USIA director urged the president to "take every step possible," before the mission took place, to explain that the chemical operations conducted against crops would be nontoxic to humans. This, he argued, would prevent the USIA from having to go on the defensive once the communists placed their own spin on the "imperialist attack."[63]

Regardless of American efforts, the situation in South Vietnam continued to deteriorate. In March 1962, Viet Cong attacks reached an all-time high, with 1,861 attacks targeting the South Vietnamese population or security forces.[64] Communist propaganda continued to call Diem's government a puppet regime propped up by the United States. Rusk opened a press conference on March 1, 1962, by addressing the criticism emanating from Hanoi, Beijing, and Moscow: "These comments from Communist capitals wholly neglect the fact that the Republic of Viet-Nam is under attack by Communist guerrillas who are directed, trained, supplied and re-enforced by north Viet-Nam—all in gross violation of the 1954 Geneva Accords."[65] The USIA continued its information campaign by explaining that U.S. military and economic aid enabled the peaceful people of South Vietnam to maintain their independence and protect themselves.

Although the USIA's media services used highlights from Rusk's press conference, not everyone in the agency accepted the administration's current strategy in South Vietnam. Chester Opal, deputy director of the USIA Television Service, sent Deputy Director Wilson a detailed memorandum expressing his views on counterinsurgency. Opal knew a great deal about the situation in Vietnam from his previous service as the public affairs officer in Saigon, a liaison officer at Fort Bragg in the 1950s, and a graduate of the U.S. Army War College. Opal opened his letter with an observation: the second stage of revolutions in the Third World increasingly led to military officers taking the reins of government, ostensibly in order to stabilize their countries' affairs. Perhaps, Opal suggested, the USIA should engage the foreign military officers enrolled in U.S. military schools to inform them about American institutions and traditions. Wilson passed the memo on to Murrow, who liked it so much that he told Opal that he would now be his special assistant. For his first task, Murrow wanted Opal to draft a memorandum that Murrow would send to McNamara with the contents of Opal's internal document. Removing only one paragraph from the draft, Murrow signed the final copy.[66]

Several days later, Opal found himself representing the USIA at General Taylor's counterinsurgency task force at the White House. The representative from McNamara's office mentioned to Opal that the defense secretary had received a memo from Murrow, and it was his responsibility to prepare the secretary's response. Because Opal worked at the USIA, the other staffer asked him how McNamara should respond to Murrow's recommendation about training the foreign military officers. Opal suggested a response, and the defense secretary's reply to Murrow contained what Opal provided at the task force meeting. This tickled Opal who recalled, "Here I was in a position of answering my own memorandum." More substantially, this led to the USIA preparing books for foreign military officers and coordinating additional meetings through the Defense Department about its international education program.[67]

The administration cautiously celebrated news received on June 12, 1962, that Lao political factions had unified in a viable neutral government behind Prince Souvanna. Although Kennedy had been tempted to make a more dramatic military intervention to achieve this in the months prior, the movement of U.S. forces into the region provided sufficient "veiled ambiguity" to bring the Pathet Lao back to the negotiation table.[68] Khrushchev even congratulated Kennedy for his role in bringing stability to the small country. The president responded to Khrushchev's cable by encouraging him to help him resolve other international problems.[69] The USIA celebrated the achievement of Lao neutrality through its media services, as evidence of how the United

Counterinsurgency Propaganda

States could help to foster diplomatic agreements without exacerbating Cold War tensions.[70]

With neutrality in Laos, the USIA increased efforts to bolster Diem and discredit the Viet Cong within South Vietnam through its radio broadcasts and mobile information programming that brought films and simple exhibits to remote villages. By August 1962, the agency provided Radio Saigon, a station similar to West Berlin's Rundfunk im amerikanischen Sektor, with the equipment to transmit its broadcast across all of North Vietnam.[71] In addition to the USIA and Defense Department support for South Vietnamese psychological warfare operations, the British Foreign Office sent a team to Saigon, as part of its South East Asian Treaty Organization commitment to advise Diem's regime on how to craft counterinsurgency propaganda. The so-called Thompson Mission consisted of British officers with considerable experience in countersubversion techniques developed during the Malayan Emergency of 1948–60.[72]

The use of defoliants remained the one aspect of the U.S. counterinsurgency strategy for Vietnam that continued to alarm Murrow. He objected to chemical munitions on moral grounds as well as for their negative impact on the USIA's messages about America's desire to promote peace and security in the region. In a memorandum to McGeorge Bundy on August 16, 1962, Murrow reminded the national security adviser that the United States did not use food as a weapon, but the chemical destruction of 2,500 acres of the Phu Yen Province would deny the Vietnamese their food supply. If the president thought that the United States could achieve its objectives in Vietnam by using the chemical, then, Murrow said, he should authorize its use. However, if his security advisers only thought that their deployment "might" allow the United States to win, then "we had better consider the implications before undertaking the project." Murrow assured Bundy that the USIA would be prepared to explain why the U.S. military used defoliants, but there would be a cost: "I am convinced that we cannot persuade the world—particularly that large part of it which does not get enough to eat—that defoliation 'is good for you.'"[73]

Due in large part to the Cuban Missile Crisis, Southeast Asian policy did not dominate international headlines in the fall of 1962, and the security situation in Saigon and Vientiane remained generally stable. However, by January 1963, intelligence emerged from both capitals of an imminent communist resurgence. On January 3, Murrow told the Special Group (Counterinsurgency) that he worried about the integrity of public information facilities in Laos, which the USIA anticipated the communists would usurp from prodemocracy local nationals. Most disconcerting, the new Lao minister of information identified himself as a communist, and he announced his intent to assume control of the *Lao Photo News*, a USIA-supported newspaper.[74] In Vietnam, Diem's lethargy toward ameliorating political and social discontent worried the Kennedy administration.[75] The USIA had to acknowledge publicly the increase in communist subversion, but its media services remained wary of crediting growing popular support for the Pathet Lao and Viet Cong to broadening disfavor with Souvanna or Diem.

When Murrow voiced his concern about winning the ideological Cold War, he worried about the United States losing credibility over Vietnam. Although not a major headline in 1962 or early 1963, anytime that South Vietnam did appear in the international press, it normally pertained to a scathing critique of Diem's regime. Murrow maintained that if the Kennedy administration believed in the strategic value of a democratic Republic of Vietnam, the administration also needed to emphasize the tenets of a free society and representative government through its words and actions. McGeorge Bundy recalled that Kennedy did not devote significant time to U.S. Vietnam policy until the summer of 1963, which may explain the lackluster results achieved by U.S. advisers during the first two years of his administration.[76]

It did not help that Kennedy tacitly permitted the Defense Department to usurp control of U.S. policy in Vietnam from the State Department. Despite the counterinsurgency training initiated by the USIA and the State Department, William Bundy, the deputy assistant secretary of state for international security affairs, felt that the Kennedy administration had failed to prepare advisers and diplomats to operate in Vietnam. Evidenced by the limited number of Americans

Counterinsurgency Propaganda

trained to speak Vietnamese, Bundy did not think that Americans understood the Vietnamese's sensitivity about their colonial past: "We went along on the idea that [speaking] French was what was necessary."[77] In June 1963, Murrow organized a new two-week course for USIA employees, titled "Problems of Developing Areas," and he asked McGeorge Bundy to serve as the keynote speaker at its conclusion.[78]

As the political situation in South Vietnam continued to deteriorate in the fall of 1963, key administration officials began to suggest to Kennedy that Diem needed to step down from power. In mid-September, the Defense Department accepted Diem's crackdown on student demonstrations, arguing that the U.S. government would respond similarly at home if faced with a comparable challenge to its authority. From Foggy Bottom, however, Harriman and Roger Hilsman advocated for a policy of disengagement from Diem—not necessarily from South Vietnam, but from its current chief of state. The administration's inability to agree upon who could legitimately replace Diem complicated the debate. Kennedy did not believe that Vietnam could adopt the neutrality arrangement that had emerged in Laos, and in August 1963, he rejected public calls by French president Charles de Gaulle for an international conference to advance Vietnam's neutrality. At home, Kennedy feared that withdrawing support for Diem would lead to a wave of criticism from congressional moderates, the Pentagon, and the press.[79]

Vietnam began to make its way into domestic headlines and editorials after the Battle of Ap Bac on January 3, 1963, especially because of *New York Times* reporter David Halberstam's vivid coverage from Vietnam. William Bundy realized only in retrospect that journalists on the ground understood the serious shortfalls of the South Vietnamese army before U.S. generals or the embassy began articulating their concerns to Washington.[80] George Ball voiced his reservations about the deployment of advisers to Vietnam in a personal conversation with the president. Ball cited the "soggy political base" and the poor terrain of jungles and rice paddies as an undesirable location in which to combat communism, and he suspected that even a small American presence would grow to three hundred thousand men within five years. "George," Kennedy replied, "you're just crazier than hell! This decision doesn't mean that." However, with 16,500 troops in place in November 1963, Ball considered the administration to be "caught in a developing situation where it was manifestly difficult to turn back."[81]

The situation in South Vietnam concerned Murrow as well. Not only did Diem's rule undermine USIA messages about democracy; communist terrorist activity also threatened USIA personnel serving in the country. The director was "horrified" when he learned that the Viet Cong had killed several USIA workers who had been riding in a jeep with projectors to show films in the jungle.[82] "USIA is literally in the front lines there," Murrow explained in a speech to the Advertising Federation of America. He described the mobile teams who traveled between villages accompanied occasionally by an American doctor who provided basic medical treatment to the Vietnamese. To gain access to the most remote locations, USIA members hitched rides on army and U.S. Agency for International Development helicopters.[83] Public affairs officers earned the ire of the Viet Cong after they began to report on the toll of terrorism on innocent Vietnamese civilians.[84] Tom Sorensen considered the Viet Cong to be the USIA's "greatest problem" by 1963, and the agency posthumously awarded its first medals ever for combat bravery to Vietnamese employees.[85]

Although the elevation of hostilities upset Murrow, he never dropped his opposition to the use of defoliants. He told Harriman that the U.S. government should provide the international public with complete details about defoliation and destruction of crops. In a Special Group (Counterinsurgency) meeting on September 6, 1963, Murrow pressed the military to verify the absolute necessity for crop destruction in Vietnam. General Paul Harkins, the Military Assistance Command, Vietnam (MACV) commander, who happened to be in Washington and in attendance at the meeting, reaffirmed the chemicals' tactical value.[86] He maintained that the defoliant denied the Viet Cong the sanctuaries necessary to attack villagers and local security forces. Murrow encouraged public affairs officers to make an extra effort to inform third-country correspondents in Saigon about the chemicals, since "ours won't do much good," in countering communist criticism of American military operations.[87] As Nicholas Cull has observed, USIA personnel in Saigon "saw its target as international opinion, rather than merely Vietnamese 'hearts and minds.'"[88]

The USIA and the embassy in Saigon briefed the press about the military's employment of Agent Orange, calling the defoliant chemical a "relatively harmless operation" to combat the Viet Cong. Such talking points were technically true, but only if the wind never carried the mist into a populated area, or if farmers remained nowhere near their crops or the jungles at the time of its employment. This was a very big "if." Unsurprisingly, communist propaganda lambasted the American "imperialists" for denying Vietnamese peasants food and wantonly decimating the countryside.[89]

Seeking to inform Kennedy about the dire situation in South Vietnam, Murrow brought John Mecklin, his public affairs officer from Saigon, with him to a White House meeting on Vietnam on September 10, 1963. A former *Time* foreign correspondent, Mecklin had volunteered for the difficult post believing optimistically that he could provide honest and influential information to his host-nation audience. However, his in-country experience greatly troubled him, particularly the strong-handed tactics of the Diem regime and the inaccuracy of other U.S. government agency reports sent from Saigon.[90] Mecklin distributed an information paper around the cabinet table and stated that opinions of the United States in South Vietnam suffered from the administration's tolerance of Diem's abuse of the populace. He urged senior administration officials to "go hog wild" and consider deploying combat forces to remove Diem's entire regime because the suspension of aid would do nothing but upset the peasants and urban poor. Perhaps the presence of the U.S. military would be enough for Diem to step aside, just as the threat of U.S. intervention had influenced Lao national leaders finally to create a neutral government the year prior. None of the senior administration officials questioned the public affairs officer's presentation.[91]

That evening Murrow described to an interagency committee at the State Department the glaring difference between military and civilian perceptions of the situation in Vietnam. For the military, both in the Pentagon and at MACV headquarters, generals believed that the Viet Cong could be eliminated with Diem remaining in charge. Foreign Service Officers, journalists, and public affairs officers strongly disagreed, contending that continued support for Diem would not contribute to the collapse of resistance to the Viet Cong. The inter-agency meeting ended so inconclusively that Murrow asked to be spared from writing press guidance for his agency until "our policy was clear" in Washington.[92] Since the spring, Murrow had recom-mended that the administration improve its information manage-ment in Saigon by designating one U.S. spokesperson, rather than having parallel military and diplomatic press secretaries hosting simul-taneous engagements with the press.[93] However, by mid-September, McNamara's office had made no effort to cooperate more effectively with the USIA in Saigon.

Young journalists reporting from South Vietnam, including David Halberstam and Peter Arnett, helped to turn Western opinion against Diem, by filing detailed stories about his brutality toward dissenters, especially the Buddhist majority. For months Diem had appeared par-anoid about a possible coup against him, and he ordered the arrest of twenty army officers in March and a midnight raid of Buddhist pago-das in August.[94] Veteran French reporter Bernard Fall, who witnessed firsthand the violence toward Buddhist protesters, considered this "an unmistakable symptom of the unraveling of the South Vietnam-ese social fabric," and he opined that this provided Kennedy with an excuse for disengagement that would be difficult for staunch anticom-munists to criticize.[95] Diem called the reporters liars and threatened to rescind their media accreditation, while Kennedy administration officials grew increasingly uncomfortable with the media's stories, even if they privately acknowledged their accuracy. This did little to enhance U.S. government–media relations.

On September 14, Murrow informed Bundy that USIA surveys only found significant sympathy for Diem in South Korea and the Philip-pines. He added a personal note at the end of his memo to Bundy: "I conclude that the degree of the dilemma and the complexity of the issues involved is almost as well understood abroad as it is in Wash-ington!"[96] While Murrow found Diem to be an obstacle to stabiliz-ing South Vietnam, he objected to the United States supporting a coup. The agency director encouraged Kennedy to pressure Diem

Counterinsurgency Propaganda

to dismiss his brother, Ngo Dinh Nhu, as his top political adviser. Bundy said Murrow's option would leave Diem in power, which the administration increasingly realized was not plausible because trying to preserve Diem as a "figurehead" would prove equally challenging.[97] Bundy's view was clearly shaped by a cable sent days earlier by Ambassador Henry Cabot Lodge Jr.: "If, in spite of all your efforts, Diem remains obdurate and refuses, then we must face the possibility that Diem himself cannot be preserved."[98] In the final weeks of his life, Diem stopped answering cables from Washington with any regularity, and the police tactics authorized by his brother became viler. Following the viewing of a USIA film in the White House family theater, on September 28, Harriman told Don Wilson that when it came to U.S. policy in Vietnam, the country's "moral position" in the world needed to drive U.S. foreign policy.[99] In the minds of senior administration officials, a break with Diem became essential to preserving their commitment to South Vietnam.

On November 2, South Vietnamese generals initiated a coup that resulted in the brutal murder of Diem and Nhu. General Duong Van Minh, who assumed the presidency for a brief period after the coup, argued that he had no alternative: "They had to be killed. Diem could not be allowed to live because he was too much respected among simple, gullible people in the countryside, especially the Catholics and the refugees. We had to kill Nhu because he was so widely feared—and he had created organizations that were the arms of his personal power."[100] Photos of the bloody corpses, with their hands tied behind their back, on the floor of an American-made armored personnel carrier, evoked international disgust. The USIA found international opinion "universally" disapproving of the coup and blaming the United States either directly or implicitly. Soviet radio did not accuse the Americans of directing the coup, but its commentators reported that the United States government "controlled" the Republic of Vietnam and could have "lifted a finger" to prevent the murders if it wanted to.[101]

Jacqueline Kennedy observed that her husband felt "just sick" after receiving the news. Although the president disapproved of Diem's performance as chief of state, Kennedy recalled that Diem fought against communists for twenty years, so surely, he should not have been ousted in such a horrific manner.[102] Murrow paid scant attention to the coup, due to his weakened state, following his lung-removal surgery on October 6 and ongoing cobalt radiation treatment to combat the remnants of his lung cancer. Neither Kennedy nor his advisers anticipated the gruesome end to Diem's regime, but as the U.S. Senate Select Committee to Study Governmental Operations with Respect to Intelligence Activities (the Church Committee) noted in 1975, "American officials had exaggerated notions about their ability to control the actions of [South Vietnamese] coup leaders."[103]

Tainted by the stigma of being complicit in the coup, the administration knew that it could not walk away from South Vietnam that November. The final public statements made by Kennedy prior to his own assassination indicated his desire to maintain U.S. support for the physical and economic security of the Republic of Vietnam. During his last White House press conference, on November 14, Kennedy voiced his personal support for General Harkins, the MACV commander, and restated his desire to "intensify the struggle" against the communist insurgency. In his very last public address, on November 22, Kennedy told the Fort Worth Chamber of Commerce, "Without the United States, South Viet-Nam would collapse overnight."[104]

William Bundy suspected that senior U.S. officials felt that in a "psychological sense" they had become more deeply committed in Vietnam because of their tacit approval of the coup. "Once we were taken to have done this," Bundy explained, "people in Saigon counted more on us, expected more from us."[105] During its November 14 meeting, the Special Group (Counterinsurgency) seemed cautiously optimistic about the new South Vietnamese regime of army officers.[106] In contrast, an alarmed State Department reported that between July and October 1963, the number of Viet Cong casualties, defections, and weapon losses dropped, while the number of Viet Cong attacks increased significantly.[107] Coupled with the muddled political scene following the coup, it appeared that the Viet Cong would remain influential. Therefore, so long as the U.S. government believed that the Viet Cong posed a threat to Southeast Asian regional security and to American credibility in the larger Cold War, its soldiers, USAID

Counterinsurgency Propaganda

workers, and USIA public affairs officers would remain committed to the security of South Vietnam.

By December 1963, it is unlikely that USIA director Murrow would still have agreed with CBS reporter Ed Murrow's 1954 conjecture that "compromise in Indo-China could be a defeat for this country [the United States] of immeasurable magnitude."[108] The political, security, and social turmoil that plagued South Vietnam not only impeded nurturing a genuine democracy, but the correlation between America's commitment to Saigon and its status as leader of the free world had grown increasingly dubious to most Western observers. As scholars Leslie Gelb and Richard Betts observed, "incrementalism would preserve flexibility" for Kennedy, but it also contributed to the absence of a decisive strategy.[109] Torn between destroying an enemy or building a stable country, the Kennedy administration failed to respond cohesively, making USIA broadcasts and programs about a brighter democratic future for South Vietnam ring hollow by the end of 1963.

The potential for achieving a free and noncommunist Southeast Asia seemed further uncertain in light of developments in Vientiane. The State Department assessed the situation in Laos quite bleakly in November 1963: "There has been no real progress towards the unification of Laos nor on the demobilization and integration of forces."[110] Among its recommendations, the department called for increasing U.S. propaganda efforts to highlight communist violations of the Geneva Agreements. As with efforts in Latin America to develop the Alliance for Progress, such an information campaign by the USIA would not succeed if economic and military aid did not follow the messages. After November 22, that quandary belonged to a new American president. Yet the same agencies and familiar advisers seated around the Cabinet Room table remained charged with helping Johnson advance peace in Southeast Asia. Among the faces conspicuously missing from the Cabinet Room would be Ed Murrow's.

The strain of articulating the USIA's message from Saigon physically exhausted John Mecklin, the hard-charging public affairs officer who told Kennedy to "go hog wild" and act decisively to correct the political and security situation in South Vietnam. His replacement, Douglas Pike, found himself equally challenged to influence the local population to support the rule of law, trust their politicians, and reject the alluring promises of the Viet Cong. Shortly after Johnson arrived in the White House, Ellsworth Bunker, who replaced Lodge as the U.S. ambassador to the Republic of Vietnam, invited Pike to join him for a meeting in the Oval Office. The president praised Pike for the USIA's efforts in Vietnam and said that he would give him whatever he asked for. When Pike asked for more time, Johnson slammed his fist on the coffee table and erupted bitterly, "That's the one goddamn thing I cannot give you."[111]

10

Good Luck, Ed

I have never worked harder in my life and never
been happier. I haven't had such satisfaction since
the days of covering the London blitz.
—EDWARD R. MURROW, March 15, 1964

Midway through his lunchtime address before the Federal Bar Association in Philadelphia on September 26, 1963, USIA director Murrow suffered a throat hemorrhage that spontaneously transformed
his deep, confident voice into the whispering rasp akin to someone
recovering from laryngitis. Begging the pardon of the assembled
attorneys, he still completed his speech about the "fishbowl world"
of the United States in the Cold War and responded to several questions from audience members. That afternoon Murrow napped at
the Bellevue-Stratford Hotel in an effort to regain his strength, while
his general counsel, Stanley Plesent, stood in for him during a previously scheduled interview. Against Plesent imploring him to cancel the remainder of his itinerary, Murrow insisted on honoring his
evening commitment, a black-tie affair, where he captivated guests
with extemporaneous remarks about his time as deputy director of
the Institute of International Education in the early 1930s. His affable demeanor could not fully disguise his discomfort. On the red-
eye flight back to Washington DC, Murrow slammed two scotch and
waters—alarming Plesent who knew his boss as a whiskey sipper—
and complained of a pain in his throat before trying to get some sleep.[1]

Following a medical exam the next day, Murrow's doctor scheduled surgery to correct a bronchial tube blockage caused by the hemorrhage. On October 6, as surgeons at the Washington Hospital Center began to cut, they discovered cancer, tracing it to Murrow's left lung. During a three-hour operation, they removed his left lung but knew that he would still require cobalt radiation therapy to eradicate the cancer.[2]

Throughout his tenure at the USIA, from 1961 to 1963, Murrow suffered from bouts of illness often attributed to his heavy smoking, with the most severe instances keeping him from his office for several weeks at a time. His most conspicuous absence occurred while convalescing from pneumonia in October 1962, when he missed participating in the Cuban Missile Crisis Executive Committee meetings. Until the lung-removal surgery, Murrow always rebounded from his ailments and returned to his self-imposed, fifteen-hours-a-day work schedule. He continued to depart his home near American University at 8:30 a.m., with his driver, Manzy Swiegert, and worked late into the night, six days a week.[3] Since the missile crisis, however, coworkers noticed him looking thinner, appearing fatigued, and, on occasion, sniping at them for minor mistakes. It is likely that doctors misdiagnosed the black spots on x-rays of his lungs as scar tissue, as opposed to cancerous tumors, in September 1962.[4] In retrospect, Murrow's 1963 physical and mood changes most likely stemmed from the insidious disease.

The October 6 surgery proved much more debilitating than earlier setbacks. Although Murrow tried earnestly to return to his 1776 Pennsylvania Avenue office in November, he struggled to remain at his desk for more than a couple of hours before exhaustion overwhelmed him. Tom Sorensen attributed Murrow's determination to his "Puritan sense of responsibility," but he confided in a British official that his boss only dealt with a few executive decisions.[5] Murrow's deputy, Donald Wilson, stepped in again as acting director and remained in daily contact with Murrow in an effort to lift his spirits with updates on the Kennedy administration, agency business, and world affairs. While convalescing at home, Murrow received a copy of *The Rise of the West* accompanied by a hand-written note from Robert Kennedy: "We need you back here desperately. The whole place is falling apart."[6]

Good Luck, Ed

Seven weeks after the operation, Murrow remained so weak that, on the day of President John F. Kennedy's assassination, his wife, Janet, put him to bed prior to breaking the tragic news. Determined to pay his final respects, a wheezing and exhausted Murrow hauled himself up the stairs from the ground floor of the White House to the East Room, where the president's body lay in state.[7] The following month, Murrow tendered his resignation to President Lyndon B. Johnson, citing his lengthy recovery as making him incapable of leading the USIA.

Biographer Ann Sperber believed that Murrow would have left the USIA imminently, even if doctors had not discovered lung cancer. She cited his increasing discontent with the Kennedy administration's handling of Vietnam, his exclusion from the president's inner policymaking circle, and his interest in returning to journalism by the fall of 1963. To support her argument, Sperber relies heavily on ABC News president Elmer Lower's efforts to entice Murrow to join his network. However, this seems unconvincing given that Lower sought out Murrow, not the other way around. Murrow agreed to hear Lower's proposal and scheduled a time to talk in person, but that meeting never occurred after Murrow canceled the day prior due to his surgery.[8]

Alexander Kendrick and Joseph Persico present a different interpretation in their respective biographies for Murrow's departure from the USIA. Kendrick acknowledges that a mid-1963 *Variety* article reported on Murrow's disenchantment with the Washington bureaucracy and constant battle with Congress. However, Kendrick also points out that Murrow publicly and privately voiced satisfaction with his job.[9] Persico agrees with Kendrick's assessment, noting that nearly everyone whom he interviewed for his own book—administration members, USIA colleagues, journalist friends, his wife—agreed that Murrow thoroughly enjoyed the challenges associated with the directorship.[10]

Murrow's son, Casey, rejects the notion that his father seriously considered leaving the USIA over philosophical differences with Kennedy or angst over budget battles with Congress. Casey points instead to the debilitating effects of the cancer treatment, drugs that were damaging in themselves in the early 1960s. For weeks after the lung removal, Murrow did not seriously consider leaving the USIA. "He didn't want to give up," Casey recalled. "He never wanted to give up on anything." His father felt it his duty to remain with the administration, at least through the end of its first term. However, Murrow returned home from his brief office visits in November to confide in Janet, "I am beat," and it exasperated him that he could not regain his stamina.[11]

Further evidence to suggest that Murrow did not intend to resign from the USIA can be found by examining his performance as agency director from January through September 1963. Instead of finding a cynical or beleaguered bureaucrat, researchers will find a political appointee fully committed to his agency's well-being and improving the efficacy of the Kennedy administration's public diplomacy. The USIA began 1963 with a new mission statement, which Murrow had proposed in September 1962 to the White House, based on the agency's expanding role in foreign affairs. Ever mindful of the USIA's legitimacy within the U.S. government, he asked Kennedy to issue the statement as an executive order, rather than making the agency's mission a tasking from the National Security Council. Murrow convinced the president to release the USIA's mission as an unclassified document, in order for other government agencies to appreciate the agency's responsibilities. "We no longer need a statement to hang on the wall," Murrow explained. "We desire a realistic, meaningful definition of the Agency's mission for internal use within the Government."[12] The president signed the USIA's new mission statement on January 25, 1963, although the last paragraph remained "Confidential" because it authorized the USIA to work with the CIA.[13]

Seeking ways to improve intra-agency cooperation between the USIA's various divisions, Murrow came to realize that despite the clever address, 1776 Pennsylvania Avenue did not adequately support the USIA's organization. Staffers crowded into a building only two-thirds the size required by federal statute based on the number of occupants, and the Voice of America and Motion Picture Service required larger studios. On April 3, 1963, Murrow asked the president directly for help in securing thirty thousand to fifty thousand square feet of new office space in Washington. He explained in his memorandum that he had "long hesitated to do so," but felt compelled to seek assistance, since the General Services Administration remained indifferent to his requests.[14]

While continuing his involvement with the complex issues of nuclear test ban treaties and counterinsurgency operations in Southeast Asia, Murrow looked for new methods to train public affairs officers assigned around the world. In April 1963, he endorsed the creation of a National Academy of Foreign Affairs because he believed that it would improve interagency relations. "Diplomacy today involves more than negotiation and passive reporting," he told the Senate Foreign Relations Committee, especially with the increasing value of the psychological and public elements. Murrow believed that an academy would better help government agencies to understand the USIA's capabilities, and public affairs officers would be more knowledgeable about the concerns and jargon of diplomats, aid workers, and defense attachés. To reach the minds of diverse people around the world, his employees needed "specialized attention to specialized problems, placed at the disposal and contemplation of ALL the best minds from all the foreign affairs community." If such a school opened, he planned to enroll some of his 6,500 foreign-national employees.[15]

Murrow's greatest demonstration of dedication to the USIA in 1963 could be seen in his continued fight with Congress for greater funding to improve the quantity and quality of his agency's programming. Murrow told senators that the USIA could not expect foreign journalists to explain U.S. foreign policy adequately; to assume otherwise would be tantamount to a senator allowing "a stranger to explain his voting record to his constituents."[16] When Murrow appeared before Congress, he focused on the deficiencies that money could correct: the need for more powerful transmitters for Voice of America, access to commercial satellites for television programming, and the financial means to hire more journalists to report expediently under the demands of emerging electronic media. When members of Congress asked Murrow if he could measure the influence of the USIA's overseas programming, he acknowledged the difficulty of quantifying its effectiveness: "No computer clicks, no cash register rings when a man changes his mind or opts for freedom." In March 1963, he told a

House foreign policy subcommittee that despite its limitations, America's "arsenal of persuasion must be as ready as our nuclear arsenal, and used as never before."[17]

A skeptical Congress did not equate the influence of public diplomacy with the hard power of aircraft carriers, strategic bombers, or army divisions. Representative John J. Rooney, chair of the House Appropriations Subcommittee on Foreign Operations, Export Financing, and Related Programs, planned to cut the USIA's 1964 budget supplemental from nine million to five million dollars.[18] The cut represented the mixed results of Murrow's three-year public engagement campaign across the United States. Although he succeeded in improving the domestic image of the USIA from its post-McCarthy-era low, Congress remained unconvinced that the United States needed to spend significant money to explain its policies or national story abroad. Recalling America's moral victory in defeating fascism in World War II, many members of Congress continued to consider communism a monolithic evil and assumed that the rest of the world agreed with them. This mentality hindered Murrow's efforts to convince them of the urgency for expanding USIA broadcasting, film, and literature behind the Iron Curtain, much less the developing world.

Before his illness, Murrow voiced his outrage with Congress in several public engagements in which he urged legislators, via their constituents, to reconsider their plan to cut his budget in 1964. Addressing an Advertising Federation of America convention, Murrow compared U.S. and Soviet spending: "We are being out-spent, out-published, and out-broadcast. We are a first-rate power. We must speak with a first-rate voice abroad." For the benefit of next-day headlines, Murrow told the advertisers that the USIA faced a serious danger: "Either the House of Representatives believes in the potency of ideas and the importance of information or it does not. On the record it does not so believe."[19]

A week after nearly collapsing on the White House steps to view Kennedy's pall, Murrow rose from his bed to make a special appeal to Representative Rooney to increase his budget. Stan Plesent watched Murrow struggle to haul himself up the steps of the House Office Building—not daring to help him—then listened as Murrow gasped for enough air to plead with Rooney for nine million dollars. Murrow's feeble condition unnerved Rooney, who told Murrow that he would increase the USIA's budget. However, Rooney only raised the appropriations to eight million. Plesent recalled Murrow's disappointment: "It was stupid! Three million! What is that? One missile or bomber costs more than our whole operation! But it was important to Murrow. It was for the Agency."[20]

Although his budget did not allow Murrow to realize all of his aspirations, the USIA's broadcasts and programs still improved America's prestige during the Kennedy administration. In the spring of 1963, a Soviet newspaper called the USIA "a truly tremendous monster of the cold war," but also acknowledged begrudgingly that the agency had succeeded in "making the stakes in freedom" better understood around the world.[21] One Soviet commentary stated that the USIA had "no equal in other capitalist countries . . . [it] extols the American way of life on every road crossing."[22] In late October 1963, the USIA's Office of Public Information released an eighteen-page paper that enumerated many of the changes within the agency since Murrow had assumed the directorship. Foremost, the paper hailed the agency's contribution to policymaking:

> The role of the Director and his senior officers in the formulation of foreign policy has been greatly strengthened. No longer is USIA handed a policy and told to make the best of it. The Agency's counsel is now sought whenever national policies with foreign implications are being formulated. . . . President Kennedy's January 25, 1963, statement of mission for USIA charged the Agency with the responsibility for "advising the President, his representatives abroad, and the various departments and agencies on the implications of foreign opinion for present and contemplated United States policies, programs and official statements." That statement is very much an operational fact.[23]

Murrow first submitted his resignation to President Johnson on December 19, 1963, citing his deteriorating health. In addition to mentioning to Johnson that he had already discussed with Kennedy the possibility of resigning due to his lung cancer, Murrow gave Don Wilson a resounding recommendation as his permanent successor. Wilson had served as acting director during several of the Kennedy administration's most difficult challenges, including the rise of the Berlin Wall, the Cuban Missile Crisis, and the coup in South Vietnam.[24] However, Johnson would not hear of Murrow leaving his administration, and he sent the director back to 1776 Pennsylvania Avenue with his resignation in hand. A month later Murrow returned to the Oval Office, insisting that he be permitted to resign for health reasons, and this time the president agreed.[25]

Johnson did not initially accept Murrow's resignation because he wanted to be able to announce Murrow's replacement simultaneously with his departure. While Wilson's performance as acting director made him an obvious choice, Casey Murrow speculates that the president did not pick him because he was not well known nationally.[26] Instead, Johnson chose Ambassador Carl Rowan, a former deputy assistant secretary of state for public affairs, whom the president recalled from the U.S. embassy in Helsinki, Finland, to become the first African American to serve on the National Security Council. Prior to joining the State Department, Rowan had worked as a reporter at the *Minneapolis Tribune*, where he earned his own trove of journalism awards. Johnson assumed political risk in selecting Rowan; however, he wanted to demonstrate his commitment to the civil rights movement. Many newspapers opined that selecting Rowan would help to advance the image of U.S. racial integration for the USIA's overseas audiences as well as African Americans at home.[27]

To improve the likelihood of Rowan's confirmation, the president personally called friends on Capitol Hill. On January 16, Johnson told Senator John McClellan (D-AR), the chair of the Senate Government Operations Committee, "I don't want you to cut his gut out because he's Negro."[28] The evening before announcing Murrow's resignation, Johnson phoned Senator Richard Russell Jr. (D-GA) asking him to "hold your hat" but also assuring him that Rowan would be a fine director. Russell said that he did not care one way or the other about the appointment, so long as Rowan did not have "some great ambition that he's going to take over and be the spokesman for the Negroes by denouncing the South before the world."[29]

News of Murrow's resignation on January 21, 1964, disappointed many members of the Johnson administration and national press.

Media coverage widely credited Murrow with serving in a position "eminently right" for a man with a name "synonymous with integrity," and for restoring the morale and credibility of the agency at home and abroad.[30] The *New York Times* headline assessed Murrow's achievement pithily: "USIA Moved from Doghouse into White House."[31] New York radio station WBBF offered an apology for predicting a bleak forecast of his directorship three years earlier: "We are delighted to say we were wrong about Edward R. Murrow. We share the sorrow of his subordinates as he leaves government service."[32] To recognize his oversight of Voice of America, the Broadcast Pioneers awarded Murrow with his fifth Peabody.[33]

Within the USIA, members praised Murrow for his service. Among the letters of condolence that flowed in after his resignation, the public affairs officer in Cairo thanked Murrow for giving the USIA the "structure and recognition that were much needed." Another officer in Mali believed that Murrow's demand "of having the Agency stick to the truth and not embark on cheap, tempting, short-run propaganda victories has given our information and cultural programs a solid and untarnishable value." From Moscow, diplomat Lee Brady wrote, "When we said, 'We'd go through fire for him!' we came as close to meaning it literally as one can."[34] Henry Loomis, who some historians portray as frustrated with Murrow's heavy-handed approach to dealing with Voice of America, had nothing but public and private praise for Murrow's leadership. Traveling through Europe, Loomis learned of the resignation, fittingly, from a VOA broadcast and penned a handwritten letter from an Air France passenger seat:

> I am now flying from Munich to Paris—in that suspended state where you look down on the world in a detached fashion, a good platform to start to assess the impact you have made on the agency. . . . We felt sheltered by your courage, enlivened by your humor but above all we knew you cared—about the world, about our goal, about the agency—even about us as individuals—but never about yourself.[35]

From within the administration, Murrow received dozens of tributes. National Security Adviser McGeorge Bundy not only appreciated the reports generated from the USIA's research department but also Murrow's personal assessments on global public opinion that often accompanied the reports sent to the White House.[36] In a leather-bound, farewell-message album, assembled by Wilson with contributions from senior officials, Bundy wrote, "You did your job so well that you leave it larger than you found it in every way." The State Department's Walt Rostow lauded Murrow for speaking "without abstraction or intermediaries," and, he confided, "No one I ever admired from afar turned out so much bigger close-up." Richard Helms, the Director of Central Intelligence, told Murrow that he had taken the USIA "out of the world of controversy and have given it, not only domestically but throughout the world, a standing which it never had before." Undersecretary of State George Ball understood what Murrow brought to the president's cabinet: "Even when many of us were caught up in the collective excitement of the moment, pontificating around the table in the Cabinet Room, you were always the barrister with a brief for sanity."[37]

In the album, Jackie Kennedy praised her late husband for bringing Murrow to Washington: "And the greatest thing of all he did was inspiring men like you—to leave comfortable lives and come to serve your country."[38] Attorney General Robert Kennedy added, "When you spoke—everyone listened—When you raised questions you caused all to think—and when you recommended courses of action whether they were always followed or not they always made sense."[39] In the forward to Tom Sorensen's 1968 book, *The Word War: The Story of American Propaganda*, Kennedy hailed Murrow as an "extraordinary man" who understood that the agency alone could not be held responsible for international perceptions of the United States abroad.[40] It was a stirring endorsement from the same man who, in 1954, had walked out in protest from the Junior Chamber of Commerce's Ten Outstanding Young Men awards ceremony as Murrow approached the podium to deliver the keynote address.

Fully appreciating Murrow's relationship with President Kennedy remains somewhat difficult. No personal correspondence between the two men exists in the archives, with the rare exception of a personal comment interjected into one of Murrow's weekly USIA reports to the White House. Most disappointingly, Murrow continued to put off requests in his retirement to sit for an oral history for the new Kennedy Presidential Library.[41] Murrow privately shared his thoughts about Kennedy in a letter to physicist J. Robert Oppenheimer on August 18, 1964. The president had remained elusive to Murrow: "I have had great difficulty in trying to reach some judgment regarding that young man's relation to his time. I saw him at fairly close range under a variety of circumstances and there remains for me a considerable element of mystery . . . I always knew where his mind was, but I was not always sure where his heart was." In the same letter, he offered a humorous description of Kennedy's successor: "My experience with Lyndon Johnson was rather the reverse—I was never in doubt as to where his heart was, as he was generally beating me over the head with it."[42]

Murrow told longtime confidant Raymond Hare that he considered his time in Washington as "probably the most rewarding experience of my life."[43] Shortly after his resignation, Murrow assessed his tenure at the agency during an interview for the *Washington Post*: "I have never worked harder in my life and never been happier. I haven't had such satisfaction since the days of covering the London blitz."[44] He congratulated Rowan for assuming "the most interesting, as well as the most complicated job in Washington," adding that Johnson had selected the right man for the job.[45] Rowan, in turn, credited Murrow with renewing the spirit of the agency and elevating its status within the Washington bureaucracy.[46]

Tom Sorensen assessed Murrow's contributions within the context of his own eleven years at the USIA: "Until 1961, frustration always followed hope and progress usually trailed off into decay. Now it will never be the same again. . . . You made a greater contribution in 34 months than your predecessors made in all their years."[47] Sorensen could quantify his praise by citing the growth of the agency's capabilities and audience. In 1963, six hundred million people in one hundred and four countries viewed USIA films every month; Voice of America provided two thousand hours of broadcasts a day in nearly forty languages, and over three hundred cultural and educational exhibits circulated around the world that year.[48]

During his confirmation hearings, Murrow had laid out three priorities for the USIA: the need for the agency's headquarters to become more flexible in supporting the unique requirements of each country post, as opposed to blanket regional directives; improving the signal strength of Voice of America; and requiring the agency's research division to carefully analyze the audience and purpose of every documentary film produced.[49] Three years later, the USIA had made progress in all three areas. Murrow split the Eastern European countries and USSR from the European division in order for assistant directors and their public affairs officers to create the most appropriate message for two very different regions. He slimmed down the number of priority agency messages to no more than five at any one time and instructed his staff to say them dynamically and repetitively.[50] To espouse the messages, he had created the USIA's "fast media" to synchronize the operations of Voice of America, the press service, the Motion Picture Service, and the Television Service.[51] By empowering Tom Sorensen's plans and policy office to establish and enforce information priorities, Murrow ensured that the fast media responsibly supported the administration during crises. The USIA's ability to stay on message influenced much of its audience to hold Soviet premier Nikita Khrushchev accountable for the Berlin and Cuban crises.

Murrow supported Kennedy's strategic pivot toward the Third World. Beyond the direction that he gave to the USIA, Murrow made suggestions to his colleagues in the National Security Council on how they could improve America's prestige south of the equator. He encouraged the administration to refer to the Third World as "developing" or "modernizing," as a sign of respect.[52] When he learned that Sargent Shriver intended to send the first group of Peace Corps volunteers to the Philippines, Murrow encouraged Shriver to send them to Africa instead, for fear of communist propagandists drawing parallels to the United States' seizure of the archipelago in 1898.[53] He convinced Vice President Johnson to make the first telephone–radio satellite broadcast in history to an African country, rather than to Europe. Although the USIA's research division reported that the majority of Europeans believed that the United States lagged behind the Soviet Union in scientific advancement in 1963, Murrow still believed the public diplomacy value of communicating with Africa to be more consequential.[54]

Good Luck, Ed

The quality of the Motion Picture Service's documentaries improved greatly under the direction of George Stevens Jr., whom Murrow hired from Hollywood. The human-interest-story approach that replaced the heavily didactic, anticommunist films of the Eisenhower administration resonated with audiences around the world. Stevens attracted imaginative directors from the private sector to work on USIA projects, and the Motion Picture Service earned international acclaim at film festivals from 1962 to 1964.[55]

Stevens's most widely viewed film posthumously honored John F. Kennedy. Just hours after learning of his assassination, Stevens developed a plan to produce a USIA documentary on Kennedy's presidency.[56] Bruce Herschensohn directed *John F. Kennedy: Years of Lightning, Days of Drums*, an hour-and-a-half tribute to the slain president's legacy released on the anniversary of his death. The narrator, Gregory Peck, contrasts the optimism of the Washington crowds on Kennedy's inauguration day to the three billion people of the world, "most of [whom] were not happy or free or at peace." Scenes explain Kennedy's quest to help alleviate suffering and promote security by highlighting the six "faces" of the New Frontier: the Peace Corps, the space race, the Alliance for Progress, civil rights, freedom, and peace. Images from Africa, Latin America, and Asia stress the cooperative nature of U.S. efforts, where locals work alongside Americans.[57]

The film captured Kennedy's international popularity, from the showering of confetti on his open-air limousine in Mexico City, to the wild reaction of West Berliners to his speech from their town hall, to the thousands of smiling faces that greet him in his ancestral home of Ireland. A significant portion of the production follows the three days of national mourning that culminated with the lighting of the memorial flame during Kennedy's burial at Arlington National Cemetery. Muffled drums and "Hail to the Chief," performed at a slow tempo, serve as the stirring soundtrack. Peck stresses that neither the Peace Corps nor the Alliance for Progress died with Kennedy; rather, they would grow under President Johnson's leadership. Over images from the March on Washington, Peck explains that Johnson had evoked his predecessor's memory to advance the 1964 Civil Rights Act through Congress.[58] Interweaving Johnson as a national leader into the documentary helped allay international concerns about U.S. political stability in the aftermath of the tragedy.

"Sentimental and dramatic," the documentary appeared commercially in sixty-seven countries and for free in fifty others, compliments of the USIA.[59] Wilson hailed Stevens's production as a "true smash hit" around the world.[60] It helped that United Artists and MGM Studio presented the USIA documentary prior to major releases overseas in the winter of 1964–65.[61] The prime minister of Nigeria, Alhaji Sir Abubakar Balewa, attested to the documentary's power: "Men and women who were illiterate who saw the film of his death, who only heard of him, were really very sad that the man died. . . . That was a mark of greatness for people who lived thousands of miles away."[62] Undersecretary of State for Political Affairs W. Averell Harriman believed that the world mourned Kennedy's death because it had come to know and understand the president's "spirit" through the USIA's work.[63]

Despite the accolades and the measurable achievements, Murrow did not succeed in fully revamping the agency. The key obstacles remained parochial members of Congress who continued to cut the agency's budget; substandard staff members; and officials from the State and Defense Departments who increasingly aired messages that were not concordant with the agency's broadcasts, particularly to South Vietnam. In retirement, Murrow continued to lambast Congress. Writing to Senator Jacob Javits (R-NY) in April 1964, he opined, "The hard fact is that the Congress of the United States does not believe in the potency of ideas or the importance of information. . . . They won't even use their own instruments to tell the story of what the U.S. Information Agency is doing." He had a solution in mind: "God knows I failed to persuade our Appropriation subcommittees of the importance of the work. Maybe Rowan will have better luck, but I assure you that what our information effort needs is not advice, counsel, or ideas. It is money."[64]

Beyond Washington, the USIA's messages achieved mixed results, but only a portion of the blame could fall on the reticence of Congress to supply adequate funding, because public diplomacy can only be as effective as the foreign policies it advocates. Kennedy's major Latin American initiative, the Alliance for Progress, failed to achieve any of its goals. Lao neutrality seemed to be crumbling before 1964; and political instability, following the coup against Ngo Dinh Diem, made the challenges facing U.S. military advisers in South Vietnam much more complicated. However, the administration advanced portions of its foreign policy agenda. Kennedy and Khrushchev avoided a violent superpower clash over the Berlin Wall or Cuban Missile Crisis. Coupled with the June 1963 signing of the nuclear test ban treaty, the likelihood of peaceful coexistence seemed more plausible than when President Dwight Eisenhower left office in January 1961.

With Murrow's departure, the USIA's role in the new administration appeared uncertain to insiders. Wilson feared that the State Department would renew its efforts to absorb the USIA.[65] By August 1964, Sorensen and Wilson had grown impatient with Rowan's poor management of the agency. In a letter to Murrow, Wilson wrote, "Carl is a very good guy but has no particular interest or aptitude for running the place."[66] As he had already begun to do over Vietnam information operations, Defense Secretary Robert McNamara continued to marginalize the USIA, and Wilson felt that he had to go through an obstacle course every time he or Rowan tried to participate in a Vietnam strategy session.[67] In the fall of 1964, Murrow learned that senior officials in the Defense Department were pushing for the South Vietnamese government to develop television programs, while media experts from the USIA and the U.S. Agency of International Development warned that the Vietnamese needed to master radio broadcasting first. They believed that it would be a waste to sink money into a television station in Saigon when television sets were largely unavailable in the countryside.[68]

Although too weak to respond to a great deal of his correspondence, Murrow continued to receive well wishes from old friends and many USIA employees as he fought his cancer from Glen Arden farm. Being in his mid-fifties, Murrow should have had another ten good years of interesting work, but his illness tired him. Offers continued to arrive by mail or phone to return to journalism. ABC encouraged him to "do a little radio or television" with their network.[69] NBC president Robert Kintner encouraged Murrow to meet once he was rested enough to "come back into the business."[70] He received a variety of letters from publishing houses encouraging him to write a book, which he told a friend, "I am not about to do."[71] Frank Stanton suggested that Murrow rejoin CBS in the spring of 1964, but Murrow told his former radio colleague Edward Morgan, "Right now I feel I aint [*sic*] going anywhere."[72] Casey Murrow believes that there was a serious possibility that, had he lived, his father would have found a new niche with the early development of the Public Broadcasting Service. In any event, the network offers "gratified" Murrow because he remained viscerally interested in journalism, but he was simply too sick to take any of the options seriously.[73]

Murrow tired so easily after leaving Washington that he rarely traveled or socialized. Janet confided in Marie Harriman that her husband had "faded a bit" by September 1964, but she hoped that he could find a project that would not be too taxing to keep him upbeat. "What that can be," she wrote sadly, "I *don't* know." The Murrows returned to Washington for a few days in mid-September 1964, and Johnson awarded Murrow the Presidential Medal of Freedom on September 14 at a noontime ceremony at the White House. Among the people they saw in Washington were the Harrimans, who hosted a party, the first one that the Murrows had attended in a year. "It was fun to attend," wrote Janet to Marie, "though I don't really like *big* parties."[74]

Murrow's health began to deteriorate rapidly by October 1964. In the final public appearance of his life on October 24, 1964, Murrow delivered an acceptance speech after receiving the Family of Man Award from the Protestant Council of New York. A dying man, he could have talked about anything from his life, but he chose to discuss the USIA. He recognized the challenge that the USIA continued to face in conducting public diplomacy, observing that, despite technological innovation in broadcasting, the agency often proved unsuccessful in carrying its message "the last few feet from the loudspeaker to the minds of the foreign listeners."[75]

Murrow spent the winter of 1964–65 in and out of hospitals. In March doctors discovered that the cancer had spread to his brain, and they wanted to keep him in the hospital for permanent care. He summoned the strength to grab hold of the arm of his friend, CBS announcer Bob Dixon, and insisted that Dixon take him home, even if that meant carrying him out against doctors' orders. Murrow did not want to die in a hospital; he wanted to go home to Pawling. The doctors and Janet made arrangements, and Murrow arrived at Glen Arden farm on April 6 to find nurses on hand and a hospital bed in his room. He passed away in his sleep on April 27, 1965, with Janet by his side. His family sprinkled his ashes over the estate's glen, and a simple plaque with his name, date of birth, and date of death marks the site affixed to a nearby boulder.[76] Under "usual occupation," his death certificate listed newscaster and director of the USIA.[77]

Hearing the news of Murrow's passing, Harriman cabled Janet the same day: "I can't believe that Ed is gone. He has been so much a part of my life in the last 25 years." The diplomat released a press statement praising Murrow for his service at the USIA, which "has done much to bring the truth of American ideals and thought to the people of the world." For Harriman, the foundations of Murrow's vision for the USIA stemmed from his wartime experience as a journalist, where he forged his own path to help his audience "understand and interpret the feelings" of the people about whom he reported.[78] The *Foreign Service Journal*'s obituary lauded Murrow for forging "new luster to American prestige."[79] The Overseas Press Club Foundation honored Murrow's memory by establishing the Edward R. Murrow Memorial Fund, and by 1967, it had raised five hundred thousand dollars for a three-year educational program emphasizing the "responsibilities of the news media in international news coverage."[80] Sponsors included Robert Kennedy, Chief Justice Earl Warren, and CBS president Frank Stanton. To generate funding, the club began hosting a series called the Edward R. Murrow World Affairs Forum, the first taking place on September 21, 1967, to discuss Israel's policy toward its Arab neighbors. In a fundraiser letter, written on behalf of the Press Club, Harriman lauded Murrow as "a rare breed of a man—quiet and somewhat shy, yet consumed by many drives and a talent for doing well and with great flair, whatever he undertook (as exemplified by the last years of his life as Director of the United States Information Agency)."[81]

Biographer Joseph Persico argued that Murrow's frustrations with CBS stemmed from his inability to reconcile with the profit-minded executives who increasingly marginalized him for taking television too seriously. "Murrow wanted the world to be a better place than it is, and he wanted television to serve that end," Persico opined. "He credited adults with adult minds, and so he wanted them to face hard truths."[82] Persico could have easily extended this analysis to explain Murrow's frustrations with government service. In his desire to improve the United States' position as leader of the free world, Murrow arrived in Washington expecting the president, his administration, the Congress, and the entire USIA staff to embrace fully the notion of telling America's story, warts and all.

Similarly, Kennedy arrived in the Oval Office believing that he could pursue a more dynamic Cold War foreign policy than had President Eisenhower. His youthfulness served as an outward sign of his New Frontier, as did the dynamism of many of his closest advisers who hailed from academia, the business world, and, as in Murrow and Wilson's case, journalism. British ambassador David Ormsby-Gore admired the way that Kennedy looked beyond the civil service to find the advisers and key national leaders "necessary under modern conditions."[83]

Once ensconced in the federal bureaucracy, however, Murrow gained a front-row seat to learning how party politics, congressional parochialism, regional prejudices, superpower rivalries, and downright irrational human behavior forced Kennedy to compromise his own ideals and policies, both foreign and domestic. Just as Bill Paley had adjusted CBS's programming schedule throughout the 1950s to secure the greatest ratings for his network, so too did Kennedy redefine what it meant to "assure the survival and the success of liberty" following his inauguration on January 20, 1961.[84] Murrow could have resigned on principle in April 1961, when Kennedy went forward with the Bay of Pigs invasion, or in October 1962, when Kennedy failed to call for a civil rights act in the wake of the James Meredith–University of Mississippi standoff, or in September 1963, when General Paul Harkins told Murrow that he needed Agent Orange to defeat the Viet Cong. Instead, Murrow remained at the USIA and strove to tell a truthful American story without dishonoring his own oath of office.

Although a liberal critic might say that Murrow had "sold out" to the administration, because Kennedy failed to pursue a robust progressive policy agenda, Murrow would have failed to contribute in the significant way that he did to the United States' position in the world had he walked away from the USIA prior to January 1964. Murrow's personal conversations and correspondence as director indicate that he remained an idealist, but he was also a political realist who accepted what he could not influence. He never romanticized about the New Frontier, and his celebrity status kept him grounded when other members of the administration became captivated by the Washington social scene or the mystique of the White House. Murrow supported the Special Group (Augmented) in encouraging the Cuban people to overthrow Fidel Castro, but he unequivocally opposed the possibility of assassinating dictators.[85] The same rationale applied to Murrow's position on Diem, even after the South Vietnam president's mistreatment of the Buddhist majority.

Those critics who maintain that Voice of America should remain entirely above government affairs may fault Murrow for usurping editorial control from Loomis on a handful of occasions. However, Voice of America was not CBS News. While both competed for a broader audience, Voice of America served, and continues to serve, as a federal agency responsible for explaining the policies of the United States government. As one of America's most seasoned journalists, Murrow understood the value of a free press as well as anyone at Voice of America, but he also recognized his responsibility as USIA director to ensuring that Voice of America serve as an advocate for the Kennedy administration. In an agency-wide memorandum in April 1961, Murrow assured his broadcasters that he would not dictate to them what all of their programs should sound like. However, he emphasized that oversight from the fourth floor of 1776 Pennsylvania Avenue would improve Voice of America's contribution to the larger USIA mission to speak with one voice and to amplify that voice as loudly as possible.[86] Murrow believed that this could be accomplished in a dynamic way. Following his advice, Voice of America began a program in late August 1964 titled *Viewpoints*. Akin to his 1950s CBS program *See It Now*, *Viewpoints* introduced different perspectives on a variety of controversial issues, such as the nuclear test ban treaty, birth control, the value of the United Nations, and the March on Washington.[87]

Throughout his time in Washington, Murrow referred to himself as a bureaucrat or propagandist but never as a policymaker. Writing to the American Federation of Television and Radio Artists in February 1961, he politely explained why he needed to end his affiliation: "I regret to say that now that I have become a Washington bureaucrat, I feel obliged to resign."[88] In April 1962, he told the *Miami Herald*, "I don't mind being called a propagandist so long as the propaganda is based on the truth."[89] Perhaps the disadvantage of hiring someone from outside of the Beltway is that the individual may feel overwhelmed by the politics and red tape of Washington. Sometimes, however, organizations need the fresh perspective of an outsider to improve their capabilities.

It is not surprising that Murrow felt overwhelmed when he first arrived at the USIA, or that he occasionally became emotionally repulsed by Byzantine congressional or bureaucratic stubbornness. Nevertheless, he strove to change what he could influence within the bureaucracy. Murrow relied on outsiders like himself—Don Wilson and George Stevens Jr.—to help rejuvenate the agency's operations. He pulled Tom Sorensen up several rungs in the agency hierarchy to fill the USIA's number three position, in order to craft and enforce internal agency policies that would more effectively ensure that messages reflected the administration's priorities. Murrow reached down into his agency to get time-sensitive information. He reprimanded supervisors for writing meaningless performance evaluations and personally cabled public affairs officers who missed deadlines for submitting their semiannual reports.[90]

Overall, Murrow's tenure at the USIA should be judged as positive for the agency and the quality of U.S. public diplomacy during the Cold War. His tremendous experience as a journalist, familiarity with world leaders, and acute sense of audience interests improved morale at the USIA after the McCarthy scourges of the 1950s. Many of his pithy quotes remained in the repertoire of USIA employees for decades: "warts and all," "in on the takeoff," and "the last three feet." Most importantly, Murrow's fervent belief that truth is the best propaganda served as the guiding principle for his directorship. He required the media services, public affairs officers, and overseas library workers to drop the simplistic Cold War platitudes of good versus evil and enter into a dialogue with their international audience. Although not always successful in advancing every administration policy, this approach generated a conversation, particularly in the developing world, where curious people evaluated America's role in the Cold War.

White House adviser and historian Arthur M. Schlesinger Jr. had privately noted Kennedy's lack of an inner conviction at the time of the 1960 Democratic convention.[91] Murrow, however, possessed that inner conviction about the value of public affairs and the real threats to freedom and democracy. In 1937 he called for the United States to join with the United Kingdom against the Third Reich before Hitler became unmanageable. In 1954 he explained how McCarthy threatened American liberties more tangibly than Soviet spies and sympathizers in the United States. From 1961 to 1963, he reminded Kennedy of the unique potential of the United States to serve as a genuine beacon of liberty in a world divided by Cold War polarities. Murrow understood the difference between the American image and the nation's ideals, and he wanted the USIA to explain the latter as the impetus behind the country's ongoing evolution toward a more genuine democracy. Under Murrow's leadership, USIA officers educated foreigners about America's complicated social and political culture, which influenced Kennedy's decisions on a wide variety of challenges at home and abroad. The USIA went about this in a fashion that did not insult the intelligence of its global audience, and it helped to create the widespread international appeal for Kennedy that became so apparent following his assassination.

NOTES

Abbreviations

ASJ   Arthur Schlesinger Jr. Journals, New York Public Library, New York NY

BNA   British National Archives, Kew Gardens, London, United Kingdom

CIA-FOIA   Central Intelligence Agency Freedom of Information Act, Electronic Reading Room, http://www.foia.cia.gov/

DA   Departments and Agencies

ERMP   Edward R. Murrow Papers, c. 1890–1992. Tufts University, Tisch Library, Digital Collections and Archives, Medford MA

ERMP-MHC   Edward R. and Janet Brewster Murrow Papers, Mount Holyoke College, Archives and Special Collections, South Hadley MA

FGO   Federal Government–Organizations

FO   Foreign Office

JFKLOHP   John F. Kennedy Presidential Library and Museum, Oral History Project, Boston MA

JFKPL   John F. Kennedy Presidential Library and Museum, Boston

LBJPL   Lyndon Baines Johnson Presidential Library, Austin TX

MM   Meetings and Memoranda

NA   National Archives and Records Administration II, College Park MD

NNPC   Nuclear Non-Proliferation Collection, National Security Archive, Gelman Library, George Washington University, Washington DC

NSA   National Security Archive, Gelman Library, George Washington University, Washington DC

NSF   National Security Files

POF   Presidential Office Files

SF   Security Files

USIAAA   United States Information Agency Alumni Association
VPP   Vice Presidential Papers
WAH   W. Averell Harriman Papers, Library of Congress, Washington DC
WHCSF   White House Central Subject Files

Introduction

1. Murrow, address before the National Convention of the Federal Bar Association, Washington DC, September 26, 1963, Box 17, E1069, RG 306, NA.

2. Murrow, speech before the National Press Club, Washington DC, May 24, 1961, Box 132, ERMP.

3. Crocker Snow Jr., "Public Diplomacy Practitioners: A Changing Cast of Characters," *Readings on Public Diplomacy*, The Edward R. Murrow Center of Public Diplomacy at the Fletcher School of Law and Diplomacy, Tufts University, http://fletcher.tufts.edu/murrow/readings/aboutpd.html.

4. Murrow, quoted in Philip Meyer, "How U.S. Is Getting Its Message Abroad," *Miami Herald*, April 29, 1962.

5. Donald M. Wilson, "Persuasion Overseas: An Element of Power," *Vassar Alumni Magazine*, February 1964, Box 37, E1069, RG 306, NA.

6. Cull, *Cold War and the United States Information Agency*, xv.

7. Arndt, *First Resort of Kings*, 4.

8. Morgan, *Benjamin Franklin*, 243.

9. Nye, *Soft Power*, 11.

10. Creel, *How We Advertised America*, 4.

11. Bernays, *Propaganda*, 38.

12. William Benton, excerpts from a letter written to an associate; enclosed with letter, Oliver McKee to Frances Jamieson, March 21, 1947, Box 2, RG 4, Nelson A. Rockefeller Washington DC Files, Rockefeller Archive Center, Tarrytown NY. I am indebted to Dr. Victoria Phillips for sharing this letter with me.

13. Wagnleiter, *Coca-Colonization and the Cold War*.

14. "The American Twang," *Time*, May 26, 1947, 21.

15. Hunt, *Ideology and U.S. Foreign Policy*, 15.

16. Susan Bachrach and Steven Luckert provide a masterful study of Nazi propaganda related to the Holocaust in *State of Deception: The Power of Nazi Propaganda*. B. R. Myers explains how two generations of Kims used racial propaganda to convince the North Korean people to remain loyal to the regime in *The Cleanest Race: How North Koreans See Themselves and Why It Matters*.

17. Dizard, *Strategy of Truth*, 26.

18. Thomas Sorensen, address before the Mid-Western Unitarian Universalist Conference, Omaha NE, April 4, 1963, Box 1, E20, RG 306, NA.

19. Cull, *Cold War and the United States Information Agency*, xiv–xvi.

20. Murrow, speech before the National Press Club, Washington DC, May 24, 1961, Box 132, ERMP.

21. Manheim, *Strategic Public Diplomacy*, 7.

22. Although many Office of Research and Analysis reports remain classified as secret, a wide variety is available in RG 306 at the National Archives. However, the Office of Research and Analysis does not have one single entry with all reports available in chronological order. Several entries proved very helpful in researching for this book: E1005, E1010, E1012, and E1039. Additionally, E1069 contains Murrow's personal copies of several key research reports related to Cuba, Berlin, nuclear testing, the space race, and the Alliance for Progress that are not available in the previously cited entries.

23. Murrow's weekly reports to the president are available in Boxes 4–5 (microfilm), E1006, RG 306, NA.

24. JFK, Inaugural Address, January 20, 1961, *Public Papers of the Presidents: John F. Kennedy*, vol. 1961, 2.

25. David E. Bell, recorded interview by William T. Dentzer Jr., January 2, 1965, JFKLOHP.

26. Memorandum, Arthur Schlesinger Jr. to JFK: "Organizing the Democratic Parties of the World," September 29, 1961, WAH.

27. Fried, *Nightmare in Red*, 136; and Schrecker, *Many Are the Crimes*, 256–57.

28. Cable: "Developments in Communist Bloc International Broadcasting in 1961," February 7, 1962, FO 1110/1522, BNA.

29. "The Truth Must Be Our Guide, But Dreams Must Be Our Goals," *Newsweek*, September 18, 1961, 26.

30. Tudda, *Truth Is Our Weapon*, 10–14.

31. In November 1954, when Soviet troops arrived in Budapest to put down the revolt, many Hungarian freedom fighters continued to resist insurmountable odds because they said that broadcasters on the CIA's Radio Free Europe had promised that American forces would cross Austria to support their cause. A post-uprising CIA investigation into the RFE's role remained inconclusive since the station did not maintain transcripts or recordings of its broadcasts, and RFE officials said that Hungarians exaggerated the content of their programs. See Sebestyen, *Twelve Days*, 181–83, 294–96.

32. Tudda, *Truth Is Our Weapon*, 128.

33. Report, President's Committee on Information Activities Abroad, December 23, 1960, quoted in Cull, *Cold War and the United States Information Agency*, 183.

34. Domer, "Sport in Cold War America," 260–61.

35. "George A. Smathers, United States Senator, 1951–1969," Oral History Interviews, Senate Historical Office, Washington DC, http://www.senate.gov/artandhistory/history/oral_history/George_A_Smathers.htm.

36. Memorandum, George A. Smathers to JFK: "Need for New Type of Leadership and Reorientation for the United States Information Agency," January 1961, Box 91, DA, POF, JFKPL.

37. James Reston, "Policy and Propaganda–Murrow's Assignment," *New York Times*, January 29, 1961.

38. Anonymous editorial appearing in numerous newspapers, "More than Job of 'Telling,'" February 7, 1963, Box 15, E1069, RG 306, NA.

39. Memorandum, Donald Wilson to JFK, January 26, 1961, Box 91, DA, POF, JFKPL.

40. Letter, JFK to William Benton, February 18, 1961, Box 184, FGO, WHCSF, JFKPL.

41. Press clippings, Box 15, E1069, RG 306, NA.

42. Press clippings, Box 10, ERMP-MHC.

43. Letter, Chester Bowles to Murrow, January 11, 1961, Box 26, ERMP.

44. In 1959 Murrow received a $300,000 salary from CBS ($2.3 million today). When he departed the network, CBS Executive Vice President James Seward continued to manage Murrow's accounts, and the network subsidized his living expenses; see letter, Murrow to James M. Seward, January 30, 1963, Box 5, ERMP-MHC.

45. Kendrick, *Prime Time*, 452; Sperber, *Murrow*, 625; and Persico, *Edward R. Murrow*, 470.

46. Letter, Raymond G. Swing to Murrow, January 2, 1961, Box 49, ERMP.

47. Winfield and DeFleur, eds., *Edward R. Murrow Heritage*, 51. The text of his speeches delivered as a CBS journalist are available in Bliss, ed., *In Search of Light*, and they reveal his criticism toward network executives, advertisers, and the corporate side of producing news in the television age of the late 1950s.

48. Letter, Murrow to Wilmott Ragsdale, January 18, 1961, Box 26, ERMP.

49. Charles Casey Murrow, interview by author, July 30, 2012, Dummerston VT.

50. Sperber, *Murrow*, xi.

51. Susanne Belovari, archivist for Reference and Collections, Tufts University Archive, conversation with author, March 16, 2010, Medford MA.

52. Arndt, *First Resort of Kings*, 315.

53. Letter, Arthur Hoffman to Martin Manning, February 24, 1986, Box 18, E1069, RG 306, NA.

54. Thomas C. Sorensen, *Word War*.

55. Belmonte, *Selling the American Way*.

56. Hixson, *Parting the Curtain*.

57. Heil, *Voice of America*; and Nelson, *War of the Black Heavens*.

58. Arndt, *First Resort of Kings*, 314–37.

59. Cull, *Cold War and the United States Information Agency*, 190.

60. Cull, *Cold War and the United States Information Agency*, 212.

61. Memorandum, Murrow to Turner B. Shelton: "Proposal by Stuart Schulberg," May 17, 1961, Box 18, E1069, RG 306, NA.

62. Anonymous USIA official, quoted in Art Edson, "Murrow of the USIA," AP *Newsfeatures*, August 6, 1961, p. 11-E, Box 16, E1069, RG 306, NA.

63. Charles Casey Murrow, interview by author, July 30, 2012, Dummerston VT.

64. "USIA's Murrow: Is Truth the Best Weapon?" *Newsweek*, September 18, 1961.

65. Edward M. Kennedy, speech before the John F. Kennedy B'nai B'rith Lodge, Washington DC, May 27, 1965, Box 10, ERMP-MHC.

66. Kendrick, *Prime Time*, 467.

67. Edward T. Folliard, "When Mr. K Bullies, How Best to Answer Him?" *Washington Post*, September 3, 1961.

68. Murrow, speech before the Radio Television News Directors Association convention, Washington DC, September 30, 1961, Box 132, ERMP.

1. *Good Night,* CBS

1. Charles Casey Murrow, interview by author, July 30, 2012, Dummerston VT.

2. Letter, Murrow to James Seward, October 26, 1959, Box 5, ERMP-MHC.

3. CBS statement quoted in letter, James Seward to Murrow, March 26, 1960, Box 5, ERMP-MHC.

4. Letter, Murrow to James Seward, November 21, 1959, Box 5, ERMP-MHC.

5. Letter, Marge to Murrow, November 16, 1959, Box 5, ERMP-MHC.

6. Telegram, Murrow to Edward Morgan, December 12, 1959, Box 5, ERMP-MHC.

7. Telegram, Murrow to Ethel Murrow, December 12, 1959, Box 5, ERMP-MHC.

8. Telegram, Murrow to Ethel Murrow, January 5, 1960, Box 5, ERMP-MHC.

9. Telegram, Murrow to Edward Morgan, January 15, 1960, Box 5, ERMP-MHC.

10. Telegram, Murrow to Edward Morgan, February 2, 1960, Box 5, ERMP-MHC.

11. Anderson clearly impressed Murrow because shortly after his appointment as USIA director, Murrow promoted him to associate deputy director for policy and plans. See Burnett Anderson, recorded USIAAA interview by Jack O'Brien, January 5, 1990, Box 8, E1073, RG 306, NA.

12. Telegram, Murrow to Edward Morgan, February 2, 1960, Box 5, ERMP-MHC.

13. Sperber, *Murrow*, 593.

14. Jack Gould, "Newsmen at Odds," *New York Times*, February 21, 1960.

15. Letter, James Seward to Murrow, February 21, 1960, Box 5, ERMP-MHC.

16. Cable, Murrow to Edward Morgan, March 1, 1960, Box 5, ERMP-MHC.

17. Cable, Murrow to James Seward, March 20, 1960, Box 5, ERMP-MHC.

18. Letter, James Seward to Murrow, March 26, 1960, Box 5, ERMP-MHC.

19. Cable, Murrow to James Seward, April 6, 1960, Box 5, ERMP-MHC.

20. Letter, James Seward to Murrow, April 8, 1960, Box 5, ERMP-MHC.

21. Certificate of Death, April 27, 1965, Box 10, ERMP-MHC.

22. "Edward R. Murrow, Broadcaster and Ex-Chief of U.S.I.A., Dies," obituary, *New York Times*, April 28, 1965.

23. Kendrick, *Prime Time*, 81–82.

24. Charles Casey Murrow, interview by author, July 30, 2012, Dummerston VT.

25. Persico, *Edward R. Murrow*, 29.

26. Sperber, *Murrow*, 20.

27. Murrow, quoted in Persico, *Edward R. Murrow*, 34.

28. Cloud and Olson, *Murrow Boys*, 21.

29. Kendrick, *Prime Time*, 109. That $25 equals about $350 today.

30. Sperber, *Murrow*, 36.

31. Kendrick, *Prime Time*, 114, 116–17.

32. Dorothy McCardle, "USIA's Boss, Communication Is a Single-Minded Means to an End," *Washington Post*, February 18, 1962.

33. Edwards, *Edward R. Murrow*, 24.

34. Kendrick, *Prime Time*, 135.

35. Persico, *Edward R. Murrow*, 110–12.

36. Sperber, *Murrow*, 121.

37. Although various writers dispute who all comprised the Murrow Boys, Stanley Cloud and Lynne Olson provide the most acceptable list: Cecil Brown, Charles Collingwood, William Downs, Thomas Grandin, Richard C. Hottelet, Larry LeSueur, Eric Sevareid, William Shirer, Howard K. Smith, and Mary Marvin Breckinridge. However, the reporters did not all begin working for CBS at the same time, and some left Europe early in the war to cover the Pacific theater. Others also left CBS during the war or shortly thereafter to pursue opportunities with other networks or publishers. The most notable break to the group's cohesion occurred between Murrow and Shirer, the first person hired by Murrow, and their differences remained irreconcilable for the remainder of their lives. See Cloud and Olson, *Murrow Boys*.

38. Murrow, quoted in Seib, *Broadcasts from the Blitz*, 9.

39. Edwards, *Edward R. Murrow*, 15.

40. Seib, *Broadcasts from the Blitz*, 80.

41. Olson, *Citizens of London*, 142.

42. Eleanor Roosevelt, quoted in Seib, *Broadcasts from the Blitz*, 156.

43. Smith, *FDR*, 538.

44. Murrow, quoted in Kendrick, *Prime Time*, 240.

45. Murrow, quoted in Seib, *Broadcasts from the Blitz*, 112.

46. *Scribner's*, quoted in Olson, *Citizens of London*, 30.

47. Department of Defense Personnel Security Questionnaire, Form 1 AUG 48, undated, Box 45, ERMP.

48. Murrow, quoted in Olson, *Citizens of London*, 318.

49. Murrow did not display many mementos in his CBS or USIA offices; however, he always displayed the microphone that he used from London. Following his last broadcast, the British Broadcasting Corporation sound engineers cut the wires to his microphone and presented it to him with the following inscription: "This microphone, taken from Studio B4 of Broadcasting House, London, is presented to Edward R. Murrow who used it there with such distinction for so many broadcasts to CBS New York during the war years 1939 to 1945. March 8th 1945." See Edwards, *Edward R. Murrow*, 90.

50. Department of Defense Personnel Security Questionnaire, Form 1 AUG 48, undated, Box 45, ERMP.

51. Murrow, in Arthur Herzog, "The Voice of Uncle Sam," *True*, June 1963, Box 17, E1069, RG 306, NA.

52. Charles Casey Murrow, interview by author, July 30, 2012, Dummerston VT.

53. Edwards, *Edward R. Murrow*, 100.

54. Collins, "Murrow and Friendly's Small World," 4. Fred Friendly recounts his relationship with Murrow and their television series in *Due to Circumstances beyond Our Control*.

55. Edwards, *Edward R. Murrow*, 107.

56. Charles Casey Murrow, interview by author, July 30, 2012, Dummerston VT.

57. Larry LeSueur, quoted in Arthur Herzog, "The Voice of Uncle Sam," *True*, June 1963, Box 17, E1069, RG 306, NA.

58. Charles Casey Murrow, interview by author, July 30, 2012, Dummerston VT.

59. Photo caption, photo MS025.002.045.00261b.00012, Box 45, ERMP.

60. Schrecker, *Many Are the Crimes*, 159.

61. Letter, Marvin Sledge to Murrow, June 11, 1954, Box 5, ERMP-MHC.

62. Murrow, CBS broadcast, February 12, 1954, in *Selected Murrow Manuscripts*, Box 6, ERMP.

63. Although the HUAC is the most infamous government component of McCarthyism, Senator Patrick McCarran (D-NV) chaired the Senate's counterpart. See Ybarra, *Washington Gone Crazy*.

64. Murrow, CBS broadcast, March 9, 1954, in *Selected Murrow Manuscripts*, Box 6, ERMP.

65. Murrow, CBS broadcast, March 12, 1954, in *Selected Murrow Manuscripts*, Box 6, ERMP.

66. Murrow, CBS broadcast, April 13, 1954, in *Selected Murrow Manuscripts*, Box 6, ERMP.

67. Murrow, CBS broadcast, April 21, 1954, in *Selected Murrow Manuscripts*, Box 6, ERMP.

68. Herbert Brownell Jr., address before the National Editorial Association Convention, June 17, 1954, Baltimore MD, http://www.justice.gov/ag/aghistory / brownell/1954/06–17–1954.pdf. Arthur Schlesinger Jr. called this extraordinary claim the "most absolute assertion of presidential right to withhold information from Congress ever uttered to that day in American history." See Schlesinger, *Imperial Presidency*, 156.

69. Murrow, CBS broadcast, May 28, 1954, in *Selected Murrow Manuscripts*, Box 6, ERMP.

70. Joseph N. Welch, quoted in Fried, *Nightmare in Red*, 139.

71. Murrow, CBS broadcast, June 10, 1954, in *Selected Murrow Manuscripts*, Box 6, ERMP.

72. Citation, quoted in CBS news release, July 9, 1954, Box 42, ERMP.

73. Murrow, acceptance speech, Annual Freedom House Award Dinner, New York NY, October 3, 1954, Box 42, ERMP.

74. Murrow, CBS broadcast, May 2, 1957, in *Selected Murrow Manuscripts*, Box 6, ERMP.

75. Kendrick, *Prime Time*, 384, 386.

76. Murrow, speech before the Convention of Radio and Television News Directors, Chicago IL, October 15, 1958, in *Selected Murrow Manuscripts*, Box 6, ERMP.

77. Murrow, CBS broadcast, July 3, 1960, in *Selected Murrow Manuscripts*, Box 6, ERMP.

78. Farm owner, quoted in script, *Harvest of Shame*, aired on CBS, November 25, 1960, in *Selected Murrow Manuscripts*, Box 6, ERMP.

79. Murrow, quoted in script, *Harvest of Shame*, aired on CBS, November 25, 1960, in *Selected Murrow Manuscripts*, Box 6, ERMP.

80. Murrow also received Peabody awards for *See It Now* in 1951 and 1957, and a personal award in 1953. See "The Peabody Winners," http://www.peabody.uga .edu/ winners/winners_1950s.php.

81. Sperber, *Murrow*, 611–12.

82. "Report to the Honorable John F. Kennedy by the Task Force on United States Information Agency," December 31, 1960, Box 1072, Transition, Pre-Presidential Papers, JFKPL.

83. Chester B. Bowles, recorded interview by Robert R. R. Brooks, February 2, 1965, JFKLOHP.

84. Thomas C. Sorensen, recorded USIAAA interview by Larry Hall, June 25, 1990, Box 10, E1073, RG306, NA.

85. Charles Casey Murrow, interview by author, July 30, 2012, Dummerston VT.

86. Murrow, CBS broadcast, January 21, 1957, in *Selected Murrow Manuscripts*, Box 6, ERMP.

87. Charles Casey Murrow, interview by author, July 30, 2012, Dummerston VT.

88. Thomas C. Sorensen, recorded USIAAA interview by Larry Hall, June 25, 1990, Box 10, E1073, NA.

89. Memorandum, Donald M. Wilson to JFK, January 26, 1961, Box 290, DA, NSF, JFKPL.

90. Olson, *Citizens of London*, 30.

91. Thomas, *Robert Kennedy*, 67.

92. "United States Information Agency: Deputy Director," undated, Box 423, White House Staff Files of Dorothy Davies, JFKPL. Today, $21,000 equals about $160,000; and $300,000 equals $2.3 million.

93. Murrow, speech to the Radio-Television Executives Society Newsmakers Luncheon, New York NY, January 12, 1961, Box 132, ERMP.

94. Murrow, CBS broadcast, January 22, 1961, in *Selected Murrow Manuscripts*, Box 6, ERMP.

2. *1776 Pennsylvania Avenue*

1. Sperber, *Murrow*, 627.

2. Henry Jackson, quoted in U.S. Senate, *Nominations of Edward R. Murrow and Donald M. Wilson*, Box 14, E1069, RG 306, NA.

3. Statement by Murrow at the Senate Foreign Relations Committee hearing regarding his nomination as director, USIA, March 14, 1961, Box 14, EI069, RG 306, NA.

4. U.S. Senate, *Nominations of Edward R. Murrow and Donald M. Wilson*.

5. Arthur Schlesinger Jr., January 25, 1962, Folder 312.1, ASJ.

6. Bourke Hickenlooper and Murrow, quoted in U.S. Senate, *Nominations of Edward R. Murrow and Donald M. Wilson*.

7. J. William Fulbright, quoted in U.S. Senate, *Nominations of Edward R. Murrow and Donald M. Wilson*.

8. See clippings, Box 10, ERMP-MHC.

9. For a variety of articles, editorials, pamphlets, and letters, see Box 41, ERMP.

10. Zubok and Pleshakov, *Inside the Kremlin's Cold War*, 240.

11. JFK, quoted in ASJ, January 31, 1964, Folder 313.6.

12. Caroline Kennedy, forward to *Jacqueline Kennedy*, xvi.

13. JFK, quoted in Caroline Kennedy, ed., *Jacqueline Kennedy*, 304.

14. Foreign Office Steering Committee on Neutralism, report: "Neutralism: The Role of the Uncommitted Nations in the Cold War," January 19, 1961, FO 371/159679, BNA.

15. Murrow, speech before the Poor Richards Club, Philadelphia PA, September 14, 1961, Box 132, ERMP.

16. "Telling Our Story," *Boston Daily Record*, March 24, 1961.

17. Cull, *Cold War and the United States Information Agency*, 190.

18. USIA announcement: "Effective Date of Appointments of Director and Deputy Director," March 20, 1961, Box 18, EI069, RG 306, NA.

19. Memorandum, Donald Wilson to P. Kenneth O'Donnell, March 16, 1961, Box 184, WHCSF, FGO, JFKPL.

20. Allen left the USIA two weeks after the general election to head the Tobacco Institute, much to the criticism of agency personnel for both his lack of loyalty to the agency as well as the moral dubiousness of his new organization. See John N. Hutchison, recorded USIAAA interview by G. Lewis Schmidt, December 28, 1988, Box 4, EI073, RG 306, NA.

21. Notification of Personnel Action (Presidential Appointment), March 15, 1961, and Notification of Personnel Action (Resignation), January 20, 1964, Box 120, ERMP.

22. Photo caption, undated clipping, Box 10, ERMP-MHC.

23. Charles Casey Murrow, interview by author, July 30, 2012, Dummerston VT.

24. Dorothy McCardle, "USIA's Boss, Communication Is a Single-Minded Means to an End," *Washington Post*, February 18, 1962.

25. Dorothy, McCardle, "USIA's Boss," *Washington Post*, February 18, 1962.

26. Mildred Marcy, recorded USIAAA interview by Dorothy Robins-Mowry, February 15, 1991, Box 12, EI073, RG 306, NA.

27. Dorothy McCardle, "USIA's Boss," *Washington Post*, February 18, 1962.

28. Betty Beale, "When a Party Is Not a Party," *New York World-Telegram*, April 8, 1961.

29. Dorothy McCardle, "USIA's Boss," *Washington Post*, February 18, 1962.

30. Charles Casey Murrow, interview by author, July 30, 2012, Dummerston VT.

31. Despite their professional disagreements over how to manage Voice of America, this did not carry over to their personal lives. See Henry Loomis, recorded USIAAA interview by Claude Groce, March 1987, Box 3, E1073, RG 306, NA.

32. Charles Casey Murrow, interview by author, July 30, 2012, Dummerston VT.

33. Edward T. Folliard, "When Mr. K Bullies, How Best to Answer Him?" *Washington Post*, September 3, 1961.

34. Arthur Herzog, "The Voice of Uncle Sam," *True*, June 1963, Box 17, E1069, RG 306, NA.

35. Charles Casey Murrow, interview by author, July 30, 2012, Dummerston VT.

36. Listing, members of the Special Group (Counterinsurgency) and their assistants for counterinsurgency, September 17, 1963, Doc No/ESDN: CIA-RDP80B01676R001900150021–5, CIA-FOIA.

37. "High-Level Reading," *Washington Post*, January 20, 1963.

38. "The Truth Must Be Our Guide, But Dreams Must Be Our Goals," *Newsweek*, September 18, 1961, 26.

39. Murrow, quoted in Robert A. Lincoln, recorded USIAAA interview by G. Lewis Schmidt, April 18, 1989, Box 5, E1073, RG 306, NA.

40. Memorandum, Lowell Bennett to Murrow, September 4, 1963, Box 18, E1069, RG 306, NA.

41. G. Lewis Schmidt, recorded USIAAA interview by Allen Hansen, February 8, 1988, Box 3, E1073, RG 306, NA.

42. Robert A. Lincoln, recorded USIAAA interview by G. Lewis Schmidt, April 18, 1989, Box 5, E1073, RG 306, NA.

43. Letter, Murrow to the American Federation of Television and Radio Artists, February 17, 1961, Box 26, ERMP.

44. Murrow, quoted in Dickson Preston, "Murrow: 'I'm Trying to Acquire Anonymity,'" *Washington Daily News*, September 17, 1962.

45. USIA Feature, "Donald M. Wilson, Deputy Director, United States Information Agency," Box 37, E1069, RG 306, NA.

46. Murrow, quoted in "People on the Way Up," *Saturday Evening Post*, January 20, 1962.

47. Charles Casey Murrow, interview by author, July 30, 2012, Dummerston VT.

48. Mildred Marcy, recorded USIAAA interview by Dorothy Robins-Mowry, February 15, 1991, Box 12, E1073, RG 306, NA.

49. USIA fact sheet prepared for Murrow's appearance on *Open Mind*, September 17, 1963, Box 22, E1069, RG 306, NA.

50. Charles Casey Murrow, interview by author, July 30, 2012, Dummerston VT.

51. Murrow, speech before the National Press Club, Washington DC, May 24, 1961, Box 132, ERMP.

52. See memoranda in Box 18, E1069, RG 306, NA.

53. Murrow, speech before the USIA Honor Awards Ceremony, Washington DC, June 9, 1961, Box 132, ERMP.

54. National column appearing in *Miami Herald*, April 13, 1961.

55. Hans N. Tuch, recorded USIAAA interview by G. Lewis Schmidt, August 4, 1989, Box 7, E1073, RG 306, NA.

56. Kendrick, *Prime Time*, 298.

57. Donald Wilson, memorial dinner remarks, May 1965, Box 120, ERMP.

58. Memorandum, Murrow to All Officers Who Prepare and Review Foreign Service Evaluation Reports: "Foreign Service Personnel Evaluation Reports," June 21, 1963, microfilm, Reel 65, Box 5, E1006, RG 306, NA.

59. Robert A. Lincoln, recorded USIAAA interview by G. Lewis Schmidt, April 18, 1989, Box 5, E1073, RG 306, NA.

60. Murrow, quoted in Robert A. Lincoln, recorded USIAAA interview by G. Lewis Schmidt, April 18, 1989, Box 5, E1073, RG 306, NA.

61. Memorandum, Murrow to All Foreign Service Employees: "Eliminating Two-Year Assignments for Foreign Service Personnel," July 7, 1961, Box 18, E1069, RG 306, NA.

62. Memorandum, Murrow to All Foreign Service Employees: "Assignments to Duty," July 28, 1961, Box 18, E1069, RG 306, NA.

63. Memorandum, Murrow to Staff, April 22, 1963, Box 290, DA, NSF, JFKPL.

64. Murrow, "Director Spells out USIA Philosophy to House Group," *USIA Correspondent*, April 1963, Box 17, E1069, RG 306, NA.

65. Murrow, speech at Washington State University, Pullman WA, June 3, 1962, Box 132, ERMP.

66. Murrow, quoted in Philip Meyer, "How U.S. Is Getting Its Message Abroad," *Miami Herald*.

67. Arthur Herzog, "A Visit with Edward R. Murrow," *Think*, October 1962, Box 17, E1069, RG 306, NA.

68. Murrow, quoted in *Newsweek*, September 18, 1961.

69. Murrow, speech to employees of USIA, April 24, 1961, in "A Selection of Quotations from Edward R. Murrow (1908–1965)," Box 43, ERMP.

70. Murrow, speech before the National Press Club, Washington DC, May 24, 1961, Box 132, ERMP.

71. Murrow, quoted in Marquis Childs, "Murrow's Methods," *New York Post*, November 27, 1961.

72. Murrow, quoted in Thomas C. Sorensen, recorded USIAAA interview by Larry Hall, June 25, 1990, Box 10, E1073, RG 306, NA.

73. Memorandum, Murrow to USIA staff, April 22, 1961, Box 290, DA, NSF, JFKPL.

74. Thomas C. Sorensen, recorded USIAAA interview by Larry Hall, June 25, 1990, Box 10, E1073, RG 306, NA.

75. Memorandum, Murrow to Dean Rusk: "usia Planning and Action on Berlin," July 10, 1961, Item no. bc02158, Berlin Crisis Collection, nsa.

76. John N. Hutchison, recorded usiaaa interview by G. Lewis Schmidt, December 28, 1988, Box 4, e1073, rg 306, na. Richard Arndt provides a scathing review of Wilson and Sorensen's role at usia in *First Resort of Kings*.

77. John N. Hutchison, recorded usiaaa interview by G. Lewis Schmidt, December 28, 1988, Box 4, e1073, rg 306, na.

78. G. Lewis Schmidt, recorded usiaaa interview by Allen Hansen, February 8, 1988, Box 3, e1073, rg 306, na. Sorensen acknowledged that his abrasive personality, somewhat akin to Robert Kennedy's, ruffled feathers within the usia, but he believed that his stubbornness was essential to realize the reform that he and Murrow hoped to achieve. See Thomas C. Sorensen, recorded usiaaa interview by Larry Hall, June 25, 1990, Box 10, e1073, rg 306, na.

79. Thomas C. Sorensen, recorded usiaaa interview by Larry Hall, June 25, 1990, Box 10, e1073, rg 306, na.

80. Cull, *Cold War and the United States Information Agency*, 191.

81. Thomas C. Sorensen, *Word War*, 220.

82. Hans N. Tuch, recorded usiaaa interview by G. Lewis Schmidt, August 4, 1989, Box 7, e1073, rg 306, na.

83. During a 1987 oral history, Loomis did not expand on what battles he "lost," but he clearly articulated his reason for resigning during the Johnson administration: "because of a direct order not to carry [the story] that our planes had been over Cambodia, when everybody knew they had," including the foreign media. See Henry Loomis, recorded usiaaa interview by Claude Groce, March 1987, Box 3, e1073, rg 306, na.

84. Thomas C. Sorensen, recorded usiaaa interview by Larry Hall, June 25, 1990, Box 10, e1073, rg 306, na.

85. Edward T. Folliard, "When Mr. K Bullies, How Best to Answer Him?" *Washington Post*, September 3, 1961.

86. Kennedy called to ask Murrow to join him in the Cabinet Room for an announcement that he would resume nuclear testing in response to Khrushchev's recent breech of the tacit test ban. See "usia's Murrow: Is Truth the Best Weapon?" *Newsweek*, September 18, 1961.

87. Charles Casey Murrow, interview by author, July 30, 2012, Dummerston vt.

88. Burnett Anderson, recorded usiaaa interview by Jack O'Brien, January 5, 1990, Box 8, e1073, rg 306, na.

89. Charles Casey Murrow, interview by author, July 30, 2012, Dummerston vt.

90. Letter, Robert Evans to Robert Lochner, September 8, 1961, microfilm, Reel 42, Box 4, e1006, rg 306, na.

91. "It Takes Time to Connect Names, Faces," *Texas Times*, Wichita Falls, April 12, 1961.

92. Memorandum, McGeorge Bundy to Murrow, June 22, 1961, Box "McGeorge Bundy Correspondence," nsf, jfkpl.

93. Memorandum, McGeorge Bundy: "Useful Terminology," July 26, 1961, Box 184, DA, WHCSF, JFKPL.

94. McGeorge Bundy, recorded interview by Richard Neustadt, March 1964, JFKLOHP.

95. Memorandum, Murrow to JFK, February 10, 1961, Box 91, DA, POF, JFKPL.

96. Letter, Charles P. Cabell to Murrow, October 30, 1961, Doc No/ESDN: CIA-RDP80B01676R001000210001–9, CIA-FOIA.

97. Letter, LBJ to Thomas J. Deegan, December 30, 1960, Box 66, VPP, LBJPL.

98. Letter, Murrow to LBJ, March 16, 1961, Box 66, VPP, LBJPL.

99. Letter, LBJ to Murrow, March 23, 1961, Box 66, VPP, LBJPL.

100. Charles Casey Murrow, interview by author, July 30, 2012, Dummerston VT; and Murrow's correspondence in RG 306, NA.

101. Dean Rusk, *As I Saw It*.

102. Memorandum, Donald Wilson to All Heads of Elements, March 13, 1961, microfilm, Reel 48, Box 4, E1006, RG 306, NA.

103. Letter, W. Averell Harriman to Janet Murrow, August 13, 1966, Box 491, WAH. Janet confirmed this in her own note to Harriman after her husband's passing: "You know how Ed cherished your friendship. He loved you [and Marie Harriman] both. And so do I." See greeting card, Janet Murrow to W. Averell Harriman, undated, Box 491, WAH.

104. Murrow, quoted in *Newsweek*, November 25, 1963.

105. William H. Weathersby, recorded USIAAA interview by Jack O'Brien, August 1, 1989, Box 7, E1073, RG 306, NA.

106. Memorandum, Murrow to McGeorge Bundy: "Overseas Cultural Activities by the U.S. Government," February 8, 1961, Box 290, DA, NSF, JFKPL.

107. Henry Loomis, recorded USIAAA interview by Claude Groce, March 1987, Box 3, E1073, RG 306, NA.

108. Charles Casey Murrow, interview by author, July 30, 2012, Dummerston VT.

109. Nicholas Cull argued that Murrow never regained fully his reputation with VOA employees after the media frenzy over the *Harvest of Shame* incident. See Cull, "'The Man Who Invented Truth,'" 27.

110. Henry Loomis, recorded USIAAA interview by Claude Groce, March 1987, Box 3, E1073, RG 306, NA.

111. Murrow, quoted in "Murrow Admits Error On 'Harvest of Shame,'" *Washington Post*, March 26, 1961.

112. Author unknown, "Almost Unique," numerous newspapers, April 6, 1961, Box 16, E1069, RG 306, NA.

113. Cassandra Column, *Daily Mirror*, London, quoted in cable, USIA London to USIA Washington: "CBS television program 'Harvest of Shame' seen in Britain," March 28, 1961, Box 18, E1069, RG 306, NA.

114. Murrow, statement during the Hearing before the Subcommittee of the Committee on Appropriations, U.S. House of Representatives, March 14, 1962, Box 14, E1069, RG 306, NA.

115. See Box 121, ERMP.

116. Murrow, speech before the National Press Club, Washington DC, May 24, 1961, Box 132, ERMP.

117. Murrow, response to question during the Hearing before the Subcommittee of the Committee on Appropriations, U.S. Senate, July 10, 1961, Box 14, E1069, RG 306, NA.

118. Murrow, statement before the Subcommittee on Africa Committee on Foreign Affairs, U.S. House of Representatives, March 5, 1963, Box 17, E1069, RG 306, NA.

119. G. Lewis Schmidt, recorded USIAAA interview by Allen Hansen, February 8, 1988, Box 3, E1073, RG 306, NA.

120. In 2008 the subcommittee changed its name to the House Appropriations Subcommittee on State, Foreign Operations, and Related Programs.

121. Persico, *Edward R. Murrow*, 478.

122. John J. Rooney, quoted in Persico, *Edward R. Murrow*, 479.

123. "House Unit Trims Budget for USIA," *Chicago Sun-Times*, May 30 1961.

124. Although uninterested in expanding the budgets of the State Department or the USIA, Rooney frequently traveled abroad to inspect U.S. diplomatic facilities. He became infamous for expecting the country team wherever he visited to provide him with female escorts during his overseas junkets. Disgusted with Rooney's behavior, Murrow instructed information officers to take photos of Rooney with his "girlfriends." Privately he threatened to blackmail the representative with the photos, although he never did. His son recalls Murrow saying, "If he tries to screw up my appropriation one more time, I'll take these pictures over and show them to him!" Charles Casey Murrow, interview by author, July 30, 2012, Dummerston VT.

125. Arthur Herzog, "A Visit with Edward R. Murrow," *Think*, October 1962, Box 17, E1069, RG 306, NA.

126. Cover letter, Lowell Bennett to Murrow, June 8, 1961, Box 16, E1069, RG 306, NA.

127. Murrow, remarks before the Educational Press Association, Washington DC, May 17, 1962, Box 21, E1069, RG 306, NA.

128. Murrow, speech before the Conference of the National Association of Broadcasters, Chicago, March 2, 1962, Box 18, E1069, RG 306, NA.

129. Murrow, quoted in "The United States Lags in the Propaganda War," *Charlotte Observer*, May 28, 1961.

130. Murrow, speech before the Annual Conference of the International Council of Industrial Editors, Cleveland OH, April 5, 1962, Box 20, E1069, RG 306, NA.

131. Murrow, statement at press conference on U.S. book publishers, Overseas Press Club, New York, December 14, 1962, Box 21, E1069, RG 306, NA.

132. Murrow, speech before the American Council on Education, Washington DC, October 5, 1961, Box 20, E1069, RG 306, NA.

133. Murrow, speech before the Public Relations Society of America, Houston TX, November 13, 1961, Box 132, ERMP.

134. Murrow, commencement address at the Johns Hopkins University, Baltimore MD, June 13, 1961, Box 20, E1069, RG 306, NA.

135. Murrow, the Anna Putterman Memorial Lecture, Bucknell University, Lewisburg PA, April 23, 1962, Box 21, E1069, RG 306, NA.

136. Murrow, commencement address at Washington State University, Pullman WA, June 3, 1962, Box 21, E1069, RG 306, NA.

137. Murrow, "America's Intellectual Image Abroad," *Educational Record*, 30.

138. Murrow, speech before the USIA Honor Awards Ceremony, Washington DC, June 9, 1961, Box 132, ERMP.

3. *From Fiasco to Progress*

1. *Manual on the Fundamentals of Marxism-Leninism*, translated by Clemens Dutt (Moscow: Foreign Languages Publishing, 1963); quoted in the Eighteenth Report of the United States Advisory Commission on Information, January 1963, 12–13; in Box 21, E1069, RG 306, NA.

2. Jacqueline Kennedy, quoted in Caroline Kennedy, ed., *Jacqueline Kennedy*, 197.

3. JFK, presidential campaign speech, Hillsborough County Courthouse, Tampa FL, October 18, 1960, Box 913, Senate Files, Pre-Presidential Papers, JFKPL.

4. Charles R. Burrows, recorded interview by Dennis J. O'Brien, September 4, 1969, JFKLOHP.

5. Adolph A. Berle, recorded interview by Joseph E. O'Connor, July 6, 1967, JFKLOHP.

6. Chester B. Bowles, recorded interview by Robert R. R. Brooks, February 2, 1965, JFKLOHP.

7. ASJ, June 25, 1961, Folder 311.13.

8. David E. Bell, recorded interview by William T. Dentzer Jr., January 2, 1965, JFKLOHP.

9. Memorandum, JFK to Arthur Schlesinger Jr., in ASJ, February 3, 1961, Folder 311.9.

10. Arturo Frondizi , quoted in ASJ, February 14, 1961, Buenos Aires, Folder 311.9.

11. ASJ, February 14, 1961, Buenos Aires, Folder 311.9.

12. Donald F. Barnes, recorded interview by John Plank, June 30, 1964, JFKLOHP.

13. JFK, Address at a White House Reception for Members of Congress and for the Diplomatic Corps of the Latin American Republics, March 13, 1961, *Public Papers of the Presidents: John F. Kennedy*, vol. 1961, 171–75.

14. USIA Office of Analysis, report R-11-61: "Reactions to President Kennedy's Address on Latin America," March 22, 1961, Box 91, DA, POF, JFKPL.

15. Donald F. Barnes, recorded interview by John Plank, June 30, 1964, JFKLOHP.

16. ASJ, March 23, 1961, Folder 311.10.

17. Murrow, statement before the Subcommittee of the Committee on Appropriations, U.S. House of Representatives, March 27, 1961, Box 14, E1069, RG 306, NA.

18. David E. Bell, recorded interview by William T. Dentzer Jr., January 2, 1965, JFKLOHP.

19. Ball recalled that Rusk "always used to say that he regarded economics as a dismal science. And he left it all to me." See George W. Ball, recorded interview by Joseph Kraft, March 29, 1968, JFKLOHP.

20. Memorandum, Murrow to Sargent Shriver, March 14, 1961, microfilm, Reel 48, Box 5, E1006, RG 306, NA.

21. U.S. Peace Corps, Interactive Timeline, Decades of Service, 1960s, http://www.peacecorps.gov/about/history/decades/1960/.

22. Founded in 1947 to counter communist influence over European labor movements, the British Foreign Office's Information Research Department conducted clandestine operations similar to the cultural and information programs sponsored by the CIA. Christopher Mayhew, a member of the British Foreign Office credited with inventing the agency, explained, "It was only black propaganda in the sense that our work was all undercover and the existence of the department was confidential." The British government disbanded the IRD in 1977. See David Leigh, "Death of the Department that Never Was," *Guardian*, January 27, 1978.

23. Agenda item, Information Problems and Prospects in Latin America, United States–United Kingdom Information Working Group Meeting, April 1961, FO 953/2028, BNA.

24. Agenda item, "Comments on United States Paper on 'Psychological Problems and Prospective Changes in United States Policy,'" United States–United Kingdom Information Working Group Meeting, April 1961, FO 953/2012, BNA.

25. Cable, British ambassador in Lima to Foreign Office, November 22, 1961, FO 953/2031, BNA.

26. Agenda item, "Note on United States Paper on 'Colonialism,'" United States–United Kingdom Information Working Group Meeting, April 1961, FO 953/2012; and Cable, R. H. K. Marett to British ambassadors in Latin America, October 16, 1961, FO 1110/1561, BNA.

27. Allen W. Dulles, recorded interview by Thomas Braden, December 5 and 6, 1964, JFKLOHP.

28. Jack B. Pfeiffer, *Central Intelligence Agency Official History of the Bay of Pigs Operation, Volume I, Air Operations, March 1960–April 1961*, 1979, in National Security Archive Electronic Briefing Book no. 353, posted August 1, 2011.

29. Adolph A. Berle, recorded interview by Joseph E. O'Connor, July 6, 1967, JFKLOHP.

30. Bird, *Color of Truth*, 195.

31. JFK, quoted in Robert Amory Jr., recorded interview by Joseph E. O'Connor, February 9, 1966, JFKLOHP.

32. Ultimately, the Department of Defense shared in the blame, since its senior officials supported the invasion under the rationale that the CIA had invested so much in training the Cuban brigade. The Joint Staff sent Army Major General David Gray to review the CIA plan for the invasion of Cuba. See George H. Decker, recorded interview by Larry J. Hackman, September 18, 1968, JFKLOHP.

33. Theodore C. Sorensen, recorded interview by Carl Kaysen, April 6, 1964, JFKLOHP.

34. JFK, quoted in ASJ, Friday, April 7, 1961, Folder 311.11. After the invasion, National Security Adviser McGeorge Bundy reminded the president that Schlesinger had written a memo opposing the invasion. The president responded, "Oh sure, Arthur wrote me a memorandum that will look pretty good when he gets around to writing his book on my administration—only he better not publish that memorandum while I'm still alive! And I know what the book will be called—*Kennedy: The Only Years*." See JFK, quoted in ASJ, April 21, 1961, Folder 311.11. Schlesinger included quotations from the memo in *A Thousand Days*, 253–55.

35. Lloyd Free, director of the Institute for International Social Research recounted in a 1965 lecture that Schlesinger came across the survey sometime after the invasion. After reading the report, Schlesinger wrote to Free, lamenting that he wished that the White House had a copy before Kennedy authorized the operation. See Thomas C. Sorensen, *Word War*, 140–41.

36. Although it is impossible to know what Kennedy would have done with this information, Richard Bissell observed that the operation should have been canceled in November 1960, once the CIA realized that Cubans were not creating an elaborate underground insurgency to support the arrival of the exiles. Bissell knew that the Revolutionary Council could not take charge of the military operation: "The Council was neither sufficiently unified, sufficiently free of its internal political rivalries, nor sufficiently respected by the military group to permit the giving to the Council of a really majority command and control role in the operation." See Richard M. Bissell, recorded interview by Joseph E. O'Connor, July 5, 1967, JFKLOHP.

37. Dallek, *An Unfinished Life*, 360.

38. Adolph A. Berle, recorded interview by Joseph E. O'Connor, July 6, 1967, JFKLOHP.

39. McGeorge Bundy and JFK, quoted in ASJ, April 16, 1961, Folder 311.11.

40. Donald Wilson stated in interviews with authors and the USIAAA that he met with Szulc on April 15. This date also appears in Sperber, *Murrow*, 623. However, Szulc told Nicholas Cull during an interview that he breakfasted with Wilson on April 5. April 5 is most likely the accurate date, since Szulc's story about strange activities in Florida appeared in the *New York Times* on April 7. See Cull, *Cold War and the United States Information Agency*, n8, 191.

41. Donald Wilson, quoted in Sperber, *Murrow*, 623.

42. Thomas C. Sorensen, *Word War*, 139. Undersecretary of State Chester Bowles argued that he and Murrow voiced the loudest opposition to the invasion, but neither was involved in the planning process. See Chester B. Bowles, recorded interview by Dennis J. O'Brien, July 1, 1970, JFKLOHP.

43. See Rasenberger, *Brilliant Disaster*; Lynch, *Decision for Disaster*; Kornbluth, ed., *Bay of Pigs Declassified*; Higgins, *Perfect Failure*; and Wyden, *Bay of Pigs*.

44. JFK, Message to Chairman Khrushchev Concerning the Meaning of Events in Cuba, April 18, 1961, *Public Papers of the Presidents: John F. Kennedy*, vol. 1961, 286.

45. Murrow, quoted in Sperber, *Murrow*, 624.

46. Murrow, quoted in Henry Loomis, recorded USIAAA interview by Claude Groce, March 1987, Box 3, E1073, RG 306, NA.

47. When the United States broke off relations with Cuba in January 1961, the USIA established a radio station in Miami for Cuba. Twice a day, it produced news analysis on the Castro regime and interviewed émigrés who had recently fled to Florida. Programming material originated from two sources primarily. From Key West the agency received the audio of Cuban television, and the Cuban Court Reporters Association provided the USIA with the full text of Castro's speeches. See C. Conrad Manley, recorded USIAAA interview by John Hogan, January 30, 1989, Box 5, E1073, RG 306, NA.

48. Henry Loomis, recorded USIAAA interview by Claude Groce, March 1987, Box 3, E1073, RG 306, NA.

49. Charles Casey Murrow, interview by author, July 30, 2012, Dummerston VT.

50. Memorandum, Murrow to JFK: "Weekly Report," April 18, 1961, microfilm, Reel 46, Box 4, E1006, RG 306, NA. Murrow recalled this achievement with pride, asking his former colleagues at the National Press Club, "What network could undertake such an expansion on such short notice with no change in personnel allowance?" See Murrow, speech before the National Press Club, Washington DC, May 24, 1961, Box 132, ERMP.

51. "Rumors that Never Cease," *Shreveport Times*, May 4, 1961.

52. Letter, Murrow to Allen Dulles, April 18, 1961, microfilm, Reel 46, Box 4, E1006, RG 306, NA.

53. McKeever, *Adlai Stevenson*, 466.

54. ASJ, April 22, 1961, Folder 311.11.

55. JFK, quoted in Caroline Kennedy, ed., *Jacqueline Kennedy*, n11, 182–83.

56. William P. Bundy, recorded interview by Elspeth Rostow, November 12, 1964, JFKLOHP.

57. Theodore C. Sorensen, recorded interview by Carl Kaysen, April 6, 1964, JFKLOHP.

58. White House Press Statement, April 24, 1961, quoted in Dallek, *An Unfinished Life*, 367–68.

59. JFK, Address before the American Society of Newspaper Editors, April 20, 1961, *Public Papers of the Presidents: John F. Kennedy*, vol. 1961, 304.

60. David Ormsby-Gore, report: "Annual Review for 1961," January 2, 1962, FO 371/162578, BNA.

61. *Herald Tribune*, April 22, 1961, quoted in ASJ, April 22, 1961, Folder 311.11.

62. *Neue Presse*, April 22, 1961, quoted in ASJ, April 22, 1961, Folder 311.11.

63. Memorandum, Murrow to JFK: "Weekly Report," April 25, 1961, microfilm, Reel 46, Box 4, E1006, RG 306, NA; $500 equals about $3,850 today.

64. Cuba benefited directly from economic aid and renewed political solidarity with other communist countries in the wake of the failed invasion. See cable, British embassy in Bonn to Foreign Office, May 18, 1961, FO 371/160528, BNA.

65. Donald M. Wilson, statement before the Inter-American Affairs Subcommittee, U.S. House of Representatives, February 21, 1963, Box 37, E1069, RG 306, NA.

66. A variety of articles speculating about Murrow's disenchantment with the Kennedy administration, including the cartoon about his transition to the CIA, are available in the staff file clippings, Box 16, E1069, RG 306, NA.

67. Murrow, quoted in "Murrow Categorically Denies He Will Quit as USIA Chief?" *Radio Daily–Television Daily*, May 25, 1961.

68. Charles Casey Murrow, interview by author, July 30, 2012, Dummerston VT.

69. "67th St. Mansion Sold by Institute," *New York Times*, May 8, 1961.

70. *Santa Barbara News-Press*, June 5, 1961.

71. JFK, Special Message to the Congress on Urgent National Needs, May 25, 1961, *Public Papers of the Presidents: John F. Kennedy*, vol. 1961, 404.

72. Memorandum, Murrow to JFK: "Weekly Report," May 2, 1961, microfilm, Reel 46, Box 4, E1006, RG 306, NA.

73. Memorandum, Murrow to JFK: "Weekly Report," May 9, 1961, microfilm, Reel 46, Box 4, E1006, RG 306, NA; and memorandum of conversation, Chester Bowles and Anatoly Dobynin, November 15, 1962, Box 428, WAH.

74. Murrow, quoted in Alexander A. Klieforth, recorded USIAAA interview by Claude Groce, August 1988, Box 1, E1073, RG 306, NA.

75. Memorandum, Murrow to JFK: "Our Latin American Program," May 15, 1961, Reel 46, Box 4, E1006, RG 306, NA.

76. The USIA conducted the survey in Brazil, Mexico, Argentina, Columbia, Peru, Venezuela, and Uruguay. See USIA Office of Research and Analysis, "The Climate of Opinion in Latin America for the Alliance for Progress: A Report of Survey Findings from Seven Countries," August 1961, Box 2, E1010, RG 306, NA.

77. Memorandum, Murrow to JFK: "Weekly Report," October 3, 1961, microfilm, Reel 42, Box 4, E1006, RG 306, NA.

78. Charles Casey Murrow, interview by author, July 30, 2012, Dummerston VT.

79. Edmund Murphy, recorded USIAAA interview by Allen Hansen, January 30, 1990, Box 8, E1073, RG 306, NA.

80. Attachment, "Castro's Current Standing in Latin America," to memorandum, Donald M. Wilson to JFK, October 19, 1961, Box 91, DA, POF, JFKPL.

81. Although Swan Radio's name changed, its cover proved to be "revealingly thin" and exposed by journalists David Wise and Thomas Ross in *Invisible Government.*

82. In October 1962, Lansdale coordinated with the USIA to provide a leaflet drop by balloon over Cuba as part of Operation Mongoose; however, the discovery of Soviet missile sites on the island led them to cancel the mission. A collection of documents relating the psychological warfare component of Operation Mongoose appears in chapter 2 of Elliston, *Psywar on Cuba.*

83. John McCone, quoted in Thomas C. Sorensen, recorded USIAAA interview by Larry Hall, June 25, 1990, Box 10, E1073, RG 306, NA.

84. Thomas C. Sorensen, recorded USIAAA interview by Larry Hall, June 25, 1990, Box 10, E1073, RG 306, NA.

85. Fidel Castro, speech, December 1, 1961, quoted in Editorial Note, Document 279, *Foreign Relations of the United States, 1961–1963,* vol. 10, *Cuba,* 689.

86. Murrow, statement before a hearing of the Subcommittee of the Committee on Appropriations, U.S. House of Representatives, March 14, 1962, Box 14, E1069, RG 306, NA.

87. Cable, British ambassador in Havana to Foreign Office, November 23, 1961, FO 953/2037, BNA.

88. Cable, Foreign Office to Certain of Her Majesty's Representatives, February 14, 1962, FO 1110/1561, BNA.

89. USIA Research and Reference Service, "Public Opinion toward the Alliance for Progress in Bogota and Other Latin American Cities," December 1961, Box 2, E1010, RG 306, NA.

90. USIA Research and Reference Service, "The Impact of the Alliance for Progress on Mexican Public Opinion and Some Related Economic Attitudes," March 1962, Box 2, E1010, RG 306, NA.

91. Dispatch, David Ormsby-Gore to Foreign Office, May 4, 1962, FO 371/162603, BNA.

92. Robert McNamara, quoted in ASJ, June 7, 1961, Folder 311.12.

93. Vice President Richard Nixon received a hostile welcome in Caracas in May 1958. *Time* reported: "Over the rigid shoulders of a line of Venezuelan soldiers at Maiquetía Airport, streams of spittle arced through humid sunlight, splattered on the neatly pressed grey suit of the Vice President of the U.S. and on the red wool suit of his wife." As the motorcade entered Caracas, a mob surrounded Nixon's car in a city traffic jam, banging sticks against the doors and shattering one of the windows with a large stone. See "The Americas: The Guests of Venezuela," *Time,* May 26, 1958.

94. Donald F. Barnes, recorded interview by John Plank, June 30, 1964, JFK-LOHP.

95. Memorandum, Murrow to JFK: "Weekly Report," December 19, 1961, microfilm, Reel 40, Box 4, E1006, RG 306, NA.

96. USIA Motion Picture Division, *Forging the Alliance-President Kennedy Visits Venezuela and Columbia, December 1961: 15–18*, USG:IA, JFKPL, online collection, http://www.jfklibrary.org/Asset-Viewer/Archives/USG-1A.aspx.

97. Memorandum, Donald Wilson to Pierre Salinger, December 6, 1961, microfilm, Reel 40, Box 4, E1006, RG 306, NA.

98. JFK, quoted in Donald F. Barnes, recorded interview by John Plank, June 30, 1964, JFKLOHP.

99. Memorandum, Donald M. Wilson to Ralph A. Dungan, July 17, 1962, Box 91, DA, POF, JFKPL.

100. USIA Motion Picture Division, *Progress through Freedom: The President's Trip to Mexico, 1962, June 28–30*, USG:IJ, JFKPL, online collection, http://www.jfklibrary.org/Asset-Viewer/Archives/USG-1J.aspx.

101. Jacqueline Kennedy, quoted in Caroline Kennedy, ed., *Jacqueline Kennedy*, 198.

102. Cable, David Ormsby-Gore to Foreign Office, January 2, 1962, FO 371/162586, BNA.

103. Cable, British Embassy in Moscow to Foreign Office, April 3, 1962, FO 371/162603, BNA.

104. Roberto de Oliveira Campos, recorded interview by John E. Reilly, May 29, 1964, JFKLOHP.

105. Frank M. Coffin, recorded interview by Elizabeth Donahue, March 2–3, 1964, JFKLOHP. Kennedy referred to Kelly Services, a Michigan-based company providing temporary administrative staffing for businesses across the country. See Kelly Services, "About Us," http://www.kellyservices.com/Global/About US/.

106. Schlesinger, *A Thousand Days*, 251.

107. ASJ, June 9, 1961, Folder 311.13.

108. ASJ, July 23, 1962, Folder 312.7.

109. Adolph A. Berle, recorded interview by Joseph E. O'Connor, July 6, 1967, JFKLOHP.

110. Adolph A. Berle, recorded interview by Joseph E. O'Connor, July 6, 1967, JFKLOHP.

111. Memorandum, Murrow to JFK, August 14, 1962, microfilm, Reel 54, Box 4, E1006, RG 306, NA.

112. Memorandum, Donald M. Wilson to JFK, July 6, 1962, Box 91, DA, POF, JFKPL; $13,000 equals approximately $100,000 today.

113. Guard Report on the United States–United Kingdom Information Working Group, which met in Washington, June 4–6, 1962, FO 1110/1522, BNA.

114. The British, for example, only provided 200,000 British pounds worth of technical assistance in 1962. See Agenda Item, "The Alliance for Progress," United States–United Kingdom Information Working Group, June 4–6, 1962, FO 953/2084, BNA.

115. Guard Report on the United States–United Kingdom Information Working Group, June 4–6, 1962, FO 1110/1522, BNA.

116. ASJ, August 19, 1962, Folder 312.8.

117. Nicholas J. Cull used the term "magic bullet" to explain what members of national security planning circles incorrectly assume that public diplomacy can provide to address international challenges. Cull, keynote address, "International Broadcasting as Public Diplomacy: The News and National Identity," Blinken European Institute series on New Diplomacy, Columbia University, New York, November 26, 2012.

118. Murrow, transcript of *Issues and Answers*, August 4, 1963, Box 21, E1069, RG 306, NA.

119. Cull, *Cold War and the United States Information Agency*, xv.

120. ASJ, October 15, 1962, Folder 312.10.

4. This . . . Is Berlin

1. The U.S. government created the RIAS (in English, Broadcasting in the American Sector) in 1946 to broadcast as a station independent from Voice of America and Radio Free Europe in Berlin. Germans comprised the majority of the staff, and they prided themselves in "remaining committed to the tradition of rational, critical American journalism." See RIAS Berlin Commission, "History and Purpose of RIAS Berlin and the RIAS Berlin-Commission," http://www.riasberlin.de/rias-hist/rius-hist-history.html.

2. "Robert Lochner; Helped Kennedy in Berlin Speech," obituary, *Boston Globe*, September 24, 2003.

3. Robert Lochner, recorded USIAAA interview by G. Lewis Schmidt, October 17, 1991, Box 12, E1073, RG 306, NA.

4. Charles Casey Murrow, interview by author, July 30, 2012, Dummerston VT.

5. Memorandum of conversation, secretary of state's meeting with European ambassadors in Paris, August 9, 1961, Box 499, WAH.

6. Albert E. Hemsing, recorded USIAAA interview by Robert Amerson, April 18, 1989, Box 8, E1073, RG 306, NA.

7. Months later, Murrow asked his assistant, Chester Opal, about the status of the implementation of the European report. Opal told him that the personnel division "is acting as though it never heard of it." Stunned, Murrow immediately called his assistant director for personnel and instructed him to implement the plans to reduce the staff sizes. See Chester H. Opal, recorded USIAAA interview by G. Lewis Schmidt, January 28, 1989, Box 5, E1073, RG 306, NA.

8. Albert E. Hemsing, recorded USIAAA interview by Robert Amerson, April 18, 1989, Box 8, E1073, RG 306, NA.

9. Nikita Khrushchev, quoted in memorandum of conversation: "Meeting between the President and Chairman Khrushchev in Vienna," June 4, 1961, 10:15 a.m., Vienna, Austria, Document 32, U.S. Department of State, *Foreign Relations of the United States, 1961–1963*, vol. 14, *Berlin Crisis, 1961–1962*, 90.

10. Charles E. Bohlen, recorded interview by Arthur Schlesinger Jr., May 21, 1964, JFKLOHP.

11. Kempe, *Berlin 1961*, 486.

12. Freedman, *Kennedy's Wars*, 58.

13. Albert E. Hemsing, recorded USIAAA interview by Robert Amerson, April 18, 1989, Box 8, E1073, RG 306, NA.

14. Historian Hope Harrison points to this press conference as the first public mention of GDR-Soviet discussions about constructing a wall. See Harrison, *Driving the Soviets up the Wall*, 179–80.

15. Zubok and Pleshakov, *Inside the Kremlin's Cold War*, 250.

16. Khrushchev, *Memoirs of Nikita Khrushchev*, 3:301–2.

17. Jian, *Mao's China*, 82–84.

18. Beschloss, *Crisis Years*, 150.

19. Giglio, *Presidency of John F. Kennedy*, 74.

20. While the *Foreign Relations of the United States, 1961–1963*, vol. 14, *Berlin Crisis, 1961–1962* contains the memorandum of conversation for each of the summit's bilateral meetings, the emotion of the dialogue is absent. Better sources are provided by historians who relied on interviews and notes from advisers to both chiefs of state during the conference. See Freedman, *Kennedy's Wars*, 55–57; Kempe, *Berlin 1961*, 234–35, 251–53; and Beschloss, *Crisis Years*, 215–20, 223–24.

21. JFK, quoted in memorandum of conversation: "Meeting between the President and Chairman Khrushchev in Vienna," June 4, 1961, 3:15 p.m., Vienna, Austria, Document 33, U. S. Department of State, *Foreign Relations of the United States, 1961–1963*, vol. 14, *Berlin Crisis, 1961–1962*, 98.

22. Khrushchev, *Memoirs of Nikita Khrushchev*, 307.

23. Harold Macmillan, quoted in Harold Brandon, recorded interview by Joseph E. O'Connor, February 7, 1967, JFKLOHP.

24. Hans N. Tuch, recorded USIAAA interview by G. Lewis Schmidt, August 4, 1989, Box 7, E1073, RG 306, NA.

25. McGeorge Bundy, recorded interview by Richard Neustadt, March 1964, JFKLOHP.

26. Cable, British Embassy, Washington, to the Foreign Office, June 8, 1961, FO 371/156456, BNA.

27. USIA Research and Reference Service, "The Current State of Confidence in the U.S. among the West European Public," August 1961, Box 5, E1010, RG 306, NA.

28. Amintore Fanfani, quoted in ASJ, June 18, 1961, Folder 311.13.

29. JFK, Radio and Television Report to the American People on Returning from Europe, June 6, 1961, *Public Papers of the Presidents: John F. Kennedy*, vol. 1961, 441–46.

30. Memorandum, Murrow to McGeorge Bundy, June 7, 1961, Box 290, DA, NSF, JFKPL.

31. Dallek, *An Unfinished Life*, 418–19.

32. Robert McNamara, quoted in ASJ, August 2, 1961, Folder 311.15.

33. ASJ, July 9, 1961, Folder 311.14.

34. Michael Beschloss credits Murrow's contribution in *Crisis Years*, 260.

35. JFK, Radio and Television Report to the American People on the Berlin Crisis, July 25, 1961, *Public Papers of the Presidents: John F. Kennedy*, vol. 1961, 533–40.

36. USIA Circular USITO 63, July 31, 1961, Box 2, E12, RG 306, NA.

37. Cable, C. Parrott to Donald Hopson, July 13, 1961, FO 1110/1430, BNA.

38. Albert E. Hemsing, recorded USIAAA interview by Robert Amerson, April 18, 1989, Box 8, E1073, RG 306, NA.

39. Robert Lochner, recorded USIAAA interview by G. Lewis Schmidt, October 17, 1991, Box 12, E1073, RG 306, NA.

40. Albert E. Hemsing, recorded USIAAA interview by Robert Amerson, April 18, 1989, Box 8, E1073, RG 306, NA.

41. Albert E. Hemsing, recorded USIAAA interview by Robert Amerson, April 18, 1989, Box 8, E1073, RG 306, NA.

42. Frederick Kempe argues that Allan Lightner, the chief of mission in Berlin, wanted to collect enough facts about the East German operation prior to reporting to Washington for fear that the U.S. government might overreact if he did not provide a complete story. See Kempe, *Berlin, 1961*, 351. This indicates that Hemsing's proactive reporting did in fact provide Kennedy with the earliest news from Berlin.

43. Robert Lochner, recorded USIAAA interview by G. Lewis Schmidt, October 17, 1991, Box 12, E1073, RG 306, NA.

44. James Hoofnagle, recorded USIAAA interview by G. Lewis Schmidt, March 3, 1989, Box 5, E1073, RG 306, NA.

45. Charles Casey Murrow, interview by author, July 30, 2012, Dummerston VT.

46. James Hoofnagle, recorded USIAAA interview by G. Lewis Schmidt, March 3, 1989, Box 5, E1073, RG 306, NA.

47. Robert Lochner, recorded USIAAA interview by G. Lewis Schmidt, October 17, 1991, Box 12, E1073, RG 306, NA.

48. Albert E. Hemsing, recorded USIAAA interview by Robert Amerson, April 18, 1989, Box 8, E1073, RG 306, NA.

49. So too were nearly all officials behind the Iron Curtain. The impulsive decision to authorize Ulbricht to construct the Berlin Wall served as the "benchmark of Khrushchev's statesmanship" and it surprised his closest comrades at the Kremlin. See Zubok and Pleshakov, *Inside the Kremlin's Cold War*, 251.

50. Robert Amory Jr., recorded interview by Joseph E. O'Connor, February 9, 1966, JFKLOHP.

51. Willy Brandt, letter sent in a telegram from the mission at Berlin to the Department of State, August 16, 1961, Document 117, U.S. Department of State, *Foreign Relations of the United States, 1961–1963*, vol. 14, *Berlin Crisis, 1961–1962*, 346.

52. Robert Amory Jr., recorded interview by Joseph E. O'Connor, February 9, 1966, JFKLOHP.

53. James Hoofnagle, recorded USIAAA interview by G. Lewis Schmidt, March 3, 1989, Box 5, E1073, RG 306, NA.

54. Robert Lochner, recorded USIAAA interview by G. Lewis Schmidt, October 17, 1991, Box 12, E1073, RG 306, NA.

55. Albert E. Hemsing, recorded USIAAA interview by Robert Amerson, April 18, 1989, Box 8, E1073, RG 306, NA.

56. Memorandum, JFK to Dean Rusk, August 14, 1961, Document 109, U.S. Department of State, *Foreign Relations of the United States, 1961–1963*, vol. 14, *Berlin Crisis, 1961–1962*, 332.

57. Cable, E. Allan Lightner to Dean Rusk, August 16, 1961, Item no. BC02326, Berlin Crisis Collection, NSA.

58. Albert E. Hemsing, recorded USIAAA interview by Robert Amerson, April 18, 1989, Box 8, E1073, RG 306, NA.

59. Cable, Murrow at the mission at Berlin to the Department of State, August 16, 1961, Document 114, U.S. Department of State, *Foreign Relations of the United States, 1961–1963*, vol. 14, *Berlin Crisis, 1961–1962*, 339–41.

60. Edward T. Folliard, "When Mr. K Bullies, How Best to Answer Him?" *Washington Post*, September 3, 1961.

61. Albert E. Hemsing, recorded USIAAA interview by Robert Amerson, April 18, 1989, Box 8, E1073, RG 306, NA.

62. Robert Lochner, recorded USIAAA interview by G. Lewis Schmidt, October 17, 1991, Box 12, E1073, RG 306, NA.

63. Record of meeting of the Berlin Steering Group, August 17, 1961, Document 118, U.S. Department of State, *Foreign Relations of the United States, 1961–1963*, vol. 14, *Berlin Crisis, 1961–1962*, 347–49.

64. Memorandum, Robert Kennedy to JFK, August 17, 1961, Item no. BC02329, Berlin Crisis Collection, NSA.

65. James Hoofnagle, recorded USIAAA interview by G. Lewis Schmidt, March 3, 1989, Box 5, E1073, RG 306, NA. Murrow departed Berlin impressed with Hemsing's performance as the acting public affairs officer—the actual officer was on leave in the United States at the time of the crisis. Six months later, Murrow recalled Hemsing to Washington to promote him to public affairs officer. See Albert E. Hemsing, recorded USIAAA interview by Robert Amerson, April 18, 1989, Box 8, E1073, RG 306, NA.

66. Edward T. Folliard, "When Mr. K Bullies, How Best to Answer Him?" *Washington Post*, September 3, 1961.

67. Murrow, speech before the Public Relations Society of America, Houston TX, November 13, 1961, Box 132, ERMP.

68. Thomas C. Sorensen, *Word War*, 148.

69. Memorandum, Murrow to JFK: "Weekly Report," August 22, 1961, microfilm, Reel 43, Box 4, E1006, RG 306, NA.

70. Murrow, speech before the Public Relations Society of America, Houston TX, November 13, 1961, Box 132, ERMP.

71. Joseph W. Alsop, recorded interview by Elspeth Rostow, June 18, 1964, JFKLOHP.

72. Khrushchev, *Memoirs of Nikita Khrushchev*, 311.

73. Lucius D. Clay, recorded interview by Richard M. Scammon, July 1, 1964, JFKLOHP.

74. Cable 261, U.S. mission, West Berlin, to secretary of state, August 20, 1961, Box 1, SF, VPP, LBJPL.

75. Cable 262, section 1 of 2, U.S. mission, West Berlin, to secretary of state, August 20, 1961, Box 1, SF, VPP, LBJPL.

76. Albert E. Hemsing, recorded USIAAA interview by Robert Amerson, April 18, 1989, Box 8, EI073, RG 306, NA.

77. LBJ, report: "Visitation to Germany," August 19–20, 1961, Box 290, DA, NSF, JFKPL.

78. Willy Brandt, quoted in ASJ, March 13, 1962, Folder 312.3.

79. LBJ, report: "Visitation to Germany," August 19–20, 1961, Box 290, DA, NSF, JFKPL.

80. Albert E. Hemsing, recorded USIAAA interview by Robert Amerson, April 18, 1989, Box 8, EI073, RG 306, NA.

81. Cable 264, U.S. mission, West Berlin, to secretary of state, August 20, 1961, Box 1, SF, VPP, LBJPL.

82. Memorandum, Walt W. Rostow to Foy D. Kohler, August 18, 1961, Box 2, SF, VPP, LBJPL.

83. Murrow, speech before the Poor Richards Club, Philadelphia PA, September 14, 1961, Box 132, ERMP.

84. East Berlin *Neues Deutschland*, August 20, 1961, quoted in Cable 262, two of two, U.S. mission, West Berlin, to secretary of state, August 20, 1961, Box 1, SF, VPP, LBJPL. From July 19 to 23, 1961, the Tunisian military blockaded the French navy base at Bizerte in an effort to force the French government to abandon its last garrison on Tunisian soil. France deployed eight hundred paratroopers to end the blockade. In 1963 the French returned the base to the Tunisians. See "Tunisia: The Wages of Moderation," *Time*, July 28, 1961.

85. JFK, quoted in Thomas C. Sorensen, recorded interview by Theodore H. White, April 15, 1964, JFKLOHP.

86. Memorandum, LBJ to JFK, August 21, 1961, Box 2, SF, VPP, LBJPL.

87. While traveling with Brandt through Berlin, the mayor showed off his boots to the Texas rancher. When Johnson mentioned that he would like a pair, Brandt arranged for a visit to the store in Berlin. Johnson explained to the owner that he needed two boots of two separate sizes since his feet measured differently. The owner said that he would need to purchase two pairs of boots, which Johnson found to be outrageous. The American escort officer stepped in to quell the incident, personally paying for the second pair of boots. See James Hoofnagle, recorded USIAAA interview by G. Lewis Schmidt, March 3, 1989, Box 5, EI073, RG 306, NA. The same day, Johnson asked Brandt to visit a china shop,

since his wife had instructed him to return with a set for thirty-six place settings. When the owner showed him the price, Johnson said that he could not afford it. The owner suggested purchasing seconds, which Johnson agreed to, but he still wanted to order thirty-six full sets. Since seconds cannot be ordered but had to be found from those accidentally chipped, Brandt realized the absurdity of the situation and stepped in: "Mr. Vice President, this is a gift from the city of Berlin." Johnson accepted the offer but said that he would take the first quality. See James Hoofnagle interview mentioned above. Albert E. Hemsing, who was present with Johnson in the china factory, said he ordered service for twenty-four; see recorded USIAAA interview by Robert Amerson, April 18, 1989, Box 8, E1073, RG 306, NA.

88. Memorandum, LBJ to JFK, August 21, 1961, Box 2, SF, VPP, LBJPL.

89. Memorandum, Donald Wilson to Pierre Salinger, August 23, 1961, microfilm, Reel 43, Box 4, E1006, RG 306, NA.

90. USIA Circular USITO 131, August 30, 1961, Box 2, E12, RG 306, NA.

91. Memorandum, Donald M. Wilson to McGeorge Bundy, October 19, 1961, Box 290, DA, NSF, JFKPL.

92. Memorandum, Kenneth R. Hansen to McGeorge Bundy: "Distribution of pamphlet on Berlin," October 31, 1961, Box 290, DA, NSF, JFKPL.

93. Memorandum, Murrow to JFK: "Weekly Report," October 3, 1961, microfilm, Reel 42, Box 4, E1006, RG 306, NA.

94. Memorandum, Donald M. Wilson to Pierre Salinger, April 26, 1963, Box 184, FGO, WHCSF, JFKPL.

95. "Murrow Tells of Information Agency Aims," *Los Angeles Times*, November 7, 1961.

96. USIA poster, "Mother's hand and ring," undated, Box 290, DA, NSF, JFKPL.

97. Cables, Michael Pistor to Edward V. Roberts, October 5, 1961, Box 1, E12, RG 306, NA.

98. Agenda item, "Berlin and Germany," United States–United Kingdom Information Working Group, November 1961, FO 953/2030, BNA.

99. Letter, John Peck to Leslie Glass, October 25, 1961, FO 1110/1434, BNA.

100. JFK, quoted in ASJ, September 5, 1961, Folder 311.16.

101. Memorandum, Murrow to JFK, September 22, 1961, Box 91, DA, POF, JFKPL.

102. Attachment, "Western European Public Confidence in the United States," to memorandum, Donald M. Wilson to JFK, October 19, 1961, Box 91, DA, POF, JFKPL.

103. Murrow, speech before the Poor Richards Club, Philadelphia PA, September 14, 1961, Box 132, ERMP.

104. Murrow, speech before the annual Freedom House Award luncheon, New York, October 6, 1961, Box 132, ERMP.

105. Foreign Office, report: "Access to East Berlin," October 27, 1961, FO 371/160572, BNA.

106. Albert E. Hemsing, recorded USIAAA interview by Robert Amerson, April 18, 1989, Box 8, E1073, RG 306, NA.

107. Albert E. Hemsing, recorded USIAAA interview by Robert Amerson, April 18, 1989, Box 8, E1073, RG 306, NA.

108. Telegram, R. Delacombe to Foreign Office, November 20, 1961, FO 371/160572, BNA. The U.S. Army did not develop plans for an unprovoked invasion of East Berlin or the GDR, but it anticipated the need to counter an invasion of West Berlin or Western Europe by Warsaw Pact forces. In contrast, the GDR prepared detailed military plans for the invasion of the three western sectors of Berlin. In 1965, the communist planners went so far as to mint a medal for the campaign—the Blücher Order, named in honor of the Prussian field marshal Gebhard Leberecht von Blücher who fought against Napoleon at Leipzig and Waterloo. See the GDR armed forces display, Deutsche Demokratische Republik Museum, Berlin, Germany.

109. Memorandum, Murrow to JFK, December 5, 1961, Box 290, DA, NSF, JFKPL.

110. Guard report on the United States–United Kingdom Information Working Group, June 4–6, 1962, FO 1110/1522, BNA.

111. Memorandum, Murrow to JFK, December 6, 1961, microfilm, Reel 40, Box 4, E1006, RG 306, NA.

112. Cover letter, David Ormsby-Gore to Foreign Office, to report: "Annual Review for 1961," January 2, 1962, FO 371/162578, BNA.

113. Murrow, speech before the annual Freedom House Award luncheon, New York, October 6, 1961, Box 132, ERMP.

114. ASJ, March 13, 1962, Folder 312.3.

115. Robert Kennedy, quoted in ASJ, March 13, 1962, Folder 312.3.

116. Memorandum, Howard Burris to LBJ: "Unrest in East Germany," June 19, 1962, Box 5, SF, VPP, LBJPL.

117. Murrow, speech before the Conference of the National Association of Broadcasters, Washington DC, March 2, 1962, Box 132, ERMP.

118. Cable, David Ormsby-Gore to Foreign Office, January 18, 1963, FO 371/168414, BNA.

119. USIA statement: "European Trip Seen Carrying out Long-Held Kennedy Aim," June 21, 1963, FO 371/168414, BNA.

120. U.S. Department of State, Briefing Book for the President's European Trip, June 14, 1963, Box 3, SF, VPP, LBJPL.

121. Lucius D. Clay, recorded interview by Richard M. Scammon, July 1, 1964, JFKLOHP.

122. Angier Biddle Duke, recorded interview by Frank Sieverts, July 29, 1964, JFKLOHP.

123. Robert Lochner, quoted in Voices of U.S. Diplomacy and the Berlin Wall, U.S. Diplomacy Center, http://diplomacy.state.gov/berlinwall/www/archive /OHI005.html. The words directly translated to "I am a jelly doughnut," and

Lochner should have written "Ich Bin Berliner." Nevertheless, the enthusiastic crowds only grew more excited with Kennedy.

124. JFK, remarks in the Rudolph Wilde Platz, Berlin, June 26, 1963, *Public Papers of the Presidents: John F. Kennedy*, vol. 1963, 524–25.

125. Thomas C. Sorensen, *Word War*, 152.

126. Dallek, *An Unfinished Life*, 623.

127. USIA Research and Reference Service, report R-125-63 (AE), "Western European Reaction to President Kennedy's Trip," July 8, 1963, Box 91, DA, POF, JFKPL.

128. Memorandum, Donald M. Wilson to JFK: "Reactions to Your European Trip," July 9, 1963, Box 91, DA, POF, JFKPL.

129. Murrow, speech before the Public Relations Society of America, Houston TX, November 13, 1961, Box 132, ERMP.

5. Mr. Murrow Goes to Hollywood

1. One week after the president's assassination, Jacqueline Kennedy told journalist Theodore White that her husband enjoyed listening to the last song from the score of *Camelot* before turning in at night. White may have been too emotionally wrapped up in the murder of the president when he equated the Kennedy administration to a second Camelot: "a magic moment in American history, when gallant men danced with beautiful women, when great deeds were done, when artists, writers, and poets met at the White House, and the barbarians beyond the walls held back." See White, "For President Kennedy an Epilogue," *Life*, December 6, 1963. This sparked the Camelot legend of the Kennedy White House that has been discounted by administration members and historians alike. Historian Robert Dallek argues that it is an inappropriate analogy, and he speculates that Jackie's "effort to lionize Kennedy must have provided a therapeutic shield against immobilizing grief." See Dallek, *An Unfinished Life*, 697.

2. Jacqueline Kennedy, inscription in USIA Farewell Message Album to Murrow, March 1964, Box 41, ERMP-MHC.

3. The antecedents for U.S. government employment of film propaganda are found in the Office of War Information (OWI) during World War II, which created information films that OWI personnel trekked into South Pacific jungles and European cities. The federal government also forged a close partnership with Hollywood during this period to create films for domestic and international consumption. See Bennett, *One World, Big Screen*.

4. A. William Bluem, introduction to MacCann, *The People's Films*, xvii.

5. Whitfield, *Culture of the Cold War*, 127–36.

6. Founded in 1944, the Motion Picture Alliance for the Preservation of American Ideals attracted an array of prominent and politically conservative producers, directors, and actors dedicated to eradicating communist and fascist infiltration. Notable members included Walt Disney, Clark Gable, Ronald Reagan, and John Wayne, who served as the organization's president for four

consecutive one-year terms. See Ceplair and Englund, *Inquisition in Hollywood*, 210–214; and Roberts and Olson, *John Wayne*, 338.

7. Shaw, *Hollywood's Cold War*, 4.

8. Wagnleitner, *Coca-Colonization and the Cold War*, 275.

9. Hollywood films delivered anticommunist messages to domestic audiences as well. American movies reaffirmed stereotypes about world communist revolution and the Third World, thereby helping to build national cohesion for containing communism. In *Cold War Orientalism*, Christina Klein reveals the paternal and sentimental tones of 1950s movies, such as *The King and I*, that depicted Asians as childlike. Such movies not only presented Westerners as more enlightened than individuals like the King of Siam, but also reminded Westerners of their obligation to educate the East about democracy, women's rights, and capitalism. Films like *South Pacific* evoked memories of World War II in an effort to rejuvenate postwar sentimentality about remaining resolute in defending countries like the Republics of Korea and Vietnam.

10. Shaw, *Hollywood's Cold War*, 302.

11. Presentation notes, Jack Patterson, July 20, 1962, FO 953/2084, BNA.

12. MacCann, *The People's Films*, 174.

13. Murrow, lecture, "Television and Politics," Guildhall, London, November 18, 1959, Box 14, E1069, RG 306, NA.

14. MacCann, *The People's Films*, xi. Bob Edwards lauds Murrow's television innovations in *Edward R. Murrow*, 107.

15. Thomas C. Sorensen, *Word War*, 183.

16. Murrow, CBS broadcast, July 3, 1960, in *Selected Murrow Manuscripts*, Box 6, ERMP.

17. NASA launched Telstar 1 on July 10, 1962, but the satellite became inoperable only seven months later when the transmitter cease to function on February 21, 1963. See "Telstar 1," http://nssdc.gsfc.nasa.gov/nmc/spacecraftDisplay .do?id=1962–029A.

18. Letter, Murrow to Joseph E. Johnson, February 17, 1961, Box 120, ERMP; $500 equals about $3,850 today.

19. Memorandum, Murrow to JFK, July 24, 1961, Box 91, DA, POF, JFKPL.

20. Memorandum, Murrow to Arthur Schlesinger Jr., October 4, 1961, microfilm, Reel 42, Box 4, E1006, RG 306, NA.

21. Memorandum, Murrow to JFK: "Luncheon for Television Network Executives, Thursday, October 5," October 2, 1961, Box 91, DA, POF, JFKPL.

22. The formation of the Motion Picture Export Association in 1946 served ostensibly to topple trade barriers, in order to sell American films overseas. However, until rebranding itself as the Motion Picture Association, the association advocated for the production of pro-American films and considered themselves the "Little State Department" by propagating American culture through their films. See Shaw, *Hollywood's Cold War*, 169.

23. Guard Report on the United States–United Kingdom Information Working Group, June 4–6, 1962, FO 1110/1522, BNA.

24. Kendrick, *Prime Time*, 367.

25. Charles Casey Murrow, interview by author, July 30, 2012, Dummerston VT.

26. Memorandum, Anthony Guarco to Murrow, June 27, 1961, Box 18, E1069, RG 306, NA.

27. Memorandum, Turner Shelton to Murrow, September 6, 1961, Box 18, E1069, RG 306, NA.

28. Hans N. Tuch, recorded USIAAA interview by G. Lewis Schmidt, August 4, 1989, Box 7, E1073, RG 306, NA.

29. USIA memorandum: "The U.S. Information Program since July 1953," circa 1960, quoted in Cull, "Film as Public Diplomacy," 265.

30. Letter, Murrow to Jack L. Copeland, December 5, 1961, microfilm, Reel 40, Box 4, E1006, RG 306, NA.

31. Memorandum, Tuner B. Shelton to Frederick G. Dutton, February 13, 1961, microfilm, Reel 50, Box 4, E1006, RG 306, NA.

32. Memorandum, Turner Shelton to Murrow, March 3, 1961, Box 18, E1069, RG 306, NA. Universal Pictures proceeded with the production and released *The Ugly American* in April 1963, with Marlon Brando starring as Ambassador Harrison MacWhite, a diplomat who could not distinguish between Sarkan's struggle for self-determination and communist infiltration. See "Plot Summary for *The Ugly American*," http://www.imdb.com/title/tt0056632/plotsummary.

33. Memorandum, Murrow to Evelyn Lincoln, May 9, 1962, Box 18, E1069, RG 306, NA.

34. "It's Schooldays Again as MM Ends Vacation," *New York Journal-American*, June 19, 1961.

35. John P. Leacocos, "USIA Gains Status under Ed Murrow," *Cleveland Plain Dealer*, November 26, 1961.

36. "Hollywood Error," *New York Times*, November 12, 1961.

37. Martin Quigley Jr., "Edward R. Murrow, 'Smatterer,'" *Motion Picture Herald*, November 22, 1961.

38. Art Buchwald, "We Like the Image," *New York Herald-Tribune*, November 21, 1961.

39. Memorandum, Murrow to Turner Shelton, September 30, 1961, microfilm Reel 42, Box 4, E1006, RG 306, NA.

40. Memorandum, Lowell Bennett to Turner Shelton: "ERM's Hollywood Visit," October 13, 1963, Box 18, E1069, RG 306, NA.

41. Cull, *Cold War and the United States Information Agency*, 209.

42. Eric Johnston and Milton Sperling, quoted in "Murrow in Hollywood," *Variety*, November 15, 1961.

43. Letter, Samuel Goldwyn to Murrow, August 1, 1962, Box 18, E1069, RG 306, NA.

44. Memorandum, Murrow to JFK, November 9, 1961, Box 91, DA, POF, JFKPL.

45. Memorandum, Arthur B. Krim to Evelyn N. Lincoln, September 14, 1962, Box 91, DA, POF, JFKPL.

46. Memorandum, Murrow to Evelyn N. Lincoln, September 26, 1962, Box 91, DA, POF, JFKPL.

47. For an examination of jazz ambassadors, see Von Eschen, *Satchmo Blows up the World*.

48. Memorandum, Murrow to JFK, September 21, 1963, Box 91, DA, POF, JFKPL.

49. Cull, "Film as Public Diplomacy," 261 and 264.

50. Letter, Murrow to Morris K. Udall, September 5, 1961, microfilm, Reel 42, Box 4, E1006, RG 306, NA.

51. Murrow, speech on television and politics, Guildhall, London, November 1959, Box 14, E1069, RG 306, NA.

52. John Grierson, quoted in MacCann, *The People's Films*, 11.

53. Memorandum, Leon Poullada to Murrow, February 5, 1962, Box 18, E1069, RG 306, NA.

54. Shaw, *Hollywood's Cold War*, 175.

55. Memorandum, Turner Shelton to Murrow, May 17, 1961, Box 18, E1069, RG 306, NA.

56. Marquis Childs, "Murrow's Methods," *New York Post*, November 27, 1961.

57. USIA Circular 1362: "Motion Pictures: Identification of TODAY Footage," November 24, 1961, Box 2, E12, RG 306, NA.

58. See memoranda in Box 2, E12, RG 306, NA.

59. Report, LBJ to JFK: "Mission to Africa, Europe," April 15, 1961, Box 2 SF, VPP, LBJPL.

60. JFK, speaking in *The Task Begun: President Kennedy in Europe, 1961: 30 May–5 June*, "USG-11," JFKPL, online collection, http://www.jfklibrary.org/Asset-Viewer /Archives/USG-01-i.aspx.

61. Turner Shelton describes the production plans for the documentary in memorandum, Shelton to Murrow, July 1, 1961, Box 18, E1069, RG 306, NA.

62. Cull, "Film as Public Diplomacy," 267.

63. Memorandum, Murrow to Pierre Salinger, December 19, 1961, microfilm, Reel 40, Box 4, E1006, RG 306, NA.

64. Jacqueline Kennedy, speaking in *White House Tour with Mrs. John F. Kennedy*, Film Archives channel, YouTube, http://www.youtube.com/watch ?v=CbFt4h3dkkw.

65. Attachment, "Reactions to Telecast," to memorandum, Donald M. Wilson to JFK, June 21, 1962, Box 91, DA, POF, JFKPL.

66. Interdepartmental Committee on Visual and Auditory Materials for Distribution Abroad list of participants, Box 3, E28, RG 306, NA.

67. Memorandum, Murrow to Arthur Sylvester, October 3, 1961, microfilm, Reel 42, Box 4, E1006, RG 306, NA.

68. Murrow, quoted in John P. Leacocos, "USIA Gains Status under Ed Murrow," *Cleveland Plain Dealer*, November 26, 1961.

69. Thomas C. Sorensen, *Word War*, 183.

70. George Stevens Sr. earned two Oscars for Best Director for *A Place in the Sun* (1951) and *Giant* (1956) and served in World War II as an army lieutenant colonel. The War Department awarded him the Legion of Merit for directing the army Signal Corps' documentaries on the Normandy landings and liberation of Dachau concentration camp. Prosecutors at the Nuremberg war crimes tribunal used the latter documentary as evidence against senior Nazi officials. See Jon C. Hopwood, "Biography for George Stevens," http://www.imdb.com /name/nm0828419/bio.

71. George Stevens Jr., quoted in MacCann, *The People's Films*, 183–84.

72. George Stevens Jr., "Always on the Side of the Heretics," *New York Times Review of Books*, July 6, 1986.

73. Charles Casey Murrow, interview by author, July 30, 2012, Dummerston VT.

74. Letter, Murrow to Samuel Goldwyn, July 27, 1962, Box 18, E1069, RG 306, NA.

75. Cull, *Cold War and the United States Information Agency*, 207.

76. Jacqueline Kennedy, in Caroline Kennedy, ed., *Jacqueline Kennedy*, 300–02.

77. Memorandum, Donald Wilson to Murrow, December 14, 1961, microfilm, Reel 40, Box 4, E1006, RG 306, NA.

78. Memorandum, George Stevens Jr. to Murrow, April 6, 1962, Box 18, E1069, RG 306, NA.

79. *Invitation to India*, U.S. Information Agency, JFKPL, online collection, http://www.jfklibrary.org/Asset-Viewer/Archives/USG-01-10.aspx.

80. *Invitation to Pakistan*, U.S. Information Agency, JFKPL, online collection, http://www.jfklibrary.org/Asset-Viewer/Archives/USG-01-14.aspx.

81. Galbraith, *Ambassador's Journal*, 339.

82. The amount of $73,000 equals about $560,000 today.

83. Cull, *Cold War and the United States Information Agency*, 208.

84. Memorandum, Donald M. Wilson to JFK, October 17, 1962, Box 91, DA, POF, JFKPL.

85. Between 1961 and 1963, Warner Brothers Studios president Jack Warner made it his personal crusade to produce *PT 109*, the first movie ever released on the life of a sitting U.S. president. The Kennedy administration's concern about presenting the president as a hero, without appearing self-serving, contributed to extended delays. Warner hired and fired writers, directors, and actors, and the disruptions ultimately led to a production cost of $6.5 million (half the cost of the war epic *The Longest Day*, produced in 1962). See Cull, "Anatomy of a Shipwreck."

86. George Stevens Jr., quoted in MacCann, *The People's Films*, 185.

87. Burnett Anderson, recorded USIAAA interview by Jack O'Brien, January 5, 1990, Box 8, E1073, RG 306, NA.

88. MacCann, *The People's Films*, 198.

89. Shaw, *Hollywood's Cold War*, 177.

90. Memorandum, George Stevens Jr. to Murrow, August 15, 1963, Box 18, E1069, RG 306, NA.

91. Alan Fisher, recorded USIAAA interview by G. Lewis Schmidt, July 28, 1988, Box 3, E1073, RG 306, NA.

92. Memorandum, George Stevens Jr. to Murrow, February 27, 1962, Box 18, E1069, RG 306, NA.

93. George Stevens Jr., quoted in MacCann, *The People's Films*, 198–99.

94. Memorandum, Murrow to George Stevens Jr., September 5, 1963, Box 18, E1069, RG 306, NA.

95. Radio and Television Interview, "After Two Years: A Conversation with the President," edited version: Parts 1 and 2, December 17, 1962, White House Audio Collection, Recordings 153 and 154, JFKPL.

96. Memorandum, Murrow to JFK, February 14, 1963, Box 91, DA, POF, JFKPL.

97. Stevens forged a close working relationship with Guggenheim, hiring him to produce *Nine from Little Rock*, an important civil rights documentary, and *Night of the Dragon*, a description of U.S. efforts to bolster South Vietnam. The latter documentary attracted criticism by American journalists during its production for canned shots and "mock battles." See MacCann, *The People's Films*, 188.

98. *United in Progress*, U.S. Information Agency, JFKPL, online collection, http://www.jfklibrary.org/Asset-Viewer/Archives/USG-01-04.aspx.

99. Memorandum, George Stevens Jr. to Murrow, August 22, 1963, Box 18, E1069, RG 306, NA.

100. Memorandum, George Stevens Jr. to Murrow, May 2, 1963, Box 18, E1069, RG 306, NA.

101. *The March* is examined in greater depth in chapter 8.

102. MacCann, *The People's Films*, 188–89.

103. Memorandum, George Stevens Jr. to Murrow, June 7, 1963, Box 18, E1069, RG 306, NA.

104. JFK, quoted in *Five Cities in June*, U.S. Information Agency, JFKPL, online collection, http://www.jfklibrary.org/Asset-Viewer/Archives/USG-01-15.aspx.

105. MacCann, *The People's Films*, 193.

106. "Video: Master Filmmaker Terry Sanders," School of Theater, Film and Television, University of California, Los Angeles, http://www.tft.ucla.edu/2010/03/video-master-filmmaker-terry-sanders/.

107. "Kent Mackenzie: Writer, Producer, and Director," *The Exiles*, http://www.exilesfilm.com/filmmaker.html.

108. Cull, "Film as Public Diplomacy," 280.

109. Memorandum, George Stevens Jr. to Murrow, March 21, 1963, Box 18, E1069, RG 306, NA.

110. USIA Circular 3925: "Local Employee Regional Training Program (Africa)," June 18, 1964, Box 1, E12, RG 306, NA.

111. Memorandum, George Stevens Jr. to Murrow, July 27, 1963, Box 18, E1069, RG 306. NA.

112. Letter, Murrow to W. Averell Harriman, January 30, 1963, Box 491, WAH.

113. Memorandum, Murrow to Pierre Salinger, February 1963, Box 184, FGO, WHCSF, JFKPL.

114. Cable, Murrow to USIS Usumbura: "Motion Picture Statistical Report for Calendar 1962," July 29, 1963, Box 2, E12, RG 306, NA.

115. USIA Circular 304: "Sino-Soviet Bloc Film Activities," July 26, 1963, Box 2, E12, RG 306, NA.

116. Murrow, transcript of *Issues and Answers*, August 4, 1963, Box 21, E1069, RG 306, NA.

117. Letter, Murrow to Sidney Poitier, August 21, 1963, Box 18, E1069, RG 306, NA.

118. Memorandum, George Stevens Jr. to Murrow, June 10, 1963, Box 18, E1069, RG 306, NA.

119. Letter, Murrow to Tony Curtis, August 2, 1963, Box 18, E1069, RG 306, NA.

120. Memorandum, Murrow to JFK, July 25, 1963, Box 18, E1069, RG 306, NA.

121. Memorandum, Murrow to JFK, July 30, 1963, Box 91, DA, POF, JKFPL.

122. Letter, Foy Kohler to Murrow, July 30, 1963, Box 18, E1069, RG 306, NA.

123. Letter, Murrow to Foy Kohler, August 9, 1963, Box 18, E1069, RG 306, NA.

124. Cull, "Film as Public Diplomacy," 268.

125. USIA Research and Reference Service, report R-91–62: "World Reaction to Vostok III and IV," Box 5, SF, VPP, LBJPL.

126. Murrow, speech before the joint session of the Missouri Legislature, Jefferson City MO, May 1, 1961, Box 132, ERMP.

127. Commenting on the launch of Sputnik, on October 4, 1957, Murrow proposed to his CBS audience that, without new taxes or government involvement, the United States would remain inferior. He challenged Americans to consider the consequences of not participating in the space race: "It is whether we, as a free people, care more for our own security than the dictators care for theirs." Two days later, after assessing the American public's reaction to Sputnik, Murrow told listeners that the Soviet satellite "may be the best alarm clock that ever waked a country up." See Murrow, CBS broadcasts, October 7 and October 9, 1957, in *Selected Murrow Manuscripts (January 12, 1953–January 22, 1961)*.

128. Murrow, speech before the First National Conference on Peaceful Uses of Space, Tulsa OK, May 27, 1961, Box 132, ERMP.

129. Notes on Points of Significance and to be Followed Up, United States–United Kingdom Information Working Group Meeting, May 9–10, 1963, FO 953/2126, BNA.

130. Guard Report on the United States–United Kingdom Information Working Group, June 4–6, 1962, FO 1110/1522, BNA.

131. Murrow, testimony before the Committee on Science and Astronautics, U.S. House of Representatives, July 14, 1961, Box 132, ERMP.

132. Chester H. Opal, recorded USIAAA interview by G. Lewis Schmidt, January 28, 1989, Box 5, E1073, RG 306, NA.

133. Memorandum, George Stevens Jr. to Murrow, June 3, 1963, Box 18, E1069, RG 306, NA.

134. Notes on meeting between W. Averell Harriman, George Stevens Jr., and Charles Hill, May 24, 1963, Box 517, WAH.

135. Memorandum, Edward V. Roberts to USIA Public Affairs Officers in Africa, November 8, 1961, Box 18, E1069, RG 306, NA.

136. See Box 84, Statements of LBJ, LBJPL.

137. Murrow, speech to the Advertising Federation of America, Atlanta GA, June 19, 1963, Box 30, ERMP.

138. Walter Tucker, address before the Jamestown Chapter, Virginia Society Colonial Dames XVII Century, October 26, 1963, Box 2, E20, RG 306, NA.

139. Arthur Schlesinger Jr., quoted in MacCann, *The People's Films*, 195. During the late 1930s, Pare Lorentz produced documentaries for the Roosevelt administration designed to inform the American people about the value of New Deal programs. The domestic public relations value of the Films of Merit series created by Lorentz convinced President Franklin Roosevelt to establish the U.S. Film Service in 1938. See Kathleen Hogan, "Reaping the Golden Harvest," http://xroads.virginia.edu/~1930s/film/lorentz/front.html.

140. Cable, USIS Athens to USIA Washington: "Annual Assessment Report," January 9, 1963, Box 47, E56, RG 306, NA.

141. MacCann, *The People's Films*, 192.

142. Memorandum, Office of Public Information to USIA Employees: "Some Changes in USIA since March 1961," October 28, 1963, Box 18, E1069, RG 306, NA.

143. Cull, "Film as Public Diplomacy," 281.

144. George Stevens Jr., quoted in Shaw, *Hollywood's Cold War*, 167.

145. Shaw, *Hollywood's Cold War*, 176.

6. *USIA and Cuban Missile Crisis*

1. Schlesinger, *A Thousand Days*, xiv; Dean Rusk, quoted in Bruce W. Nelan, "Armageddon's Echoes," *Time*, October 13, 1997; and Robert Kennedy, *Thirteen Days*.

2. Central Committee of the Communist Party of the Soviet Union, Presidium, Protocol No. 60, Session of October 22–23, 1962, in the Woodrow Wilson International Center for Scholars, *Cold War International History Project*, 306.

3. Khrushchev, *Memoirs of Nikita Khrushchev*, 320–24.

4. Zubok and Pleshakov, *Inside the Kremlin's Cold War*, 258.

5. George W. Anderson Jr., recorded interview by Joseph E. O'Connor, April 25, 1967, JFKLOHP.

6. Edward Lansdale, "The Cuba Project," January 18, 1962, Item no. CC00141, Cuban Missile Crisis Collection, NSA.

7. The Senate Select Committee to Study Governmental Operations with

Respect to Intelligence Activities, known as the Church Committee, after its chairman, Senator Frank Church (D-ID), made Operation Mongoose public knowledge in 1975. The committee noted that the "most ironic" assassination plot unfolded on November 22, 1963, the day of Kennedy's own assassination. A CIA case officer provided Cuban army major Rolando Cubela, codename "AM/LASH," with a ballpoint pen containing a hypodermic needle. The needle was so fine that the victim would not realize its insertion, and the case officer recommended that Cubela use the commercially available poison Blackleaf-40 to kill Castro at a forthcoming meeting between Castro and a U.S. diplomat (ironically, to consider a rapprochement). Cubela never used the pen. See U.S. Senate, *Alleged Assassination Plots Involving Foreign Leaders*, 88–89.

8. Schoultz, *That Infernal Little Cuban Republic*, 196.

9. U.S. Senate, *Alleged Assassination Plots Involving Foreign Leaders*, 105.

10. John McCone, quoted in U.S. Senate, *Alleged Assassination Plots Involving Foreign Leaders*, 164.

11. U.S. Senate, *Alleged Assassination Plots Involving Foreign Leaders*, 320.

12. Memorandum, Murrow to McGeorge Bundy: "Cuban MIGS," June 24, 1961, Item no. CC00095, Cuban Missile Crisis Collection, NSA.

13. Memorandum, Murrow to Edward Lansdale, May 23, 1962, Item no. CU00267, Cuban Missile Crisis Revisited Collection, NSA.

14. Memorandum, Murrow to John McCone, December 1962, cited in Schoultz, *That Infernal Little Cuban Republic*, 92n, 628.

15. James G. Hershberg, "Before 'The Missiles of October,'" 181–87.

16. Amintore Fanfani, quoted in ASJ, June 18, 1961, Folder 311.13.

17. Jon Lee Anderson, *Che Guevara*, 509.

18. USIA Research and Reference Service, reports, February and March 1962, Box 2, E1010, RG 306, NA.

19. Their book not only explores Kennedy's decision to curb U-2 flights over Cuba after September 1, 1962, but it also reveals the administration's deliberate efforts during and after the crisis to counter journalists and congressional representatives who began to inquire into why U.S. intelligence did not locate the missile sites earlier. Republican politicians raised the possibility of a Soviet buildup in Cuba weeks prior to the crisis. On October 6, Representative Robert Dole (R-KS) added the following to the *Congressional Record*:

> Today, just 90 miles from the United States, anti-aircraft missiles are being installed by the Soviet technicians . . . it becomes increasingly apparent that the Soviet Union is establishing a base in the Western Hemisphere from which an attack might one day be mounted against the United States. Who can say that the next step will not be the installation of short- and intermediate-range ballistic missiles which could be launched against the United States?

> Dole, quoted in Barrett and Holland, *Blind over Cuba*, 16.

20. Murrow, speech before the Poor Richards Club, Philadelphia PA, September 14, 1961, Box 132, ERMP.

21. Guard Report on the United States–United Kingdom Information Working Group, June 4–6, 1962, FO 1110/1522, BNA.

22. G. Lewis Schmidt, recorded USIAAA by Allen Hansen, February 8, 1988, Box 3, E1073, RG 306, NA; and Sperber, *Murrow*, 663.

23. Dobbs, *One Minute to Midnight*, 3.

24. Barrett and Holland, *Blind over Cuba*, 14–15.

25. Jacqueline Kennedy, quoted in Caroline Kennedy, ed., *Jacqueline Kennedy*, 88.

26. Memorandum, McGeorge Bundy to JFK: "The Use of the National Security Council," January 24, 1961, Box 405, McGeorge Bundy Correspondence, NSF, JFKPL.

27. Donald M. Wilson, recorded interview by James Greenfield, September 2, 1964, JFKLOHP.

28. Donald M. Wilson, recorded interview by James Greenfield, September 2, 1964, JFKLOHP.

29. Thomas C. Sorensen, recorded USIAAA interview by Larry Hall, June 25, 1990, Box 10, E1073, RG 306, NA.

30. Cull, *Cold War and the United States Information Agency*, 214; and Thomas C. Sorensen, *Word War*, 199.

31. Thomas C. Sorensen, recorded USIAAA interview by Larry Hall, June 25, 1990, Box 10, E1073, RG 306, NA.

32. Henry Loomis, recorded USIAAA interview by Claude Groce, March 1987, Box 3, E1073, RG 306, NA. In his interview, Loomis recalled Wilson calling him to his office on Thursday, October 18. Based on other sources, it seems evident that Loomis misspoke, and Wilson did not speak to him until Saturday, October 20, when Wilson received permission from the White House to involve Loomis. See Thomas C. Sorensen, *Word War*, 199; and Cull, *Cold War and the United States Information Agency*, 214.

33. Memorandum, Donald M. Wilson: "Radio Propaganda Plan," October 20, 1962, in Elliston, *PsyWar on Cuba*, 132–34.

34. George W. Ball, recorded interview by Joseph Kraft, April 16, 1965, JFKLOHP.

35. Dallek, *An Unfinished Life*, 553.

36. Memorandum, Donald M. Wilson: "Psychological Program," October 20, 1962, in Elliston, *PsyWar on Cuba*, 136–37.

37. Twenty-three nations adopted the Inter-American Treaty of Reciprocal Assistance on September 2, 1947, in Rio de Janeiro, Brazil, and the agreement entered into force on December 8, 1948. As a signatory, the United States could cite Article 1 during the missile crisis: "The High Contracting Parties formally condemn war and undertake in their international relations not to resort to the threat or the use of force in any manner inconsistent with the provisions of the

Charter of the United Nations or of this Treaty." See Department of International Law, OAS, http://oas.org/juridico/english/sigs/b-29.html.

38. Underlining appears in the original text. See cable, Thomas Sorensen: "Information Policy Guidance on Cuba (Output to Cuba)," October 22, 1962, in Elliston, *PsyWar on Cuba*, 138–41.

39. Burnett Anderson, recorded USIAAA interview by Jack O'Brien, January 5, 1990, Box 8, E1073, RG 306, NA.

40. One indication that Loomis did not resent Anderson's presence at VOA during the crisis emerged several years later. When Loomis became the head of the Corporation for Public Broadcasting, he asked Anderson to join him as his deputy. See Burnett Anderson, recorded USIAAA interview by Jack O'Brien, January 5, 1990, Box 8, E1073, RG 306, NA .

41. Henry Loomis, recorded USIAAA interview by Claude Groce, March 1987, Box 3, E1073, RG 306, NA.

42. Henry Loomis, recorded USIAAA interview by Claude Groce, March 1987, Box 3, E1073, RG 306, NA

43. Cull, *Cold War and the United States Information Agency*, 214. Alan Heil Jr. who served in VOA's Worldwide English division at the time of the crisis, observed Anderson sitting at the end of the central desk before the window to the Teletype operators room. Heil found the censorship "unnecessary," and the commentaries "reminiscent of the darkest days of the Campaign of Truth," referring to overtly propagandistic broadcasts during the early 1950s. See Heil, *Voice of America*, 71.

44. Sperber, *Murrow*, 663.

45. Thomas C. Sorensen, *Word War*, 199.

46. Kendrick, *Prime Time*, 484–85.

47. Memorandum, Murrow to Staff, April 22, 1961, Box 290, DA, NSF, JFKPL.

48. G. Lewis Schmidt, recorded USIAAA interview by Allen Hansen, February 8, 1988, Box 3, E1073, RG 306, NA.

49. JFK, Radio and Television Report to the American People on the Soviet Arms Buildup in Cuba, October 22, 1962, *Public Papers of the Presidents: John F. Kennedy*, vol. 1962, 806–07.

50. Emphasis in original text. See *Public Papers of the Presidents: John F. Kennedy*, vol. 1962, 809.

51. Thomas C. Sorensen, *Word War*, 204.

52. James Pettus, recorded USIAAA interview by G. Lewis Schmidt, May 30, 1990, Box 9; and John N. Hutchison, recorded USIAAA interview by G. Lewis Schmidt, December 28, 1988, Box 4, E1073, RG 306, NA.

53. After reviewing the intelligence presented by Ambassador Bruce, a prominent Labour Member of Parliament, Dennis Healy, told *The Daily Telegraph*, "I made myself very unpopular with the Americans because I opposed the official line. I thought they were making a ghastly error and searching for a pretense

to invade Cuba." Healy became defense minister in 1964. Healy, quoted in Jon Swaine, "Cuban Missile Crisis Cables Reveal Bomb Threats at US Embassy in London," *Daily Telegraph*, October 11, 2012.

54. James Pettus, recorded USIAAA interview by G. Lewis Schmidt, May 30, 1990, Box 9, E1073, RG 306, NA.

55. Donald M. Wilson, recorded interview by James Greenfield, September 2, 1964, JFKLOHP.

56. Thomas C. Sorensen, *Word War*, 204.

57. Thomas C. Sorensen, *Word War*, 202.

58. Zelikow and May, eds., *Presidential Recordings, John F. Kennedy*, 3:234.

59. USIA leaflet, "LA VERDAD," annex A to Joint Chiefs of Staff appendix: "CINCLANT Psychological Leaflet Program," October 27, 1962, in Ellison, *Psywar on Cuba*, 144.

60. After the crisis, Wilson reminded Kennedy about the six million leaflets that the military never dropped, causing the president to laugh. Eventually, the army burned the handouts at Fort Bragg NC. See Donald M. Wilson, recorded interview by James Greenfield, September 2, 1964, JFKLOHP.

61. Robert F. Kennedy, quoted in ASJ, October 28, 1962, Folder 312.10.

62. ASJ, October 28, 1962, Folder 312.10.

63. Dobbs, *One Minute to Midnight*, 131–32.

64. McGeorge Bundy, quoted in Zelikow and May, eds., *Presidential Recordings, John F. Kennedy*, 3:299.

65. JFK, quoted in Zelikow and May, eds., *Presidential Recordings, John F. Kennedy*, 3:299; and summary record of NSC Executive Committee Meeting no. 6, October 26, 1962, 10:00 a.m., Box 316, MM, NSF, JFKPL.

66. James Pettus, recorded USIAAA interview by G. Lewis Schmidt, May 30, 1990, Box 9, E1073, RG 306, NA.

67. Garthoff, "Cuban Missile Crisis," 61.

68. Hans N. Tuch, recorded USIAAA interview by G. Lewis Schmidt, August 4, 1989, Box 7, E1073, RG 306, NA.

69. JFK, quoted in Dallek, *An Unfinished Life*, 565.

70. Letter, Nikita Khrushchev to JFK, sent as cable, U.S. Embassy in the Soviet Union to the Department of State, October 26, 1962, Document 84, U.S. Department of State, *Foreign Relations of the United States, 1961–1963*, vol. 11, *Cuban Missile Crisis and Aftermath*, 240.

71. Dobbs, *One Minute to Midnight*, 231.

72. See Nikita Khrushchev, quoted in Jon Lee Anderson, *Che Guevara*, 525.

73. Donald Wilson, quoted in Zelikow and May, eds., *Presidential Recordings, John F. Kennedy*, 3:391.

74. JFK, Message in Reply to a Broadcast by Chairman Khrushchev on the Cuban Crisis, October 28, 1962, *Public Papers of the Presidents: John F. Kennedy*, vol. 1962, 814–15.

75. Dobbs, *One Minute to Midnight*, 306–07.

76. Donald M. Wilson, recorded interview by James Greenfield, September 2, 1964, JFKLOHP.

77. JFK, quoted in Gaddis, *Strategies of Containment*, 212.

78. Memorandum, George Reedy to LBJ, October 26, 1962, Box 8, Vice Presidential Aide's Files of George Reedy, LBJPL.

79. Khrushchev, *Memoirs of Nikita Khrushchev*, 354–55.

80. Freedman, *Kennedy's Wars*, 236.

81. Theodore C. Sorensen, recorded interview by Carl Kaysen, March 26, 1964, JFKLOHP. The public diplomacy value of Kennedy's American University speech is explored in chapter 7.

82. Summary record of NSC Executive Committee Meeting no. 13, October 30, 1962, 10:00 a.m., Box 316, MM, NSF, JFKPL.

83. NSC Executive Committee Record of Action, October 31, 1962, 6:00 p.m., Meeting no. 15, Box 316, MM, NSF, JFKPL.

84. Summary record of NSC Executive Committee Meeting no. 17, November 2, 1962, 11:00 a.m., Box 316, MM, NSF, JFKPL.

85. Memorandum, Donald M. Wilson to JFK, November 2, 1962, in Elliston, *Psywar on Cuba*, 147–48.

86. NSC Executive Committee Record of Action, November 6, 1962, 6:15 p.m., Meeting no. 21, Folder "Executive Com. Meetings 17–24," Box 316, MM, NSF, JFKPL.

87. Memorandum, Murrow to JFK, November 19, 1962, Box 91, DA, POF, JFKPL.

88. NSC Executive Committee Record of Action, November 19, 1962, 10:00 a.m., Meeting no. 27, Box 316, MM, NSF, JFKPL.

89. Summary record of NSC Executive Committee Meeting No. 33, December 6, 1962, 11:00 a.m., Box 316, MM, NSF, JFKPL.

90. Summary record of NSC Executive Committee Meeting no. 34, December 10, 1962, 5:40 p.m., Box 316, MM, NSF, JFKPL.

91. One example of this emerged in April 1963, when Murrow advised the president against authorizing the CIA's plan to balloon half a million anti-Castro leaflets over Havana on May Day. Operationally, the director worried about the CIA's experimental plan of launching balloons from twelve miles offshore to drift over the island. Murrow called it a "gimmick" that would "embarrass" the U.S. government. He harkened back to the Bay of Pigs by arguing, "If the call for 'uprisings' is not coupled with a plan of support and actions, we could seriously compromise any possibility of future support from the Cuban people." See memorandum, Murrow to McGeorge Bundy: "Cuban Balloon/Leaflet Project," April 5, 1963, Box 91, DA, POF, JFKPL.

92. Memorandum, Murrow to JFK: "Airborne Television Capability," December 3, 1962, Box 91, DA, POF, JFKPL.

93. The Eighteenth Report of the United States Advisory Commission on Information, January 1963, Box 21, E1069, RG 306, NA.

94. William Randolph Hearst Jr., in USIA editorial file, November 19, 1962, Box 21, EI069, RG 306, NA.

95. Murrow, note on letter, Lowell Bennett to Reed Harris, November 19, 1962, Box 21, EI069, RG 306, NA.

96. "Radio Stations Cited for Service in Cuban Crisis," *Washington Post*, December 5, 1962.

97. Henry Loomis, recorded USIAAA interview by Claude Groce, March 1987, Box 3, EI073, RG 306, NA.

98. Memorandum, Murrow to JFK, December 11, 1962, Box 290, DA, NSF, JFKPL.

99. Memorandum, Murrow to McGeorge Bundy, December 13, 1962, Box 290, DA, NSF, JFKPL.

100. Chester Bowles, "Report of Mission to Africa: October 15–November 9, 1962," Box 438, WAH.

101. USIA Research and Reference Service, reports, February-July 1963, Box 91, DA, POF, JFKPL.

102. Cable, USIS Athens to USIA Washington: "Annual Assessment Report," January 9, 1963, Box 47, E56, RG 306, NA.

103. Agenda item, "Propaganda about the Soviet Union," United States–United Kingdom Information Working Group Meeting, May 9–10, 1963, FO 953/2125, BNA.

104. Murrow, transcript of *Issues and Answers*, ABC, August 4, 1963, Box 21, EI069, RG 306, NA.

105. Fidel Castro, quoted in Donald M. Wilson, statement before the Inter-American Affairs Subcommittee, U.S. House of Representatives, February 21, 1963, Box 37, EI069, RG 306, NA.

106. See memorandum for record: "Minutes of the Meeting of the Special Group (CI), 2 p.m., Thursday, January 31, 1963," January 31, 1963, Doc No/ESDN: CIA-RDP80B01676R001900150085–5, CIA-FOIA.

107. Charles Casey Murrow, interview by author, July 30, 2012, Dummerston VT.

108. Murrow, statement before the Subcommittee on International Organizations and Movements of the Committee on Foreign Affairs, U.S. House of Representatives, March 28, 1963, Box 132, ERMP.

109. Henry Loomis, recorded USIAAA interview by Claude Groce, March 1987, Box 3, EI073, RG 306, NA.

7. Advocates for a Test Ban

1. Memorandum, Murrow to Dean Rusk: "USIA Planning and Action on Berlin," July 10, 1961, Item no. BC02158, Berlin Crisis Collection, NSA.

2. Memorandum, Murrow to Roswell Gilpatric: "U.S. Public Position on our Defense Capability," March 8, 1961, Box 290, DA, NSF, JFKPL.

3. Harlan Cleveland, recorded interview by Sheldon Stern, November 30, 1978, JFKLOHP.

4. Memorandum, Murrow to all USIS posts: "Special Program Emphasis," July 24, 1961, Box 1, DA, NSF, JFKPL.

5. Murrow, CBS broadcast, March 18, 1954, in *Selected Murrow Manuscripts*, Box 6, ERMP.

6. Murrow, CBS broadcast, September 6, 1954, in *Selected Murrow Manuscripts*, Box 6, ERMP.

7. Emphasis in original text, memorandum, Murrow to Chester Bowles: "The Nuclear Test Ban Issue," June 24, 1961, Box 290, DA, NSF, JFKPL.

8. USIA Research and Reference Service, "West European Attitudes toward Disarmament," August 1961, Box 5, E1010, RG 306, NA.

9. "The Crisis in the Nuclear Test-Ban Negotiations," FO 953/2083, BNA.

10. Freedman, *Kennedy's Wars*, 80–85.

11. Harold Brown, recorded interview with interviewer no. 1, 1964, JFKLOHP.

12. Report of the ad hoc panel on nuclear testing, July 21, 1961, Box 5, SF, VPP, LBJPL.

13. Murrow, quoted in Beschloss, *Crisis Years*, 295.

14. Memorandum, Murrow to JFK, August 31, 1961, microfilm, Reel 43, Box 4, E1006, RG 306, NA.

15. Founded in 1957, in response to Eisenhower's New Look policy, the Committee for a Sane Nuclear Policy (SANE) also petitioned Kennedy to maintain the U.S. moratorium on atmospheric testing. In 1987, SANE merged with Freeze to form Peace Action, which remains an outspoken activist organization today. See "Peace Action History," http://www.peace-action.org/history.

16. Memorandum, Murrow to JFK, August 31, 1961, microfilm, Reel 43, Box 4, E1006, RG 306, NA.

17. Edward T. Folliard, "When Mr. K Bullies, How Best to Answer Him?" *Washington Post*, September 3, 1961.

18. JFK, White House Statement Following the President's Meeting with the National Security Council and Congressional Leaders on the Resumption of Nuclear Tests by the USSR, August 31, 1961, *Public Papers of the Presidents: John F. Kennedy*, vol. 1961, 584–85.

19. Edward T. Folliard, "When Mr. K Bullies, How Best to Answer Him?" *Washington Post*, September 3, 1961.

20. ASJ, September 4, 1961, Folder 311.16.

21. Memorandum, Murrow to JFK, September 1, 1961, Box 91, DA, POF, JFKPL.

22. USIA Research Service, Research Note 24–61, "Initial Worldwide Reactions to the Soviet Nuclear Test Announcement," September 1, 1961, Box 91, DA, POF, JFKPL.

23. Memorandum, Murrow to JFK: "Reactions to Nuclear Tests," undated, Box 91, DA, POF, JFKPL.

24. Cull, *Cold War and the United States Information Agency*, 203.

25. "The Truth Must Be Our Guide, But Dreams Must Be Our Goals," *Newsweek*, September 18, 1961, 24–25.

26. ASJ, September 5, 1961, Folder 311.16.

27. JFK, Statement by the President on Ordering Resumption of Underground Nuclear Tests, September 5, 1961, *Public Papers of the Presidents: John F. Kennedy*, vol. 1961, 589–90.

28. Memorandum, Murrow to JFK: "Weekly Report," September 5, 1961, microfilm, Reel 43, Box 4, E1006, RG 306, NA.

29. Memorandum, Murrow to Thomas Sorensen, September 16, 1961, microfilm, Reel 42, Box 4, E1006, RG 306, NA.

30. "The Truth Must Be Our Guide, But Dreams Must Be Our Goals," *Newsweek*, September 18, 1961, 24–25.

31. Memorandum, Murrow to JFK, September 11, 1961, Box 290, DA, NSF, JFKPL.

32. Cable, Murrow to Wireless File, September 26, 1961, Box 184, FGO, WHCF, JFKPL.

33. Murrow, speech before the Public Relations Society of America, Houston TX, November 13, 1961, Box 132, ERMP.

34. Letter, Donald J. Irwin to H. William Ihrig, October 10, 1961, Box 6, SF, VPP, LBJPL.

35. Notes on National Security Council Meeting, November 2, 1961, Item no. NP00812, NNPC, NSA.

36. Harold Brown, recorded interview with interviewer no. 1, 1964, JFKLOHP.

37. Notes on National Security Council Meeting, November 2, 1961, Item no. NP00812, NNPC, NSA.

38. Claude Groce, recorded USIAAA interview by Jack O'Brien, February 8, 1988, Box 1, E1073, RG 306, NA.

39. Hans N. Tuch, recorded USIAAA interview by G. Lewis Schmidt, August 4, 1989, Box 7, E1073, RG 306, NA.

40. Memorandum, Murrow to McGeorge Bundy, October 30, 1961, Box 290, DA, NSF, JFKPL.

41. Cull, *Cold War and the United States Information Agency*, 205.

42. Claude Groce, recorded USIAAA interview by Jack O'Brien, February 8, 1988, Box 1, E1073, RG 306, NA.

43. Agenda item, "United States General and Complete Disarmament Programme," United States–United Kingdom Information Working Group, November 1961, FO 953/2030, BNA.

44. USIA Research and Reference Service, "The Impact of U.S. versus Soviet Science in West European Public Opinion: A Survey in Four Western European Countries," October 1961, Box 5, E1010, RG 306, NA.

45. Giglio, *Presidency of John F. Kennedy*, 154.

46. Theodore C. Sorensen, recorded interview by Carl Kaysen, March 26, 1964, JFKLOHP.

47. Murrow, Some Guidelines for United States Overseas Exhibits, August 21, 1961, microfilm, Reel 43, Box 4, E1006, RG 306, NA.

48. JFK, Special Message to the Congress on Urgent National Needs, May 25, 1961, *Public Papers of the Presidents: John F. Kennedy*, vol. 1961, 404.

49. USIA Research and Reference Service, "Trends in the U.S. and Soviet Economic Images in Western Europe," January 1962, Box 5, EI010, RG 306, NA.

50. Memorandum, Howard Burris to LBJ: "Atmospheric Nuclear Testing," February 26, 1962, Box 5, SF, VPP, LBJPL.

51. Memorandum, Lyman Lemnitzer to JFK: "Joint Chiefs of Staff Views on Resumption of Nuclear Testing," February 16, 1962, Box 5, SF, VPP, LBJPL.

52. Notes on National Security Council Meeting, February 27, 1962, Item no. NP00840, NNPC, NSA.

53. JFK, Radio and Television Address to the American People: "Nuclear Testing and Disarmament," March 2, 1962, *Public Papers of the Presidents: John F. Kennedy*, vol. 1962, 187, 192.

54. Memorandum, Murrow to JFK: "Soviet Jamming of your Nuclear Testing Speech," March 3, 1962, Box 91, DA, POF, JFKPL.

55. USIA Research and Reference Service, report R-21–62: "Reaction to the Presidential Announcement on Nuclear Testing," March 6, 1962, Box 91, DA, POF, JFKPL.

56. Dallek, *An Unfinished Life*, 502.

57. Murrow, speech before the Columbia University Scholastic Press Association, New York NY, March 17, 1962, Box 132, ERMP.

58. Cable, Darrell I. Drucker to USIA Washington, March 20, 1962, Box 1, EI2, RG 306, NA.

59. Cable, USIS Athens to USIA Washington: "Annual Assessment Report," January 9, 1963, Box 47, E56, RG 306, NA.

60. Memorandum, Murrow to JFK: "Overseas Exhibition of 'Friendship 7' Space Capsule," February 27, 1962, Box 91, DA, POF, JFKPL.

61. Murrow, introduction to U.S. Information Agency, "19th Report to Congress, July 1–December 31, 1962," Item no. CC2808, Cuban Missile Crisis Collection, NSA.

62. Memorandum, Oren Stephens to Murrow: "Trend in West European Confidence in the U.S.," August 14, 1962, Box 91, DA, POF, JFKPL.

63. U.S. Arms Control and Disarmament Agency, memorandum of conversation: "Meeting of Committee Principals, May 31, 1962," Doc No/ESDN: CIA-RDP80B01676R002900150014–2, CIA-FOIA.

64. Agenda Item, "Disarmament and Nuclear Testing," United States–United Kingdom Information Working Group Meeting, Washington DC, June 4–6, 1962, FO 953/2083, BNA.

65. Memorandum, Murrow to JFK: "Weekly Report," August 22, 1962, microfilm, Reel 54, Box 4, EI006, RG 306, NA.

66. Memorandum of conversation, Chester Bowles and Anatoly Dobrynin, November 15, 1962, Box 428, WAH.

67. Thomas C. Sorensen, recorded USIAAA interview by Larry Hall, June 25, 1990, Box 10, EI073, RG 306, NA.

68. JFK, Commencement Address at American University in Washington, June 10, 1963, *Public Papers of the Presidents: John F. Kennedy*, vol. 1963, 459–64.

69. Thomas C. Sorensen, *Word War*, 212.

70. Thomas C. Sorensen, recorded USIAAA interview by Larry Hall, June 25, 1990, Box 10, E1073, RG 306, NA.

71. Thomas C. Sorensen, *Word War*, 212–13.

72. Nikita Khrushchev, quoted in Moscow TASS, June 14, 1963, Box 479, WAH.

73. ASJ, July 28, 1963, Folder 313.1.

74. JFK, quoted in Caroline Kennedy, ed., *Jacqueline Kennedy*, 250.

75. Memorandum of conversation, W. Averell Harriman and Nikita Khrushchev, July 26, 1963, Box 480, WAH.

76. USIA Research and Reference Service, report R-143–63 (A): "Initial Media Reaction to the U.S.-U.K.-USSR Test Ban Agreement," July 30, 1963, Box 91, DA, POF, JFKPL.

77. Murrow, transcript of *Issues and Answers*, ABC, August 4, 1963, Box 21, E1069, RG 306, NA.

78. Murrow, quoted in William McGaffin, "Murrow Sees No Letup Now in Cold War," *New York Post*, July 29, 1963.

79. Memorandum, Donald M. Wilson to JFK: "First Effort to Measure World Opinion," July 10, 1963, Box 91, DA, POF, JFKPL.

80. Memorandum, Murrow to JFK: "Psychological Factors in Manned Space Flight Decisions," March 29, 1963, Box 91, DA POF, JFKPL.

81. LBJ, "Our Five Years of Space Progress," USIA Celebration of NASA Fifth Anniversary, Box 84, Statements of LBJ, LBJPL.

8. Birmingham

1. Freedom Riders sought to generate national support for federal enforcement of the December 1960 Supreme Court ruling in *Boynton v. Virginia* that declared segregated interstate bus terminals unconstitutional. See Arsenault, *Freedom Riders*.

2. L. B. Sullivan, speaking in WSB-TV news interview, Montgomery AL, May 21, 1961; in Civil Rights Digital Library, http://crdl.usg.edu/cgi/crdl?format=_video &query=id%3Baugabma_wsbn_35162&_cc=1.

3. Murrow, address before the National Press Club, Washington DC, May 25, 1961, Box 23, E1069, RG 306, NA. The same day, Kennedy spoke before a joint session of Congress to commit the United States to landing a man on the moon before the end of the decade. See JFK, Special Message to the Congress on Urgent National Needs, May 25, 1961, *Public Papers of the Presidents: John F. Kennedy*, vol. 1961, 404.

4. "Color in Foreign Affairs," *Des Moines Register*, May 28, 1961.

5. Cable, British Embassy in Washington to Foreign Office, June 7, 1961, FO 371/156508, BNA.

6. Harry Truman, quoted in Von Eschen, *Race Against Empire*, 126.

7. When Arkansas authorities defied the 1954 Supreme Court decision *Brown v. Board of Education*, by having police escort nine black children out of Little Rock Central High School on September 23, 1957, Eisenhower deployed troops from the 101st Airborne Division to return the students to their classroom. Historian Mary Dudziak argues that Eisenhower worried less about improving the plight of African Americans than preserving the positive global opinion of the United States. Speaking publicly after the incident, the president explained that he had deployed soldiers to "restore the image of America," saying nothing about upholding the Supreme Court decision to overturn the 1896 precedent of "separate but equal" established by *Plessy v. Ferguson*. See Dudziak, "Birmingham, Addis Ababa, and the Image of America," 183.

8. Lauren, "Seen from the Outside," 34.

9. Dean Rusk, quoted in Borstelmann, *Cold War and the Color Line*, 136.

10. Herve Alphand, recorded interview by Adalbert de Segonzac, October 14, 1964, JFKLOHP.

11. William H. Attwood, recorded statement, November 8, 1965, JFKLOHP.

12. Dudziak, *Cold War Civil Rights*, 156.

13. Cable, U.S. Agency for International Development officer, Dakar to International Cooperation Administration, April 10, 1961, Box 1, SF, VPP, LBJPL.

14. Borstelmann, *Cold War and the Color Line*, 138.

15. Democratic candidate Hubert Humphrey received a much warmer reception at the same meeting. See ASJ, July 10, 1960, Folder 311.8.

16. Robert F. Kennedy, quoted in ASJ, July 11, 1960, Folder 311.8.

17. Berl I. Bernhard, recorded interview by John Stewart, June 17, 1968, JFKLOHP.

18. Martin Luther King Jr., quoted in Harry Belafonte, recorded interview by Victoria Daitch, May 20, 2005, JFKLOHP.

19. Wofford, *Of Kennedys and Kings*, 103.

20. Cable, British Consul-General in New Orleans to Foreign Office, "Southern Reflections, 1961," June 29, 1961, FO 371/156508, BNA.

21. Schlesinger, *A Thousand Days*, 930; and Theodore C. Sorensen, *Kennedy*, 255–56. In his second memoir, written nearly forty years after the first, Sorensen provided a less-glowing portrayal of Kennedy. Sorensen calls the president "slow" to respond to the immoral problem of racial discrimination in America as a senator and president. See Theodore C. Sorensen, *Counselor*, 270–71.

22. Patterson, *Grand Expectations*, 466.

23. Kendrick, *Prime Time*, 112–13; and Charles Casey Murrow, interview by author, July 30, 2012, Dummerston VT.

24. Murrow, CBS broadcast, May 18, 1954, in *Selected Murrow Manuscripts*, Box 6, ERMP.

25. Murrow, CBS broadcast, September 10, 1957, in *Selected Murrow Manuscripts*, Box 6, ERMP.

26. Letter, C. Herbert Oliver to Murrow, January 26, 1961, Box 26, ERMP.

27. Charles Casey Murrow, interview by author, July 30, 2012, Dummerston VT.

28. Dudziak, *Cold War Civil Rights*, 13.

29. Wofford, *Of Kennedys and Kings*, 103.

30. Memorandum, Frederick G. Dutton to JFK: "Proposed Cabinet Agenda for Thursday, February 16th," February 13, 1961, Box 92, DA, POF, JFKPL.

31. Report, LBJ to JFK: "Mission to Africa, Europe," April 15, 1961, Box 1, SF, VPP, LBJPL.

32. Murrow, quoted in "American Reality," *Redbook*, February 1961.

33. Letter, Murrow to Morris Ernst, March 28, 1961, Box 18, E1069, RG 306, NA.

34. Memorandum, Murrow to Turner B. Shelton, June 12, 1961, Box 18, E1069, RG 306, NA.

35. Murrow, statement before the Subcommittee on Africa, Committee on Foreign Affairs, March 5, 1963, Box 17, E1069, RG 306, NA.

36. Memorandum, Murrow to Turner B. Shelton, August 21, 1961, Box 18, E1069, RG 306, NA.

37. Memorandum, Murrow to JFK, March 21, 1961, Box 91, DA, POF, JFKPL. For a study of 1950s jazz ambassadors, see Von Eschen, *Satchmo Blows up the World*.

38. Murrow, address before the joint session of the House and Senate of the Missouri Legislature, Jefferson City MO, May 1, 1961, Box 21, E1069, RG 306, NA.

39. Jean White, "Racial Snubs Here Seen More Hurtful than Riots," *Washington Post*, May 25, 1961.

40. Murrow, address before the joint session of the House and Senate of the Missouri Legislature, Jefferson City MO, May 1, 1961, Box 21, E1069, RG 306, NA.

41. Murrow, speech before the National Press Club, May 25, 1961, Box 21, E1069, RG 306, NA.

42. Murrow and Eleanor Roosevelt, quoted in transcript, "America's Propaganda Capabilities," *Mrs. Eleanor Roosevelt: Prospects of Mankind*, May 26, 1961, Box 21, E1069, RG 306, NA.

43. Habib Bourguiba Jr., recorded interview by David Schoenbrun, April 1, 1964, JFKLOHP.

44. U.S. State Department press statement, September 19, 1961, FO 371/156508, BNA.

45. "Big Step Ahead on a High Road," *Life*, December 8, 1961.

46. "Washington: A Hardship Post," *Cincinnati Enquirer*, May 30, 1961; and cable, British Embassy in Washington to Foreign Office, June 7, 1961, FO 371/156508, BNA.

47. Borstelmann, *Cold War and the Color Line*, 166; and "Practicing what We Preach," *Harrisburg Patriot-News*, May 29, 1961.

48. "Congress Can End This," *American Evening Sunday*, May 26, 1961.

49. "Color in Foreign Affairs," *Des Moines Register*, May 28, 1961.

50. JFK, quoted in Caroline Kennedy, ed., *Jacqueline Kennedy*, 313.

51. Anonymous student, quoted in USIA Research and Reference Service report: "A Study of Three VOA Programs," March 1962, Box 5, E1012, RG 306, NA.

52. Murrow, quoted in "Dixie Violence Dealt U.S. Sharp Blow, Murrow Says," *Louisville Times*, June 24, 1961.

53. "Murrow Says Race Violence Hurts U.S. Image Abroad," *Philadelphia Bulletin*, June 25, 1961.

54. "Negro Leaders Seek Halt in Freedom Ride Testing," *New York Times*, June 25, 1961.

55. Harry Golden, "Kennedy Declaration," October 20, 1961, Box 91, DA, POF, JFKPL.

56. Memorandum, Murrow to JFK, November 2, 1961, Box 91, DA, POF, JFKPL.

57. Memorandum, Murrow to Dean Rusk: "Proposed Campaign to Ensure Public Understanding of United States Foreign Policy," November 14, 1961, Box 18, E1069, RG 306, NA.

58. "The Fight for Men's Minds," *New York Journal*, December 3, 1961.

59. Memorandum, Edward V. Roberts to USIA Public Affairs Officers in Africa, November 8, 1961, Box 18, E1069, RG 306, NA.

60. Murrow, speech before the American Association of Colleges and Teacher Education, Chicago IL, February 16, 1962, Box 132, ERMP.

61. Murrow, speech before the annual dinner of the Lincoln Group of DC, Washington DC, February 10, 1962, Box 20, E1069, RG 306, NA.

62. Murrow, statement before the Subcommittee on Africa, Committee on Foreign Affairs, March 5, 1963, Box 17, E1069, RG 306, NA.

63. JFK, remarks on the Twentieth Anniversary of the Voice of America, Washington DC, February 26, 1962, Box 14, E1069, RG 306, NA.

64. David Ormsby-Gore, report: "Annual Review for 1961," January 2, 1962, FO 371/162578, BNA.

65. Cable, British Consul-General in New Orleans to British Embassy in Washington, November 24, 1961, FO 371/156508, BNA.

66. ASJ, October 2, 1962, Folder 312.10.

67. Borstelmann, *Cold War and the Color Line*, 159.

68. Robert F. Kennedy, quoted in Thomas C. Sorensen, *Word War*, 175.

69. USIA Circular 932, October 9, 1962, Box 2, E12, RG 306, NA.

70. Cable, USIA Usumbura to USIA Washington DC, October 26, 1962, Box 2, E12, RG 306, NA.

71. USIA Research and Reference Service, report R-109–62 (A): "Media Comment on the Mississippi Crisis," October 5, 1962, Box 91, DA, POF, JFKPL.

72. Murrow, speech before the Twenty-third Annual Distinguished Service Award Banquet, Kinston Junior Chamber of Commerce, Kinston NC, February 11, 1963, Box 121, ERMP.

73. Chester Bowles, "Report of Mission to Africa: October 15–November 9, 1962," Box 438, WAH.

74. "Summary Description of President's Major Legislative Proposals," February 7, 1962, Box 92, DA, POF, JFKPL.

75. Cull, *Cold War and the United States Information Agency*, 212.

76. See Murrow's exchange with P. Kenneth O'Donnell, September 11–20, 1962, Box 184, FGO, WHCSF, JFKPL.

77. USIA, "20th Review of Operations: January 1–June 30, 1963," Box 121, ERMP.

78. "80th Report of the United States Advisory Commission on Information," January 1963, Box 22, EI069, RG 306, NA.

79. Memorandum, Murrow to JFK: "Opinions of African Students in West Germany," March 7, 1963, Box 91, DA, POF, JFKPL.

80. Murrow, statement before the Subcommittee on Africa, Committee on Foreign Affairs, March 5, 1963, Box 17, EI069, RG 306, NA.

81. Murrow, statement before the Subcommittee on International Organizations and Movements of the Committee on Foreign Affairs, U.S. House of Representatives, March 28, 1963, Box 8, ERMP-MHC.

82. Patterson, *Grand Expectations*, 480.

83. Transcript, *Washington Report*, CBS, June 2, 1963, Box 18, EI069, RG 306, NA.

84. Dudziak, *Cold War Civil Rights*, 169–70.

85. Department of State, Bureau of Intelligence and Research, research memorandum: "Soviet Media Coverage of Current U.S. Racial Crisis," June 14, 1963, Box 295A, DA, NSF, JFKPL.

86. ASJ, June 2, 1963, Folder 312.17.

87. Dean Rusk, Murrow, and LBJ, quoted in press clippings, May–June 1963, Box 18, EI069, RG 306, NA.

88. Theodore C. Sorensen, *Kennedy*, 489.

89. JFK, quoted in letter, Spark M. Matsunaga (D-HI) to Kennedy, June 13, 1963, Box 91, DA, POF, JFKPL.

90. JFK, televised speech, the White House, June 11, 1963, *Public Papers of the Presidents: John F. Kennedy*, vol. 1963, 469.

91. USIA, "20th Review of Operations: January 1–June 30, 1963," Box 121, ERMP-MHC.

92. Circular 2143, Dean Rusk to all American diplomatic and consular posts, June 14, 1963, Box 295A, DA, NSF, JFKPL.

93. Cable, U.S. Embassy, Kigali, to Dean Rusk, June 26, 1963, Box 295A, DA, NSF, JFKPL. The folder also contains similar cables from twelve other ambassadors stationed in Africa.

94. Memorandum, Murrow to JFK: "Reactions to Your June 11 Civil Rights Speech," June 14, 1963; and report R-98–63 (R): "Public Opinion trends in Western Europe in the Wake of the Cuban Crisis," July 1963, Box 91, DA, POF, JFKPL.

95. "Suggested Agenda for the Cabinet Meeting, Wednesday, June 19, 1963, at 10:00 a.m.," June 17, 1963, Box 92, DA, POF, JFKPL.

96. Dean Rusk, quoted in Dudziak, "Birmingham, Addis Ababa, and the Image of America," 193.

97. Murrow, speech before the Fifty-ninth Annual Convention, Advertising Federation of America, Atlanta GA, June 19, 1963, Box 132, ERMP.

98. JFK, quoted in Theodore C. Sorensen, *Kennedy*, 506.

99. "The Image at Home," *Washington* DC *Evening Star*, May 31, 1963.

100. USIA, Research and Reference Service, report R-135–63 (A): "Recent World-wide Comment on the U.S. Racial Problem," July 19, 1963, Box 295A, DA, NSF, JFKPL.

101. James W. Canan, "Lack of Money (and Words) Hampers Information Unit," *Utica Observer Dispatch*, June 23, 1963.

102. John C. O'Brien, "Dixie Riots, Color Bar in Washington Help Reds, Murrow Warns," *Philadelphia Inquirer*, May 25, 1961.

103. Emphasis in original text; John Pauker, USIA News Policy Note no. 28–63: "Civil Rights and Race Relations," July 26, 1963, Box 22, E1069, RG 306, NA.

104. John Pauker, USIA News Policy Note no. 28–63: "Civil Rights and Race Relations," July 26, 1963, Box 22, E1069, RG 306, NA.

105. USIA Circular 173: "Press Conference USA (Martin Luther King)," July 16, 1963, Box 2, E12 NA.

106. *The March*, National Archives channel, YouTube, http://www.youtube.com/watch?v=DQYzHIIQ1O4.

107. Thomas C. Sorensen, *Word War*, 178.

108. Murrow, quoted in Persico, *Edward R. Murrow*, 483.

109. Letter, Donald M. Wilson to Murrow, March 14, 1964, Box 6, ERMP-MHC.

110. Letters, March–April, 1964, Box 6, ERMP-MHC.

111. Murrow, address before the National Convention of the Federal Bar Association, Philadelphia PA, September 26, 1963, Box 17, E1069, RG 306, NA.

112. Thomas C. Sorensen, *Word War*, 171–73.

113. Murrow, transcript of *Issues and Answers*, August 4, 1963, Box 21, E1069, RG 306, NA.

114. Murrow, quoted in Jean White, "Luster Rubbed off on USIA," *Washington Post*, March 15, 1964.

9. *Counterinsurgency Propaganda*

1. JFK, quoted in Elie Abel, recorded interview by Dennis O'Brien, April 10, 1970, JFKLOHP.

2. Giglio, *Presidency of John F. Kennedy*, 47.

3. Winthrop G. Brown, recorded interview with Larry J. Hackman, February 1, 1968, JFKLOHP.

4. JFK, The President's News Conference, March 23, 1961, *Public Papers of the Presidents: John F. Kennedy*, vol. 1961, 213.

5. Freedman, *Kennedy's Wars*, 293.

6. Thomas C. Sorensen, recorded interview with Theodore H. White, April 15, 1964, JFKLOHP.

7. ASJ, March 20, 1961, Folder 311.10.

8. W. Averell Harriman, memorandum for files, August 29, 1961, Box 479, WAH.

9. Winthrop G. Brown, recorded interview with Larry J. Hackman, February 1, 1968, JFKLOHP.

10. Kennedy told this to Theodore Sorensen on at least two occasions; see Sorensen, recorded interview with Carl Kaysen, April 6, 1964, JFKLOHP.

11. JFK, quoted in ASJ, May 7, 1961, Folder 311.11.

12. W. Averell Harriman, quoted in Dallek, *An Unfinished Life*, 351.

13. McGeorge Bundy, recorded interview by Richard Neustadt, March 1964, JFKLOHP.

14. JFK, quoted in Caroline Kennedy, ed., *Jacqueline Kennedy*, 112–13.

15. Robert McNamara, recorded interview with Arthur Schlesinger Jr., April 4, 1964, JFKLOHP.

16. George W. Ball, recorded interview by Joseph Kraft, February 16, 1968, JFKLOHP.

17. Memorandum, Roger Hilsman to Ambassador Young, May 5, 1961, Box 483, WAH.

18. Murrow, CBS broadcast, February 9, 1954, in *Selected Murrow Manuscripts*, Box 6, ERMP.

19. National Security Action Memorandum no. 180: "Membership of the Special Group (Counterinsurgency)," August 13, 1962, Item no. PD00911, Presidential Directives Collection, NSA.

20. Memorandum for record: "CI Group discussion of Charter," January 24, 1963, Doc No/ESDN: CIA-RDP80B01676R001900150088–2, CIA-FOIA.

21. John M. Anspracher, recorded USIAAA interview by G. Lewis Schmidt, March 22, 1988, Box 4, E1073, RG 306, NA.

22. John M. Anspracher, recorded USIAAA interview by G. Lewis Schmidt, March 22, 1988, Box 4, E1073, RG 306, NA.

23. Letter, Murrow to Marshall S. Carter, May 16, 1962, Doc No/ESDN: CIA-RDP80B01676R002900170002–3; and letter, Marshall S. Carter to Murrow, unreadable date, 1962, Doc No/ESDN: CIA-RDP80B01676R002900170005–0, CIA-FOIA.

24. Memorandum for record: "Minutes of the Meeting of the Special Group (CI), 2:00 p.m., Thursday, July 11, 1963," July 11, 1963, Doc No/ESDN: CIA-RDP80B01676R001900150036–9, CIA-FOIA.

25. Si Nadler, recorded USIAAA interview by Jack O'Brien, November 21, 1989, Box 8, E1073, RG 306, NA.

26. Letter, Murrow to W. Averell Harriman, August 23, 1961, Box 491, WAH.

27. Keith Adamson, recorded USIAAA interview with Earl Wilson, January 12, 1988, Box 1, E1073, RG 306, NA.

28. Letter, Murrow to Robert McNamara, September 22, 1961, microfilm, Reel 42, Box 4, E1006, RG 306, NA.

29. Memorandum, Office of Public Information to USIA Employees: "Some Changes in USIA since March 1961," October 28, 1963, RG 306, NA.

30. Stephen Ailes, recorded interview by Larry J. Hackman, September 26, 1968, JFKLOHP.

31. Terms of Reference between the Department of Defense and the U.S. Information Agency for the Assignment of Senior USIA Officers to Each of Certain Unified Commands, May 9, 1961, included with memorandum, Murrow to JFK: "Weekly Report," April 25, 1961, microfilm, Reel 46, Box 4, E1006, RG 306, NA.

32. Chester B. Bowles, recorded interview with Dennis J. O'Brien, July 1, 1970, JFKLOHP.

33. Murrow, speech before the Public Relations Society of America, Houston TX, November 13, 1961, Box 132, ERMP.

34. Memorandum, Murrow to G. Lewis Schmidt: "Change to Procedures for Promoting Officers to Class 1," December 5, 1961, microfilm, Reel 40, Box 4, E1006, RG 306, NA.

35. JFK, Inaugural Address, January 20, 1961, *Public Papers of the Presidents: John F. Kennedy*, vol. 1961, 1.

36. Thomas C. Sorensen, recorded interview with Theodore H. White, April 15, 1964, JFKLOHP.

37. McGeorge Bundy, recorded interview with Richard Neustadt, March 1964, JFKLOHP.

38. McGeorge Bundy, recorded interview with William Moss, February 22, 1971, JFKLOHP.

39. JFK, quoted in ASJ, November 14, 1961, Folder 311.18.

40. McGeorge Bundy, recorded interview with William Moss, February 22, 1971, JFKLOHP.

41. William Bundy, recorded interview with William Moss, March 6, 1972, JFKLOHP.

42. Emphasis in original text; see Murrow, CBS broadcast, May 10, 1957, in *Selected Murrow Manuscripts*, Box 6, ERMP.

43. JFK, Special Message to the Congress on Urgent National Needs, May 25, 1961, *Public Papers of the Presidents: John F. Kennedy*, vol. 1961, 404.

44. Task Force on Viet-Nam, Presidential Program for Vietnam, May 23, 1961, Box 2, SF, VPP, LBJPL.

45. Cable, U.S. ambassador, Karachi, to the Secretary of State, May 22, 1961, Box 2, SF, VPP, LBJPL.

46. Cable, U.S. ambassador, Saigon, to Secretary of State, May 15, 1961, Box 2, SF, VPP, LBJPL.

47. USIA Office of Research and Analysis, report R-28–61: "Press Reaction to Vice President Lyndon Johnson's Visit to Asia," June 2, 1961, Box 33, Personal Files, Vice Presidential Aide's Files of George Reedy, LBJPL.

48. Cable, U.S. ambassador, Saigon, to Secretary of State, May 15, 1961, Box 2, SF, VPP, LBJPL.

49. Memorandum, LBJ to JFK: "Mission to Southeast Asia, India and Pakistan," May 23, 1961, Box 2, SF, VPP, LBJPL.

50. Murrow, speech at the Johns Hopkins University, Baltimore MD, June 13, 1961, Box 132, ERMP.

51. Murrow, quoted in transcript, "America's Propaganda Capabilities," *Mrs. Eleanor Roosevelt: Prospects of Mankind*, WGBH-TV, May 26, 1961, Box 21, E1069, RG 306, NA.

52. Memorandum, Murrow to USIA Staff, April 22, 1961, microfilm, Reel 46, Box 4, E1006, RG 306, NA.

53. Memorandum, Murrow to USIA Directors, April 24, 1961, microfilm, Reel 46, Box 4, E1006, RG 306, NA.

54. "The Fight for Men's Minds," *New York Journal*, December 3, 1961.

55. Howard Needham, recorded UISAAA interview with G. Lewis Schmidt, March 29, 1990, Box 9, E1073, RG 306, NA.

56. USIA paper on colonialism for the 1961, United States–United Kingdom Information Working Group Meeting, April 1961, FO 953/2028, BNA.

57. Charles F. Baldwin, recorded interview by Dennis J. O'Brien, March 13, 1969, JFKLOHP.

58. Freedman, *Kennedy's Wars*, 345–46.

59. Notes on the National Security Meeting, November 15, 1961, Item no. V100873, U.S. Policy in the Vietnam War Collection, 1954–1968, NSA.

60. The military advisers focused on training the South Vietnamese army for a conventional counterattack against a North Vietnamese invasion. They applied the same advisory techniques adopted since 1953 by U.S. forces stationed in South Korea. See Chester L. Cooper, recorded interview by Joseph E. O'Connor, June 9, 1966, JFKLOHP. For a study of how the early U.S. advisers trained the Republic of Vietnam's army, see Spector, *Advice and Support*.

61. Freedman, *Kennedy's Wars*, 316–17.

62. Memorandum, Paul Nielson to Murrow: "Use of Defoliants in Vietnam," November 17, 1961, Document 265, *Foreign Relations of the United States, 1961–1963*, Vol.1, *Vietnam, 1961*, 641–42.

63. Memorandum, Murrow to JFK, November 27, 1961, Box 91, DA, POF, JFKPL.

64. Memorandum, Howard Burris to LBJ: "Viet-Cong Activities," April 16, 1962, Box 5, SF, VPP, LBJPL.

65. Dean Rusk, statement at a Department of State news conference, March 1, 1962, Box 92, DA, POF, JFKPL.

66. Chester H. Opal, recorded USIAAA interview with G. Lewis Schmidt, January 28, 1989, Box 5, E1073, RG 306, NA.

67. Chester H. Opal, recorded USIAAA interview with G. Lewis Schmidet, January 28, 1989, Box 5, E1073, RG 306, NA.

68. Dallek, *An Unfinished Life*, 524.

69. Telegram, Nikita Khrushchev to JFK, June 12, 1962, Document 46; and telegram, JFK to Nikita Khrushchev, Document 47, U.S. Department of State, *Foreign Relations of the United States, 1961–1963*, Vol. 6, *Kennedy-Khrushchev Exchanges*, 134–36.

70. Thomas C. Sorensen, *Word War*, 188.

71. Memorandum, Murrow to JFK: "Weekly Report," August 22, 1962, microfilm, Reel 54, Box 4, E1006, RG 306, NA.

72. Memorandum, "U.S./U.K. Information Working Group Meeting, Information Aspects of the Situation in South-East Asia," June 1962, FO 953/2083, BNA.

73. Memorandum, Murrow to McGeorge Bundy: "Defoliation," August 16, 1962, microfilm, Reel 54, Box 4, E1006, RG 306, NA

74. Memorandum for record: "Minutes of the Special Group (CI) Meeting, 2:00 p.m., Thursday, January 3, 1963," January 3, 1963, Doc No/ESDN: CIA-RDP80B01676R001900150092–7, CIA-FOIA.

75. Memorandum, Howard Burris to LBJ: "Vietnam," January 24, 1963, Box 6, SF, VPP, LBJPL.

76. McGeorge Bundy, recorded interview by William W. Moss, February 22, 1971, JFKLOHP.

77. William Bundy, recorded interview by William W. Moss, March 6, 1972, JFKLOHP.

78. Memorandum, Murrow to McGeorge Bundy, May 24, 1963, Box 184, FGO, WHCF, JFKPL.

79. ASJ, September 16, 1963, Folder 313.2.

80. William P. Bundy, recorded interview by William W. Moss, April 25, 1972, JFKLOHP.

81. George W. Ball, recorded interview by Joseph Kraft, February 16, 1968, JFKLOHP.

82. Charles Casey Murrow, interview by author, July 30, 2012, Dummerston VT.

83. ERM, speech to the Advertising Federation of America, Atlanta GA, June 19, 1963, Box 30, ERMP.

84. Memorandum for record: "Minutes of the Meeting of the Special Group (CI), 2:00 p.m., Thursday, July 11, 1963," July 11, 1963, Doc No/ESDN: CIA-RDP80B01676R001900150036–9, CIA-FOIA.

85. Thomas C. Sorensen, *Word War*, 192.

86. Memorandum for record: "Minutes of the Meeting of the Special Group (CI), 3:30 p.m., Friday, September 6, 1963," September 6, 1963, Doc No/ESDN: CIA-RDP80B01676R001900150026–0, CIA-FOIA.

87. Telephone conversation, W. Averell Harriman and Murrow, March 11, 1963, Box 491, WAH.

88. Cull, "Justifying Vietnam," 289.

89. Memorandum, Howard Burris to LBJ: "Highlights," March 12, 1963, Box 6, SF, VPP, LBJPL.

90. Thomas C. Sorensen, *Word War*, 191.

91. Memorandum of conference with the president, September 10, 1963: "Vietnam," Box 316, MM, NSF, JFKPL. The memorandum misnamed Mecklin as "Mr. Melching."

92. Meeting at the State Department, September 10, 1963: "Vietnam," Folder "Meetings on Vietnam 9/1/63–9/10/63," Box 316, MM, NSF, JFKPL.

93. Minutes of Meeting of the Special Group for Counterinsurgency, March 14, 1963, Document 59, U.S. Department of State, *Foreign Relations of the United States, 1961–1963*, vol. 3, *Vietnam, January–August 1963*, 151.

94. Memorandum, Howard Burris to LBJ: "Highlights," March 18, 1963, Box 6, SF, VPP, LBJPL.

95. Logevall, *Choosing War*, 39.

96. Memorandum, Murrow to McGeorge Bundy: "World Reaction to Developments in Viet-Nam," September 14, 1963, Box 317, MM, NSF, JFKPL.

97. Memorandum of conference with the president, August 29, 1963, 12:00 p.m.: "Vietnam," Box 316, MM, NSF, JFKPL.

98. Cable, Henry Cabot Lodge Jr. to CINCPAC/POLAD, August 24, 1963, Box 316, MM, NSF, JFKPL.

99. ASJ, October 2, 1963, Folder 313.3.

100. Duong Van Minh, quoted in Jones, *Death of a Generation*, 435.

101. Memorandum, Murrow to JFK: "Foreign Reaction to Diem Repression and U.S. Foreign Policy," August 28, 1963, Box 91, DA, POF, JFKPL.

102. Jacqueline Kennedy, quoted in Caroline Kennedy, ed., *Jacqueline Kennedy*, 305.

103. U.S. Senate, *Alleged Assassination Plots Involving Foreign Leaders*, 256.

104. JFK, The President's News Conference of November 14, 1963, and Remarks at the Breakfast of the Fort Worth Chamber of Commerce, November 22, 1963, *Public Papers of the Presidents: John F. Kennedy*, vol. 1963, 846, 889.

105. William P. Bundy, recorded interview by William W. Moss, April 25, 1972, JFKLOHP.

106. Memorandum for record: "Minutes of the Meeting of the Special Group (CI), 2:00 p.m., Thursday, November 14, 1963," November 14, 1963, Doc No/ESDN: CIA-RDP80B01676R001900150009–9, CIA-FOIA.

107. The State Department's Bureau of Intelligence and Research added to the report its doubts that South Vietnamese security forces would have done any better at destroying the insurgency if Diem had remained in power. See memorandum, Thomas L. Hughes to Dean Rusk: "Statistics on the War Effort in South Vietnam Show Unfavorable Trends," October 22, 1963, Box 13, SF, VPP, LBJPL.

108. Murrow, CBS broadcast, February 9, 1954, in *Selected Murrow Manuscripts*, Box 6, ERMP.

109. Gelb with Betts, *Irony of Vietnam*, 77.

110. Talking paper on Laos for meeting with the president, November 8, 1963, Box 483, WAH.

111. Douglas Pike, recorded USIAAA interview by John Hutchison, February 1989, E1073, RG 306, NA.

10. Good Luck, Ed

1. Sperber, *Murrow*, 683.

2. Persico, *Edward R. Murrow*, 487.

3. Arthur Herzog, "The Voice of Uncle Sam," *True*, June 1963.

4. G. Lewis Schmidt, recorded USIAAA interview by Allen Hansen, February 8, 1988, Box 3, E1073, RG 306, NA.

5. Cable, Michael Robb to Anthony Moore, December 18, 1963, FO 953/2126, BNA.

6. Letter, Robert F. Kennedy to Murrow, November 2, 1963, Box 5, ERMP-MHC.

7. Sperber, *Murrow*, 684.

8. Sperber, *Murrow*, 681–82.

9. Kendrick, *Prime Time*, 493.

10. Murrow's old CBS friend William Paley was the one exception, who told Persico that Murrow "never complained to me when I saw him, but he made you understand he was not happy down there." In Persico's opinion, Murrow may have voiced his frustrations with Paley as a subconscious way of telling Paley that he still belonged at his old network, "that he had been driven from his true métier." See Persico, *Edward R. Murrow*, 489–90.

11. Charles Casey Murrow, interview by author, July 30, 2012, Dummerston VT.

12. Memorandum, Murrow to Bromley Smith: "Your Memorandum of August 9, 1962," September 26, 1962, Box 91, DA, POF, JFKPL.

13. Memorandum, JFK to Murrow, January 25, 1963, Box 290, DA, NSF, JFKPL.

14. Memorandum, Murrow to JFK, April 3, 1963, Box 91, DA, POF, JFKPL.

15. Murrow, statement before the Senate Foreign Relations Committee, April 5, 1963, Box 132, ERMP.

16. Murrow, response to question during a hearing before the Subcommittee of the Committee on Appropriations, U.S. Senate, September 20, 1962, Box 14, E1069, RG 306, NA.

17. Murrow, statement before the Subcommittee on International Organizations and Movements of the Committee on Foreign Affairs, U.S. House of Representatives, March 28, 1963, Box 17, E1069, RG 306, NA.

18. Sperber, *Murrow*, 685.

19. Murrow, speech before the Fifty-ninth Annual Convention, Advertising Federation of America, Atlanta GA, June 19, 1963, Box 17, E1069, RG 306, NA.

20. Stanley Plesent, quoted in Sperber, *Murrow*, 685.

21. Thomas C. Sorensen, address before the Mid-Western Unitarian Universalist Conference, Omaha NE, April 4, 1963, Box 1, E20, RG 306, NA.

22. Soviet media quotes in Donald M. Wilson, statement before the Subcommittee on Departments of State, Justice, and Commerce, the Judiciary, and Related Agencies, Committee on Appropriations, U.S. Senate, October 29, 1963, Box 120, ERMP.

23. Memorandum, USIA, Office of Public Information to USIA Employees: "Some Changes in USIA since March, 1961," October 28, 1963, Box 17, E1069, RG 306, NA.

24. Cover letter to resignation letter, Murrow to LBJ, December 19, 1963, Box 5, ERMP-MHC.

25. Letter, LBJ to Murrow, January 20, 1964, Box 41, ERMP.

26. Charles Casey Murrow, interview by author, July 30, 2012, Dummerston VT.

27. Newspaper editorials available in Box 22, E1069, RG 306, NA.

28. LBJ, quoted in telephone conversation with John McClellan, Thursday, January 16, 1964, 4:20 p.m., in Beschloss, ed., *Taking Charge*, 165.

29. LBJ and Richard Russell, quoted in telephone conversation, Monday, January 20, 1964, 7:20 p.m., in Beschloss, ed., *Taking Charge*, 169–70.

30. "Murrow Steps Down," *Washington Post*, January 22, 1964.

31. James Reston, "Under Ed Murrow USIA Moved from Doghouse into White House," *New York Times*, January 22, 1964.

32. Editorial, WBBF, Rochester NY, January 22, 1964, Box 22, E1069, RG 306, NA.

33. Val Adams, "Peabody Awards Due Wednesday," *New York Times*, April 24, 1964.

34. See letters to Murrow, Box 6, ERMP-MHC.

35. Letter, Henry Loomis to Murrow, January 22, 1964, Box 6, ERMP-MHC.

36. Memorandum, McGeorge Bundy to Murrow, March 11, 1963, Box 290, DA, NSF, JFKPL.

37. I am grateful to Casey Murrow for showing me the original album following his interview, July 30, 2012, Dummerston VT.

38. Jacqueline Kennedy in USIA Farewell Message Album to Murrow, March 1964, Box 41, ERMP.

39. Robert Kennedy in USIA Farewell Message Album to Murrow, March 1964, Box 41, ERMP.

40. Robert F. Kennedy, forward to Thomas C. Sorensen, *Word War*, vii–viii.

41. See letters, John F. Kennedy Library administrators to Murrow, 1963–1964, Boxes 6 and 7, ERMP-MHC.

42. Letter, Murrow to J. Robert Oppenheimer, August 18, 1964, "Aug 1–16, 1964," Box 6, ERMP-MHC.

43. Letter, Murrow to Raymond A. Hare, April 23, 1964, Box 6, ERMP-MHC.

44. Murrow, quoted in Jean White, "Luster Rubbed Off on USIA," *Washington Post*, March 15, 1964.

45. Letter, Murrow to Carl T. Rowan, March 27, 1964, Box 41, ERMP.

46. Letter, Carl T. Rowan to Murrow, March 24, 1964, Box 41, ERMP.

47. Thomas C. Sorensen in USIA Farewell Message Album to Murrow, March 1964, Box 41, ERMP.

48. USIA fact sheet prepared for Murrow's appearance on *Open Mind*, September 17, 1963, Box 22, E1069, RG 306, NA.

49. U.S. Senate, *Nominations of Edward R. Murrow and Donald M. Wilson*, Box 14, E1069, RG 306, NA.

50. Marquis Childs, "Murrow's Methods," *New York Post*, November 27, 1961.

51. Memorandum, Murrow to Dean Rusk: "USIA Planning and Action on Berlin," July 10, 1961, Item no. BC02158, Berlin Crisis Collection, NSA.

52. Memorandum, Murrow to McGeorge Bundy: "Useful Terminology," July 26, 1961, Box 184, FGO, WHCF, JFKPL.

53. Memorandum, Murrow to Sargent Shriver, March 14, 1961, microfilm, Reel 48, Box 5, E1006, RG 306, NA.

54. Box 84, Statements of LBJ, LBJPL.

55. MacCann, *The People's Films*, 174; and Shaw, *Hollywood's Cold War*, 176.

56. Cull, "Film as Public Diplomacy," 269.

57. *John F. Kennedy: Years of Lightning, Days of Drums*. PublicResourceOrg channel. YouTube video. http://www.youtube.com/watch?v=PvN5ecqCFk0.

58. *John F. Kennedy: Years of Lightning, Days of Drums*. PublicResourceOrg channel. YouTube video. http://www.youtube.com/watch?v=PvN5ecqCFk0.

59. Thomas C. Sorensen, *Word War*, 257. In October 1965, Johnson signed an exemption for the release of the film in the United States. Congress maneuvered around the Smith-Mundt Act restriction against propagating within the United States when Senator Mike Mansfield (D-MT) instructed the Senate Foreign Relations Committee to write instructions into a bill for USIA to sell the film to the newly established John F. Kennedy Center for the Performing Arts Foundation for $122,000 (a $42,000 profit for the agency, which spent only $80,000 on its production). Not only could the foundation show the film domestically, but profits from ticket sales would contribute to the construction of the center on the bank of the Potomac in Washington DC. See "President Signs Bill Releasing Film on Kennedy," *Washington DC Evening Star*, October 22, 1965; and "Senate Bans Film on Johnson," *Chicago Tribune*, Box 145, Records of the Democratic National Committee, LBJPL.

60. Letter, Donald Wilson to Murrow, December 14, 1964, Box 7, ERMP-MHC.

61. Cull, "Film as Public Diplomacy," 270.

62. Alhaji Sir Abubakar Tafawa Balewa, recorded interview by Emmanuel Omatsola, May 7, 1964, JFKLOHP.

63. W. Averell Harriman in USIA Farewell Message Album to Murrow, March 1964, Box 41, ERMP.

64. Letter, Murrow to Jacob K. Javits, April 2, 1964, Box 26, ERMP.

65. Letter, Donald Wilson to Murrow, March 14, 1964, Box 6, ERMP-MHC.

66. Letter, Donald Wilson to Murrow, August 19, 1964, Box 6, ERMP-MHC.

67. Wilson thought that McNamara's dominance might actually be good for the USIA, so as "not to have our names associated with that benighted country [South Vietnam] because, alas, it is going [downhill] fast." See Donald Wilson to Murrow, December 23, 1964, Box 7, ERMP-MHC.

68. Letter, Stuart Hannon to Murrow, October 14, 1964, Box 7, ERMP-MHC.

69. Letter, Jene Zousmer to Murrow, January 16, 1964, Box 6, ERMP-MHC.

70. Letter Robert Kintner to Murrow, January 23, 1964, Box 6, ERMP-MHC.

71. Cable, Murrow to Edward Morgan, February 12, 1964, Box 6, ERMP-MHC.

72. Letter, Murrow to Edward Morgan, Spring 1964, Box 6, ERMP-MHC.

73. Charles Casey Murrow, interview by author, July 30, 2012, Dummerston VT.

74. Emphasis in original text. Letter, Janet Murrow to Marie Harriman, September 23, 1964, Box 491, WAH.

75. Murrow, speech before the Protestant Council of New York NY, October 24, 1964, Box 18, E1069, RG 306, NA.

76. Persico, *Edward R. Murrow*, 495; and Sperber, *Murrow*, 702–03.

77. Certificate of Death, April 27, 1965, Box 10, ERMP-MHC.

78. Press release, April 27, 1965, and letter, W. Averell Harriman to Janet Murrow, April 27, 1965, Box 491, WAH.

79. Murrow obituary, *Foreign Service Journal* (May 1965), enclosure to letter, W. Averell Harriman to Dean Acheson, May 8, 1965, Box 429, WAH.

80. Letter, Walter Cronkite to W. Averell Harriman, March 1, 1966, Box 491, WAH.

81. W. Averell Harriman, approved letter for mailing list, May 1966, Box 491, WAH.

82. Persico, *Edward R. Murrow*, 499.

83. Letter, David Ormsby-Gore to Alec Douglas-Home, December 20, 1963, PREM 11/5011, BNA.

84. JFK, Inaugural Address, January 20, 1961, *Public Papers of the Presidents: John F. Kennedy*, vol. 1961, 1.

85. John McCone, quoted in U.S. Senate, *Alleged Assassination Plots Involving Foreign Leaders*, 320.

86. Memorandum, Murrow to USIA staff, April 22, 1961, Box 290, DA, NSF, JFKPL.

87. Letter, Alexander Klieforth to Murrow, July 14, 1964, Box 6, ERMP-MHC.

88. Letter, Murrow to the American Federation of Television and Radio Artists, February 17, 1961, Box 26, ERMP.

89. Murrow, quoted in Philip Meyer, "How U.S. Is Getting Its Message Abroad," *Miami Herald*, April 29, 1962.

90. Memorandum, Murrow to All Officers Who Prepare and Review Foreign Service Evaluation Reports: "Foreign Service Personnel Evaluation Reports," June 21, 1963, microfilm, Reel 65, Box 5, E1006, RG 306, NA; and cable, Murrow to USIS, Usumbura: "Motion Picture Statistical Report for Calendar 1962," July 29, 1963, Box 2, E12, RG 306, NA.

91. ASJ, July 15, 1960, Folder 311.8.

BIBLIOGRAPHY

Abramson, Rudy. *Spanning the Century: The Life of W. Averell Harriman, 1891–1986*. New York: William Murrow, 1992.

Anderson, David. *Trapped by Success: The Eisenhower Administration and Vietnam, 1953–1961*. New York: Columbia University Press, 1991.

Anderson, Jon Lee. *Che Guevara: A Revolutionary Life*. New York: Grove Press, 1997.

Armistead, Leigh, ed. *Information Operations: Warfare and the Hard Reality of Soft Power*. Washington DC: Brassey's, 2004.

Arndt, Richard T. *The First Resort of Kings: American Cultural Diplomacy in the Twentieth Century*. Washington DC: Potomac, 2005.

Arsenault, Raymond. *Freedom Riders: 1961 and the Struggle for Racial Justice*. New York: Oxford University Press, 2006.

Ayers, Margaret C. *Promoting Public and Private Reinvestment in Cultural Exchange-Based Diplomacy*. Series on International Cultural Engagement. New York: Robert Sterling Clark Foundation, April 16, 2010.

Bachrach, Susan, and Steven Luckert. *State of Deception: The Power of Nazi Propaganda*. Washington DC: U.S. Holocaust Memorial Museum, 2009.

Baldwin, Kate A. *Beyond the Color Line and the Iron Curtain: Reading Encounters between Black and Red, 1922–1963*. Durham NC: Duke University Press, 2002.

Ball, George. *The Past Has Another Pattern: Memoirs*. New York: W. W. Norton, 1982.

Barrett, David M., and Max Holland. *Blind over Cuba: The Photo Gap and the Missile Crisis*. College Station: Texas A&M University Press, 2012.

Bass, Warren. *Support Any Friend: Kennedy's Middle East and the Making of the U.S.-Israel Alliance*. New York: Oxford University Press, 2003.

Baughman, James. *The Republic of Mass Culture: Journalism, Filmmaking, and Broadcasting in American since 1941*. Baltimore: Johns Hopkins University Press, 1992.

Belmonte, Laura A. *Selling the American Way: U.S. Propaganda and the Cold War*. Philadelphia: University of Pennsylvania Press, 2008.

Bender, Thomas, ed. *Rethinking American History in a Global Age*. Berkeley: University of California Press, 2002.

Bennett, M. Todd. *One World, Big Screen: Hollywood, the Allies, and World War II*. Chapel Hill: University of North Carolina Press, 2012.

Bernays, Edward. *Propaganda*. London: Routledge, 1928. Reprint, Brooklyn NY: Ig Publishing, 2005.

Berry, Joseph P., Jr. *John F. Kennedy and the Media: The First Television President*. Lanham MD: University Press of America, 1987.

Beschloss, Michael R. *The Crisis Years: Kennedy and Khrushchev, 1960–1963*. New York: Harper Collins, 1991.

———. *Mayday: Eisenhower, Khrushchev, and the U-2 Affair*. New York: Harper and Row, 1988.

———, ed. *Taking Charge: The Johnson White House Tapes, 1963–1964*. New York: Simon and Schuster, 1998.

Bird, Kai. *The Color of Truth: McGeorge Bundy and William Bundy: Brothers in Arms*. New York: Touchstone, 1998.

Bliss, Edward, Jr. "Edward R. Murrow and Today's News." *Television Quarterly*, Fall 1970.

———, ed. *In Search of Light: The Broadcasts of Edward R. Murrow, 1938–1961*. New York: Knopf, 1967.

Bogart, Leo. "A Study of the Operating Assumptions of the U.S. Information Agency." *Public Opinion Quarterly* 19, no. 4 (Winter 1955–56).

Bohlen, Charles E. *Witness to History, 1929–1969*. New York: W. W. Norton, 1973.

Borstelmann, Thomas. *The Cold War and the Color Line: American Race Relations in the Global Arena*. Cambridge MA: Harvard University Press, 2001.

———. "'Hedging Our Bets and Buying Time': John Kennedy and Racial Revolutions in the American South and Southern Africa." *Diplomatic History* 24 (Summer 2000).

Bowles, Chester. *Promises to Keep: My Years in Public Life, 1941–1969*. New York: Harper and Row, 1971.

Brauer, Carl. *John F. Kennedy and the Second Reconstruction*. New York: Columbia University Press, 1977.

Brinkley, Douglas. *Cronkite*. New York: Harper, 2012.

Bundy, McGeorge. *Danger and Survival: Choices about the Bomb and the First Fifty Years*. New York: Random House, 1988.

Burk, Robert F. *The Eisenhower Administration and Black Civil Rights*. Knoxville: University of Tennessee Press, 1984.

Center for Strategic and International Studies. *International Information, Education and Cultural Relations: Recommendations for the Future*. Washington DC: Center for Strategic and International Studies, 1975.

Ceplair, Larry, and Steven Englund. *The Inquisition in Hollywood: Politics in the Film Community, 1930–1960*. Berkeley: University of California Press, 1983.

Cleveland, Harlan. *The Obligation of Power: American Diplomacy in the Search for Peace*. New York: Harper and Row, 1966.

Coleman, David. *The Fourteenth Day: JFK and the Aftermath of the Cuban Missile Crisis: The Secret White House Tapes.* New York: W. W. Norton, 2012.

Collins, Kathleen. "Murrow and Friendly's Small World: Television Conversation at the Crosswords." *Journal of Popular Film and Television* 40, no. 1 (2012).

Conniff, Michael L., ed. *Populism in Latin America.* Tuscaloosa: University of Alabama Press, 1999.

Coombs, Philip H. *The Fourth Dimension of Foreign Policy: Educational and Cultural Affairs.* New York: Council on Foreign Relations, 1964.

Craig, Campbell, and Fredrik Logevall. *America's Cold War: The Politics of Insecurity.* Cambridge MA: Belknap Press, 2009

Creel, George. *How We Advertised America.* New York: Harper and Brothers, 1920.

Cull, Nicholas J. "Anatomy of a Shipwreck: Warner Bros., the White House, and the Celluloid Sinking of *PT 109.*" In *Hollywood and the American Historical Film,* edited by J. E. Smyth. London: Palgrave Macmillan, 2012.

———. "Auteurs of Ideology: USIA Documentary Film Propaganda in the Kennedy Era as Seen in Bruce Herschensohn's *The Five Cities of June* (1963) and James Blue's *The March* (1964)." *Film History* 10, no. 3 (1998).

———. *The Cold War and the United States Information Agency: American Propaganda and Public Diplomacy, 1945–1989.* Cambridge: Cambridge University Press, 2008.

———. "Film as Public Diplomacy: The USIA's Cold War at Twenty-Four Frames per Second." In *Diplomatic Studies.* Vol. 5, *United States and Public Diplomacy: New Directions in Cultural and International History,* edited by Kenneth A. Osgood and Brian Etheridge. Leiden, the Netherlands: Martinus Nijhoff Publishers, 2010.

———. "Justifying Vietnam: The United States Information Agency's Vietnam Campaign for International Audiences." In *Justifying War: Propaganda, Politics and War in the Modern Age,* edited by Jo Fox and David Welch. London: Palgrave, 2012.

———. "'The Man Who Invented Truth': The Tenure of Edward R. Murrow as Director of the United States Information Agency." *Cold War History* 4, no. 1 (October 2003).

Cummings, Richard H. *Cold War Radio: The Dangerous History of American Broadcasting in Europe, 1950–1989.* Jefferson: McFarland, 2009.

Dallek, Robert. *An Unfinished Life: John F. Kennedy, 1917–1963.* New York: Back Bay, 2003.

De Grazia, Victoria. *Irresistible Empire: America's Advance through Twentieth-Century Europe.* Cambridge MA: Belknap Press, 2006.

Deibel, Terry L., and Walter R. Roberts. *Culture and Information: Two Foreign Policy Functions.* Washington DC: Center for Strategic and International Studies, 1976.

Delaney, Robert F., and John S. Gibson, eds. *American Public Diplomacy: The Perspective of Fifty Years*. Medford MA: Lincoln Filene Center for Citizenship and Public Affairs, 1967.

Dinerstein, Herbert S. *Intervention Against Communism*. Baltimore: Johns Hopkins University Press, 1967.

Dizard, Wilson P. *The Strategy of Truth: The Story of the U.S. Information Service*. Washington DC: Public Affairs Press, 1961.

Dobbs, Michael. *One Minute to Midnight: Kennedy, Khrushchev, and Castro on the Brink of Nuclear War*. New York: Knopf, 2008.

Domer, Thomas M. "Sport in Cold War America, 1953–1963: The Diplomatic and Political Use of Sport in the Eisenhower and Kennedy Administrations." PhD diss., Marquette University, 1976.

Douglas, Susan J. *Listening In: Radio and the American Imagination, from Amos 'n' Andy and Edward R. Murrow to Wolfman Jack and Howard Stern*. New York: Random House, 1999.

Dudziak, Mary L. "Birmingham, Addis Ababa, and the Image of America: International Influence on U.S. Civil Rights Politics in the Kenney Administration." In *Windows of Freedom: Race, Civil Rights, and Foreign Affairs*, edited by Brenda Gayle Plummer. Chapel Hill: University of North Carolina Press, 2003.

———. "Brown as a Cold War Case." *Journal of American History* 32 (2004).

———. *Cold War Civil Rights: Race and the Image of American Democracy*. Princeton NJ: Princeton University Press, 2000.

———. "The Global Impact of Brown v. Board of Education." SCOTUSBlog, February 18, 2010. http://www.scotusblog.com/2010/02/the-global-impact -of-brown-v-board-of-education.

Edwards, Bob. *Edward R. Murrow and the Birth of Broadcast Journalism*. Hoboken NJ: Wiley, 2004.

Elliston, Jon. *Psywar on Cuba: The Declassified History of U.S. Anti-Castro Propaganda*. Melbourne, Australia: Ocean Press, 1999.

Endress, Valerie A. "The Limits of Presidential Rhetorical Power: A Case Study of Cold War Ideology and Its Influence." PhD diss., Indiana University, 1997.

Ferrell, Robert H. *American Diplomacy: The Twentieth Century*. New York: W. W. Norton, 1988.

Fox, Jo, and David Welch, eds. *Justifying War: Propaganda, Politics and War in the Modern Age*. London: Palgrave, 2012.

Fraser, Matthew. *Weapons of Mass Distraction: Soft Power and American Empire*. New York: St. Martin's Press, 2003.

Freedman, Lawrence. *Kennedy's Wars: Berlin, Cuba, Laos, and Vietnam*. New York: Oxford University Press, 2000.

Fried, Richard M. *Nightmare in Red: The McCarthy Era in Perspective*. New York: Oxford University Press, 1990.

Friendly, Fred. *Due to Circumstances beyond Our Control.* New York: Random House, 1967.

Gaddis, John Lewis. *The Cold War: A New History.* New York: Penguin, 2006.

———. *Strategies of Containment: A Critical Appraisal of American National Security Policy during the Cold War.* Rev. ed. New York: Oxford University Press, 2005.

———. *We Now Know: Rethinking Cold War History.* New York: Oxford University Press, 1997.

Galbraith, John K. *Ambassador's Journal: A Personal Account of the Kennedy Years.* New York: Houghton Mifflin, 1969.

———. *Letters to Kennedy.* Cambridge MA: Harvard University Press, 1998.

Garthoff, Raymond. "Cuban Missile Crisis: The Soviet Story." *Foreign Policy* 72 (Autumn 1988).

———. *Reflections on the Cuban Missile Crisis.* Washington DC: Brookings Institution, 1987.

Geduld, Victoria Phillips. "Dancing Diplomacy: Martha Graham and the Strange Commodity of Cold-War Cultural Exchange in Asia, 1955 and 1974." *Dance Chronicle* 33 (2010).

Gelb, Leslie H., with Richard K. Betts. *The Irony of Vietnam: The System Worked.* Washington DC: Brookings Institution, 1979.

Giglio, James N. *John F. Kennedy: A Bibliography.* Westport CT: Greenwood Press, 1995.

———. *The Presidency of John F. Kennedy.* 2nd ed. Lawrence: University Press of Kansas, 2006.

Giglio, James N., and Stephen G. Rabe. *Debating the Kennedy Presidency.* Lanham MD: Rowman and Littlefield, 2003.

Girling, John L. S. *America and the Third World: Revolution and Intervention.* London: Routledge and Kegan Paul, 1980.

Gordon, George N., and Irving A. Flak. *The War of Ideas: America's International Identity Crisis.* New York: Hastings House, 1973.

Gromyko, Andrei. *Through Russian Eyes: President Kennedy's 1036 Days.* Washington DC: International Library, 1973.

Haddow, Robert H. *Pavilions of Plenty: Exhibiting American Culture abroad in the 1950s.* Washington DC: Smithsonian Institution Press, 1997.

Haefele, Mark. "John F. Kennedy, USIA and World Opinion." *Diplomatic History* 25 (Winter 2001).

Halberstam, David. *The Best and the Brightest.* New York: Random House, 1969.

Harrington, Daniel F. *Berlin on the Brink: The Blockade, the Airlift, and the Early Cold War.* Lawrence: University Press of Kansas, 2012.

Harrison, Hope M. *Driving the Soviets up the Wall: Soviet-East German Relations, 1953–1961.* Princeton NJ: Princeton University Press, 2003.

Harvey, James C. *Civil Rights during the Kennedy Administration.* Hattiesburg: University and College Press of Mississippi, 1971.

Heather, David. *North Korean Posters: The David Heather Collection*. New York: Prestel, 2008.

Heil, Alan L., Jr., ed. *Local Voices/Global Perspectives: Challenges Ahead for U.S. International Media*. Washington DC: Public Diplomacy Council, 2008.

———. *Voice of America: A History*. New York: Columbia University Press, 2003.

Henderson, John W. *The United States Information Agency*. New York: Praeger, 1969.

Herring, George C. *America's Longest War: The United States and Vietnam, 1950–1975*. New York: Wiley, 1979.

———. *From Colony to Superpower: U.S. Foreign Relations since 1776*. New York: Oxford University Press, 2008.

Hershberg, James. "Before 'The Missiles of October': Did Kennedy Plan a Military Strike against Cuba?" *Diplomatic History* 14 (Spring 1990).

Hewitt, Don. *Tell Me a Story: Fifty Years and 60 Minutes in Television*. New York: PublicAffairs, 2002.

Higgens, Trumbull. *The Perfect Failure: Kennedy, Eisenhower, and the CIA at the Bay of Pigs*. New York: W. W. Norton, 1987.

Hilsman, Roger. *To Move a Nation: The Politics of Foreign Policy in the Administration of John F. Kennedy*. Garden City NY: Doubleday, 1967.

Hixon, Walter L. *Parting the Curtain: Propaganda, Culture, and the Cold War, 1945–1961*. New York: St. Martin's Press, 1997.

Hoffman, Arthur S., ed. *International Communication and the New Diplomacy*. Bloomington: Indiana University Press, 1968.

Hoffman, Elizabeth C. *All You Need Is Love: The Peace Corps and the Spirit of the 1960s*. Cambridge MA: Harvard University Press, 1998.

Hogan, Kathleen. "Reaping the Golden Harvest: Pare Lorentz, Poet and Filmmaker." *1930s Project*. Department of American Studies, University of Virginia, 1998. http://xroads.virginia.edu/~1930s/film/lorentz/front.html.

Hogan, Michael J., ed. *America and the World: The Historiography of American Foreign Relations since 1941*. New York: Cambridge University Press, 1995.

———, ed. *Paths to Power: The Historiography of American Foreign Relations to 1941*. New York: Cambridge University Press, 2000.

Hogan, Michael J., and Thomas G. Paterson, eds. *Explaining the History of American Foreign Relations*. 2nd ed. New York: Cambridge University Press, 2007.

Hunt, Michael H. *Ideology and U.S. Foreign Policy*. New Haven CT: Yale University Press, 1997.

Isaacson, Walter and Evan Thomas. *The Wise Men: Six Friends and the World They Made*. New York: Simon and Schuster, 1986.

Jian, Chen. *Mao's China and the Cold War*. Chapel Hill: University of North Carolina Press, 2001.

Jones, Howard. *Death of a Generation: How the Assassinations of Diem and JFK Prolonged the Vietnam War*. New York: Oxford University Press, 2003.

Joyce, Walter. *The Propaganda Gap*. New York: Harper and Row, 1963.

Judge, Edward H., and John W. Langdon. *A Hard and Bitter Peace: A Global History of the Cold War*. Upper Saddle River NJ: Prentice Hall, 1996.

Kahin, George. *Intervention: How America Became Involved in Vietnam*. New York: Knopf, 1986.

Kaiser, David. *American Tragedy: Kennedy, Johnson, and the Origins of the Vietnam War*. Cambridge MA: Belknap Press, 2000.

Kalb, Madeline G. *The Congo Cables: The Cold War in Africa–From Eisenhower to Kennedy*. New York: Macmillan, 1982.

Kaplan, Lawrence S., Ronald D. Landa, and Edward J. Drea. *History of the Office of the Secretary of Defense*. Vol. 5, *The McNamara Ascendancy, 1961–1965*. Washington DC: U.S. Government Printing Office, 2006.

Kempe, Fredrick. *Berlin 1961: Kennedy, Khrushchev, and the Most Dangerous Place on Earth*. New York: Putnam, 2011.

Kendrick, Alexander. *Prime Time: The Life of Edward R. Murrow*. Boston: Little, Brown, 1969.

Kennedy, Caroline, ed. *Jacqueline Kennedy: Historic Conversations on Life with John F. Kennedy: Interviews with Arthur M. Schlesinger, Jr., 1964*. New York: Hyperion, 2011.

Kennedy, John F., Lyndon B. Johnson, Hubert H. Humphrey, and Thomas H. Kuchel. *Moral Crisis: The Case for Civil Rights*. Minneapolis: Gilbert, 1964.

Kennedy, Robert. *Thirteen Days: A Memoir of the Cuban Missile Crisis*. New York: W. W. Norton, 1968.

Khrushchev, Nikita. *Memoirs of Nikita Khrushchev*. Vol. 3, *Statesman [1953–1964]*, edited by Sergei Khrushchev. University Park: Pennsylvania State University Press, 2007.

Khrushchev, Sergei. *Khrushchev on Khrushchev: An Inside Account of the Man and His Era*. Boston: Little, Brown, 1990.

Kissinger, Henry. *Diplomacy*. New York: Touchstone, 1994.

Klein, Christina. *Cold War Orientalism: Asia in the Middlebrow Imagination, 1945–1961*. Berkeley: University of California Press, 2003.

Kopp, Harry W., and Charles A. Gillespie. *Career Diplomacy: Life and Work in the U.S. Foreign Service*. Washington DC: Georgetown University Press, 2008.

Kornbluth, Peter, ed. *Bay of Pigs Declassified: The Secret CIA Report on the Invasion of Cuba*. New York: Free Press, 1998.

Krugler, David F. *The Voice of America and the Domestic Propaganda Battles, 1945–1953*. Columbia: University of Missouri Press, 2000.

Kuralt, Charles. "Edward R. Murrow." *North Carolina Historical Review* 48 (April 1971).

Lauren, Paul Gordon. "Seen from the Outside: The International Perspective on America's Dilemma." In *Windows of Freedom: Race, Civil Rights, and Foreign Affairs*, edited by Brenda Gayle Plummer. Chapel Hill: University of North Carolina Press, 2003.

Leffler, Melvyn P. *For the Soul of Mankind: The United States, the Soviet Union, and the Cold War*. New York: Hill and Wang, 2007.

Lippman, Walter. *Public Opinion*. New York: Harcourt, Brace, 1922. Reprint, Radford VA: Wilder Publications, 2010.

Lodge, Henry C. *The Storm Has Many Eyes: A Personal Narrative*. New York: W. W. Norton, 1973.

Logevall, Fredrik. *Choosing War: The Lost Chance for Peace and the Escalation of War in Vietnam*. Berkeley: University of California Press, 1999.

———. "A Critique of Containment." Bernath Lecture. *Diplomatic History* 28 (September 2004).

Lynch, Grayston L. *Decision for Disaster: Betrayal at the Bay of Pigs*. Dulles VA: Potomac, 2000.

MacCann, Richard Dyer. "Film and Foreign Policy: The USIA, 1962–67." *Cinema Journal* 9 (Autumn 1969).

———. *The People's Films: A Political History of U.S. Government Motion Pictures*. New York: Hastings House, 1973.

Macmillan, Harold. *At the End of the Day, 1961–1963*. New York: Harper and Row, 1973.

Mahoney, Richard D. *JFK: Ordeal in Africa*. New York: Oxford University Press, 1983.

Manheim, Jarol B. *Strategic Public Diplomacy and American Foreign Policy: The Evolution of Influence*. New York: Oxford University Press, 1994.

Masey, Jack, and Conway Lloyd Morgan. *Cold War Confrontations: U.S. Exhibits and Their Role in the Cultural Cold War*. Verona, Italy: Lars Müller, 2008.

McDougall, Walter A. *The Heavens and the Earth: A Political History of the Space Age*. New York: Basic, 1985.

McKeever, Porter. *Adlai Stevenson: His Life and Legacy*. New York: William Morrow, 1989.

McNamara, Robert S. *The Essence of Security: Reflections in Office*. New York: Harper and Row, 1968.

Meisler, Stanley. *When the World Calls: The Inside Story of the Peace Corps and Its First Fifty Years*. Boston: Beacon Press, 2012.

Mitter, Rana, and Patrick Major, eds. *Across the Blocs: Cold War Cultural and Social History*. London: Frank Cass, 2004.

Morgan, Edmund S. *Benjamin Franklin*. New Haven CT: Yale University Press, 2002.

Muehlenbeck, Philip E. "Betting on the Dark Horses: John F. Kennedy's Courting of African Nationalist Leaders." PhD diss., George Washington University, 2007.

Murrow, Edward R. "America's Intellectual Image Abroad." *Educational Record* 43 (January 1962).

———. *Selected Murrow Manuscripts (January 12, 1953–January 22, 1961)*. New York: Columbia Broadcasting System, 1965.

Muton, Don, and David Welch. *The Cuban Missile Crisis: A Concise History*. 2nd ed. New York: Oxford University Press, 2011.

Myers, B. R. *The Cleanest Race: How North Koreans See Themselves and Why It Matters*. New York: Melville House, 2011.

Nelson, Michael. *War of the Black Heavens: The Battles of Western Broadcasting in the Cold War*. London: Brassey's, 1997.

Nowell-Smith, Geoffrey, and Steven Ricci, eds. *Hollywood and Europe: Economics, Culture, National Identity, 1945–1995*. London: British Film Institute, 1998.

Nye, Joseph S., Jr. *Soft Power: The Means to Success in World Politics*. New York: Public Affairs, 2004.

O'Brian, Michael. *John F. Kennedy: A Biography*. New York: Thomas Dunne, 2005.

Olson, Lynne. *Citizens of London: The Americans Who Stood with Britain in Its Darkest Hour*. New York: Random House, 2010.

Olson, Lynne, and Stanley W. Cloud. *The Murrow Boys: Pioneers on the Front Lines of Broadcast Journalism*. New York: Mariner, 1997.

Osgood, Kenneth A., and Brian Etheridge, eds. *Diplomatic Studies*. Vol. 5, *United States and Public Diplomacy: New Directions in Cultural and International History*. Leiden, the Netherlands: Martinus Nijhoff Publishers, 2010.

Paterson, Thomas G., ed. *Kennedy's Quest for Victory: American Foreign Policy, 1961–1963*. New York: Oxford University Press, 1989.

Patterson, James T. *Grand Expectations: The United States, 1945–1974*. New York: Oxford University Press, 1996.

Persico, Joseph E. *Edward R. Murrow: An American Original*. New York: McGraw-Hill, 1988.

Phillips, Lucy Victoria. "The Strange Commodity of Cultural Exchange: Martha Graham and the State Department on Tour, 1955–1987." PhD diss., Columbia University, 2013.

Plummer, Brenda Gayle, ed. *Window of Freedom: Race, Civil Rights, and Foreign Affairs*. Chapel Hill: University of North Carolina Press, 2003.

Public Papers of the Presidents of the United States: John F. Kennedy. Vol. 1961. Washington DC: U.S. Government Printing Office, 1962.

Public Papers of the Presidents of the United States: John F. Kennedy. Vol. 1962. Washington DC: U.S. Government Printing Office, 1963.

Public Papers of the Presidents of the United States: John F. Kennedy. Vol. 1963. Washington DC: U.S. Government Printing Office, 1964.

Public Papers of the Presidents of the United States: Ronald W. Reagan. Vol. 1987. Washington DC: U.S. Government Printing Office, 1988.

Puddington, Arch. *Broadcasting Freedom: The Cold War Triumph of Radio Free Europe and Radio Liberty*. Lexington: University of Kentucky Press, 2000.

Rabe, Stephen G. *The Most Dangerous Area in the World: John F. Kennedy Confronts Communist Revolution in Latin America*. Chapel Hill: University of North Carolina Press, 1999.

Rasenberger, Jim. *The Brilliant Disaster: JFK, Castro, and America's Doomed Invasion of Cuba's Bay of Pigs*. New York: Scribner, 2011.

Rawnsley, Gary D. *Radio Diplomacy and Propaganda: The BBC and VOA in International Politics, 1956–64*. New York: St. Martin's Press, 1996.

Reeves, Richard. *President Kennedy: Profile of Power*. New York: Simon and Schuster, 1993.

Richmond, Yale. *Practicing Public Diplomacy: A Cold War Odyssey*. New York: Berghahn, 2008.

Risso, Linda. "Radio Wars: Broadcasting in the Cold War." *Cold War History* 13, no. 2 (2013).

Roberts, Randy, and James Stuart Olson. *John Wayne: American*. Lincoln: University of Nebraska Press, 1997.

Robin, Ron. *Enclaves of America: The Rhetoric of American Political Architecture Abroad, 1900–1965*. Princeton NJ: Princeton University Press, 1992.

Romano, Renee. "No Diplomatic Immunity: African-American Diplomats, the State Department, and Civil Rights, 1961–1964." *Journal of American History* 87 (September 2000).

Rosenberg, Jonathan, and Zachary Karabell. *Kennedy, Johnson, and the Quest for Justice: The Civil Rights Tapes*. New York: W. W. Norton, 2003.

Rostow, Walt W. *The Diffusion of Power: An Essay in Recent History*. New York: Macmillan, 1972.

Rusk, Dean. *As I Saw It*. New York: W. W. Norton, 1990.

Salinger, Pierre. *With Kennedy*. Garden City NY: Doubleday, 1966.

Saunders, Frances Stonor. *The Cultural Cold War: The CIA and the World of Arts and Letters*. New York: New Press, 1999.

Schake, Kori N. "The Case against Flexible Response: Berlin Policy and Planning in the Eisenhower and Kennedy Administrations." PhD diss., University of Maryland at College Park, 1996.

Schlesinger, Arthur M., Jr. *The Imperial Presidency*. Boston: Houghton Mifflin, 1973.
——. *Robert Kennedy and His Times*. Boston: Houghton Mifflin, 1978.
——. *A Thousand Days: John F. Kennedy in the White House*. Boston: Houghton Muffin, 1965.

Schoultz, Lars. *That Infernal Little Cuban Republic: The United States and the Cuban Revolution*. Chapel Hill: University of North Carolina Press, 2009.

Schrecker, Ellen, ed. *Cold War Triumphalism: The Misuse of History after the Fall of Communism*. New York: New Press, 2004.
——. *Many Are the Crimes: McCarthyism in America*. Princeton NJ: Princeton University Press, 1998.

Scott, Allen J. "Hollywood in the Era of Globalization." *YaleGlobal Online*. November 29, 2002. http://yaleglobal.yale.edu/content/hollywood-era-globalization.

Sebestyen, Victor. *Twelve Days: The Story of the 1956 Hungarian Revolution*. New York: Pantheon, 2006.

Bibliography

Seib, Philip. *Broadcasts from the Blitz: How Edward R. Murrow Helped Lead America into War*. Dulles VA: Potomac, 2007.

Shaw, Tony. *Hollywood's Cold War*. Amherst: University of Massachusetts Press, 2007.

Shaw, Tony, and Denise Youngblood. *Cinematic Cold War: The American and Soviet Struggle for Hearts and Minds*. Lawrence: University Press of Kansas, 2010.

Sigmund, Paul E., ed. *The Ideologies of the Developing Nations*. New York: Praeger, 1967.

Sitkoff, Howard. *Struggle for Black Equality, 1954–1980*. New York: Hill and Wang, 1981.

Skidmore, Thomas E., and Peter H. Smith. *Modern Latin America*. 6th ed. New York: Oxford University Press, 2005.

Smith, Jean Edward. *Eisenhower: At War and Peace*. New York: Random House, 2012.

————. *FDR*. New York: Random House, 2007.

Smyth, J. E., ed. *Hollywood and the American Historical Film*. London: Palgrave Macmillan, 2012.

Snow, Crocker, Jr. "Public Diplomacy Practitioners: A Changing Cast of Characters." Readings on Public Diplomacy, the Edward R. Murrow Center of Public Diplomacy at the Fletcher School of Law and Diplomacy, Tufts University. http://fletcher.tufts.edu/murrow/readings/aboutpd.html.

Sorensen, Theodore C. *Counselor: A Life at the Edge of History*. New York: Harper Collins, 2008.

————. *Kennedy*. New York: Harper and Row, 1965.

Sorensen, Thomas C. *The Word War: The Story of American Propaganda*. New York: Harper and Row, 1968.

————. "The Murrow Years: Triumph and Tragedy." *Foreign Service Journal*, May 1968.

Sparks, Kenneth R. "Selling Uncle Sam in the Seventies." *Annals of the American Academy of Political and Social Sciences* 398 (November 1971).

Spector, Ronald. *Advice and Support: The Early Years, 1941–1960*. Washington DC: U.S. Government Printing Office, 1983.

Sperber, Ann M. *Murrow: His Life and Times*. New York: Freundlich, 1986.

Spiller, Robert E. "American Studies Abroad: Culture and Foreign Policy." *Annals of the American Academy of Political and Social Sciences* 366 (Spring 1966).

Srodes, James. *Allen Dulles: Master of Spies*. Washington DC: Regnery History, 2000.

Stern, Mark. *Calculating Visions: Kennedy, Johnson and Civil Rights*. New Brunswick NJ: Rutgers University Press, 1992.

Stern, Sheldon. *The Cuban Missile Crisis in American Memory: Myths versus Reality*. Stanford CA: Stanford University Press, 2012.

Stevenson, Charles A. *The End of Nowhere: American Policy toward Laos since 1954*. Boston: Beacon Press, 1972.

Stone, Joseph. *Prime Time and Misdemeanors: Investigating the 1950s TV Quiz Scandal*. New Brunswick NJ: Rutgers University Press, 1994.

Stossel, Scott. *Sarge: The Life and Times of Sargent Shriver*. Washington DC: Smithsonian Books, 2004.

Summitt, April R. "Perspectives on Power: John F. Kennedy and U.S.–Middle East Relations." PhD diss., Western Michigan University, 2002.

Taithe, Bertrand, and Tim Thornton, eds. *Propaganda: Political Rhetoric and Identity, 1300–2000*. Stroud, Gloucestershire: Sutton Publishing, 1999.

Talbott, Strobe, ed. *Khrushchev Remembers: The Last Testament*. Boston: Little, Brown, 1974.

Thomas, Evan. *Robert Kennedy: His Life*. New York: Simon and Schuster, 2000.

Tudda, Chris. *The Truth Is Our Weapon: The Rhetorical Diplomacy of Dwight D. Eisenhower and John Foster Dulles*. Baton Rouge: Louisiana State University Press, 2006.

Turpeau, Anne B. "People to People Diplomacy." *World Affairs* 123, no. 4 (Winter 1960).

U.S. Department of State. *Foreign Relations of the United States, 1961–1963*. Vol. 2, *Vietnam, 1962*. Washington DC: U.S. Government Printing Office, 1990.

———. *Foreign Relations of the United States, 1961–1963*. Vol. 3, *Vietnam, January–August 1963*. Washington DC: U.S. Government Printing Office, 1991.

———. *Foreign Relations of the United States, 1961–1963*. Vol. 4, *Vietnam, August–December 1963*. Washington DC: U.S. Government Printing Office, 1991.

———. *Foreign Relations of the United States, 1961–1963*. Vol. 6, *Kennedy-Khrushchev Exchanges*. Washington DC: U.S. Government Printing Office, 1996.

———. *Foreign Relations of the United States, 1961–1963*. Vol. 10, *Cuba, January 1961–September 1962*. Washington DC: U.S. Government Printing Office, 1997.

———. *Foreign Relations of the United States, 1961–1963*. Vol. 11, *Cuban Missile Crisis and Aftermath*. Washington DC: U.S. Government Printing Office, 1996.

———. *Foreign Relations of the United States, 1961–1963*. Vol. 14, *Berlin Crisis, 1961–1962*. Washington DC: U.S. Government Printing Office, 1993.

———. *Foreign Relations of the United States, 1961–1963*. Vol. 15, *Berlin Crisis, 1962–1963*. Washington DC: U.S. Government Printing Office, 1994.

———. *Foreign Relations of the United States, 1961–1963*. Vol. 24, *Laos Crisis*. Washington DC: U.S. Government Printing Office, 1994.

U.S. Information Agency. *The March*. 1964. National Archives channel. YouTube video. http://www.youtube.com/watch?v=DQYzHIIQ1O4.

———. *Five Cities in June*. 1963. John F. Kennedy Presidential Library. Online collection. http://www.jfklibrary.org/Asset-Viewer/Archives/USG-01-15.aspx.

———. *Forging the Alliance: President Kennedy Visits Venezuela and Columbia*. 1961. John F. Kennedy Presidential Library. Online collection. http://www.jfklibrary.org/Asset-Viewer/Archives/USG-01-A.aspx.

———. *Invitation to India*. 1962. John F. Kennedy Presidential Library. Online collection. http://www.jfklibrary.org/Asset-Viewer/Archives/USG-01-10.aspx.

————. *Invitation to Pakistan*. 1962. John F. Kennedy Presidential Library. Online collection. http://www.jfklibrary.org/Asset-Viewer/Archives/USG-01-14.aspx.

————. *Jacqueline Kennedy's Asian Journey*. United Artists, 1962. PublicResourceOrg channel. YouTube video. http://www.youtube.com/watch?v=2OTAJ_Gmy1c.

————. *John F. Kennedy: Years of Lightning, Days of Drums*. 1964. PublicResourceOrg channel. YouTube video. http://www.youtube.com/watch?v=PvN5ecqCFk0.

————. *The President's Visit to Canada*. 1961. John F. Kennedy Presidential Library. Online collection. http://www.jfklibrary.org/Asset-Viewer/Archives/USG -01-09.aspx.

————. *Progress through Freedom: The President's Trip to Mexico*. 1962. John F. Kennedy Presidential Library. Online collection. http://www.jfklibrary.org/Asset -Viewer/Archives/USG-01-J.aspx.

————. *The Task Begun: President Kennedy in Europe, 1961: 30 May–5 June*. 1961. John F. Kennedy Presidential Library. Online collection. http://www.jfklibrary .org/Asset-Viewer/Archives/USG-01-I.aspx.

————. *United in Progress*. 1963. John F. Kennedy Presidential Library. Online collection. http://www.jfklibrary.org/Asset-Viewer/Archives/USG-01-04.aspx.

————. *White House Tour with Mrs. John F. Kennedy*. CBS, 1962. Film Archives channel. YouTube video. http://www.youtube.com/watch?v=CbFt4h3Dkkw.

U.S. Senate. *Alleged Assassination Plots Involving Foreign Leaders: An Interim Report of the Select Committee to Study Governmental Operations with Respect to Intelligence Activities*. Washington DC: U.S. Government Printing Office, 1975.

————. *Nominations of Edward R. Murrow and Donald M. Wilson: Hearing before the Committee on Foreign Relations, March 14, 1961*. Washington DC: U.S. Government Printing Office, 1961.

Von Eschen, Penny M. *Race Against Empire: Blacks, Americans and Anticolonialism, 1937–1957*. Ithaca: Cornell University Press, 2007.

————. *Satchmo Blows Up the World: Jazz Ambassadors Play the Cold War*. Cambridge MA: Harvard University Press, 2004.

Wagnleitner, Reinhold. *Coca-Colonization and the Cold War: The Cultural Mission of the United States in Austria after the Second World War*. Chapel Hill: University of North Carolina Press, 1994.

Walton, Jennifer L. "Moral Masculinity: The Culture of Foreign Relations during the Kennedy Administration." PhD diss., Ohio State University, 2004.

Wasburn, Philo C. *Broadcasting Propaganda: International Radio Broadcasting and the Construction of Political Reality*. Westport: Praeger, 1992.

Westad, Odd Arne. *The Global Cold War*. Cambridge: Cambridge University Press, 2007.

Whitfield, Stephen J. *The Culture of the Cold War*. 2nd ed. Baltimore: Johns Hopkins University Press, 1996.

Williams, William Appleman. *The Tragedy of American Diplomacy*. Cleveland OH: World Publishing, 1959. Reprint, New York: W. W. Norton, 2009.

Winfield, Betty Houchin, and Lois B. DeFleur, eds. *The Edward R. Murrow Heritage: Challenge for the Future*. Ames: Iowa State University Press, 1986.

Wise, David, and Thomas Ross. *The Invisible Government*. New York: Random House, 1964.

Wofford, Harris. *Of Kennedys and Kings: Making Sense of the Sixties*. Pittsburgh PA: University of Pittsburgh Press, 1980.

Woodrow Wilson International Center for Scholars. *Cold War International History Project Bulletin* no. 17/18 (Fall 2012).

Woods, Randall B. *LBJ: Architect of American Ambition*. Cambridge MA: Harvard University Press, 2006.

Wyden, Peter. *Bay of Pigs: The Untold Story*. New York: Simon and Schuster, 1979.

Ybarra, Michael. *Washington Gone Crazy: Pat McCarran and the Great American Communist Hunt*. Hanover NH: Steerforth, 2004.

Young, Robert J. C. *Postcolonialism: An Historical Introduction*. Malden MA: Blackwell, 2001.

Zelikow, Philip, and Ernest May, eds. *The Presidential Recordings, John F. Kennedy: Vols. 1-3, The Great Crises*. New York: W. W. Norton, 2001.

Zubok, Vladislav, and Constantine Pleshakov. *Inside the Kremlin's Cold War: From Stalin to Khrushchev*. Cambridge MA: Harvard University Press, 1996.

INDEX

In this index, ERM is used for Edward R. Murrow and JFK is used for John F. Kennedy. Figure numbers in italic indicate photographs in the gallery following p. 82.

ABC network, 116, 130, 247, 259
Acheson, Dean, 90, 107
Adamson, Keith, 224
Adenauer, Konrad, 86, 100–101
AFN (Armed Forces Network) radio station, 102, 151, 180
Africa: ERM's tour of, 202–3; JFK's focus on, 30–31, 192; racism faced by diplomats from, 191, 199–201; responses to U.S. racism, 201, 207, 208, 213; threat of communism in, 114, 192; U.S. ambassadors to, 200–201; USIA films targeting, 123, 131–32, 198; USIA operations in, 50, 138–39, 256
African Americans: in the NSFA, 195; reactions to JFK, 193–94, 204; as U.S. diplomats, 197, 203; in the USIA, xxx–xxxi, 215, 252; in USIA films, 132, 133, 198, 207. *See also* civil rights movement; racism
After Two Years (film), 130
Agent Orange, 239
Alabama, 133, 190, 208
Alexiev, Alexandr, 161
Algeria, 200
Allen, George, 31–32, 35, 275n20
Alliance for Progress: challenges to implementation, 75, 77–82, 287n114;

failure of, 258–59; garnering support for, 60–61, 72, 74–77, 146–47; JFK's proposal for, 57–59; under LBJ, 257; USIA films on, 131
Alsop, Joseph, 98
American Evening Sunday (newspaper), 200
American University speech (JFK), 185–87
Amory, Robert, Jr., 95
Anderson, Burnett: in counterinsurgency planning, 223; during the Cuban missile crisis, 152–53, 154, 161, 305n43; drafting ERM's weekly reports, 45; promotion of, 271n11; relationship with Loomis, 305n40; work with CBS filming, 3
Anderson, George, 144
Anderson, Ida Lou, 7, 12
Anderson, Marian, 15–16, 107
Anderson, Rudolf, 161
Anglo-American information working group, 62–63, 74, 91, 137, 167, 184
Anspacher, John, 223
anticolonialism, 62–63
Army-McCarthy hearings, 17–19
Arndt, Richard, xvii, xxix, xxx
Arnett, Peter, 240
Austria, 11

Balewa, Alhaji Sir Abubakar, 258
Ball, George, 61, 150, 237–38, 254, 282n19
Barmine, Alexander, 43–44
Barnes, Donald, 58–59
Barnett, Ross, 204
Barrett, David, 147
Batista, Fulgencio, 60
Bay of Pigs operation, 63–70, 283n32;
    impact on Cuba, 143, 146, 285n64;
    impact on JFK's foreign policy, 221;
    opposition to, 64–65, 283n34, 283n36,
    284n42
BBC (British Broadcasting Corporation),
    xxii, 48–49
Bell, David, xxiii, 57–58, 61
Belmonte, Laura, xxx
Belovari, Susanne, xxviii
Benjamin, Burton, *fig. 8*
Bennett, Lowell, 35
Benton, William, xx, xxvii
Berle, Adolph, 64, 66, 79–80
Berlin, 83; building of the Wall, 92–95,
    106, 289n14; and the Cuban missile cri-
    sis, 151; European attitudes toward, 103–
    4; General Clay in, 104–6; growing
    tensions over, 86–89; JFK's visit to, 108–
    10, 294n123; LBJ's visit to, 96, 99–101,
    292n87; significance of, 143; tank stand-
    off incident, 106; USIA in, 83, 84–85;
    U.S. response to crisis in, 89–90, 94–97,
    98–101, 107–8
Bernays, Edward, xviii–xix
Bernhard, Berl, 194
Betancourt, Rómulo, 59, 76
Betts, Richard, 243
Birmingham (AL), 194, 196, 208–9
Bissell, Richard, Jr., 63, 66, 69, 144, 283n36
Blue, James, 132
Bolshoi Theater Ballet Company, 164
Borstelmann, Thomas, 193, 195
Bourguiba, Habib, 200
Bowles, Chester: and the Alliance for
    Progress, 57, 72; and the civil rights
    movement, 200, 206; and the Cuban
    missile crisis, 167; on ERM for director,
    xxvii, 23–24; friendship with ERM, 47;
    on interagency cooperation, 225; and

nuclear testing, 172, 185; opposition to
    Bay of Pigs, 284n42
Brady, Lee, 253
Brandt, Willy, 27, 95, 96, 99, 100, 104,
    292n87
Breckinridge, Mary Marvin, 12, 272n37
British Foreign Office, 31, 62–63, 74, 103,
    184, 235, 282n22. *See also* Great Britain
Brown, Cecil, 272n37
Brown, Clarence J., 70
Brown, Winthrop, 220–21
Brown v. Board of Education, 195, 313n7
Bruce, David, 156, 305n53
Buchwald, Art, 120
budget and funding (USIA): cuts to, 51, 54,
    188, 250, 258; for MPS, 135; requests for,
    51–52, 60–61, 135, 137, 249–51; of the tele-
    vision service, 137; through the USAID,
    134; for VOA, 50
Bulgaria, 207
Bundy, McGeorge: and the Bay of Pigs,
    64, 66, 283n34; during the Berlin crisis,
    95; during the Cuban missile crisis, 149,
    150, 159; on foreign policy development,
    221–22; praise for ERM, 253–54; on the
    Vienna summit, 88; and Vietnam policy,
    227, 235, 236–37, 240–41; working with
    the USIA, xxxii, 45–46, 48, 145, 223, 225–26
Bundy, William, 227–28, 237, 242
Bunker, Ellsworth, 244
Burrows, Charles, 57
Burundi, 103, 183, 205

Campos, Roberto de Oliveria, 79
Canan, James, 213
Castro, Fidel: and the Bay of Pigs inva-
    sion, 63, 65–67, 70; and the Cuban mis-
    sile crisis, 143–48, 157, 163, 164; declining
    support for, 73, 168; ideology of, 74;
    impact on U.S. foreign policy, 57; rev-
    olution led by, 66; support for, 65, 67;
    U.S. attempts to assassinate, 144–45,
    303n7. *See also* Cuba
CBS network, 260; cooperation with
    USIA, 116; end of ERM's career at, xxvii–
    xxviii, 22, 23–24, 25–26; ERM's career
    at, 6, 9–22, 114; ERM's salary at, xxvii,

25, 270n44; NSFA programming on, 8; tensions between ERM and, 1–2, 3–5, 20–21, 261–62, 270n47
Central Asia, 126, 127–28
Central Intelligence Agency (CIA): and the Bay of Pigs operation, 63–70, 283n36; and Castro's regime, 144–45, 168; during the Cuban missile crisis, 82, 148–49, 150, 165, 283n32, 307n91; Hungarian Uprising (1956), 269n31; relationship with USIA, 46, 73–74, 224, 248; in Vietnam, 228; during World War II, xix
chemical defoliation, 232–33, 235, 238–39
China, xxiv, 61, 114, 201
Church Committee, 145, 242, 303n7
Churchill, Winston, 11
CIA (Central Intelligence Agency). See Central Intelligence Agency (CIA)
Civil Rights Act (1964), 212, 257
civil rights movement: under Eisenhower, 191, 313n7; ERM's impact on, xxx–xxxi, 195–99, 201–2, 206, 215, 217–18; foreign media coverage of, 188, 191, 205, 208, 211; Freedom Riders, 190, 312n1; impact of the Cold War on, 192–95, 209; under JFK, 193–95, 197, 201–2, 204–5, 206, 209–13; USIA during, 195, 196–99, 202, 205–7, 211, 213–18; USIA films on, 132, 133, 197–98, 215–17; violence during, 190, 194, 196, 204–5, 208. See also racism
Clay, Lucius, 99–100, 104–6, 107, 108–9
Cleveland, Harlan, 171
Cloud, Stanley, 272n37
Coffin, Frank, 78
Cohn, Roy, 17, 18
Cold War: film propaganda during, 112–14; impact on civil rights, 192–93, 195–96; impact on the space race, 181; public diplomacy during, xix–xx; racism's impact on, 192–93, 208–10; tensions over Berlin, 83–87, 90–91; test ban treaty's impact on, 187–88. See also communism; Soviet Union (USSR)
The Cold War and the Color Line (Borstelmann), 193, 195
The Cold War and the United States Information Agency (Cull), xvii, xxx–xxxi

Cold War Civil Rights (Dudziak), 192–93, 195
Cold War Orientalism (Klein), 296n9
Collingwood, Charles, 4, 14, 272n37
Committee for a Sane Nuclear Policy (SANE), 309n15
Committee on Public Information (CPI), xviii–xix
communism: addressed by Eisenhower, xxiv–xxv; debates on growth of, xix–xx; expansion of, xxiii, 226–27; film industry's fight against, 113; JFK's fight against, 219; in Latin America, 56–57, 73; in Southeast Asia, 222–23, 226–27, 229–30. See also Cold War; Soviet Union (USSR)
communist propaganda: highlighting colonialism, 62–63, 231; highlighting U.S. racism, xv–xvi, 191, 192, 196, 201, 208–9, 211–12; increases in, xx, xxiv; in Latin America, 61, 70, 80; on nuclear testing, 184–85; in Southeast Asia, 229–30, 233, 239
Congress (U.S.): and the Alliance for Progress, 58–59, 78–79; and the civil rights movement, 193, 194–95, 197; ERM's confirmation hearings, 27–30; and USIA film honoring JFK, 325n59; and McCarthyism, 273n63; and the space race, 181; USIA budget cuts, 51, 54, 188, 250, 258; USIA funding requests, 49–51, 60–61, 249–51, 258
Connor, Theophilus "Bull," 208
Costa Rica, 131
CPI (Committee on Public Information), xviii–xix
Cuba: and the Alliance for Progress, 57; Bay of Pigs invasion, 63–70, 283n32, 283n35, 283n36; Great Britain's relations with, 62; impact of Bay of Pigs on, 143, 146, 285n64; propaganda campaigns of, 61, 70; significance of, 143–44; USIA's strategy in, 71–72, 73–74, 151, 284n47
Cuban missile crisis: background to, 143–48; impact on test ban treaty, 167, 185; international response to, 142–43, 159–60, 166–69; resolution to, 160–65; U.S.

Cuban missile crisis (*continued*)
  discovery of missile sites, 82, 148–49,
  303n19; U.S. response to, 150–60, 165–66,
  306n60, 307n91; VOA during, 150–54, 164,
  165–66, 168, 305n43
Cuban Project, 144
Cubela, Rolando, 303n7
Cull, Nicholas: on ERM's tenure, xxx–
  xxxi, 176; on the *Harvest of Shame* incident, 279n109; on Jackie's propaganda
  role, 124; on public diplomacy, xvii, 82,
  288n117; on the USIA, xxii, 126, 136, 140,
  154, 238–39
Curtis, Tony, 135

Dallek, Robert, 109, 295n1
Deegan, Tom, 46
Defense Department: and Hollywood,
  118; interagency cooperation, 125, 225–26,
  234; role in JFK's policy development,
  64, 222; role in the Cuban missile crisis,
  145–46, 283n32; and Southeast Asia, 259
DeFleur, Lois, xxvii
defoliation, 232–33, 235, 238–39
de Gaulle, Charles, 95, 237
Diem, Ngo Dinh, 227–29, 232–33, 235, 236,
  237, 239–42
Disney, Roy, 121
Dixon, Bob, 260
Dobrosielski, Marian, 187
Dobrynin, Anatoly, 162, 164, 185
documentaries. *See* films
Dole, Robert, 303n19
Downs, William, 272n37
Dudziak, Mary, 192–93, 195, 313n7
Duke, Angier Biddle, 109
Dulles, Allen, 46, 63, 64, 66, 68, 69, 73
Dulles, John Foster, xxiv, xxvi, 17

Edwards, Bob, 9, 15
Eisenhower, Dwight: and the 1956 Hungarian uprising, xxv, 86; and the Bay of
  Pigs operation, 64; and civil rights, 191,
  313n7; foreign policy of, xxiv–xxv, xxvi,
  30, 57; and Laos, 220; and McCarthyism, 16, 18; New Look doctrine of, 172;
  and the Smith-Mundt Act, xxi

Ellender, Allen, 50–51
England. *See* Great Britain
Europe: reactions to nuclear testing,
  173, 180–81, 182; response to Cuban
  missile crisis, 167; response to the Berlin crisis, 103–4; USIA operations in,
  43, 85
Evans, Robert, 45
Evening Star (newspaper), 212
ExComm (NSC) meetings, 149, 151, 157,
  158–59, 160, 161–62, 164

Fall, Bernard, 240
Fanfani, Amintore, 89, 146
Faubus, Orval, 196
Federal Republic of Germany (FRG), 86
film division (USIA). *See* Motion Picture
  Service (USIA)
film festivals, 117, 135–36
film industry: anticommunist messages
  of, 113–14, 296n9; propagating American culture, 113–14, 119–20, 296n22; and
  the USIA, 115–21, 135–36; during World
  War II, 295n3
films: on African Americans, 132, 133,
  198, 207; about JFK, 76, 77, 123–24, 128,
  130–33, 257–58, 299n85, 325n59; during
  the Roosevelt administration, 302n139;
  George Stevens' approach to, 127–33;
  value of, 112–14, 122–23; during World
  War II, xix, 295n3. *See also* Motion Pic-
  ture Service (USIA)
Fisher, Alan, 129
Five Cities in June (film), 132–33
Flexible Response policy, 90, 103, 222, 232
Food for Peace conference, 58
France, 88, 167, 173, 292n84
Franklin, Benjamin, xvii
Free, Lloyd, 283n35
Freedman, Lawrence, 86, 162–63, 220
Freedom House Award, 19, 104
Freedom Riders, 190, 312n1
FRG (Federal Republic of Germany), 86
Friendly, Fred, 4, 15, 16, 21, 114
Frondizi, Arturo, 58
Fulbright, J. William, 28, 29, 43, 79, 216
funding. *See* budget and funding (USIA)

Gagarin, Yuri, 181
Galbraith, John Kenneth, 47, 127–28
Gallup, George, 22
Gelb, Leslie, 243
Geneva conferences, 170, 173, 177, 185
German Democratic Republic (GDR), 84,
   86–87, 89, 92–95, 100, 106, 108. *See also*
   Berlin
Giglio, James, 181, 219
Gilpatric, Roswell, 171, 173
Glass, Leslie, 103
Glen Arden Farm, 14, 34, 261
Glenn, John, 183
Golden, Harry, 201–2
Goldwyn, Samuel, Jr., 126
Goldwyn, Samuel, Sr., 121, 125–26
Good Neighbor program, 57, 58, 81
Good Night, and Good Luck (film), 20
Goodwin, Richard, 57
Goulart, João, 78
Grandin, Thomas, 272n37
Gray, David, 283n32
Great Britain: during the Berlin crisis, 106;
   and Castro's regime, 62, 148; during the
   Cuban missile crisis, 156, 159; ERM's time
   in, 10–12. *See also* British Foreign Office
The Great Escape (film), 135–36
Greece, 167, 183
Greene, Sir Hugh Carlton, 48
Grierson, John, 122
Groce, Claude, 179
Guevara, Che, 70, 146
Guggenheim, Charles, 130–31, 140, 300n97
Gullion, Edmund, xvi

Halberstam, David, 237, 240
Hansen, Kenneth, 102
hardship tours, 39–40
Harkins, Paul, 238, 242, 262
Harriman, Marie, 134, 260, 279n103
Harriman, W. Averell, 238; friendship with
   the Murrows, 47, 260, 261, 279n103; on
   JFK's legacy, 258; and Laos negotiations,
   221, 224; programming targeting Africa,
   138; and the test ban treaty, 187; and USIA
   films, 134; and Vietnam policy, 241
Harrison, Hope, 289n14

Harvest of Shame (documentary), 21–22,
   48–49, 279n109
Harvey, William, 144–45
Have You Been Told? (radio program),
   179–80
Healy, Dennis, 305n53
Hear It Now (radio program), 15
Hearst, William Randolph, Jr., 165–66
Heil, Alan, Jr., 154, 305n43
Helms, Richard, 74, 144, 254
Hemsing, Albert, 91–92, 94, 96, 99, 105–6,
   110–11, 290n42, 291n65, 293n87
Herschensohn, Bruce, 132, 257
Heston, Charlton, 117, 132–33
Hickenlooper, Bourke B., 28–29, 46
Hill, Chuck, 137–38
Hilsman, Roger, 222
Hitler, Adolf, 10–11, 265
Hixson, Walter, xxx
Hodges, Luther, 45
Holland, Max, 147
Hollywood. *See* film industry
Honor Awards Ceremony (USIA), 37
Hoofnagle, James, 85, 91, 93–94, 97
Hottelet, Richard C., 272n37
House Committee on Space and Astro-
   nautics, 137
House of Representatives (U.S.), 49–51,
   60–61, 79, 188, 250–51
House Un-American Activities Commit-
   tee (HUAC), 113, 273n63
Hughes, Langston, 203
Hungarian Uprising (1956), xxv, 86,
   269n31
Hunt, Michael, xxi
Hutchison, John, 42

India, 126, 127–28
Institute of International Education, 9
Invitation to India (film), 127–28
Invitation to Pakistan (film), 127–28
Iran, 3, 148
Israel, 3
Issues and Answers (TV program), 82, 168, 187

Jackson, Henry M., 27
Javits, Jacob, 258

John F. Kennedy (film), 257–58, 325n59

Johnson, Lyndon B. (LBJ): and the Alliance for Progress, 75; during the Berlin crisis, 96, 99–101, 292n87; and civil rights, 193, 197, 210, 257; on Congress, 79; and ERM's resignation, 247, 251–52, 260; image of, *fig. 11*; during nuclear tensions, 178; on portrayals of JFK, 123; as president, 243, 244, 255, 257–58, 260, 325n59; relationship with ERM, 46–47; satellite conference call by, 138–39, 256; and the space program, 181, 188–89; Vietnam tour, 228–29

Johnston, Eric, 77, 119, 120

Joint Chiefs of Staff: during the Bay of Pigs operation, 64, 69; and the Berlin crisis, 90; on nuclear testing, 173, 181–82; role in the Cuban missile crisis, 157–58, 283n32

Journey Across Berlin (film), 97, 102, 103

Jurey, Jack, 102

Kaye, Danny, 117, 135

Kayibanda, Grégoire, 211

Kelly, Robert, 8

Kempe, Frederick, 86, 290n42

Kendrick, Alexander, xxix, xxxii, 154, 247

Kennedy, Caroline, 30

Kennedy, Edward, xxxii

Kennedy, Ethel, 24, 107–8

Kennedy, Jacqueline "Jackie," 57, 69, 164, 222, 241, 254; and the Camelot legend, 112, 295n1; during the Cuban missile crisis, 148–49; international appeal of, 30, 124; tour of Central Asia, 126–28; tour of Latin America, 76; and USIA films, 77, 112

Kennedy, John F. (JFK): and the 1961 Vienna summit, 55, 87–89; assassination of, 247; and the Bay of Pigs operation, 63–70, 283n34, 283n36; and the Berlin crisis, 55, 89–90, 93, 94–97, 98–99, 103–4, 107, 108–10, 294n123; and the Camelot legend, 112, 295n1; and Castro's regime, 71, 144, 146, 147; and civil rights, 192–95, 196, 197, 201, 202, 203–5, 206, 209–13, 313n21; and the film industry, 116, 121; films about, 76, 77, 123–24,

128, 130–33, 257–58, 299n85, 325n59; foreign policy development, 221–22; foreign policy focus of, xvi, xxiii, 26, 30–31, 56–61, 85–86, 107; images of, *fig. 1, fig. 2*; involvement in Southeast Asia, 219–22, 226–29, 232–33, 234, 236–38, 241–43; and a nuclear test ban treaty, 170–71, 173–74, 184, 185–87, 189; nuclear testing resumed by, 173–79, 181–82, 189, 278n86; obstacles faced by, 262–63; relationship with ERM, xxxii–xxxiii, 44–45, 254–55, 265; selecting ERM as director, xxv–xxvii, 22–25, 31; and the space race, 180–81, 183, 188, 312n3; tour of Latin America, 75–77; and USIA films, 112, 128; and the USIA's mission, 248

Kennedy, Joseph, Sr., 25

Kennedy, Robert: during the Berlin crisis, 97, 107–8; and civil rights, 193, 194, 204–5, 209, 212, 216; and counterinsurgency training, 224; and the Cuban missile crisis, 142, 149–50, 158, 161–62; and the Overseas Press Club, 261; relationship with Donald Wilson, 24, 36; relationship with ERM, 25, 246, 254; and the USIA, 119

"Kennedy Declaration," 201–2

Khrushchev, Nikita: at the 1961 Vienna summit, 55, 87–89; and the Bay of Pigs invasion, 67; and the Berlin crisis, 55, 86–87, 90, 97–98, 103–4, 108; and Castro's regime, 145–46; communist propaganda of, xxiv, 62–63, 185; and the Cuban missile crisis, 142–44, 151, 155, 160–65, 168–69; during Eisenhower's administration, xxv; expanding communism, 30, 56; resumption of nuclear testing, 173, 175–77; and satellite countries, 91; and Southeast Asia, 220, 234; and the space race, 136, 183, 185; and a test ban treaty, 171, 183, 185, 186–87; on West Berlin, 85

King, Martin Luther, Jr., 132, 190, 194, 215–16

Kintner, Robert, 259

Klauber, Edward, 9, 10

Klein, Christina, 296n9

Klieforth, Alexander, 71
Kohler, Foy, 94, 136
Kong Le, 220
Kreisky, Bruno, 88
Krell, Gerald, 133–34
Krim, Arthur B., 121

Lansdale, Edward, 73, 144, 286n82
Laos, 220–24, 226, 231–32, 234–35, 236, 243
Latin America: and the Alliance for Progress, 77–82; and the Bay of Pigs operation, 63–70; and the Cuban missile crisis, 155, 163–64, 167–68; impact of Castro's regime on, 146; JFK's interest in, 31, 56–61; JFK's tour of, 75–77; OAS treaty, 152, 304n37; reactions to nuclear testing, 182; USIA work in, 31, 131, 146–47, 163–64
Lemnitzer, Lyman, 69, 181–82, 222
LeSueur, Larry, 15, 33, 272n37
Let's Learn English (TV program), 138
libraries (USIA), xxiv, 50, 52–53, 183–84, 203
Lightner, E. Allan, Jr., 92, 94, 95, 100, 105–6, 110–11, 290n42
Lincoln, Evelyn, 121
Lincoln, Robert, 35
Lippmann, Walter, 88, 220–21
Little Rock (AR), 196, 313n7
Lochner, Robert, 83, 91–93, 95, 96–97, 109, 110–11, 294n123
Lodge, Henry Cabot, Jr., 241
Loewe, Lothar, 92–93
Loomis, Henry: access to intelligence reports, 46; and the Bay of Pigs operation, 67–68; and Burnett Anderson, 305n40; conflicts with Tom Sorensen, 186; during the Cuban missile crisis, 150, 152–54, 165, 166, 168, 304n32; and the *Harvest of Shame* incident, 48–49; image of, *fig. 9*; under the Johnson administration, 278n83; relationship with ERM, 33, 44, 179–80, 253, 276n31; reporting on nuclear testing, 177, 179–80
Lorentz, Pare, 302n139
Lowe, David, 21–22
Lower, Elmer, 247
Lundahl, Arthur, 148

MacCann, Richard, 114
Mackenzie, Kent, 133
Macmillan, Harold, 88, 95, 156
Manheim, Jarol, xxii
Mansfield, Mike, 325n59
Manual on the Fundamentals of Marxism-Leninism, 56
The Manufactured Crisis (radio program), 98
Mao Zedong, xxiv, 70, 87
March, Mildred, 32–33
The March (film), 132, 215–17
March on Washington rally, 215
Markey, James, 224
Marshall, George, xx, xxi
Mayhew, Christopher, 282n22
McCarran, Patrick, 273n63
McCarthy, Joseph, xxiv, 16–19, 25, 273n63
McClellan, John, 252
McCloy, John, 173, 175
McCone, John, 73, 145, 225–26
McCrandle, Dorothy, 33
McCullough, David, 42
McLeod, Scott, 16
McMenamin, William, 101
McNamara, Robert: and the Alliance for Progress, 75; on assassinating Castro, 144–45; during the Berlin crisis, 90; during the Cuban missile crisis, 159; interagency cooperation of, 225; marginalizing the USIA, 259; on nuclear testing, 173, 181–82; role in Southeast Asia policies, 222; during Vietnam, 234, 325n67
Mecklin, John, 239, 243
Meet the Press (program), 54
Meredith, James, 204–5
Mexico, 74–75, 76–77
migrant workers, 21–22
Minh, Duong Van, 241
Mohlams, 226
Montalban, Carlos, 138
Montalban, Ricardo, 138
Montgomery (AL), 190
Morgan, Edward, 4, 260
Morgenthau, Hans, 89
Moscow International Film Festival, 135–36

Moscow Radio, 211–12

Mosley, Lionel, 39, *fig. 7*

Moss, Lee, 17

Motion Picture Alliance for the Preservation of American Ideals, 113, 295n6

Motion Picture Export Association, 117, 296n22

motion pictures. *See* films

Motion Picture Service (USIA): during the Berlin crisis, 97–98, 102; covering civil rights issues, 132, 133, 197–98, 207, 211, 215–17; ERM's impact on, 40, 41–43, 255; and the film industry, 130–33, 139–41, 300n97; films about JFK, 325n59; funding for, 135; importance of, 113–14, 121–23; JFK's praise for, 112; message focus of, 40, 123–24; under George Stevens, 125–30, 133–36, 257–58

Mount Holyoke College, 8–9

movie stars, 117, 119, 135

MPS (Motion Picture Service). *See* Motion Picture Service (USIA)

Mundt, Karl, xx, 17

Murphy, Edmund, 73

Murrow, Charles Casey: on ERM's career options, 1, 24, 260; on ERM's leadership style, 84; on ERM's love of radio, 15; on ERM's personality, xxviii, 33; on ERM's resignation, 71, 247–48; at ERM's swearing-in, 31, *fig. 2*; on ERM's time at USIA, xxxii, 44, 45, 49, 51, 196; on the Murrows' homes, 14, 32, 34

Murrow, Dewey, 6–7

Murrow, Edward R. (ERM): administrative changes made by, 36–44, 47–48, 54–55, 226, 230, 288n7; and the Alliance for Progress, 60–63, 80–82; appointed USIA director, xxvi–xxviii, 22–25, 31; approach to propaganda, xvi, xxxiii, 27–29, 36, 40–42, 55, 147–48, 218, 229–30; and the Bay of Pigs operation, 65–68, 284n42; during the Berlin crisis, 83, 84–85, 90–92, 93–94, 95–98, 101–3, 104, 106–7, 110–11; birth and childhood of, 6–7; career with CBS, xxviii–xxix, 6, 9–22, 114, 222–23; CBS sabbatical, 1–4, 21; on chemical defoliation, 232–33, 235,

238–39; and the civil rights movement, 195–99, 201–7, 213–18; confirmation hearings, 27–30, 255–56; conflicts with CBS, 1–2, 3–5, 20–21, 261–62, 270n47; during the Cuban missile crisis, 143, 149, 164–65, 166, 168, 307n91; death of, 261; dedication to the USIA, 247–51, 260, 262–63, 323n10; early career of, 7–9; and the film industry, 115–16, 116–21; fostering interagency cooperation, 46, 224–26, 249; and funding challenges, 51–52, 60–61, 249–51, 258; and the *Harvest of Shame*, 21–22, 48–49, 279n109; health problems, 148, 242, 245–48, 259–61; homes of, 14, 32, 34; honors received by, 253, 260, 274n80, *fig. 11*; images of, *fig. 1, fig. 2, fig. 4, fig. 5, fig. 6, fig. 7, fig. 8, fig. 9, fig. 10, fig. 11*; impact on USIA, 251, 253–54, 255–57, 264–65; leadership style, 72–73, 83–84, 85, 111, 264; leaving CBS, xxvii–xxviii, 22, 23–24, 25–26; marriage of, 9; and the MPS, 113–14, 121–26, 130, 132, 134–36, 139–40; on nuclear testing, 171–72, 174–76, 177–80, 187, 189, 278n86; obstacles faced by, 54–55, 125, 258, 262–63, 264; office of, 34–35, 272n49, *fig. 4*; overseas travel, 72–73, 148, 202–3; personality of, xxviii, 35; on racism, xv–xvi, 188, 190–91, 195–99, 201–2, 210, 217–18; relationship with JFK, xxiii, xxxii–xxxiii, 44–47, 70–71, 254–55; resignation from USIA, 247–48, 251–52; salary of, 25, 32, 270n44; social life, 32–34, 279n103; and Southeast Asia tensions, 222–26, 228, 232–34, 235, 238–41; and the space race, 180–81, 183–84, 188, 301n127; speaking engagements, 51–54, 250; swearing-in ceremony, 31, *fig. 2*; and the USIA television service, 115, 136–39; vision for the USIA, xxxi–xxxii; and the VOA, 179–80, 186, 263–64, 284n50; work habits of, 6, 34–35, 39, 246

Murrow, Ethel F. (née Lamb), 6–7

Murrow, Janet Huntington Brewster: dinner with the Roosevelts, 13; and ERM's health, 247, 248, 260, 261; at ERM's swearing-in, 31, *fig. 2*; friendship with the Harrimans, 279n103; homes of, 14, 32, 34; marriage of, 9; at Mount Holyoke College, 8–9; overseas travel, 2–3, 4, 10, 72; social life, 32–34

Murrow, Lacey, 6–7

Murrow, Roscoe C., 6

Murrow Boys, xxix, 11–12, 14, 272n37

NASA (National Aeronautics and Space Administration), 124, 181, 188, 296n17

Nasser, Gamal Abdel, 175

National Security Council (NSC): and the Bay of Pigs operation, 65; during the Berlin crisis, 102; ExComm meetings, 149, 151, 157, 158–59, 160, 161–62, 164; JFK's use of, 221; and nuclear testing, 172, 173–74, 178–79, 182, 184; and Southeast Asia tensions, 232; USIA director on, xxii, xxvi, xxxii–xxxiii, 23, 44–45, 256; and the VOA, 46

National Student Federation of America (NSFA), 7–9, 195

Nazi Germany, xvi, 10–14, 265

NBC network, 10, 116, 259

Needham, Howard, 230–31

The Negro American (film), 198, 213

Nehru, Jawaharlal, 175

neocolonialism, 62–63

New Frontier policies, xvi, 257, 262

New York Ballet, 160

Nhu, Ngo Dinh, 241

Nielson, Paul, 233

NIE (National Intelligence Estimate) reports, 46

Nigeria, 138–39, 200, 203

Night of the Dragon (film), 300n97

Nixon, Richard, 75, 286n93

Nolting, Frederick, 229

Non-Aligned Movement, 31, 175, 176, 208

NSC (National Security Council). *See* National Security Council (NSC)

NSFA (National Student Federation of America), 7–9, 195

nuclear missile base (Turkey), 161–62, 166

nuclear test ban treaty: global opinions on, 184, 189; impact of Cuban missile crisis on, 163, 167, 185; negotiations, 170,

177, 185, 186–87; signing of, 187; U.S. work toward, 170–73, 184, 185–87, 189

nuclear testing: communist propaganda on, 184–85; global reactions to, 176, 182; opposition to, 172, 174–76, 178–79, 309n15; by the Soviet Union, 173, 176–77; by the United States, 176–79, 181–82, 185, 278n86

Nye, Joseph, Jr., xviii

OAS treaty, 152, 304n37

Office of Research and Analysis (USIA). *See* research division (USIA)

Office of War Information (OWI), xix, 295n3

Okamoto, Yoichi, 101

Oliver, C. Herbert, 196

Olson, Lynne, 272n37

Opal, Chester, 137–38, 233–34, 288n7

Operation Lantphibex 1-62, 145–46

Operation Mongoose, 73, 144, 286n82, 303n7

Operation Northwoods, 69

Operation Phibriglex 62, 145–46

Oppenheimer, J. Robert, 17, 255

Ormsby-Gore, David, 75, 77, 107, 204, 262

Overseas Press Club Foundation, 261

OWI (Office of War Information), xix, 295n3

Oxford (MS) race riots, 204–5

Pakistan, 126, 127–28

Paley, William, 9–10, 14, 24, 323n10

Patterson, James, 208

Pauker, John, 213–14

Paz Estensorro, Victor, 78

Peace Corps, 61–62, 257

Peck, Gregory, 257

Peck, John, 103

Persico, Joseph, xxix–xxx, 51, 247, 261–62, 323n10

Person to Person (TV program), 2, 4

Pervukhin, Mikhail, 87

Pettus, James, 156, 159

Phillips, Joe, 85, 91, 93, 96

Phouma, Souvanna, 220–21, 234

Picker, Arnold, 134

Pike, Douglas, 243–44
Plesent, Stanley, 216, 245, 250–51
Poitier, Sidney, 135
policy and planning office (USIA), 41–43, 55, 154, 186, 230–31, 256, 264. *See also* Sorensen, Thomas
"Potomac Cable" (commentary), 98
Poullada, Leon, 122
Progress through Freedom (documentary), 77
Promise to History (documentary), 91, 103
propaganda: need for truth in, xxxiii, 27–29, 36, 40–42, 199, 203, 253; negative connotations of, xvi–xvii, xviii; use of film in, 114; value to historians, xxi; during World War II, 295n3. *See also* communist propaganda; public diplomacy
Prospects of Mankind (TV program), 199, 230
PT 109 (film), 128, 299n85
public diplomacy: countering communism, xx; definitions of, xvi, xvii; need for assessment of, xxii–xxiii; racism's impact on, 193, 199–200; relation to foreign policy, xvii, xxvi, 258–59; as soft power, xvii–xviii; use of film in, 112–14; value to historians, xxi. *See also* propaganda

Quigley, Martin, 120

racism: Africans' responses to, 201, 207, 208, 213; communist propaganda highlighting, xv–xvi, 191, 192, 196, 201, 208–9, 211–12; experienced by African diplomats, 191, 199–201; impact on public diplomacy, 199–200; impact on the Cold War, 192–93, 208–10; impact on U.S. image, xv–xvi, 190–93, 205, 217; in the Soviet Union, 207. *See also* civil rights movement
Radio Americas, 73
radio broadcasting: in Berlin, 110; during the Cold War, xix, 160; and the Hungarian Uprising, 269n31; Soviet use of, 161; targeting Cuba, 73, 284n47; during World War I, xviii; during World War II, 10–11, 13–14. *See also* Voice of America (VOA)

radio division (USIA). *See* Voice of America (VOA)
Radio Free Europe, xix, 110, 179, 269n31
Radio Havana, 70, 168
Radio Liberty, xix, 160, 179
Radio Moscow, xxiv, 160, 162
Radio Saigon, 235
Ragsdale, Wilmott, xxviii
Reedy, George, 36, 47
research division (USIA): on the Alliance for Progress, 59; attempts to quantify success, xxiii, 54; on the Berlin crisis, 109–10; on civil rights, 205, 212–13; ERM's plan for, 28; following the Cuban missile crisis, 164, 166–67; on nuclear testing, 173, 176, 179, 184, 188; role of, xxii; and Southeast Asia, 240
Reston, James, xxvi
RIAS (Rundfunk im amerikanischen Sektor), 83, 93, 95, 102, 288n1
Rockefeller, Nelson, xx
Rooney, John J., 51, 79, 250–51, 280n124
Roosevelt, Eleanor, 13, 16, 190, 199, 230, *fig. 5*
Roosevelt, Franklin D., 12–13, 57, 302n139
Ross, Thomas, 286n81
Rostow, Walt, 232, 254
Rowan, Carl, 215, 252, 255, 259
Rusk, Dean, 30, 201; and the Bay of Pigs operation, 66, 68; during the Berlin crisis, 84, 94, 95, 105; and civil rights, 209–10, 212, 216; and communist expansion, 192; and the Cuban missile crisis, 142; on ERM's appointment, 22, 23; interagency cooperation of, xxxii, 47, 225–26; JFK's assessment of, 222; on nuclear testing, 174, 175, 181–82; and the USAID, 61, 282n19; during Vietnam, 233
Russell, Richard, Jr., 252
Russia. *See* Soviet Union (USSR)
Ryan, Hewson, 150

Saerchinger, Caesar, 10
Salant, Richard, *fig. 8*
Salinger, Pierre, xxvii, 76, 124, 134, 150, 153–54
Sanders, Terry, 133

SANE (Committee for a Sane Nuclear Policy), 309n15
satellite communications, 136–37, 138–39
Scali, John, 82, 135, 187
Schlesinger, Arthur M., Jr., 221, 227, 265; and the Alliance for Progress, 57, 58, 60, 79, 81, 82; assessment of Hickenlooper, 28; and the Bay of Pigs, 65, 66, 68–69, 283n34, 283n35; during the Berlin crisis, 99, 107–8; on combating communism, xxiii; and the Cuban missile crisis, 142, 158; on Eisenhower's claim, 273n68; on JFK's civil rights record, 194; on the MPS, 139; on nuclear testing, 175, 177
Schmidt, Lewis, 42, 51, 155
Schoultz, Lars, 144
Schrecker, Ellen, 16
Seaborg, Glen, 181–82
See It Now (TV program), 4, 15–16, 20, 114
Seltzer, Leo, 127
Senate (U.S.), 27–30, 54, 181, 273n63
Senate Foreign Relations Committee (SFRC), 27–30, 54
Sevareid, Eric, 272n37
Seward, James, 2, 4–5, 270n44
SFRC (Senate Foreign Relations Committee), 27–30, 54
Shaw, Tony, 113, 122, 141
Shelton, Turner, 118, 123, 125
Shepard, Alan, 181
Shermarke, Abdirashid Ali, 129
Shirer, William, 272n37
Shriver, Sargent, 61–62, 256
Small World (TV program), 4, 5
Smathers, George, xxv–xxvi
Smith, Howard Alexander, xx
Smith, Howard K., 272n37
Smith, Walter Bedell, xx, xxi
Smith-Mundt Act (1948), xx–xxi, 52, 150, 325n59
Sorensen, Theodore, 24; and the Bay of Pigs operation, 64–65, 69; during the Berlin crisis, 100; and brother Tom, 41, 46, 185; and civil rights, 194, 210, 313n21; during the Cuban missile crisis, 149–50, 161–62, 163; speechdrafting of, 185

Sorensen, Thomas: during the Berlin crisis, 109; and brother Ted, 46; and civil rights, 216, 217–18; during the Cuban missile crisis, 149–50, 152, 154, 157, 165; directing the policy office, 41–43, 55, 154, 185–86, 230, 264; and ERM's biographies, xxix; on ERM's nomination, 23–24; and George Stevens, 129; and Henry Loomis, 44, 186; image of, *fig. 10*; nuclear testing messages of, 177; personality of, 278n78; praise for ERM, 114, 246, 254, 255; relationship with the CIA, 73–74; on Rowan's management, 259; on USIA's mission, xxi–xxii, 42; and USIA's promotion process, 226, 264; on USIA's shortfalls, 125; on the Viet Cong, 238
Soviet Union (USSR): and the Bay of Pigs operation, 67, 143; and the Berlin crisis, 84, 86–87, 89, 105, 106, 108; Berlin's significance to, 143; Cuba's significance to, 143–44; Eisenhower's policy toward, xxiv–xxv; in Latin America, 61, 80, 146; New York Ballet tour in, 160; and the nuclear test ban treaty, 163, 170–71, 180, 185, 186–87; nuclear testing by, 173, 175–77, 178; propaganda highlighting U.S. racism, 192, 201, 208–9, 211–12; propaganda of, xx, xxiv, 61, 80, 114, 231; racism in, 207; and Southeast Asia, 220, 229–30; space program of, 136–37, 181, 188–89, 301n127; on successes of USIA, 251; USIA operations in, 43, 179–80, 182. *See also* Cold War; communism; Cuban missile crisis
space race, 136–37, 180–81, 183–84, 188–89, 301n127, 312n3
Sperber, Ann, xxviii, xxix–xxx, 23, 154, 247
Sperling, Milton, 121
Spivak, Lawrence E., 54
Sprague, Mansfield, xxv
Springer, Axel, 102
Stanton, Frank, 2–5, 22, 23, 260, 261
State Department: during the Berlin crisis, 98, 105; budget concerns, 54; and civil rights, 197, 208; criticism of, 81–82,

State Department (*continued*)
192; and cultural programs, 48; interagency cooperation, 47, 225–26; and
public diplomacy, xx; and racial insen-
sitivity, 200–201; role in policy development, 64, 222; and Southeast Asia, 242,
243, 322n107
Stevens, George, Jr.: ERM's hiring of, 115,
126, 264; film producers recruited by,
77, 130–33, 140, 300n97; image of, *fig.*
7; impact of, 115, 126–30, 133–36, 140–
41, 257; and the Television Service, 138;
vision for MPS, 128, 140
Stevens, George, Sr., 126, 299n70
Stevens, Robert, 18
Stevenson, Adlai, 68, 157, 158, 171, 177, 200
stratovision, 164, 165
Success Stories from America (pamphlet),
207
Sullivan, L. B., 190
Supreme Court (U.S.), 195, 204
Swan Island radio station, 68, 73, 150,
286n81
Swiegert, Manzy, 34, 246
Swing, Raymond, xxvii
Sylvester, Arthur, 125
Szulc, Tad, 66, 283n40

The Task Begun (film), 123–24
Taylor, Maxwell, 95, 157, 223, 232, 234
television industry, xix, xxvii–xxviii,
14–15, 114, 115–16, 208
television service (USIA), 107, 136–39, 164
Telstar I satellite, xix, 296n17
Third World countries: JFK's focus on,
30–31, 56–57, 256; USIA's focus on, 43,
45–46, 50; views of the United States, xv–
xvi, 192. *See also* Africa; Latin America
Thompson, Llewellyn, 88
Thompson Mission, 235
Thorneycroft, Peter, 156
Three Faiths (film), 133–34
Truman, Harry, 113, 191
Tuch, Hans, 88, 117, 160
Tudda, Chris, xxiv–xxv
Tunisia, 292n84
Turkey, 161–62, 166

The Ugly American (film), 118, 297n32
Ulbricht, Walter, 86–87, 89, 97, 98, 106,
108, 290n49
United in Progress (film), 131
United Nations, 158
United States Information Agency (USIA):
administrative changes under ERM,
36–44, 47–48, 54–55, 226, 230, 288n7;
and the Alliance for Progress, 59–61,
74–75, 79–82; approach to propaganda,
xxxiii, 27–29, 36, 40–42, 55, 60–63; during the Bay of Pigs operation, 65–68;
during the Berlin crisis, 84–85, 90, 91,
92–94, 96, 97–98, 101–3, 104, 107, 109–
11; countering communist propaganda,
231, 233–34; covering civil rights issues,
195, 196–99, 201–7, 211, 213–18; covering
JFK's Latin America tour, 76–77; covering nuclear testing, 177–78, 184, 187, 189;
covering the space race, 180–81, 183–84;
creation of, xxi; in Cuba, 143, 146–47,
149–54, 163–64, 168–69, 284n47; under
Eisenhower, xxiii–xxiv, xxv, 31–32;
ERM's confirmation hearings, 27–30,
255–56; ERM's impact on, 253–54, 255–
57, 261, 264–65; ERM's resignation from,
247–48, 251–52; European operations,
85, 288n7; film industry relationship,
115–21; funding of, xxiv, 28, 31, 49–50,
51–52, 54, 60–61, 80, 249–51; headquarters of, 34, 248–49; interagency cooperation of, xxii, 223–26, 234; under JFK,
xxvi–xxvii, 22–25, 31; in Latin America,
71–75, 163–64; mission of, xvii, xxi–xxii,
248; modes of communication, xvi,
xxii; negative assessments of, xxiii–xxiv,
xxv–xxvi; policy and planning division,
41–43, 186, 230–31; relationship with
CIA, 73–74; role in foreign policy, xxii,
xxvi, xxxi–xxxii, 170, 251; under Rowan,
252, 259; in Southeast Asia, 222–23, 226,
228, 231, 233–37, 238–41, 259, 325n67;
Soviet praise for, 251; television service,
107, 136–39; women in, 32–33. *See also*
budget and funding (USIA); Motion Picture Service (USIA); research division
(USIA); Voice of America (VOA)

United States Information Service (USIS), xxi. *See also* United States Information Agency (USIA)

Universal Pictures, 118, 297n32

USAID (U.S. Agency for International Development), 61, 78–79, 81–82, 134, 192

USIA (United States Information Agency). *See* United States Information Agency (USIA)

USIS (U.S. Information Service), xxi. *See also* United States Information Agency (USIA)

USSR. *See* Soviet Union (USSR)

Venezuela, 75–76, 286n93

Vienna summit (1961), 55, 87–88, 171

Viet Cong, 226–27, 233, 238, 242

Vietnam, 226–29, 231, 232–33, 235–44, 259, 320n60

Viewpoints (radio program), 263–64

Voice of America (VOA): during the Bay of Pigs operation, 67–68; during the Berlin crisis, 89, 97, 98, 102; covering civil rights issues, 205–6, 207, 211, 214; covering nuclear testing, 179–80, 186; in Cuba, 71, 145, 150–54, 164, 165–66, 168, 284n47, 305n43; ERM's impact on, 28, 40, 41–43, 44, 255; establishment of, xix; and the film industry, 119; funding for, 50; interagency cooperation in, 46; and McCarthyism, xxiv; mission of, 186, 203, 263–64; use of satellite communication, 138–39

Wachuku, Jaja, 139

Wagnleitner, Reinhold, xx, 113

Warner, Jack, 128, 299n85

Warren, Earl, 261

Washington Report (program), 210

Washington State College, 7–8, 54

Watson, Albert, Jr., 92

WBBF (radio station), 253

Weathersby, William, 47

Welch, Joseph N., 18–19

Wheeler, Romney, 137

White, Theodore, 295n1

White House Tour (film), 124

Whitfield, Stephen, 112–13

Wilson, Donald: as acting USIA director, 149–53, 246, 251–52; and the Bay of Pigs operation, 66, 283n40; during the Berlin crisis, 96, 97, 101, 102; and civil rights, 205, 216; criticism of, 42, 44; during the Cuban missile crisis, 149–53, 154, 156–57, 158–59, 161, 162, 163–64, 165, 304n32, 306n60; as deputy USIA director, 24, 42, 44, 55, 125, 264; and ERM's swearing-in, 31; image of, *fig. 3*; and JFK's Latin America tour, 76–77; praise for ERM, xxvi, 24, 38; on propaganda, xvi–xvii; qualifications of, 35–36; relationship with Robert Kennedy, 24; relationship with the CIA, 73–74; on Rowan's management, 259; and Southeast Asia tensions, 233–34, 241; on Soviet propaganda, 80; on the space race, 104; and USIA's promotion process, 226

Wilson, Susan, 24, 33

Winfield, Betty, xxvii

Wise, David, 286n81

Wofford, Harris, 194

World War I, xviii

World War II, xix, 11–14, 295n3

Zubok, Vladislav, 143–44